EL The Bread Box Papers

EL in Florence in the 1860's.

E.L. The Bread Box Papers

The high life of a dazzling Victorian lady

A Biography of
Elizabeth Chapman Lawrence
by Helen Hartman Gemmill

With an Introduction by
James A. Michener

Doylestown, Pennsylvania

The Bucks County Historical Society
Doylestown, Pennsylvania 18901

Unless otherwise stated, all photographs are from the collections of
the Spruance Library of the Bucks County Historical Society,
where the Fonthill manuscripts are deposited.
***
Photography of the Fonthill collection by Maddox Studio of Doylestown, PA.

Copyright © 1983 by Helen Hartman Gemmill
All Rights Reserved

ISBN 0-941668-02-09
Library of Congress Catalog Card No. 89-51330
Printed in the United States of America

To my husband, Kenneth

ACKNOWLEDGMENTS

Had it not been for the enthusiastic assistance of the staff of the Bucks County Historical Society and its components, the Mercer Museum, Fonthill, and the Spruance Library, this enterprise would still be on the drawing board. To Terry McNealy, Director of the Library, must go especially warm appreciation for aiding, abetting, and lending his considerable expertise.

With reluctance I must let the caption credits and reference notes express my thanks to all those helpful and imaginative archivists on both sides of the Atlantic who so generously shared their talents and resources. A special debt is owed to Dr. Charles Vandersee at the University of Virginia for alerting me to the Henry Adams connection, and providing a bibliography, and to Dr. Hans Trefousse at the City University of New York for introducing me to the Carl Schurz relationship.

Judy Bartella's uncommon common sense and critical eye were invaluable.

Finally, I must reiterate my gratitude to Baron Bernard von Friesen, EL's great-great nephew. Her story was enriched by the family documents, photographs, and recollections which he so painstakingly provided.

CONTENTS

INTRODUCTION		1
PROLOGUE		3
CHAPTER 1	Pennsylvania and Maryland (1829–1853) *"I hope you will not think I am a perfect lump of vanity."*	5
CHAPTER 2	Louisville, Kentucky (1848–1850) *"In Boston such a habit could not be allowed."*	13
CHAPTER 3	Philadelphia and Europe (1853) Bigelow *"imagines himself very much taken with me."*	23
CHAPTER 4	Boston, then London (1854) *"Victoria, Her Majesty, I regret to say, is a perfect fright."*	38
CHAPTER 5	London: "The Season" (1854) *"Exchanging your wreath for your nightcap" at dawn.*	53
CHAPTER 6	The Stately Homes *"This wonderful realization of my old Doylestown air-castles."*	63
CHAPTER 7	More Stately Homes The *"domestic arrangements"* were on a very large scale.	73
CHAPTER 8	A Cold English Winter The most stately *"feudal pile."*	85
CHAPTER 9	The Second "Season" (1855) *"The everlasting roll of the wheels of fashion."*	98
CHAPTER 10	Boston (1856–1861) *"I am getting very shaky about honest old Abe."*	110
CHAPTER 11	Florence (1862) *"Depravity worthy of Sodom itself."*	132
CHAPTER 12	Excursions and Alarms (1863–1865) *"Singing mice" and "frantic Abolitionists."*	146
CHAPTER 13	Italy and Switzerland (1865–1869) *"The Gineral who beat 'em so completely at Antietam."*	160
CHAPTER 14	Doylestown, Pennsylvania (1869–1872) *"Our bright comfortable cottage."*	175
CHAPTER 15	Europe (1874–1875) *"The courtly splendors of other days."*	188

CHAPTER 16	Washington (1875–1881)	204
	"If Blaine were a widower...."	
CHAPTER 17	Capital entertaining (1881–1884)	220
	"As age steals on, one can do nothing except to keep many interests."	
CHAPTER 18	Northeastern U.S. and Europe (1885–1899)	231
	"Out of mantel decoration" and "knee-deep in science."	
EPILOGUE	*"For EL's sake thus flash the light."*	244
NOTES		259
INDEX		269

EL The Bread Box Papers

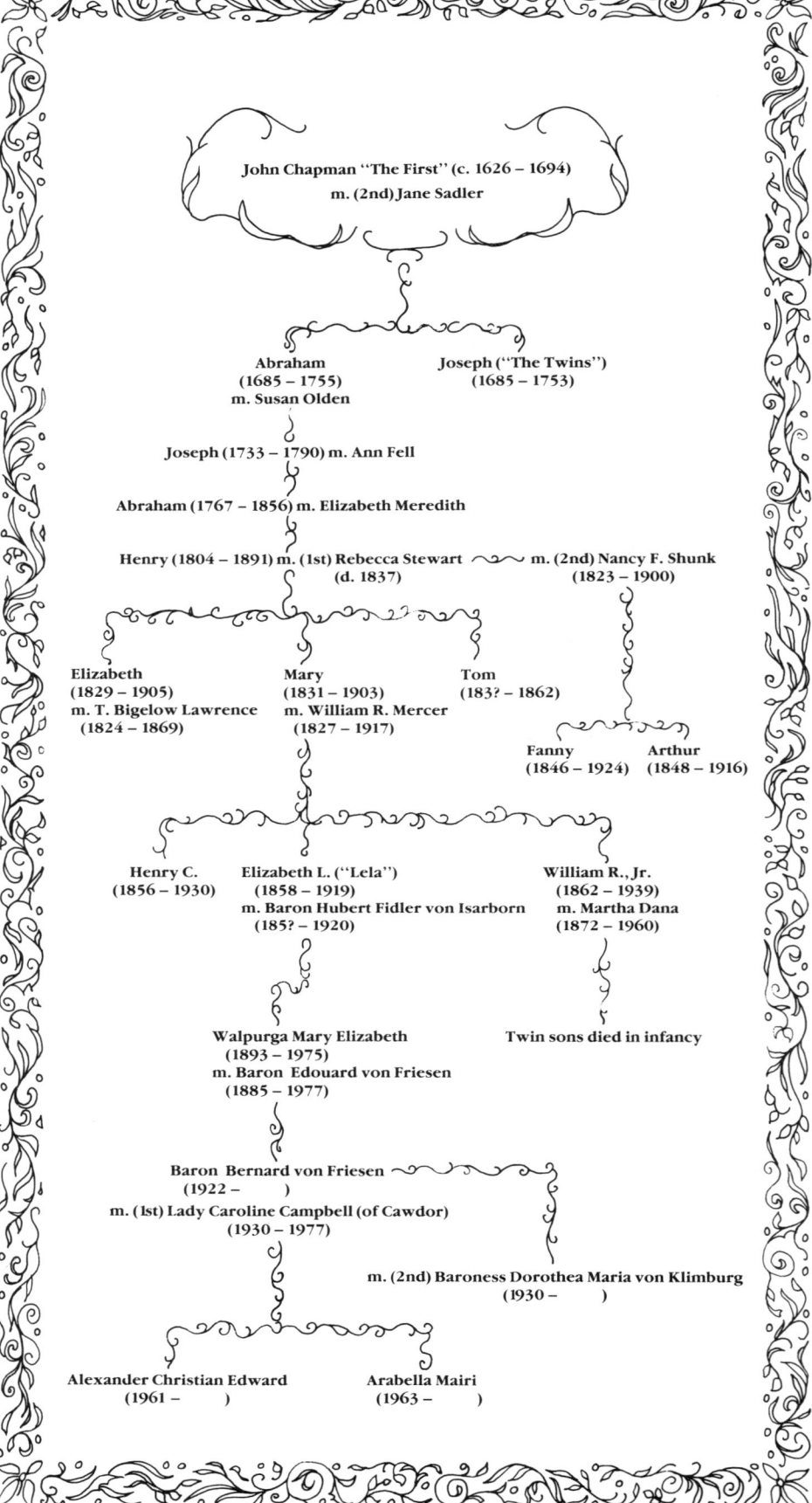

INTRODUCTION

The first thing I can remember occurred in the autumn of 1912 when I was five years old. My mother came running into our bedroom at midnight crying: "The world is on fire."

She was right. A highly individualistic neighbor had recently finished building a remarkable dwelling, and to celebrate he had lugged to its roof high in the air a huge collection of cedar, pine, oak and other combustibles and had doused them with gallons of kerosene. In the dark of night he had thrown in a match, and the conflagration could be seen for miles.

He was not an idiot, this man. In fact, he was the most intelligent and able man our village of Doylestown, Pennsylvania was to produce: intelligent in all fields, a genius in some.

You see, his house was non-flammable and formed a great base for a *Walpurgisnacht* celebration, for it was a Rhine castle, built of structural cement, and one of the craziest, most beautiful structures in this part of America. It was the castle of Henry Mercer, and I grew up right across from it. The exciting part about the Mercer story was that when he finished building this first castle on the north end of town, he had on his hands a group of German and Italian workmen who were now skilled in castle building, but their skills were not in great demand elsewhere, so he moved to the south end of our little town and built another concrete castle, which he turned into one of the world's unique museums. But that's another story.

I lived within sight of the first castle during the early years of my life, and in all that time Henry Mercer never spoke to me once, although we met on the road at least once each day. He was a tall, patrician, forbidding man not much given to idling his time with urchins. I found out later that he was able to indulge his wild fancies because a doting aunt had left him a great deal of money. This book is about that remarkable aunt.

Elizabeth Chapman was the daughter of a small-town judge. She was born in 1829 and could have had only the aspirations normal to an average, undistinguished young woman of that period. Our town was a somnolent place situated on the wrong side of the Philadelphia suburbs, and her family had been Quakers, not a very exciting group socially. Not much could have been expected of Elizabeth, but by a chain of incredible accidents she married the immensely wealthy son of a New England blue-blooded textile family, Colonel Bigelow Lawrence, a minor diplomat in the State Department.

When she was forty, her husband died leaving her an estate of more than one million dollars, which would be about thirty million at today's value. She thereupon set out to spend her fortune lavishly, but most intelligently, and she became the darling of Florence, Italy, London and especially Washington. She knew everybody. She entertained everyone. She became the constant subject of social comment, and she began to appear in reminiscences, stories and even novels.

She continued to live some months each year at her home in Doylestown, to which the great of the time repaired. She knew Charles Dickens, Bulwer-Lytton, Disraeli, James G. Blaine, and General McClellan. It seems that both Blaine and William Makepeace Thackeray had a more than passing interest in her.

She was a strong Democrat with an aversion to Abraham Lincoln, and she often said that it would have been better for America had Robert E. Lee been in the White House. Of Lincoln she once said: "What can you expect from a pig but a grunt?" Her place in literary history is based on the fact that the American novelist Henry Adams, scion of the great New England family, published in 1880 a *roman à clef*, *Democracy*, which gained

1

enormous popularity and which was based on the career and character of Elizabeth Lawrence, the little country girl from Doylestown.

I was especially interested to learn from these papers, recently found among Henry Mercer's accumulations, that it was at a house party she gave in our town that major steps were taken to found the great Boston Museum of Fine Arts. With her customary perspicacity she agreed to put up $25,000 if someone else would raise $75,000.

On and on she went. Dumas cooked dinner for her in Florence. In Washington she helped found, with the enthusiastic assistance of Carl Schurz, the famous Secretary of the Interior, a private club for the lampooning of pomposities, The National Rational International Dining Club. A casual comment in a letter home will include four names worthy of notice:

> Last night I dined at Mrs. Bancroft's. The dinner was given to Mrs. [John Jacob] Astor & it was a very distinguished party. General Sherman took me to table and I sat between him & Mr. Bayard, [Senator from Delaware].

Scandal delicately skirted Elizabeth Chapman Lawrence. Her husband's divorce from the daughter of a prominent Kentucky family was ugly to begin with, made more so when a younger brother of his former wife considered himself insulted by a schoolteacher imported from the North. Two of the boy's brothers solved that problem rather neatly by murdering the teacher. But then the Kentucky establishment gathered around, defended the killers as fine young fellows and denigrated the dead teacher. Verdict: not guilty.

Of greater interest to me is the revelation made here concerning one of the grand old ladies of my hometown. As a boy I knew and revered Fanny Chapman, younger half-sister of the dazzling Elizabeth. I remember her as kind, generous, aloof, a dear little old lady who had never married, pillar of her church and about the only respectable Democrat in town. She was the kind of winsome dear about whom I used to weave imaginary stories. In my version, she was always either knitting or doing good or serving tea or talking with the vicar.

Now I find that she was the life-long inamorata of Carl Schurz.

How important is this newly revealed portrait of a smalltown American girl on the move? First, it is delightful reading. Elizabeth had a sharp, naughty mind. Her observations were apt to be pertinent, and to share her reactions to the great people of her day in both Europe and America is fun. Second, it could well become required reading for any scholar doing research on our great American novelist Henry James, because Elizabeth can be taken as prototype for many of his heroines. And finally, her notes prove that the popular movie *Auntie Mame* was not much exaggerated.

On a more mundane note, it demonstrates yet again that a feisty widow with a million dollars can have one hell of a time.

James A. Michener

PROLOGUE

At the inauguration of President Grant on 4 March 1869, Col. T. Bigelow Lawrence caught a cold. On leave from his post as U. S. Consul-General in Florence, he and his wife had planned to stay on at the Willard Hotel while he consulted with the State Department, before returning home to Boston. For several days, therefore, he went about his business in the capital, ignoring his physical discomfort.

The cold worsened. According to the Boston newspapers, by the thirteenth he was experiencing "an irritation about the palate," and with growing alarm he called in a doctor, who diagnosed his ailment as "a malignant sore throat." When the swelling of the throat began to extend into the head, another consultant was hastily summoned, but by four o'clock in the morning of the twenty-first, both physicians informed the patient's wife the case was hopeless.

Col. Lawrence "expired" at two that afternoon. *The New York Times* summed up the end on its front page:

> ....An abcess *[sic]* had formed in his head pressing on his brain, which broke today, pushing one eye from its socket, rendering him insensible and causing speedy death. He was a man of many accomplishments, of much wealth and high social distinction, and had represented our Government at Florence for the past eight years.

A week after the funeral, Col. Lawrence's widow turned forty. By his will she became an heiress to a considerable fortune generated by the mills of New England. For the next thirty-six years, until she died in 1905, she proceeded to spend her legacy with generosity, imagination, and gusto.

Traveling as she did in élite circles at home and abroad, she could not remain completely anonymous. Her name crops up sporadically in newspapers, diaries, and journals, in footnotes to history, and even in some Presidential correspondence. But it was not until her letters to her family were recently discovered—stacked in an old tin bread box in her nephew's home, Fonthill—that she emerged as a vivid personality in her own right.

The breezy commentaries she scribbled to the folks at home in execrable handwriting were rarely paragraphed; the punctuation is decidedly casual; the spelling is occasionally erratic; and some words are illegible. Yet her writings bounce with vivacity and sparkle with curious details.

Quintessentially Victorian (indeed, her life roughly coincided with the Queen's long reign), she omitted certain things from her rollicking letters that one longs to know. Was she genuinely in love with "Mr. L.," or, as her twenty-fifth birthday loomed, was marriage to the good-looking, wealthy Boston Brahmin merely expedient? Did her outgoing, fun-loving nature chafe under his reserve? Did her deaf husband use an ear trumpet, or did she spend fifteen years shouting at him? And why were there no children?

Possibly some of the more personal letters were destroyed by her adoring nephew, the antiquarian-potter Henry C. Mercer, who is known to have edited his own voluminous papers with a sharp scissors. Convinced of the interest and value of his aunt's effusions, he made a faint attempt to put the letters in chronological order as he piled the jumble into the bread box for posterity to mull over.

The bread box containing EL's letters, found at Fonthill.

In spite of excisions and omissions (for after all, there were no letters when she was at home), a striking picture of the lady and her times emerges from the yellowed and often black-bordered envelopes.

Meet "E.L."—as most of her letters are signed—until now, a lady unknown.

1

PENNSYLVANIA AND MARYLAND (1829–1853)

"I hope you will not think I am a perfect lump of vanity."

As Elizabeth Chapman walked over the Bucks County hills to her grandfather's farm, she could hardly have imagined that one day she would marry the son of the Minister to the Court of St. James and maintain elegant residences in Boston, London, Florence, and Washington, while entertaining the important diplomats, politicians, artists, literati, and social leaders of the day.

Born in 1829 in Doylestown, Pennsylvania, a village thirty miles north of Philadelphia, Elizabeth came from a highly respected family with a heavy tilt towards medicine and law.

Her grandfather, Abraham Chapman, was a staunch Quaker and distinguished lawyer who had moved to Doylestown, along with the courts, when it replaced Newtown as the county seat in 1813. He had a predilection for art that his granddaughter would inherit. Recognizing "the peculiar talent for painting"[1] of his neighbor, the primitive artist Edward Hicks, Abraham became an early patron. For thirty dollars he purchased two landscapes, later receiving a *Peaceable Kingdom* from the painter "as a small compensation for many favors."

Elizabeth was not brought up a Quaker, however, for Abraham's son Henry (her father) married an equally staunch Presbyterian of Scotch-Irish descent, Rebecca Stewart, a dark-eyed beauty from a neighboring farm. He and Rebecca had three children, two daughters and a son. Elizabeth, the eldest, was only eight when her mother died, the void being filled by a plethora of relatives.

Furthermore, she always had a particularly close rapport with her father, a lawyer who was appointed a judge at an early age. (Eventually he became President Judge of the Bucks County Court). A scholarly, cultured man with a literary bent and a finely tuned sense of humor, he saw to it that the house was supplied with good books, music, and art. The burgeoning county seat attracted superior schoolmasters and tutors; so the three children received a well-grounded education.

A thoroughgoing romantic even as a child, Elizabeth loved to hear her father tell the story, over and over, of their ancestor, John Chapman "the First," as they called him. A persecuted Quaker, he had emigrated with his wife and children from Yorkshire to Bucks County in 1684, shortly after William Penn.[2] Delayed by a storm at sea, the dauntless family arrived too late in the year to construct a log house and were forced to live in a cave, subsisting that first severe winter on deer carcasses deposited at the entrance by friendly Indians. The next year John (nearing sixty) and Jane (forty-four) produced twin sons, from one of whom Elizabeth was descended.

To see the land of his ancestors had long been Henry Chapman's dream. Accordingly, two years after his wife's death he left his children in the care of relatives and sailed for England.[3] On his return his tales of castles and great parks fired the imagination of his elder daughter, who longed to see them for herself one day.

Elizabeth's early years were near-idyllic. With a host of relatives and friends she went fishing in the Neshaminy Creek or sliding on the frozen pond behind the brick kiln or driving in the old green wagon to get weighed on the cider mill scales. At night the family read aloud by candlelight, sang around the piano, or played charades.

(Left) Abraham Chapman—Grandpa—a daguerreotype c. 1850. (Right) Judge Henry Chapman—Papa—photographed c. 1857 during his term in Congress by Matthew Brady.

The placidity of village life was interrupted by an occasional typhoid epidemic, a runaway horse, or a drunken brawl at one of the taverns near the stagecoach stop. The courthouse across the street from her home produced an endless panorama of quaint costumes from Quaker to Mennonite, and a babel of accents from German to Welsh.

* * *

When she was sixteen, Elizabeth heard "rumors" that her father, who was then serving a term in the state Senate at Harrisburg, was bestowing his attentions on an attractive young lady just six years older than she; indeed, that he intended to marry her. Far from resenting this prospect, Elizabeth declared herself delighted. She wrote her father that the impending engagement "formed the whole topic of conversation in Doylestown, for both the drawing-rooms and kitchens of that select spot," adding that the family had heard "flaming accounts of Miss Shunk's beauty and talents."

The wedding took place in Harrisburg in July 1845. The people of Doylestown were overjoyed, for the new wife, Nancy Shunk, was not only the granddaughter of a previous governor, William Findlay, but the daughter of the present one, Francis Shunk. When Governor Shunk and his retinue rode into town some months later to visit his daughter and her new family, he was greeted by "the firing of cannon."[4]

Elizabeth, her sister Mary, and brother Tom were promptly captivated by their stepmother's sunny nature, hearty laugh, and culinary capabilities. With the aid of a couple of local "hired girls," Mama—as they all quickly took to calling her—was soon turning out quantities of preserves and relishes.

(Left) An early photograph of EL's birthplace. Still standing, it has housed a number of commercial ventures, including a newspaper publishing office. (Right) The house next door, built by Judge Chapman for his second wife, daughter of Governor Shunk of Pennsylvania. Then considered the handsomest house in Doylestown, it is now owned by the Village Improvement Association and known as the James-Lorah House.

A new house was built next door to the old one. Adorned with elaborate woodwork and marble fireplaces, the three-story grey house with white trim was considered the handsomest in town.[5] Indeed a larger house was needed, for the Judge and his wife soon had two more children, Fanny and Arthur. From the day she was born Fanny, though nearly eighteen years younger, held a special place in her half-sister Elizabeth's affections.

* * *

In her late teens, Elizabeth's education was topped off at one of the excellent female academies in Philadelphia, run by the Misses Gill in the Society Hill section of the city.[6] Her sister Mary, two years younger, soon joined her there. The girls were instructed not only in the customary singing, piano playing, and drawing, but also—as Elizabeth put it later—in some of the "ologies." She also learned to read French, but not to speak it fluently—a delinquency which she spent much of her life trying to remedy.

Both girls loved music, and their leisure time was often spent at concerts, as well as at the theater and lectures. When they went home for the holidays, they entertained the local swains at musical "soirées."[7]

Though their father was comfortably well off, he was far from affluent. His daughters were kept on a tight tether in Philadelphia, and frequent pleas were dispatched to Doylestown to "please send five dollars." At one point Elizabeth's shoes were so shabby she wore her "India rubbers" to hide them. Her washing bill ran higher then expected because the streets were "so windy and dusty." And one winter a painful tooth extraction took her last cent.

Beautiful clothes were a lifelong passion with her, but she had to content herself with frugal rearrangements by the local seamstresses. Blessed with an unerring sense of style and color, she was thriftily able to ring an astounding number of changes on her few outfits with the use of different sleeves, waists, berthas, laces, ribbons, flowers, and hairdos:

> .... I had a high-neck body put on my canton crape by Madame Otté in Walnut Street by Eighth. She only charged $1.50 and made it at once, and fitted me most exquisitely. I have got out of conceit with Mrs. Hook; she padded my brown silk until I looked like a wet nurse and charged me very extravagantly.

Such straitened circumstances seemed to have had no effect whatsoever on her social life. During "the season," she and Mary attended as many balls, assemblies, teas, soirées, "at homes," romps, routs, and "elegant suppers" as they could manage, sometimes whisking to three in one evening. The sisters were popular, and during one particularly active season Elizabeth wrote home that her dance cards were always filled "ten sets ahead." Even a doubting city aunt conceded that her country niece was blossoming into one of the city's "tearing belles."

She was quickly adopted by the Philadelphia "fashionables." The Biddles, Cadwaladers, Pauls, Norrises, Fishers, Wisters, and Wistars all were her friends:

> .... The Colemans, Scotts, Pleasantons & Miss Kate Biddle have called on me within the last week so my visiting list, you perceive, is increasing....
> .... Tomorrow night I am going to a large party at [the] Vanderkempts who left their card on me a few days since. Wednesday night I am going to both Horner's and Mrs. James Paul's.... Friday night I am going to Watson's. As I will be out so much this week I have determined not to go to Rush's although Mrs. R. did tell some of her intimate friends she was bent upon having me there. Mrs. Vincent, one of Mrs. Butler's protegées, and who gave a great ball the other night, was exceedingly anxious to ask Miss Chapman to her house but "did not know how to get at her." I am getting my blue spots done up and altered and it looks like a new dress....

Mama expressed concern about how her stepdaughter was "getting on," and begged her to describe her "successes." Trusting Mama to keep her letter "confidential," she replied:

> .... I hope you will not think I am a perfect lump of vanity and conceit, for writing all that I have about myself. If it had not been that I thought you would like to hear how I am coming on at the parties and what kind of debut I have made, I should never have troubled you with this egotistical nonsense. Do you know I have got a reputation and an extensive one too, for my unsophisticated simplicity which is called one of my greatest charms. I have laughed more in my sleeve within the last month than I ever did in my life. My "utter forgetfulness of self" is highly applauded. The remark that "if Miss Chapman does not leave Town soon her head will be completely turned" has grown into a proverb. I think they must have very little opinion of what's in my head if they think it's going to be turned with the nonsense I hear.

In the meantime she'd have to "hire a cab or something or other to return Julia Rush's visit." Would Mama please send five more dollars? "I suppose you will think I have been extravagant," she added, "but I can assure you that Girard himself [Stephen Girard, the philanthropist-banker] could not have been more saving of his money than Elizabeth Chapman."

She was not above gossip:

> You remember Harry B——? He is the father of a young son, by a South American widow with grown-up children. She tells people she did nothing more than shake hands with Mr. B——. It must have been a very emphatic shake.
>
> Bob Tyler [the President's son] has called on me three times since I have been in Town. He tells people I am half angel half rose—did you ever hear anything so ridiculous? I hope Grandpa was pleased with Walpole's letters, they are considered uncommonly amusing....

At a large party one evening she had been introduced to "Mrs. Dr. Rush," Philadelphia's most flamboyant hostess. The wife of Dr. James Rush, heiress to the Ridgway fortune, lived up to her reputation. She was wearing an imposing costume of green velvet "with a crimson cashmere turban embroidered in gold, and enough jewels to make a mine of." Within the week Elizabeth received an invitation to attend the Rushes' renowned Monday evening soirées—illuminated, it was said, by six thousand candles.[8]

A subsequent invitation that she and a school friend received from the persistent Mrs. Rush had to be refused on stout Presbyterian principle:

> .... I was invited to Mrs. Rush's last *Sunday evening* to meet Miss Cushman [Charlotte Cushman, the actress]. She gave [us] the invitation at Miss Eyre's the other afternoon & at first we were so taken aback that we could scarcely make a reply but in the end managed to stutter out that we never went anywhere on Sunday evening. Last Saturday we called to see her & she again with the most emphatic squeeze of my hand asked me if I could not for once make an exception to my rule. When I got up to go she pushed me down again on the chair & said I must stay longer, for she wanted her company to show to the best advantage—but enough of Mrs. Rush....

She thought Henry Clay, whom she passed on Chestnut Street, the "most distingué" person she ever saw, with the exception of his mouth and teeth, "which are awful."

* * *

Even after the two sisters finished school, they spent weeks at a time in the city, staying with friends and relatives, and doing what well-bred girls were expected to do: attend cultural events and parties and troll for a suitable husband. As she "thrilled" to the "arch tones" of the beautiful Jenny Lind or the "mellow notes" of Ole Bull, Elizabeth cast a critical eye on her escorts.

For a brief time young Mr. Drayton caught her fancy. Unfortunately he suffered from "the greatest curse on earth:" he was "poor but proud." One day after walking up and down the street with him for hours discussing his prospects, she was dismayed to hear he was determined to sail for Europe the following week and hoped to bring her "shoes and gloves from Paris." He would never dream of "binding" her by an engagement until he had "succeeded in business!" Whereupon, he turned on his heel and stalked off. Months passed, but the shoes and gloves—and Mr. Drayton—never materialized.

* * *

In the early 1850's Elizabeth and Mary spent several weeks each winter visiting an aunt in Annapolis, where the sisters enjoyed an even livelier social life than in Philadelphia.

During one visit even a painful ingrown toenail could not deter the irrepressible Elizabeth. After the doctor had called three times and rubbed the infection with "caustic which makes it burn and ache equal to any tooth that ever thumped," she attended two balls with a satin slipper on one foot and a red sock on the other. Although she could not dance a single set, she had more attention paid her than any one in the room—and would Mama please send five dollars for the doctor's bill?

When there wasn't a ball, they played parlor games at somebody's house. Elizabeth excelled at charades, and the enthusiasm with which she threw herself into her roles, combined with her quick wit, invariably had her audience in stitches.

For the Assembly in Annapolis she received a bouquet from her "most particular and devoted beau," Mr. Lloyd, and as he was considered the greatest catch in Maryland and "very handsome," she felt highly flattered. That she was a "success," Mama could have had no doubt:

> I feel perfectly done up from the Governor's Rout last night.... I wore my white illusion, green ivy wreath (my old one), violets, and hair [à la] Jenny Lind. Seven gentlemen asked to take me into supper, but as I had come with Mr. William Spencer I felt bound to go in with him. In the supper room I was obliged to drink healths with so many gents that if it had not been that I have a pretty strong head, I don't know what would have become of me.
>
> The Governor (one of the handsomest men I ever saw, but as bad as he is handsome) was one of the number who drank with me, & informed me he had heard a great deal of my wit! & repartee!... At one time I can assure you I felt quite stuck up, for there were seven gents around me, among whom I numbered the Governor, the Chief Justice, our ex-Minister to Vienna, & the two greatest wits in the Convention....
>
> Now for the widower with the six blessings.... I had almost made up my mind to engage myself to him, & among other inducements he offered to take me to the World's Fair; but what must he do at the Governor's the other night but get exceedingly jolly after the ladies left, & although there were plenty to keep him company, yet nothing would induce me to marry a man of that kind, for although I might not love him, yet I must at the least respect him.

* * *

The following winter the girls again visited for several weeks in Annapolis after a round of parties in Philadelphia at Christmastime. That year her gifts were more pleasing than the "smelling bottles" of the previous one: A school friend gave her "Miss Barrett's poems," and a beau presented her with a "beautiful box of sugar-plums." On December 28 she went to a ball at the Dallases (new illusion [tulle] dress, pearl earrings, and a wreath of wild strawberries), danced with Charley Biddle, and raced back at midnight to pack her trunk. By eight-thirty the next morning she was aboard the boat for Baltimore, then on to Annapolis.

Again she attended the Assembly (the same white illusion gown, but hair à la Mary Stuart). This time her "devoted beau" was Mr. McHenry, "the richest and most gentlemanly man in the convention." Part way through the evening, her shoestring broke. She "tramped it off," and instantly Mr. McHenry and another gentleman "rushed forward in the quadrille, picked it up, and flourished about with pieces of it in their buttonholes the rest of the evening." Another beau got "tipsy," and as she was "retiring," chased her all the way up the staircase shouting: "Oh, thou divinity."

In spite of all the attention, she was by now twenty-three, the years were going by, and no husband was in sight. "Why under the sun is it," she wondered, "that I could never have a single beau (but one) that I could take the slightest interest in?"

That spring Elizabeth and Mary received an invitation to visit friends on Maryland's Eastern Shore. They longed to go, if Papa had no objections, for "all the country houses round are to be filled with Baltimore belles and beaux," and they anticipated a "magnificent time."

One of the highlights of the visit (which Papa, of course, had approved) was a party given at Wye, one of the handsomest plantations in the state. The girls arrived in time to wander over the grounds, marveling that they stretched "seven miles up and down the bay." The avenue of elms and oaks leading up to the house was a mile long, and the walks reminded Elizabeth of pictures of St. Cloud. Never had she seen "anything so superb!"

The mansion itself was crowded with gentlemen who had already been there five days, each admitting to a total of six hours' sleep. "They frolick morning, noon, and night," she reported home.

A party or a ball was planned for every night that week. The sisters got to bed at two and breakfasted at ten-thirty. They agreed they had never seen "such a quantity of handsome people together in one place before," and concluded with smugness laced with a dash of humor that "the Doylestown party carry the day against belles both from Washington and Baltimore," who were "incensed beyond measure at our success, and make all kinds of nice little spiteful remarks which amuse us beyond anything. They can't make me mad, although they try their best."

In spite of the overlay of a city education, the country girl was never far below the surface:

> We live high here, I tell you what. Always four kinds of meat for dinner & strawberries & ice-cream for dessert. Everyone seems to live only to enjoy themselves.... I wish I could transport some of the pomegranate trees from here to Doylestown. Tell Grandpa I have seen no potatoes down here that can come up to his.

* * *

Two months before her twenty-fourth birthday, in January 1853, while Elizabeth was visiting in Philadelphia, she was introduced to William Makepeace Thackeray and Timothy Bigelow Lawrence. That the former made a deeper impression than the latter is clear:

> Just think, Mama, last Saturday I was introduced to Mr. Bigelow Lawrence, Sally Ward's husband, who went with me to Thackeray's lecture.... Just think of my having been introduced to Thackeray about a week ago—our conversation was one series of compliments. They say his [Thackeray's] wife is in a mad-house, and he is very much in love with Miss B—— [illegible], a great beauty in New York.... Mr. Lawrence has just been announced and I must dart.

Understandably she was more excited about her encounter with the popular novelist than with a notorious divorcé. All she knew at that point about her future husband was what all the world knew: that he was the famous—or infamous—Boston Brahmin who had been married to, then divorced from, one of the most talked-about females in America, Sallie Ward.

For the past few years Bigelow (as he was always called) had been living in London where he served as attaché to his father, Abbott Lawrence, who was the American Minister to the Court of St. James. His father had recently resigned his post; so Bigelow had returned to the States to sound out the political waters and await the appointment of the next Minister.

Just what he was doing in Philadelphia is unclear. He had made Thackeray's acquaintance in London and had heard him lecture in Boston two months before, at which time he had proffered him an invitation to dinner.[9] It is likely that, en route to or from Washington, he stopped over in Philadelphia to hear Thackeray lecture again and incidentally to visit with distant relatives who lived there.

At this stage it never crossed Elizabeth's mind to consider Bigelow as a possible husband. Divorce was looked at askance, and this one, like the wedding, had been grist to the mill of the newspaper columnists. It was enough to give most girls pause.

2

LOUISVILLE, KENTUCKY (1848–1850)

"In Boston such a habit could not be allowed."

The Ward–Lawrence nuptials five years before had been dubbed "the grandest show in Louisville history."[1]

There stood the groom, scion of one of the oldest and wealthiest families in New England. The first Lawrence had planted stakes in Massachusetts, finally becoming an original land proprietor in Groton in 1662.[2]

Bigelow's grandfather, Samuel, took part in the Battle of Bunker Hill after months of drilling a company of minutemen in a large, draughty barn. He was not quite twenty-one when the Lexington alarm sounded and they marched off to put theory into practice. Samuel's fiancée passed through the British lines under the pretext of visiting an elderly aunt, her letters sewed into the hem of her skirt. She and Samuel were married during a brief furlough.

Honorably discharged when his enlistment ran out in 1778 and the battlefield had shifted to the south, Major Sam Lawrence returned home to spend the rest of his life as a farmer, selectman, town clerk, and deacon. During the long winters he learned how to make shoes for his ten children, one of whom was Abbott, Bigelow's father.

The family could not afford to send him to college, so at fifteen, "his bundle under his arm, with less than three dollars in his pocket,"[3] he arrived in Boston to apprentice himself to his brother Amos, who conducted a mercantile importing business. Made a partner on coming of age, Abbott was sent to Manchester, England, at the conclusion of the War of 1812, to purchase much-needed manufactured goods.

He sailed on the first vessel to leave from the Boston harbor after the cessation of hostilities, accomplishing his mission with such noteworthy dispatch that he outmaneuvred his competitors, and the goods were sold at great profit. Other highly successful business trips were made to England after that.

The firm of A. & A. Lawrence acquired an interest in the Lowell cotton mills, as well as several other companies, later profiting from the China trade. Abbott Lawrence prospered. He was elected to Congress. By 1847 he was in a position to give fifty thousand dollars to Harvard to found the scientific school that bears his name. Two years later President Zachary Taylor offered him several cabinet positions, which he declined, accepting instead the post of Minister to England. (The title of Ambassador was not used until 1893). Described as possessing "peculiar urbanity and gracious manners,"[4] he was well qualified for the job.

On the maternal side Bigelow's ancestry was also distinguished. His mother, Katharine, was the daughter of the Honorable Timothy Bigelow, at one time Speaker of the House of Massachusetts, for whom he was named.

Bigelow "fitted" at Chauncy Hall in Boston and entered Harvard in 1842, at the age of fifteen, graduating four years later.[5] Keenly interested in military affairs, he became aide-de-camp to Governor Briggs, and soon attained the rank of Colonel in the militia, a title which he used throughout his life.

A serious illness in college had left him with impaired hearing; so, not long after graduation, he took off on an extended trip to Europe to consult with aural specialists. Though no cure for his deafness was found, his extensive travels enabled him to further his study of military matters—and to begin a collection of armor and ancient weapons that was destined to become one of the greatest in the country.

Then he met Sallie Ward.

It is thought their paths crossed at Saratoga Springs, where the Wards and the Lawrences had gone to take the waters. Bigelow was by no means the first—nor the last—to fall instantly head-over-heels for Sallie.

* * *

There stood the bride, the "brightest belle of Kentucky," the "idol of the ballroom"[6] whose piquant charms stemmed from a mother of aristocratic French-Huguenot descent, and an ambitious father who was Speaker of the House in Kentucky before he was thirty. With immense wealth deriving from various business enterprises, such as cotton and tobacco, Robert Ward was influential and popular. A handsome man with a proud bearing ("nature had created him to be a king,"[7] Louisvillians said), he spent with a lavish hand. Fifty thousand dollars a year, it was estimated, was dispensed for hospitality at his magnificent residence. Every morning two sturdy slaves could be seen at the market trundling wheelbarrows piled with produce ordered by Robert Ward's renowned chef.

The incomparable Sallie Ward, painted by the fashionable portraitist G.P.A. Healy in 1860. The artist thought her "the most beautiful...the most exquisite woman he had ever painted." *Courtesy of the J. B. Speed Art Museum, Louisville.*

His mansion boasted three parlors that could be closed off with massive folding doors; a greenhouse and conservatory alight with a profusion of rare plants; an aviary with a hundred birds in cages suspended from the walls; and an exotic miniature castle complete with a pool and fountain, constructed by a "stranded Prussian nobleman."[8]

Sumptuous feasts were served in this ante-bellum extravaganza by a retinue of liveried slaves. Guests dined on enormous mahogany tables glowing with quantities of silver plate and cut glass. Gossip had it that there was never a large dinner served that cost less than a thousand dollars.

Surrounded by such magnificence, Sallie learned early that the Ward family could flout convention—and get away with it. She was spoiled, high-handed, and impetuous; she could also be generous, endearing, and completely charming. Not really beautiful, with indifferent brown hair and blue eyes, the total effect she produced was nevertheless quite devastating.

Since Philadelphia had the reputation for having the best educational institutions in the country, she was sent there to "finishing" school, where her ebullience and high spirits often caused considerable consternation among students and faculty alike. "At wholly inappropriate moments" she would appear in male attire, only to be quickly forgiven when they glimpsed her beaming face and heard her tinkling laugh. Besides, she made "a very captivating youth."[9]

When she took the steamboat down the Mississippi to New Orleans to attend the Mardi Gras, it was like a "royal progress,"[10] with her train of followers. Summers were spent at White Sulphur Springs, Newport, and Saratoga, where her fame as a belle was no less firmly established.

She was the kind of person to attract legends, and separating the wheat of fact from the chaff of fancy is no small task. Household pets, babies, and race horses were supposedly named for her, and there was the "Sallie Ward glove," the "Sallie Ward hat," and even the "Sallie Ward walk"[11]—all implying the height of elegance. She was reputed to be the first person in Louisville to use opera glasses, and when she appeared in a box at the theater, she aroused more interest than the play itself.

There still exists the flag Sallie presented to the Louisville regiment as its soldiers marched off to the Mexican War. When the wind whipped the banner around the curves of her shapely figure, there was not a dry eye to be seen. Said one effusive biographer:

> There had never been a more gallant and inspiring scene in the city than when she sat in an open carriage as they passed along, each lifting his hat in homage to their queen of beauty. No honor of the ballroom, she said, had ever touched her heart so deeply, and when the war was over and they came back to Louisville, they greeted her with a tumultuous joy as she received them seated on her horse with all the majesty of a young Empress.[12]

Sallie made good copy for the rest of the century. In 1901 *The Ladies Home Journal* ran her story, along with a sketch of Sallie sitting sidesaddle on her famous white horse, reviewing the troops.

Another legend that persisted in the Bluegrass country for years told of her daredevil ride up the steps to the second floor of the Galt House, the biggest hotel in town. As her horse cantered up the staircase, she cast a backward glance at her escort, challenging him to follow. Another version has her galloping through the market, her horse's hooves scattering cucumbers and cabbages. There is even a version that places the scene of the escapade at the courthouse.

It is understandable that a straitlaced Bostonian would be enchanted by this sparkling Southerner, possessed of beauty, wealth, and background. Bigelow, in turn, would have passed muster with equally flying colors. Not only was he good-looking, with an impeccable family tree, but even more importantly, he could maintain a wife like Sallie in the manner to which she had not only become accustomed, but had no intention of changing!

The engagement was announced, and after a suitably long interval the marriage was celebrated. On 1 December 1848 Bigelow arrived in Louisville for the wedding, accompanied by his parents and a servant, several other members of his family, and friends with good Boston names like Gray and Dana.[13]

The *Boston Post* dispatched a special reporter to cover the nuptials. It was the first time the journalist had ever attended "a Western ball, wedding, or soiree,"[14] and, expecting a rough-and-ready jamboree in an uncivilized frontier town, he was overcome by the elegant lavishness of it all. Even the Ward home, he noted with awe, would "do credit to a New York upholsterer." All the hotels and boarding houses were "crammed," and "steamboats and stages brought in people from all over Kentucky for the great event."[15]

On the day of the wedding, unfortunately, there was such a deluge of rain that "coaches, carriages, cabs, and vehicles"[16] were embroiled in a muddy traffic jam, and it took an hour and a half to drive three blocks. Nevertheless the bride looked radiant in a gown that reputedly cost five thousand dollars. The eight bridesmaids looked only slightly less splendid.

After the ceremony, supper was served in the Ward's dining room. The *pièce de résistance* was "a large pyramid...supported by 20 cherubim (said to be the number of years of Sallie's life!), on top of which was mounted a huge vase which poured forth clouds of sweetly exotic incense."[17] The fact that Sallie was then twenty-*two* made little difference.

In the midst of all this splendor, the bridegroom's mother, Mrs. Abbott Lawrence, was reported to have been attired in "a plain, dark cotton dress, trimmed in cotton lace,"[18] adorned only with a single strand of "mock" pearls around her neck. Her husband, about to become the Minister to the Court of St. James, was also simply appareled. The Ward contingent, on the other hand, was decked out in the latest and most elaborate fashion.

The newlyweds spent the rest of the winter in "sweet post-nuptial seclusion"[19] in the bridal chamber prepared for them in the Ward home. It had been specially fitted out with festoons of lace, while the pitcher, bowl, and other metal fittings were of sterling silver.

When the spring thaw set in, Sallie and Bigelow made the arduous journey to Boston, taking with them her maid Eliza. At first they stayed at the Tremont House, later moving out to the Nahant Hotel for the summer. Frequent visits were paid to the senior Lawrences at their big brick townhouse on Park Street overlooking Boston Common.

Within two weeks Bigelow faced the realization that he had married an extravagant, spoiled child with schizophrenic tendencies. When refused her own way, Sallie shrieked at the top of her lungs, giving rise to gossip about her husband's "cruelty and abuse."[20] Possibly his deafness was a factor. In any case, letters and telegrams poured back to Louisville, bemoaning her "utter, perfect misery"[21]—followed by assurances that she had never been so happy.

She complained constantly of ill health. The Lawrence kin countered that her clothes were unsuitable for the Boston weather: low-cut dresses and short sleeves in April, indeed!

There was also the matter of arising in the morning at a decent hour. Mrs. Abbott Lawrence, in "school mar'm" fashion, berated her daughter-in-law for whiling away most of a perfectly good morning in bed instead of leaping up with the sun and industriously going about the business of the day. Or so the pro-Sallie Southern faction would claim.

Her worst failing, in the eyes of the proper Bostonians, was her "frequent and free use of paints and other cosmetics." Her husband, exerting his "prerogative" in proper nineteenth century fashion, attempted to break her of this vulgar habit, not only because it was "injurious" to herself, but "condemned by the sentiment of the community." Whatever she might have done in Kentucky, "in Boston such a habit could not be allowed."[22]

When Sallie complained to her mother about Bigelow's commands, Mrs. Ward advised:

> .... seem to obey, but do as you please. If you use proper caution, he can never know it... The most delicate tinge possible is all you want.... You are better looking without complexion than with too much, but if you think differently, then do what would make you happy.... Defy the opinion of the universe.... Stick to it with some of your mother's spunk.[23]

Convinced that Sallie was leaving her letters around where they could be read, Mrs. Ward urged her daughter to burn them, for this was a "serious matter" involving "the reputation of two families." She also suggested that if Sallie would "try to live quietly" with Bigelow, he might consent to let her come home for a visit:

> Your pa would come for you if it would not raise such a talk. May God forgive them all; I fear I never can. Your pa drinks almost constantly.[24]

Correspondence between the Wards and the Lawrences grew more heated. Wrote Mrs. Ward to her daughter: "The woman [i.e., Mrs. Abbott Lawrence] says your education has been neglected. She does not know what education is.... Sallie, beware of her; she is a wolf in sheep's clothing."[25]

Sallie's capers provided the Boston papers with plenty of titillating fodder. "At one of the most fashionable and brilliant levees ever given in Boston," trumpeted the *Herald*, "she appeared in a loose calico morning dress."[26] Obviously it was a matter of tit-for-tat; if that game could be played by her mother-in-law at her wedding in Louisville, then Sallie could play it in Boston.

Even worse, on another equally formal occasion she appeared in white satin *bloomers*, which exposed her dainty feet shod in a pair of jeweled Persian slippers. When she made her entrance, one concerted gasp swept the room; her in-laws stood frigid. Mrs. Abbott Lawrence is said to have asked her to withdraw and return in a *dress*. As Sallie swept out of the room, she ripped off the offending article of clothing.

The Southern version contradicted the Northern one, which implied that this was one more example of Sallie's shocking willfulness. On the contrary, claimed her champions in Louisville when they heard about the "bloomer" incident, the poor child was merely having fun satirizing the reform movement of Dr. Amelia Bloomer, who had recently lectured in Boston on the subject of women's dress. Obviously the staid city of Boston was "lost to a sense of humor."[27]

Matters came to a head in May when her mother-in-law, Mrs. Abbott Lawrence (whose husband would soon be leaving for his post in London), gave a dinner party for a visiting dignitary. Sallie made an entrance, her complexion noticeably rosy.

Though Bigelow withheld comment, at some point during the evening Sallie, in a fit of perverseness, accosted her mother-in-law with the announcement that there was no paint on her cheeks—absolutely none. Though "Bigelow thinks I have been rouging.... I swear to God, there is not a particle of color on my face," she insisted, causing the senior Mrs. Lawrence to shudder at the use of "such violent language." Sallie could prove her innocence: Bigelow's younger brother had caught her in the music room, dipped his handkerchief in cologne, and vigorously rubbed her cheeks with it—and not a single bit of color had come off![28]

17

Bigelow's brother subsequently denied ever having done any such thing, and Sallie finally confessed she had fibbed. Contrite, she relinquished "of her own free will" a large supply of cosmetics, including two dozen bottles of "liquid chalk," and two dozen "pink saucers," promising her father-in-law and her husband that she would henceforth behave herself.[29]

Another point of friction was the matter of "the hundred dollar transaction,"[30] as it was later referred to in court. Without her husband's knowledge, Sallie sent a note to her father-in-law, asking for a loan of a hundred dollars to pay her maid's back wages. "I am expecting money every day," she wrote. "When pa arrives, it will be returned to you."[31]

Without comment the Minister to the Court of St. James dispatched the money. There was no mention of repayment, nor was Bigelow apprised of the transaction. Later it was made to appear the Lawrences had dunned her for the money, and a ridiculous picture was painted of two enormously wealthy families squabbling over a mere hundred dollars.

In the meantime Bigelow had rented a house on Beacon Street, and while it was being readied, it was agreed that Sallie could spend the month of September in Louisville, ostensibly to recoup her health. Escorted by her father, she left Boston, taking with her trunks that contained eighty dresses and robes.

She never went back.

Bigelow bought furniture, engaged servants, and awaited his wife's return. By February he had given up hope. Taught by "a short but sad experience" that she bought anything she wanted, "however costly, or however foolish," and that "year after year" the wife who had "abandoned" him might present him with bills "to an almost unlimited amount" for which he would be liable,[32] he inserted the following advertisement in the *Louisville Daily Courier*:

> **NOTICE**
> WHEREAS my wife, SALLIE WARD LAWRENCE, has deserted me wilfully and without cause, this is to caution all persons against harboring or trusting her on my account, as I hold myself responsible for no debts contracted by her.
>   T. BIGELOW LAWRENCE.
> Boston Mass., February 1850.—feb25—d7t.

A thrill of horror swept through Kentucky, and the editor of the paper gallantly protested in an editorial that his sympathies were "entirely in the unfortunate lady's behalf":[33]

> .... But little more than a year has elapsed since the marriage of Mr. Lawrence, to one of the most beautiful and accomplished women of Kentucky. Some time since, it was understood that relations of an unpleasant character existed, rather from the unhappiness experienced by Mrs. Lawrence with her husband's relatives than from any other cause.
>
> Mrs. Lawrence returned to Kentucky last summer, and her husband has never been in this State since. Her health had become precarious and the consolation of home was absolutely necessary to her existence. She had suffered, and the sympathy and affection of her friends were not withheld.
>
> We inserted the advertisement because we knew that it would be made public through other channels, but we cannot but condemn, strongly condemn, its tenor.

> To all who know either Mrs. Lawrence, or her honorable father; who know the affluence by which she has been surrounded, and the indulgence and generosity of a parent who has ever gratified her slightest wishes, the idea that he would ever permit his child to become a pecuniary charge to Mr. Lawrence or his family, is preposterous....[34]

Obviously, the "hundred dollar transaction" was being bandied about with relish! The editor of the *Journal* even refused to publish Bigelow's ad, which he called "wanton and outrageous," and dashed off a scathing denouncement:

> ....We have never known a parallel case...where a lady of such lofty standing...was posted by a husband who even professed to have a claim to the character of a gentleman....
>
> There is not a lady in Kentucky more admired and beloved than Mrs. Lawrence...kind-hearted, beautiful, fascinating, accomplished, brilliant...the idol and ornament of the society in which she lives.[35]

In short, it was said that Bigelow would have been shot on sight if he appeared south of the Ohio River.

* * *

Sallie dropped an occasional note to Bigelow, declaring her health was improving so rapidly she was once more able to attend the parties and entertainments. Louisville, she wrote, had never been so gay.

Mr. Ward also contacted Bigelow, dangling before him several attractive business propositions designed to entice him to move to Kentucky. Bigelow, in turn, wrote his wife, dangling before her a long winter cruise far from Boston's inclement weather—to the West Indies or Rio or the Mediterranean—if she would only return.

All offers were rejected.

On 25 May 1850, Robert Ward appeared before the circuit judge and petitioned for a divorce on behalf of his daughter, testifying among others things that her health was "too delicate for the Boston climate."[36] Bigelow was roundly excoriated for his "meanness" and "niggardliness."[37] The case went to a jury, which took only a few minutes to decide that Sallie had been "harshly and improperly treated by her husband, and that he had slandered her by his advertisement."

Bigelow was outraged. Feeling his side of the case had not been heard, he published a fourteen-page pamphlet titled *An Exposition of the Difficulties between T. B. Lawrence and his Wife Sallie Ward Lawrence which led to their Divorce*, from which much of the above information was extracted. Though reluctant to wash the dirty linen in public, he refuted many of the charges by quoting verbatim from family letters, excerpts of which soon found their way to Boston and New York newspapers. He quoted all the notes that had accompanied the hundred-dollar business, for instance, adding: "Mrs. Lawrence asked for it and chose to consider it a loan, and its return was voluntary and unsolicited."[38] He also revealed letters written by Sallie's mother acknowledging that her daughter had given "great cause for dissatisfaction," and that she should have "acted the part of a woman and not that of a child."[39]

AN EXPOSITION

OF THE DIFFICULTIES BETWEEN

T. B. LAWRENCE,

AND HIS WIFE

SALLIE WARD LAWRENCE,

WHICH LED

To their Divorce.

PREPARED BY T. B. LAWRENCE AND HIS COUNSEL.

BOSTON:
W. LITTLE & CO., 19 State Street.

The cover of the pamphlet in which Bigelow set forth his side of the story.

Wrote the *Boston Courier:*

> It is not often that affairs of a private nature produce so widely extended a sensation through a large community and even through distant and separate portions of a nation as the recent divorce of Mrs. T. B. Lawrence.[40]

* * *

The Opening of the Great Exhibition, by Henry C. Selous, 1851. In this portion of the painting of the Crystal Palace ceremony, the U.S. Minister, Abbott Lawrence, is shown standing in the group of diplomats flanking Prince Albert, at lower right, behind the arm of the Chinaman Hee Sing, who, according to the picture's key, "happened to be present on the occasion." *Courtesy of the Victoria and Albert Museum.*

Believing he had set the record straight, Bigelow fled to London to serve as an attaché at the Legation where his father was now installed as Minister. The latter, accompanied by his wife and daughter Kitty, had rented a fine townhouse at 138 Piccadilly,[41] into which Bigelow also moved. His father's unusually comfortable living arrangements caused some comment among Englishmen who expected a more modest showing from the uncouth ex-colonists:

> .... The American Minister here, Abbott Lawrence, is said to have taken Lord Cadogan's house at the full amount of his salary [1200 pounds a year rent—a huge sum for those days[42]], so that he will appear more like the representative of Califor-

21

nia, than the frugal republic of the States. He is very wealthy and has made some magnificent endowments and donations for the advancement of education in Massachusetts....[43]

Said an American biographer:

....Possession of an ample fortune enabled him [Lawrence] to support a style of hospitality more in accordance with the higher European embassies, than is usual under the somewhat niggardly allowance of our own government....[44]

For Bigelow, a young man of twenty-four, this was a unique opportunity. In addition to such problems as overseas postal rates, fishing rights, lighthouses, and the territorial claims of the Mosquito Indians (a canal across Central America was contemplated), and ceremonial duties like congratulations on the birth of another royal baby, in all of which his father was involved,[45] there was also the stimulating preparation for the forthcoming Crystal Palace Exhibition. Recognizing the importance of having the United States worthily represented at this first great international exposition, the Minister made a point of introducing prominent visitors from the States to the leaders of the British establishment, and Bigelow was of course often included. The plunge into the arrangements for the Crystal Palace opening provided an antidote to the pain caused by the Sallie Ward debacle.

3

PHILADELPHIA AND EUROPE (1853)

Bigelow "imagines himself very much taken with me."

When Bigelow returned to the States in the fall of 1852, following his father's resignation as Minister in London, he was still referred to as "Sallie Ward's husband." It would have been readily understandable if the embittered Bostonian had searched out for his second wife a lady who was plain, retiring, and compliant, avoiding entanglement with another beautiful, effervescent, fun-loving female. That he did not succeed is a tribute to the somewhat less flamboyant charms of Elizabeth Chapman, who might attend a ball in a red sock but *never* in bloomers!

Not the least of her attractions was her lively interest in politics—past and present, at home and abroad—inherited from her father. Although her views were often at odds with Bigelow's, they were expressed with such conviction larded with humor, it could not fail to add piquancy to their encounters.

Like all her friends, Bigelow was quickly treated to her passionate opinions on everyone from "that brilliant strategist Napoleon Buonaparte" to "that scamp Simon Cameron" (the Pennsylvania Senator who would become Lincoln's first Secretary of War). When they met, her current hero was Lajos Kossuth, the Hungarian patriot. To her Kossuth represented the Central European counterpart of George Washington, struggling for the freedom of a romantic people, battling to throw off the Austrian yoke.

When "the great Magyar," as she called him, had come to Philadelphia to seek funds for his revolutionary cause, she had gone to hear him speak, beside herself with excitement. He was far handsomer than she had anticipated, but "his genius and fascinations of manner" made her "forget everything else." She proceeded to read every speech by Kossuth she could lay her hands on. Convinced of the justness of his cause, and determined to raise

"I then proceeded down Chestnut Street with a very satisfied expression of countenance, and sailing into Bayley's [sic]...I pulled out my broken eye glass,..." The jewelry store may be seen near the center of this view titled *Panorama of Philadelphia: Chestnut Street East of Fifth, 1856. Courtesy of the Historical Society of Pennsylvania.*

seventy dollars towards it, she canvassed all her friends, and when she came within ten dollars of her goal, she decided to raise the rest by selling her gold "eye-glass" to a jeweler:

> I thought it would look too much like pawning my jewels, and smacked entirely too strongly of "necessity's hard punch" to take it down looking perfectly good and new; so as I wended my way up thirteenth street, I concluded to break it. I forthwith pulled it out of my pocket and with the greatest secrecy broke it under my cloak into three pieces.
>
> I then proceeded down Chestnut Street with a very satisfied expression of countenance, and sailing into Bayley's (after asking if my ear-rings were silvered, and having a very interesting chat upon the state of the weather) I pulled out my broken eye-glass, and with quite an indifferent air, inquired the worth of the gold around these glasses.
>
> "Nothing, Miss, it is merely silver-gilt" was the laconic reply.

Elizabeth thought it "a good joke about myself"—and decided Kossuth would have to content himself with her sixty dollars.

To her delight, he had written her a letter, a treasure which she kept in her desk at home. Mama was asked to send it down to Philadelphia by the next mail pouch so it could be shown to Bigelow.

Having been in London when Kossuth visited there in 1851, the attaché must have regaled Elizabeth with tales of what Queen Victoria termed "the stupid Kossuth fever"[1] that erupted among the Liberals and Radicals who enthusiastically endorsed his cause. Even Lord Palmerston, the fractious Foreign Minister, had invited the freedom fighter to his home, until the angry Queen put her foot down. Since Elizabeth was not numbered among Victoria's admirers, opposition to her hero from *that* quarter only served to buttress her championship of him.

* * *

> Miss Chapman,
> with the compliments
> of T. B. Lawrence.
>
> Phila. Feb. 1853.

Inscription on the flyleaf of the book found at Fonthill, describing the U.S. role in the Crystal Palace Exhibition.

Before leaving Philadelphia to return to the Legation in London, Bigelow presented to Elizabeth a slim, gilt-edged volume that bore on the flyleaf in his angular hand: "To Miss Chapman, with the compliments of T. B. Lawrence, Philadelphia, Feb. 1853."[2] Far from being a volume of exquisite love poetry, the book was titled: *Proceedings at Mr. George Peabody's Parting Dinner to the Americans connected with the Great Exhibition, at the London Coffee House*.... Privately distributed, it paid tribute to the Lawrences, *père et fils*, for their efforts (among others), in making the Crystal Palace Exhibition such a notable success.

Unfortunately, Elizabeth's reaction to his parting gift is not known.

* * *

That spring the visits to Maryland bore fruit: Mary announced her engagement to William (Willie) Mercer, a tall, extraordinarily handsome midshipman whose home, Cedar Park, overlooked the West River below Annapolis. As a prospective husband, Willie Mercer had splendid qualifications. He was obviously madly in love with Mary (and she with him); he was good-looking, gentlemanly, and agreeable. A graduate of the Naval Academy, he was descended from most of the First Families of Maryland and Virginia. Byrds, Carters, Spriggs, Swanns, Harrisons could all be found on the family tree.[3] Willie's grandfather, John Francis Mercer, had studied law under Thomas Jefferson, had served as a delegate to the Continental Congress, and later became Governor of Maryland.

(Left) Sister Mary. The wedding ring gives evidence that this daguerreotype was taken after her marriage in 1853. (Right) Her husband, William R. Mercer (Willie), graduate of the U.S. Naval Academy, posing in uniform.

But Willie had one drawback: He had no income, other than his meager wages from the Navy. With considerable trepidation he had admitted this inadequacy to his future sister-in-law, confessing that, as a result, he would "rather fight a duel" than ask Judge Chapman for Mary's hand. However, he had explained to the sympathetic Elizabeth, he expected to be promoted shortly, when his pay would rise to fifteen hundred a year—surely an adequate sum? Whether Papa would agree was questionable.

Never reluctant to take matters into her own hands—especially when her beloved sister's happiness was at stake—Elizabeth had told the wretched Willie that she "felt for him very much," and had advised him, instead of calling on the Judge, to write a letter. When the relieved Willie had rushed off to find pen and paper, Elizabeth sought out her father and repeated the entire conversation. Gleefully she wrote to Mama:

> I have no doubt but that he [Father] will give his consent. Mr. Mercer has a leave of absence for fifteen days and intends spending it in Doylestown. He's a splendid fellow. I have quite a sisterly feeling for him already.... Tell Mary she must feel very much obliged to me for feeling and looking so flat [with Father] as I did for her sake.

Elizabeth's strategy worked. Mary's "enchanting" engagement was shortly announced and a fall wedding planned. A few days later Elizabeth was "sent into seventh heaven" by the news that her father was taking her along on a "grand tour" of Europe that summer. Whether the perspicacious Judge intended the trip as a form of consolation for his still-unmarried elder daughter, or whether he secretly hoped to promote Bigelow as a son-in-law is immaterial in view of the result. Most Americans in those days stopped off at the American Legation in London at some point in their European excursions, and it would be the most natural thing in the world to look up Bigelow. Mama, who would stay home with the children, and prepare for Mary's wedding, was promised at least one letter a week.

* * *

The *Atlantic* sailed from New York on a sunny June day "amidst firing of cannon, waving of handkerchiefs, and cheers of the multitude." The first to be steam-heated, it was one of the most elegantly appointed wooden paddle steamers afloat with its paneling of satinwood and rosewood, its costly mirrors, and its elaborate bronzework.[4]

The sails billowing before the breeze Elizabeth thought incredibly beautiful. Unfortunately, it was a scene which she had the "soul" to appreciate, but not the "stomach." Valiantly she laughed her way through the first dinner aboard; then:

> ...shawl-less, bonnetless, cloakless, I rushed on deck, and looking wildly around me with a sort of green stare, seated myself, and there, I must tell it, hardly was I down before everything else was up.
>
> I have sometimes thought that the most awkward feeling of one's life is to want a handkerchief and be without one, but it is a blessing, a privilege—compared to that of wanting a basin, when there is none to be had. Handkerchief, veil, gloves and skirt were all brought into requisition—but still the ceaseless cataract poured on. Some of the ladies at length came to my rescue, and stretching me out on the floor, covered me with buffalo skins.
>
> For about an hour I felt tolerably comfortable, but unfortunately, I opened my eyes and caught sight of a man walking, which made me as sick as death. I heard a girl laugh which almost gave me a spasm, and just then the gong sounded for tea, and I shrieked for a basin!

An hour later she struggled down to her berth, had the chambermaid pull off her boots, and stretched out in misery:

> Suddenly, all the diabolical rich, greasy dishes that ever were cooked, came crowding upon my memory.... Jumbles and cream haunted me like a demon,

and do what I could it was impossible to get roast pig out of my mind... shining with fat and dripping with gravy.

Finally she fell asleep trying to devise "a safe and commodious route home by way of the Bering Straits!"

Fully recovered the next day, she spent the remaining evenings up on deck with Mary Wistar, a Philadelphia friend, and Emma Fitzpatrick, a *comédienne* from London's Drury Lane Theater, who had just made her final appearance in New York, after a long run with the stock company of the Walnut Street Theater in Philadelphia.[5] While all the other ladies aboard went below, the three were the center of attention:

> We three pine-knots would sit... wrapped up in blankets and bearskins, surrounded by gentlemen and laughing, talking and singing by moonlight until twelve o'clock.
> Sometimes when the nights were dark we would watch the phosphorescence over the sides of the ship, which had the appearance of the most gorgeous fireflies, entangled in a net of foam. Miss Fitzpatrick has a most charming voice, and I can leave you to imagine how delightfully a ballad must have sounded, sung by the light of the summer moonlight. Two or three times we all joined in *Home Sweet Home*. Sometimes Miss Fitzpatrick would recite passages from different plays, and sometimes we would adjourn into the captain's room, and he would give us a little supper. Oh! the laughs that we had, and the times that we had!

A large party of Peruvians produced great excitement among the other passengers:

> One of them, a foolish fop, and valued at 23 millions, strutted up and down the deck the whole day long, and changed his white kid gloves for a fresh pair every half hour—while his sister reclined on a sofa in the ladies' cabin, arms covered with bracelets, beneath linen sheets trimmed with lace, and a coverlet of red velvet.

Ironically, she discovered during the voyage that the lady who occupied the cabin next to hers was none other than Sallie Ward! However, since the Louisville belle never left her cabin during the entire crossing (perhaps a victim of the same malady), Elizabeth got no more than a brief glimpse of her face, which she considered "neither handsome nor ladylike." With the exodus of Bigelow from Sallie's life, the paint bottles had obviously made their reappearance.

* * *

After the divorce, Sallie had gone into discreet retirement, for the status of a divorcée was an anomalous one. But it was not in her nature to remain in the background for long, and to many would-be swains, "that horrible experience" in Boston only made her more attractive. It was only a matter of months before she and her family gave a party that overshadowed anything ever seen before in Louisville: a huge fancy-dress ball. A few of the more conservative social leaders were apprehensive about such an expensive, faintly naughty frivolity, but they were soon convinced that impersonating the characters of history was actually an intellectual exercise. Others worried that appropriate costumes might be hard to find.

This proved not to be the case. Guests came from all over the South. The *Louisville Weekly* termed the evening "gorgeous," the costumes "superb," and said that the "admirable band filled the three large parlors with the most delicious tones."

Sallie appeared during the evening in not one, but two costumes. Before supper she was

Nourmahal, "the Light of the Harem," glittering in a bright pink satin skirt covered with silver lamé, from beneath which peeped satin trousers alight with gold spangles. Her bodice was embroidered with silver and studded with diamonds, and her hair was braided with pearls.

After supper she staged a second appearance as Nourmahal at the Feast of the Roses. The contrast was dramatic. Instead of a blaze of color, now she was an ethereal mist. This time her dress was white illusion, a white and silver veil cascaded down from a wreath of white roses, and her dainty feet were shod in white silk boots with silver anklets. She carried a lute.

Sallie was back in circulation, and it was just a matter of time before she would marry again.

* * *

After a calm crossing, the *Atlantic* anchored in the Mersey near Liverpool, and the passengers were taken ashore by "a miserable little steamboat":

> The whole way up the Mersey to our landing place, I was continually saying to myself: at length I am to set my foot on the shores of Old England, and determined that my first step should be an emphatic one; so accordingly as I left the steamboat, I came down on English soil with a tremendous stamp, and Oh! that I must tell it, caught my foot between two planks, and was five minutes at least in getting it loose!

The U.S. steamship *Atlantic* (3,000 tons, 1,000 horse power, Captain James West) on the Mersey River off Liverpool. On this elegantly appointed ship EL and her friends "would adjourn into the captain's room, & he would give us a little supper. Oh, the laughs that we had." *Courtesy of Kenneth M. Newman, The Old Print Shop, Inc.*

Along with most of the other passengers, she and her father spent the night at the Adelphi Hotel in Liverpool where she shared a room with Mary Wistar. Exhausted and wet, they popped into bed and ordered up tea, which arrived accompanied by an immense round of cold roast beef, which they attacked like "ravenous wolves," chorusing, "Three cheers and a bumper for the roast beef of Old England!"

The next day Mr. Harrison, a fellow passenger and "devoted attendant," sent her a basket of fruit, along with an invitation to drive through the countryside with him, discreetly suggesting that she might like to select two other guests to accompany them. Elizabeth accepted the invitation, invited two friends from the boat, and at the appointed hour met them in the hotel drawing room. Peering out the window at the street, she discovered to her horror that Mr. Harrison had hired an open barouche with four horses, mounted by two postilions dressed in red and white livery. Furthermore, the flamboyant equipage was surrounded by a mob of gawking people who were convinced that "a prince and princess were about to take an airing:"

> I flew from the window in dismay and declared that face that crowd I could not and would not—but all the ladies and gentlemen said that it would be absurd to deprive myself of a charming ride on account of a mass of gaping simpletons. And so at length down we went, and I think I may say I know what it is to be stared at by the multitude. Papa nearly killed himself laughing—and away we dashed in great style, the people bowing most reverently in every direction, and taking us for a party of Grandees from the continent!

Once away from the crowd, Elizabeth was enchanted with her first view of the English countryside, with its lakes and hedgerows and porters' lodges, "their walls all blushing with roses."

The next day they were off to London.

* * *

Within hours of their arrival, Bigelow called at the hotel. He told Elizabeth how "amazed" he was when he heard she was in town. She, in turn, was "delighted to see a face that I knew in America."

The following day Bigelow called for her in his carriage and took her to the House of Commons where they heard a "country Baronet" make such a ridiculous speech, she "longed to choke him." He kept repeating *ad nauseam:* "Ahem! This is a very important measure, gentlemen!"

Another day Bigelow escorted her and several of her shipboard friends to the House of Lords. In the crowd the two got separated from the rest of the party and finally drove on to the Zoological Gardens alone. Standing by the lake, watching the swans lazily drifting by, Bigelow suddenly became "very touching in his remarks, and I think really imagines himself very much taken with me."

The next evening he escorted her to her first ball, at Lady Brinkman's. For the occasion she had bought a new "illusion" dress that fit "like wax," for which she had to pay the outrageous sum of fifty dollars. After being announced by a "powdered footman," she was introduced by Bigelow to several gentlemen, who whisked her off to the music of the most "fashionable band in London":

> You must know that there are no such things as flirtations and belles in our sense of the word. The young ladies seat themselves on raised benches along the walls, and if they dance at all, as soon as the quadrille is finished, are led back to their Mamas.
>
> I saw there... Miss Fitzroy, who is considered the most admired girl of the season. In America she would hardly be considered pretty, and most of the evening was talking to her lady friends. You have no idea how strange it looked to see wallflowers so contented & happy.... At home the contention among the ladies at parties is for the most beaux & all the quadrilles; here it seemed to be for the most comfortable chairs in the room. The difference between an American belle & an English one is that one contends for sites, & the other for seats.

> I saw a great deal of splendid jewelry, but I give you my word that with few exceptions these high-born ladies looked far more like firemen's belles than real Countesses.
>
> We had supper at about one, but the table was anything but splendid. I ate some lobster salad dressed with cucumber & some soup.... As I was getting into the carriage the footmen called out: "There are four steps to ascend, your ladyship.... Shall I tell your Highness' coachman to drive off?"

Such titles sounded strange to an American's ears. They also sounded like a bid for a shilling tip.

* * *

To celebrate the Fourth of July, Elizabeth, her father, and the ever-attentive Mr. Harrison (who continued to shower fruit, flowers, and books upon her) took "the cars" out to Richmond to see Hampton Court. Although she could have happily spent a week exploring the vast palace, after three hours the return trip had to be considered:

> Papa was anxious to return to London by rail, but as I had set my heart on an excursion on the Thames in a steamboat, he at length gave way to my wishes, although he said he was sure we would only get among a horrid set of people & have a very disagreeable time.
>
> "Papa," said I, & felt most particularly republican when I said it, "that's the very thing I want to do. I want to get among the people, the bone & sinew of this land, among the people from whom sprang Milton & Shakespeare & Jonson..." & accordingly, as you will learn by the sequel, among the *people* I got!
>
> When we first left Richmond there were very few persons on board, & as we passed Garrick's country place & the Shakespeare villa with the willows drooping over it, I turned to Papa, & with a very triumphant expression asked him if he really thought it such a disagreeable thing to be in a steamboat on the Thames.
>
> Scarcely had I the words out of my mouth, when we stopped at a little village on the bank—& at least six hundred people rushed furiously on the boat, which certainly was never intended to carry more than two hundred with safety. Never talk to me of the rush & hurry of an American crowd!
>
> If I hadn't been frightened almost to death, I think I should have nearly killed myself laughing. In the foreground was a woman who had caught her clothes in something about two yards behind her, & in her effort to get loose, had writhed & twisted them until she stood a-Bloomer—without the pantaloons! Fortunately the weather was warm! A man got twisted round a pillar & roared to the crowd to let him get loose!
>
> On they came, cursing, swearing, jostling to join the republican ship; the specimen of American democracy... had shrunk, nearly frightened to death, into a corner. The boat rocked from side to side, & I expected every moment it would lurch over. I would have given anything I owned to get on shore, I think even the Kossuth letter, but it was impossible. Harrison tried to comfort me by saying that if anything happened, he would swim with me to shore!

At the first stop the three shaken travelers debarked, and Elizabeth announced that no matter where in future she might be thrown, "whether amongst bears, lions or wolves, whites or blacks, Hottentots or Caffers," never again did she wish to be "amongst the *people*, the bone & sinew of England!"

The following day, after sightseeing at Temple Bar, Bigelow called for her in his carriage and took her to Vauxhall Gardens where a band was playing waltzes. In compliment to Thackeray's heroine, Becky Sharp, she ordered a glass of "Rack Punch"—"which was my first & shall be my last."

The two visited practically every art gallery in town. One day they walked up and down Rotten Row, watching "the great ladies & gentlemen dashing along on horseback." She told Bigelow that if she rode no better than they, she would "dismount, walk home, & sell my horse on the first opportunity." She regretted to have to state that she was "dreadfully disappointed in the English aristocracy."

By night they attended the theater, the opera, and the circus.

On July 13 Elizabeth and her father, joined by several cousins, sailed for France, Bigelow assuring them he would be able to get away in time to join them in Germany. The Channel crossing was rough, and Elizabeth was so seasick, she cared not a whit which shore the boat headed for, Patagonia or France.

Finally ensconced at "Meurice's" in Paris, the travelers undertook a tour of the historic sites. At the Hotel des Invalides they watched the army veterans drill:

> I never beheld a more interesting spectacle: there they marched, erect & firm, the medals from Austerlitz & Marengo & the star of the Legion glittering upon their breasts, many with but a single leg, & keeping step to the music on crutches, some with frightful gashes on their faces, their coat sleeves hanging empty by their side, the old soldiers of the Empire, the sole survivors of the wars of Napoleon.
>
> What would I not have given to hear them tell the story of the battles they had fought, & the hardships they had experienced. I was introduced to the oldest soldier. He was over a hundred years of age, & his long white hair & beard nearly covered his breast & shoulders. He had fought in the wars of Louis the 15th & 16th, & was too old to fight under Napoleon. For the twentieth time I regretted my inability to speak the French language. I think, however, I managed to let the old veteran see how much I honoured & respected him, & his eyes fairly beamed with delight.

One night, they attended the theater and were "shocked & enchanted" by a troupe of Spanish dancers. In their brilliant costumes, they looked "like a bed of tulips blown about in a storm."

The Chapman party proceeded on to Brussels, traveling all night, and after a rest, drove out to Waterloo. Their elderly guide had helped to bury the dead after the battle and pointed out cannonballs embedded in the nearby trees. Cornfields now covered parts of the battlefield, but Elizabeth was quite sure she could "never eat the bread made off the waving corn."

Moving on to Cologne, they boarded the *Lorelei* and began the ascent of the Rhine. As they passed the formidable castles overlooking the river, it began to rain in torrents, but Elizabeth was undaunted. With her skirts tucked up out of reach of the water cascading over the deck, wrapped in a "blanket shawl," and clutching an umbrella, she "hailed every craggy peak & ruined castle as an old acquaintance." All the German legends she had ever read, all the ballads she had ever heard, "swarmed thick" on her memory. As the boat curved around the renowned Lorelei rock, she reached for her glass with her free hand and, all alone on the sodden deck, toasted her Doylestown family with "the most splendid hock wine."

The persistent Mr. Harrison, who had followed the Chapmans to Paris, caught up with them again on the Rhine and for several weeks made himself useful. It was he who translated at the dressmaker's when Elizabeth's wardrobe needed altering. (The delectable food was taking its toll.) What a scene it made—"this mustachiod gentleman standing dress in hand, explaining how it was to be let out under the arms!" And it was he who miraculously produced a roast chicken at a chaotic railway station, only to diminish the good deed by sending the gravy-coated bird on to her lap as he started to carve it. If she had had a pistol, she would have shot him. Instead, she smiled sweetly and informed him that the stain (a half-yard long on her only traveling dress) was "not of the least consequence."

Like most American tourists, the party stopped off at several of the glittering spas and gambling salons, where they were alternately fascinated and repelled by the elegantly dressed people playing at the tables. One gentleman, for instance, was so far gone with consumption, he was too weak to stand, and as he placed his gold pieces on the numbers, Elizabeth noticed his fingers were wasted away "to skin & bones." She had no doubt she and her father were considered "very verdant" by the onlookers, but decided she'd rather "be thought green than withered any day."

At one of the castles where Victoria and Albert had been entertained several years before, she climbed up on the bed the Prince had slept in (the guards were completely disinterested), and pronounced it "a plain French bedstead not nearly as nice as Papa & Mama sleep in at home!"

One day, strolling through one of the "pleasure gardens," they passed "the most hideous object in the shape of a woman" that they had ever beheld. Her face was covered with "white wens," and every feature was horribly distorted. Elizabeth was astonished to learn that the unfortunate lady was "the wife of Baron Rothschild of Frankfurt—and had always looked so!"

Another day she and her cousin rented a rowboat, and rowed across the lake to a town where they mounted donkeys to climb up the mountain. On the way the two girls burst into song, and when they finally struck up *Herz mein Herz*, the donkey drivers shouted *"Gut! Gut!"* Elizabeth motioned for them to join in, and they all made "the hills and woods echo with our German song!"

From Heidelberg and its student cafés they headed for Baden, where Bigelow was expected to join the party. Instead of the gentleman himself, there was a note "bemoaning his inability to do so on account of the unexpected arrival of Mr. [James] Buchanan," the new Minister. Nothing on earth, he declared, would prevent his traveling with the Chapmans to Scotland on their return from the Continent. On they pushed to Basel, then to Berne by diligence, the four horses "with their jingling bells to scare off the wolves from the mountains," the postilions with their red and blue jackets cracking their whips, the "curious jabber" of French, German, and English.

At Vevey she longed for a moonlight row on the lake, but the "prudential portion of the party got the better of the romantic!" There they were joined by other Americans; so in three carriages they set out for Chamonix. While they were all having a fine time walking on the glacier, they were suddenly overtaken by a rain squall. Since they were determined to eat lunch on the glacier, they wrapped up in shawls, put up their umbrellas, perched on the hampers, and drank wine and ate chicken and "kept ourselves warm with laughing and joking until we had finished our repast."

After lunch they were mounted on mules and led through a mountain pass made even more gloomy by another rain squall. Judge Chapman, thinking there was less danger of catching cold if he walked, dismounted and trudged slowly ahead, while Elizabeth from her perch atop her mule held her parasol over his head, but "a saucer on a stick would have been quite as serviceable."

Fortunately the sun quickly reappeared, and they rode on for miles, enjoying some of the most beautiful scenery in the world. Elizabeth had to admit, however, that she might have been "somewhat more charmed if there had been a little more skin 'where the skin ought to be.'" Eight hours of mule riding was "no joke":

> Oh, how our bones ached! I was too tired to stand, too stiff to walk, so I accordingly *sat down* and felt like *Montezuma* on a bed of coals! How I envied a *bottomless pit!*

There were misadventures, too, along the way. At an overcrowded inn, her bed was only four feet long. One mountain pass was so narrow and precipitous, she got dizzy and was forced, to her shame, to be carried over it in a sedan chair hefted by four bearers. At Nuremberg, the supper table was laden with cold chicken, roast pheasants, Westphalian ham, and boiled trout—a "deceptive feast," for it was all so spoiled, they had to open the windows and give the room an "airing."

But these setbacks were minor and often provoked hilarity rather than annoyance. They were quickly forgotten in the face of such highlights as the museum at Dresden, "the great store-house of German arts," where she feasted on the paintings and the *objets d'art*:

> I saw a silver egg which, upon opening, displayed a golden yolk; upon opening that you came to a golden chicken, which opens to a jeweled crown inside of which you found a diamond ring of immense size.

From Berlin they returned to London, to be greeted with a backlog of mail. To her dismay, the letters from home disclosed that rumor had her engaged to Mr. Harrison. "Confound Philadelphia and its reports," she fumed to Mama in a hastily dashed-off note. "If you ever hear such reports about me again, don't believe them, for I never intend to marry."

* * *

At this juncture a hiatus occurs in Elizabeth's correspondence, occasioned certainly by the fact that she would soon be home. Fortunately the progress of Bigelow's courtship can be gleaned from another source, the letters of the new American Minister (and soon-to-be President) James Buchanan, to his niece, Harriet Lane (who would serve as her bachelor uncle's hostess in the White House).

Back once again in London, the Chapmans paid a call on the new Minister. The Judge had long known Buchanan—a lawyer and former Senator from Lancaster, Pennsylvania—through their mutual interest in the Democratic party. After the Chapmans' visit, Buchanan wrote his niece that "in truth, she [Elizabeth] is a very nice girl & very handsome. Lawrence has gone to Scotland with Miss Chapman & her father, & I think he is much pleased with her."[6]

Buchanan was also much pleased with his attaché, whom he had never met before. In the short time they had been together at the Legation, he had developed a profound respect for Bigelow, finding him "industrious, gentlemanly,... and knows everybody." To his amazement he had discovered that Bigelow was serving without pay, but "works as though he received $10,000 per annum."[7]

In the next letter to his niece, Buchanan wrote:

> I shrewdly suspect that Miss Chapman has made a conquest of Col. Lawrence.... I shall not be surprised if it should be a match, though I know nothing. The Col. is quite deaf, which is very much against him.... She is delighted with her travels,... & has a great deal of vivacity. Upon the whole, I was much pleased with her.[8]

Buchanan's hunch was correct. Elizabeth had indeed made a conquest. The trip to Scotland had produced the finishing touches. The Judge had no need, this time round, to wonder about his prospective son-in-law's financial prospects, and the cloud occasioned by the divorce seemed to be dissipating. Furthermore, the two men shared many interests. Bigelow's growing collection of armor and historic artifacts, as well as rare books and manuscripts dealing with the Lawrence genealogy, must have delighted the Judge.

From Scotland Bigelow dropped a line to Buchanan requesting an extended leave of absence so that he could return to America, promising to explain the *"particular reasons ...in detail"* upon his arrival in London before sailing for home. He assured the Minister that his trip through England and Scotland had been "most agreeable," adding in an excited burst of obscure sentence structure: "as I believe you will agree with me that it could not fail of being so, accompanied as I was."[9]

As a traveling companion, Elizabeth had proved delightful. Bigelow was once again captivated by a lovely lady.

* * *

The Chapmans sailed for home the end of September, arriving just in time for Mary's wedding to Willie on October 11. Bigelow followed in November, assuring Buchanan he would be back in London with his bride in February.

Then came the blow.

On his arrival he was thunderstruck to discover that the divorce settlement had been contested by "the parties in Kentucky." On 28 January 1854 he wrote Buchanan that he was still uncertain of the outcome. The judge in Kentucky had ruled in his favor "in chambers," but felt duty-bound to appeal it to the "full bench." In the meantime the Wards were being urged by counsel to accept a settlement out of court, rather than appeal.

An appeal would, of course, take months. So Bigelow was forced to tell the Minister that, though the outcome was still unsettled, he was prepared to sail back to England "in the one case *alone*, in the other *with a wife*, for our matrimonial arrangements will be speedily adjusted." He was happy to assure Buchanan that "my engagement gives entire satisfaction to my family [who] seem *much gratified* that I have made so agreeable and fortunate a connection."[10]

Indeed, the senior Lawrences could hardly wait for their son to sever all connections with the Wards, for the Kentucky family was making the headlines once again, not only in the States, but even in the London *Times*, which devoted a half-column to the most recent example of "lawlessness" in the American West.[11] This time it was not divorce, but murder.

One of Sallie's younger brothers had been accused by his schoolmaster of eating roast chestnuts in school, which was against the rule. When the boy denied it, the schoolmaster (a Northerner) called him a liar and applied the strap. Two of the boy's brothers considered this a slur on the family honor. No one called *their* brother a liar! They seized a Bowie knife and a "self-cocking pistol that would send a bullet through a two-inch board anyhow," accosted the schoolmaster, and demanded an apology. When none was forthcoming, one of the brothers called the schoolmaster "a —— scoundrel and coward," pulled out his pistol, and shot him dead.

At the trial that followed, eighteen of the "ablest counsel that money could command" handled the defense of the two brothers. Antagonistic newspapers were "muzzled," and a steady stream of character witnesses gave evidence for the defendants, including a Senator and a former Governor. When the verdict of acquittal was handed down in May, newspapers across the land called it "a triumph of wealth over justice," and vehemently maintained the boys deserved to "stretch the hemp." Rarely did they fail to mention sister Sallie and her ill-fated marriage.[12]

* * *

While the question of his divorce appeal was still pending, Bigelow learned that Buchanan's niece, Harriet Lane, was planning a visit to her uncle that spring. He wrote the Minister that he would be delighted to act as her escort.[13] However, a hitch was thrown into Harriet's plans from an unexpected quarter. The Secretary of State circulated a memorandum to all diplomats directing them to wear "the simple dress of an ordinary American citizen," rather than "costumes" and elaborate military regalia when appearing before the Courts of Europe.[14]

Buchanan had good cause to wonder about Victoria's reaction to this latest directive from the upstart ex-colony. Would she go along with it, or would she put her foot down and insist on fancy court dress? When Buchanan had been Minister to Russia, even the Czar in St. Petersburg had not required it!

He had invited his niece primarily so that she could participate in the London "season," escorted by her well-placed uncle. What was the point of her coming if he were "socially in Coventry" and unable to attend the best functions?

AMBASSADORS IN LIVERY.

HERE are, certainly, some anomalies in our ceremonial arrangements which cannot be got rid of too speedily. We refuse to let a servant *in* livery pass into Kensington Gardens, and we refuse to let a diplomatic servant *out of* livery pass into the House of Lords. The American Minister was positively refused admission to the ceremony of opening Parliament, unless he would consent to bedizen himself with gold lace, and, in fact, to come in masquerade. Had he dropped in at any Vauxhall *costumier's*, or taken Holywell Street in his way, and hired a suit of second-hand regimentals, or disguised himself in the cast-off coat of some discharged or dishonest flunkey, he would have been at once received into the presence of Royalty with the other "Excellencies!" who had tricked themselves out in the tawdry trappings demanded by the regulations of the LORD CHAMBERLAIN. We must protest, in the joint names of common sense and common prudence, against the absurdity and the impolicy of calling on a foreign ambassador to put himself in livery, and running the risk of giving offence to a great nation by an imbecile adherence to an effete practice, which certainly ought to have gone out with Bartholomew Fair, and which might, at all events, be left to the *Bal Masqué* and the Beefeaters.

We do not blame the CHAMBERLAIN, who is the very head of all the livery servants in the kingdom, and is not only a state servant—in livery—himself, but would be nothing if the livery system were to fall into disuse at Court, where his occupation would be gone if the abolition of external show were permitted. We admire the good sense of the American Government and of the American Minister on this occasion, and we earnestly call on LORD JOHN RUSSELL, LORD PALMERSTON, SIR JAMES GRAHAM, and the other upper servants of the Crown—we have named these three as the most likely to be influenced by reasonable considerations—to get permission of their Royal Mistress to imitate the wise example of the domestic butler of the present day, by going out of livery.

Punch satirizes the U.S. Minister's dilemma: Would the Queen tolerate his appearance at Court in "the simple dress of an ordinary American citizen," or would she remain adamant and demand a "fancy costume?"

Buchanan had a "pretty animated conversation on the subject" with Sir Edward Cust, the Master of Ceremonies, who informed him that the Queen would not object to his appearance at Court in any dress he might think "proper," but he could not expect to be invited to Court balls and dinners where everybody else appeared "in costume." He "graciously" added that the Minister would be invited to Court concerts which the Bishops attended because a "uniform" was not required "on such occasions." Therefore Buchanan wrote his niece:

> Should her Majesty pursue this course, it will unquestionably be followed by her courtiers. Now I would not care a button personally for this social exclusion, but whilst it continues, *I should not be willing to have you here on any account*.... Should this difficulty be amicably adjusted, then you may come with Col. Lawrence otherwise not.... I entrust you with the secret of Col. Lawrence [i.e., his forthcoming marriage]—in the full belief that you will divulge it to no person.[15]

He also suggested to his niece that she should have no dresses made in the United States, for, though he was neither a "very close observer or accurate judge," he thought that the English ladies of the very highest rank "do not dress as expensively, with the exception of jewels, as those in the United States."[16]

So the two ladies—Harriet Lane and Elizabeth Chapman—bided their time and made preparations in case word came suddenly from London or Kentucky.

Though Harriet was advised to buy nothing in the States, Elizabeth took the opposite tack and visited Mme. Motté in Philadelphia about her trousseau. Madame was "overwhelmingly obliging," and hastily applied her needle. There was to be a brown merino for traveling, a morning dress of blue India silk covered with palm leaves, and a black velvet cloak. The most beautiful gown of all, Elizabeth thought, was to be of green antique moiré, the color of "a green pippin even by gas light."

Suddenly, all difficulties for both ladies were resolved. The Wards, persuaded no doubt that one lawsuit was enough, agreed not to take an appeal and settled out of court. Doylestown's Presbyterian minister, asked to perform the wedding ceremony, had no objections—a "great relief" to Elizabeth.

As for the "dress question" at the Court in London, Buchanan wrote his niece that it, too, was satisfactorily settled:

> I appeared at the Levée on Wednesday last, in just such a dress as I have worn at the President's one hundred times. A black coat, white waist-coat & cravat & black pantaloons & dress boots, with the addition of a very plain black-handled & black-hilted dress sword. This is to gratify them who had yielded so much & to distinguish me from the Upper Court servants.[17]

To a friend in Lancaster the Minister wrote in some disgust that he was "beginning to have a taste of what our troubles will be when the American Season for travelling fairly commences." He could hardly wait for the return of his competent attaché "with his young & beautiful wife."[18]

Since her uncle was not to be ostracized from the social life at Court after all, Harriet would be able to accompany Bigelow and Elizabeth, who had postponed their departure date on the *Atlantic* to the middle of April. That suited both ladies better, anyway, as there would be less chance of seasickness from winter storms.

On 16 March 1854, three lines appeared in the *Doylestown Intelligencer* announcing the marriage of "Col. T. B. Lawrence, of the American Legation in London to Miss Elizabeth Chapman, eldest daughter of Judge Henry Chapman." There was no mention of a previous marriage, but everybody knew about it, for even in Doylestown Bigelow's name had recently appeared in the papers in connection with the Ward brothers' murder trial.

The *New York Mirror* announced that Col. Lawrence would be returning to the Legation in London with his "fresh, blooming, and accomplished bride.... It is a matter of congratulation that the hospitalities of Col. Lawrence will be graced hereafter by one of the most beautiful of our fair country-women.... Mrs. Lawrence has every qualification of mind and person to command admiration among the most refined and courtly circles of 'England's honored dames.' "[19]

4

BOSTON, THEN LONDON (1854)

"Victoria, Her Majesty, I regret to say, is a perfect fright"

Following the ceremony at the bride's home, the newlyweds left for New York, where they spent a week shopping, going to the theater, and dining with some of Bigelow's friends. They then boarded the *Bay State* for the overnight cruise to Fall River. There they were met by two Lawrence servants with a carriage to take them on to Boston, where they planned to stay till their departure for London.

Elizabeth's heart "slightly palpitated" as they drove up to the imposing townhouse on Park Street. Bigelow's must have done so for a different reason. He could hardly fail to have been reminded of the same scene almost exactly five years before when he arrived at his parents' home overlooking the Common after the journey from Louisville with Sallie and her maid Eliza.

A view of Park Street, Boston, in 1859. The bride's heart "slightly palpitated" at the sight of the Lawrence's elegant townhouse (second from left). The house, overlooking the Common, is now part of the Union Club. *Courtesy of the Boston Athenaeum.*

The door was opened by the butler, who led them into the hall where Mrs. Abbott Lawrence awaited them, holding a huge basket of flowers that had just arrived for the bride. She had been too ill to attend the wedding; so she was meeting her son's second wife for the first time. After extending "the warmest of greetings," she dispatched them upstairs to dress, for that afternoon she was giving the first of three receptions to introduce the new bride:

> I put on my brown lace spencer & coral earrings & breast-pin & just as I had finished dressing, old Mr. Lawrence was announced at my room door. I rushed out & he greeted me in the most affectionate manner.... I descended to the drawing-room on his arm, & there was presented to a very large number of the family, all of whom had called in a pouring rain. You may imagine the extent of the connection when I tell you there were eleven Mrs. Lawrences in the room at the same time.

Mrs. Abbott Lawrence, by Chester Harding, *c.* 1855. EL's mother-in-law was so "goodhearted," she did nothing but "hoist presents on her friends." *Courtesy of the Museum of Fine Arts, Boston.*

They dine at six, & after dinner Mr. Lawrence [i.e., Bigelow] took me up to his sanctum. It is a perfect museum & one of the prettiest rooms I ever was in. He has all sorts of curiosities, from the claymore of a Highlander to the lion knife of a South African. The walls are covered with book cases, armour, & pictures.

Abbott Lawrence, an engraving by Chappel found at Fonthill. The distinguished merchant, "a perfect paragon of a man," is seated with his ledgers and a bolt of cloth from his company's mills, which are visible in the distance.

The next day the bride again stood for two hours (this time in her blue silk), and was presented as "my daughter" to two hundred and fifty people:

> I have shaken hands with all the fashion, talent,—& I was going to say, wealth—of Boston. I can name but a few of the distinguished persons who called, but I cannot refrain from mentioning Mr. Winthrop, Mr. Everett, Mr. Prescott, Mr. Greenough, Mr. Longfellow, Mr. Quincy....

There were so many parties lined up for the rest of their stay, they were forced to refuse as many as they accepted. Elizabeth was charmed by everyone, and they by her. She thought her father-in-law a "perfect paragon of a man," and her mother-in-law so goodhearted, she did nothing but "hoist presents on her friends." Indeed, her husband's family

Silhouette of the Abbott Lawrence family in their second floor drawing room. Bigelow stands at right, facing his older brother James. In this setting EL was introduced to "all the fashion, talent... & wealth of Boston." This picture now hangs in the same room, returned by family descendants. *Courtesy of the Union Club, Boston.*

was "quite a match for my own & I can pay it no higher compliment." She detected none of the chill that had frozen out poor Sallie.

Old Abbott Lawrence particularly endeared himself to her by asking "a great many questions about Grandpa, as well as about our old Quaker stock," and she took great pleasure in "recounting to him the history of John Chapman the first." She thought the folks at home would want to know he told her that her "manner of receiving people had pleased him exceedingly" and that never had a stranger come to Boston "who in so short a time made themselves so great a favorite."

Needless to say, curiosity about Bigelow's second try ran high. Whenever she entered a room, every eye was riveted. The few Bostonians who had come down for the wedding conceded (somewhat to their surprise, apparently) that they had been "perfectly charmed" with Elizabeth's family and with their visit to Doylestown.

The week after her arrival she celebrated her twenty-fifth birthday. Before she was even dressed, there was a knock on her door, and a servant handed her a box with the compliments of Mr. Augustus Lowell, who was engaged to Bigelow's younger sister, Kitty. It looked like a large box of sugarplums, but when she opened it she found a "superb white Canton crape shawl."

She had scarcely recovered from "that shock" when her husband appeared and proffered "a magnificent white camel's hair Burnoos cloak, and the most exquisite lava bracelet" she had ever beheld. She "flourished about" in them for a few minutes, when another box was handed in: a gold breastpin from Mrs. James Lawrence, Bigelow's sister-in-law (who was the daughter of William Prescott, the historian).

Then came "the finale." Abbott Lawrence handed her five hundred dollars and expressed his pleasure that she was now "his daughter." Elizabeth was quite overcome. It was more money than she had ever seen at one time in her life.

* * *

She had a marvelous time at the dinner parties, enjoying the animated conversations. One evening (dressed in her favorite "pippin"-colored dress), she sat beside the historian, Mr. Prescott, and the two laughed so hard the hostess vowed she would never seat them together again. After dinner she had a long and entertaining chat with Mr. Longfellow.

The next day she and Bigelow and a couple of relatives went in "the cars" out to Groton to see the old Lawrence homestead. As the family reminisced about playing hide-and-seek in the barn, Elizabeth was reminded of her own childhood days at her grandparents' farm. Another evening she was taken to meet the venerable Josiah Quincy, followed by a supper at Mrs. Amory's—at which all forty guests were actually "seated at table!"

Meanwhile, preparations were under way for the voyage to England. She and Bigelow sat for their daguerreotypes, to be distributed to both families. On April 13 they took the overnight boat down to New York, stopping at the Astor House. Two days later they sailed on the *Atlantic*, along with Harriet Lane, whose chaperonage had been transferred from Bigelow to the wife of Commodore Perry.[1]

Unlike the voyage with her father on the same ship the previous summer, this crossing found the banks of the bay covered with snow, a strong wind was howling, and Elizabeth felt "anything but comfortable" when she realized that in just such a gale the *San Francisco* had set off, never to return. The minute she sensed the motion of the boat, she went to her stateroom, undressed, and climbed into her berth, prepared to stay there for at least four days. However, the ship was forced to anchor off Sandy Hook for the night; so Bigelow persuaded her to get dressed and make a "reappearance" in the dining room. There she found the passengers sitting around "at as a decided a stand-still as the ship, & everyone looking as melancholy as ravens."

The captain raised anchor late the next morning, but by nightfall they ran into another violent storm, and again Elizabeth took to her berth. To her annoyance her husband never felt a qualm. Once she weakly staggered to the porthole and spotted an iceberg, and later, the wreck of a large New York packet ship, "all its boats, masts & sails gone, & a melancholy sight it was drifting about over the waves, unguided & alone."

No sooner had the ship anchored off Liverpool than a tugboat chugged alongside, bringing Buchanan to meet his niece (a year younger than Elizabeth and "a most charming person bye the bye"), and Augustus Belmont to meet "Mrs. Com. Perry," his mother-in-law. (The financier was at that time *chargé d'affaires* at The Hague.)

The Lawrence and Buchanan parties were among the last to disembark:

> We were obliged to descend a flight of steps down the sides of the steamer. A tremendous gale was blowing; every person in the crowded tug below was staring at my petticoats fluttering in the wind. As I attempted to hand my leather basket to Capt. West, it fell from my hands down into the Mersey. Instantly all eyes were on it, & I glided down the stairway most fortunately unheeded. I never was in so conspicuous a position in my life—quite as bad as the unintentional Bloomer we saw on the banks of the Thames last summer.

The party proceeded to the Adelphi Hotel, where they shared a parlor. Harriet Lane, like Elizabeth, had eaten nothing since they left New York; so they ordered "soup, salmon, roast beef, lamb, spring chicken, fried sweet breads, tarts, puddings, jellies, custards, oranges, raisins, & almonds—all these without the vegetables, mind you!"

While the two ladies were gorging themselves at the hotel, Buchanan and Belmont went out to a dinner party, "the latter with diamond buttons down his waistcoat the largest I ever saw." On their return the two men sat in the parlor discussing politics "over a cigar & a bottle of wine."

Next morning they all departed by train for London, Buchanan and Belmont telling "most amusing stories so that the hours flew like minutes." At the station the Minister's coach awaited them "with coachman & footman in livery," and they were soon "whirling" along the streets to their new home, 12 A George Street, near Hanover Square. Bigelow had rented the first floor apartment, the drawing room of which looked out at St. George's Chapel, "where all the marriages of the nobility take place." Elizabeth promised herself a great deal of enjoyment peering at the "distinguished couples" as they entered the famous church.

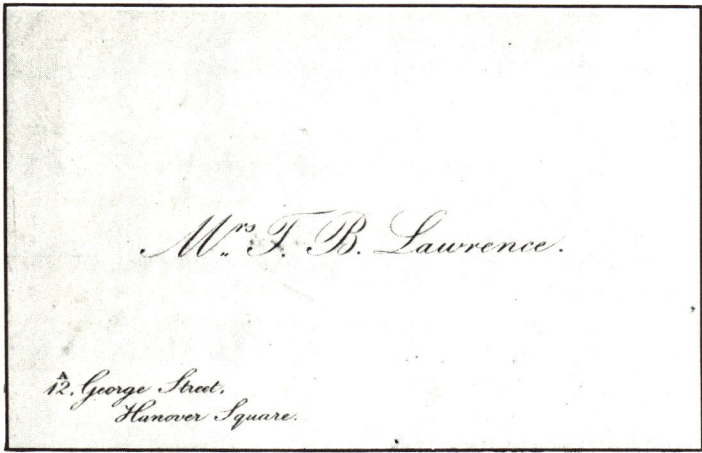

The first of many calling cards, engraved in London.

The apartment above was occupied by Prince Mahomet of Calcutta, who employed five "native servants," all dressed in Indian style. These "poor wretches", she discovered, were given two shillings a week for their meals. Consequently they were "half starved," and broke into the pantry and stole everything they could lay their hands on while "His Highness their master is perhaps away driving with the Queen."

She was plunged immediately into the whirl of the London "season." The big excitement was her approaching "presentation at the court Drawing Room," which was to take place in less than two weeks. She did not expect to be the least "flurried" about it, and Mrs. Joshua Bates had volunteered to give her and Harriet some advice about their "drapes." Since Mrs. Bates was a down-to-earth Yankee whose husband, a Boston merchant, was presently the head of the prestigious Baring Brothers bank in London, her advice would be welcome.

One of the first dinners Elizabeth attended—a meeting of the Literary Fund—amused her immensely:

> The ladies all sat in the gallery & had the pleasure of seeing the gentlemen eat in the hall below & judging of the good dishes by their olfactories alone. I regret to state that the feast of reason & the flow of soul was not quite so animating to the ladies as the feast of turtle & the flow of champagne was to the gentlemen.
>
> By the side of the President sat four Indian princes.... all arrayed in glittering drapes of cashmere & gold with turbans adorned with diamonds, but poor old Prince Mahomet was shivering with cold the whole time, & would constantly wrap his shawls more closely around his throat & seemed to be suffering both with bronchitis & neuralgia. They all looked half asleep long before the dinner was over, & I've no doubt would have given the brightest jewel they owned to have got away.

The next evening the Lawrences were off to hear Crevelli in *Fidelio* at Covent Garden, where Elizabeth caught her first glimpse of the royal family:

> In the box immediately opposite to us sat the Queen, Prince Albert, & the Prince of Wales & Prince Arthur. Victoria, Her Majesty, I regret to say, is a perfect fright, & although dressed very handsomely in a blue dress & pink opera cloak, & her head adorned with pearls, she looked neither royal nor handsome. She is very short & stout, with a retreating chin—such a short upper lip that it does not cover her teeth, a face as red as a blaze, & with a shine on it that might almost lead you to think that her hair-dresser had made a mistake & put the pomatum on her features instead of her hair.
>
> Prince Albert is very fine looking, but is growing quite bald. The royal children are pretty & pale.... They all paid the greatest attention to the music, & although I saw her Majesty yawn once behind her fan, yet they seemed to enjoy it very much, Prince Albert often keeping time with both head & hand.

As the wife of the attaché, and the daughter-in-law of a previous Minister, her days were filled with the formality of being called upon and then returning the calls. Among the first visitors was Charles Robert Leslie, a Philadelphia artist who had gone to England as a young man to study under Benjamin West and had continued to live there. He was followed by the Belgian Minister, and a steady stream of ladies of the Court:

> Yesterday morning when I reached home from a shopping expedition I found the card of the Duchess of Inverness, the wife of the Duke of Sussex, the uncle of the Queen—& an invitation to dine with her on next Wednesday.
>
> I had scarcely taken off my bonnet when the servant told me that a lady had called who wished to know if Mrs. Lawrence was in—& in a moment quite a fine looking woman entered dressed in a striped brown silk, purple bonnet & black silk mantle, who shook hands with me in a very friendly manner. She seated herself, crossed her legs in the most easy style possible, & it was not until she had been here for nearly an hour that I discovered I was talking to the Countess of Clarendon.
>
> She is at the very apex of fashion & position in England, but instead of being very upish & fly away, I think the term motherly describes her manners.... She is to present me at the next Drawing Room, which comes on the 11th of this month—oh, how I wish it was over.

Advice on dress and etiquette was proffered by the Countess, after which Elizabeth went into consultation with a dressmaker:

> My train is to be of white *poult de soie [sic]*.... It hangs loose from the shoulders, & is to be trimmed with illusion looped with bunches of pink moss rose buds & white crape leaves. The petticoat is of the same kind of silk, which is very fashionable in London, with two flounces of white Brussels lace. I am sure to wear white plumes which tower above my head, & lappets of lace to match my flounces—lappets are a kind of scarf which is fastened on the back of the head & hangs down over the shoulders.
>
> You have no idea what an expensive thing a Court dress is—you cannot go to Court in the simplest imaginable way under a hundred & twenty dollars, & for that price your dress would be rather mean.... I have a most excellent maid, who I have employed for the season, so there is no danger of my going anywhere with my dress flying wildly to the winds.

In spite of her best efforts, Elizabeth felt decidedly nervous whenever she thought about the long train she had to manage and the deep curtsy she was required to make. Her dress was not delivered until the night before, and as it lay spread out on the bed, looking "so immensely long and white," she contemplated it with "about as cheerful an expression as a winding-sheet might suggest."

On the morning of the great event, Cavalier, the popular London hairdresser, appeared:

> In half an hour my plumes were towering above my head, my lappets waving over my shoulders, & everything ready to putting on my train, which by dint of violent exertions both on Susan's [her maid] part & my own, I at length found myself arranged in, & then I commenced exercising about the room & making stately bows to all the chairs & tables that came in my way.

At half-past one the brougham drove up to the door. Bigelow, in full uniform, helped with the careful arrangement of train, plumes, and lappets, and they were off to the Palace of St. James.

Instead of going in through the main entrance "with its gloomy old towers," they were escorted through the park, between rows of infantry and cavalry lined up for the occasion. Arriving at the entrance for foreign Ministers, Elizabeth was gently propelled through the door of the brougham and shown into one of the "cosiest little rooms imaginable," where their cloaks were taken off by "two blooming-faced old Englishwomen."

On entering the waiting room set apart for the members of the diplomatic corps, they were greeted by a "most striking spectacle": titled representatives from every kingdom of Europe, the men covered with orders, the ladies dazzling in jewels and plumes. Lady Clarendon stepped forward and introduced Elizabeth to Sir Edward Cust, the Master of Ceremonies, who shone in full court dress of red and gold, then to Lord and Lady Palmerston. His Lordship's features were "delicate as a woman's," while his bright blue eyes, looking "ten times bluer" when contrasted with his snow-white hair, were "keen as a hawk's."

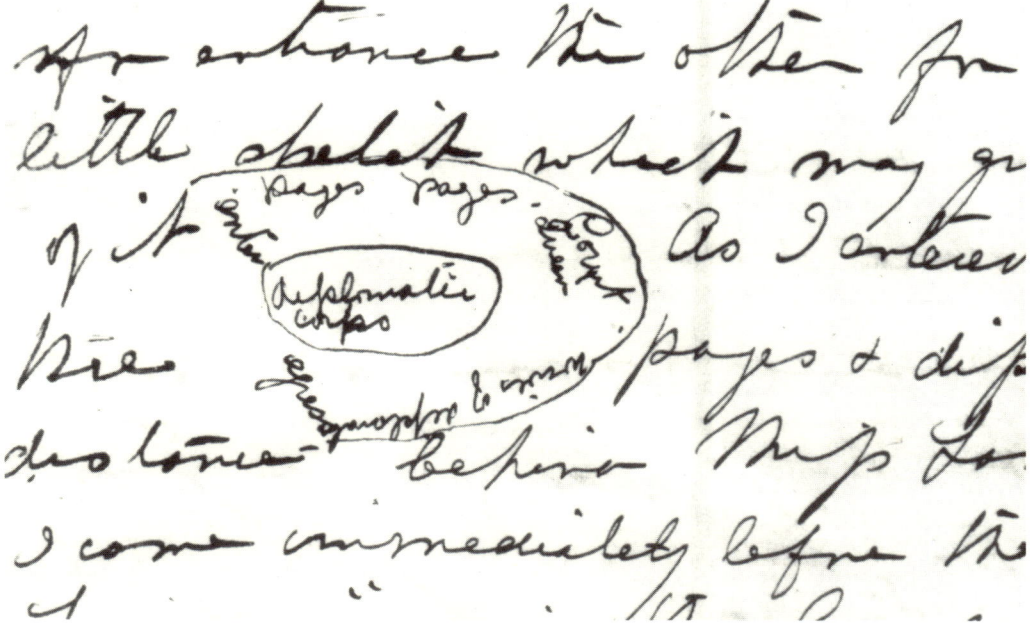

EL's rough sketch of the positioning of the participants in her presentation at Court.

Suddenly the great folding doors were thrown open, the assembled company was formed into a single line, and one by one they entered the throne room where the Queen and Prince Albert were seated on a raised dais surrounded by the ladies and gentlemen of the Court. Elizabeth took great care not to tread on the train of Harriet Lane, who preceded her.

"Mrs. Bigelow Lawrence," intoned the Countess of Clarendon.

> The Queen wore a train of green and white brocaded silk, trimmed with white tulle and blonde, and alternate bunches of violets and pink and white may-blossoms. The petticoat was of white satin, with white tulle and blonde, and bunches of violets and pink and white may-blossoms to correspond with the train.
> Her Majesty's head-dress was a wreath of violets and pink and white may-blossoms and diamonds.
> The foreign Ministers were introduced, when the following presentations to the Queen took place in the diplomatic circle :—
> By the Countess of Clarendon.—Miss Harriet Lane, niece of his Excellency the United States' Minister; Mrs. Lawrence, wife of Colonel Lawrence, Attaché to the United States' Legation.

An excerpt from *The Times* of London, Friday, 12 May, 1854. A description of the Queen's gown is followed by mention of the Countess of Clarendon's presentation of the two young ladies from Pennsylvania.

Elizabeth glided forward and managed the deep curtsy "to a little red-faced woman with a pair of immense staring light blue eyes that looked as cold & feelingless as two icebergs." On rising she shot a quick glance at the handsome Prince Albert, and found herself pitying him "having to pass all his days with the singular mixture of red pepper & ice that stood by his side." After bowing to the other members of the Court, she passed down the other side of the room to stand between the Countess of Clarendon and the wife of Sir James Graham, who whispered to her the names of the various distinguished personages.

In case the folks in Doylestown were curious to know how her performance was rated, the Master of Ceremonies reported to a friend that she had "produced a great sensation."

* * *

The following night the Lawrences were scheduled to attend a fancy-dress ball given by the French Ambassador. They had rented costumes at Moreau's, the French *costumier*. Bigelow was to go as a musketeer, Elizabeth as a Bohemian gypsy girl. Though some of the guests paid as much as three hundred dollars for their costumes, the Lawrences paid only sixty, which Elizabeth thought outlandish enough "for one single wearing!"

Two hours before the party, as the gypsy girl awaited the hairdresser, Bigelow dashed home from the Legation with the startling announcement that they could not go! He explained to his astonished wife that since Mr. Sickles, the Secretary of the Legation, had not been invited, Buchanan thought it did not behoove Bigelow—a mere attaché—to attend. The formalities and privileges of the pecking order must be observed.

Disappointed and angry, for the ball was heralded as the "most splendid" of the season, they suspected that the Minister's objections actually stemmed from the fact that Harriet Lane, his niece, had not received an invitation and Elizabeth had. But, fumed the frustrated gypsy to her musketeer, how could the French Ambassador's wife invite Miss Lane when she did not even "know of her existence" at the time the invitations were issued?

She understood why Sickles had not been asked. Not once but twice he had appeared at the Drawing Room in a black coat and pantaloons, "a thing which Mr. Buchanan never does." The last time he went so attired the Queen had commented on it, and poor Sickles was requested not to appear dressed that way again. Mrs. Sickles only made matters worse, for though she was pretty, she dressed "flashily" and talked in a loud voice "as

Queen Victoria and Prince Albert, still in Court dress, taken immediately after the ceremony on 11 May, 1854, at which EL and Harriet Lane were presented. *Reproduced by gracious permission of Her Majesty Queen Elizabeth II.*

though she had hot pudding in her mouth," causing the English ladies to titter behind their fans.

The hairdresser was canceled; the costumes were returned unworn. Salt was rubbed into the wound when the papers announced the next day that the Lawrences had attended the ball, and even described their fancy dress. The information had been obtained well ahead of time.

* * *

There were other activities to be attended, for instance, the launching of the *Royal Albert*. After the ceremonies Elizabeth returned in the carriage of the Sardinian Embassy. Since Bigelow knew most of the diplomatic corps, his wife was always "very well attended to" wherever they went. Furthermore Abbott Lawrence had written some of the dignitaries he had met while at the Court, so that doors were opened to the ex-Minister's daughter-in-law that would not have been opened to a mere attaché's wife. Elizabeth was not unappreciative of the fact that, for an American girl, she was enjoying a unique experience. Even for her first visit to the Tower, she and Harriet Lane were to be accompanied by "Mr. Sotheby, the great antiquary," who was prepared to "show all the places that the public cannot enter."

Not long after the fancy-dress debacle they attended the Queen's ball at Buckingham Palace. The diplomatic corps was ranged on one side of the throne room, the nobility on the other, and such a display of "beauty & rank & diamonds" the Doylestown girl had never before seen. Finally the doors were thrown open and a man in gold livery rushed down the aisle clapping his hands and calling "sharp, sharp," signifying the arrival of the Queen.

Four gentlemen ushers followed carrying long sticks, then two chamberlains in red and gold, who entered the room backwards. Finally in swept Victoria in a white lace dress covered with garlands of green leaves and diamonds, "the splendid Mountain of Light [the Koh-i-Noor diamond] sparkling on her bosom," her hair *à l'impératrice* crowned by a "superb" wreath of green leaves and diamonds matching the motif on her dress.

Trailing Victoria were her husband, resplendent in uniform and orders, her mother, the Duchess of Kent, and her aunt, the Duchess of Cambridge, both daughters-in-law of George III. Then came the latter's daughter, Princess Mary of Cambridge—"poor Mary,"[2] as Victoria often referred to the cousin who looked, as the novelist Bulwer-Lytton later told Elizabeth, like "a feather-bed put on two short legs."

Her Majesty was "exceedingly gracious, . . . smiling & bowing & showing not only her teeth but her gums." Some of the ladies curtsied so low the admiring American was convinced they "sat down to it."

A quadrille was struck up by the band, the Queen gave her hand to the Austrian Minister, while the Prince stepped out with bulbous Princess Mary:

> It was quite funny as the [two] ladies danced towards one another, seeing the Mountain of Light playing *vis à vis* to the mountain of fat. You can imagine nothing more coarse or vulgar than the Princess Mary both in her appearance and manners—her neck looks like one vast acre of fat, & on the back of it bloomed an immense—rose!—which I regret to state was not, however, "the rose that all are praising."

The figures of the quadrille were different from their American counterparts. The Queen flew through them "like a fairy," never moving straight forward like everybody else, but always "on the diagonal." When the dancers joined hands and formed a circle, Elizabeth suddenly found herself grasping the hand of Prince Albert!

By far the most interesting dance to her was the Highland reel, which was performed in front of the throne, the better for the little Queen to see. Most of the participants were in their clan dress, and she was fascinated by the "wild sound of the bag pipes, the tartan plaids and heron plumes" of the dancers.

At the third Drawing Room of the season (attired in sky blue silk trimmed with blue illusion, covered with bunches of blush roses, and frosted silver and brown leaves), Elizabeth was astonished to learn that the famous Lady Seymour, whom she had longed to meet, had asked to be presented to *her*. Lady Seymour's beauty had not been exaggerated. She looked "glorious in a gold crown studded with gems, & a golden veil hanging about her like a sunset cloud."

At a subsequent party at Lady Ashburton's, Elizabeth was introduced to Thomas Carlyle:

> ...how different from the calm philosophical noble portrait that graces [our] edition of his works. He is quite a small man, & although his head is splendidly shaped & his features the same as the likeness, yet instead of being sicklied over with the pale cast of thought, they are red & swollen & have perhaps a *spiritual* but certainly not an intellectual expression.

The next person she met there was John T. Delane, editor of the London *Times*, the paper that "has more influence than any man in England." She looked with respect at this "Jupiter of its thunderbolts," who certainly had nothing in face or figure to inspire much awe. His "rubicund complexion" suggested he took "his full share of beer & beef."

In the midst of all this "star-gazing," she spotted her husband advancing towards her with Thackeray in tow. The novelist put out his hand, and Elizabeth started to shake it, when she suddenly realized it was intended not for her but for the gentleman she had been talking to. Thackeray looked astonished (but not displeased), and she turned "perfectly scarlet." Quickly recovering, she said:

> "Mr. Thackeray, perhaps you don't remember me, but I was presented to you last winter in Philadelphia."
>
> "Really, Madame, I hope you'll excuse me," he replied, "but I have been introduced to so many persons lately that"—he had got this far when he suddenly stopped, looked me full in the face, & throwing up his hands, exclaimed: "Good Lord! I should think I did remember you. I was presented to you at Mrs. Rush's & was asking about you of the American Minister's niece only today at dinner."
>
> "Well," said I, "Mr. Thackeray, your memory amazes me, but I will not press it so hard as to ask you my name."
>
> "I can tell you that, too," he replied, "it began with the first letter after B" [i.e., C for Chapman].

Later that evening Elizabeth encountered Harriet Lane and proceeded to recount her meeting with the novelist. To her amazement, Harriet said Thackeray had told her he had "lost his heart" to Elizabeth in Philadelphia and had been in love with her ever since. In fact, when Thackeray learned she was now married to Bigelow, he told him the same thing!

A few nights later they were invited to Lansdowne House, where the art-loving Elizabeth was enthralled by the paintings and statuary.[3] During the course of the evening she was presented to Disraeli and his wife. The former "wandered about the rooms in a sort of political abstraction, with the curls that *Punch* has rendered so famous still waving over his head as black & glossy as ever." Among the other guests were Doyle, the caricaturist, and Sir Edwin Landseer, the artist, a "small gray-haired whiskered delicate-featured little man, & one of the most smiling gentlemanly looking persons I have ever seen."

Thursday night they dined at Orleans House, where she sat between Lord Lansdowne and Mr. Panizzi, the president of the British Museum, both of whom kept her tremendously amused throughout the dinner.

Then came the Marquis of Brendalbane's ball, which was also attended by the Queen and the royal family:

> You can imagine nothing more superb than the grand ballroom. The ceilings were arched & paneled & painted with the Campbell arms & ensigns & the walls covered with stained glass illuminated from behind & blazing with the pictures [and] legends of this noble house.
>
> I will not pretend to tell you how many apartments were thrown open, but there were three supper-rooms at about two o'clock in the morning, & just as we were going away we discovered that there was another ballroom hung in white & gold, & so far from the crimson & gold dancing room that not a note of the music could be heard.
>
> The apartments were thrown open as high up as the third story, & upon ascending a crimson carpeted staircase which led out of a charming little blue & gold boudoir, what was my amazement to find myself on a piazza covered with canvas & built on the *outside* of the house.
>
> The view from it of the park, crowded with people who were watching for the appearance of the Queen—the blazing torches of the linkmen [torchbearers], the splendid liveries of coachmen & footmen, the carriages of state all gilded & glittering as the torch-light fell upon them, the shouts of the pages as they called out: "Lord Palmerston's carriage stops this way"..."The Duke of Montrose's servant is called for",..."The Duke of Hamilton's carriage"..., together with the loud importunities of the linkmen: "Another sixpence, your Lordship",... "Shilling, your ladyship, for keeping your dress from the wheel"...—all formed one of the most remarkable scenes I ever beheld.

Friday night found Elizabeth seated at dinner next to the Dean of St. Paul's Cathedral ("who you will know better as Henry Millman, the poet"). During the course of their spirited conversation he told her:

> Miss Brontë, the authoress of *Jane Eyre*, was married about two months ago to her father's curate. She is very agreeable in conversation, & although plain, not remarkably so, with one of those iron jaws such as you see in the pictures of Napoleon.

Saturday morning the Lawrences drove in an "elegant open barouche" to the reopening of the Crystal Palace, which had been moved from Hyde Park to a hill across the Thames several miles to the south in Sydenham (where it stood until destroyed by fire in 1936). The beauty of this "fairy-like structure" was breathtaking:

> It looks as if some gigantic glass-blower had created it—or rather as if the mist of a summer's morning had formed itself into pillars & domes & suddenly congealed; indeed, it looks at once so beautiful & so transitory, as though it waited but the presence of the mid-day sun to melt & vanish forever.

Since they were members of the diplomatic corps, their seats were nearly opposite the Queen's throne, enabling Elizabeth to get a particularly close view of the ceremony. Her Majesty arrived, "punctual as clock-work," on the arm of Prince Albert, surrounded by the ladies and gentlemen of the Court. The Queen was dressed in light blue silk, "with Brussels flounces, & wore a crape bonnet with pink flowers in the face." Whenever she glanced in their direction, some of the thirty thousand people bowed and shouted and waved their handkerchiefs "in the most frantic manner."

Prince Albert looked handsome in his red uniform; the Prince of Wales she thought a "melancholy, pale-looking child." They were followed by the Duchess of Kent leading the

Princess Royal, who was in white muslin over pink silk, and a straw bonnet; then the Duchess of Cambridge, the Princess Alice, and the Princess Mary.

When the orchestra and chorus of seventeen hundred voices struck up *God Save the Queen*, it sounded like "the roar of the ocean." By the time Victoria had been presented with various medals and the lengthy ceremonies gone through, Elizabeth was so exhausted she skipped dinner, preferring a cup of tea and a nap before joining Sir Edward Bulwer-Lytton, the novelist, in his box at the opera that evening.

Elizabeth thought him "remarkably distinguished looking, with a superb head covered with light brown curls, large clear grey eyes, high & aristocratic features." Indeed, he looked rather like the hero of one of his own novels! Since it was rumored he was taciturn and entirely different in person from what he was "on paper," she was surprised to find him a delightful conversationalist:

The Countess of Blessington, by Sir Thomas Lawrence. "He [Bulwer-Lytton] thinks me exceedingly like Lady Blessington, & so do other persons who knew her." *Courtesy of the Trustees, The Wallace Collection, London.*

> We were speaking of the opera, & turning to the stage he remarked: "How beautiful that scene is, & yet how unnatural! how unreal! But the truth is, Mrs. Lawrence, all our pleasures are but illusions, while all our pains are facts."
>
> He described to me in language such as he alone can use the original hero of his novel *Lucretia*, which, you may remember, I once brought with me from Philadelphia, & the conversation, turning upon Louis Napoleon, he told me that he had known him intimately & had always thought him a man of great abilities; but that it was now as much the fashion to overrate as it once had been to underrate them, [he] possessed great moral & physical courage, with wonderful self-reliance & concentration & a will strong as iron. He also had the strongest

impulses, & . . . he had seen him shed tears over an affecting incident & often at a generous sentiment.

"Indeed", he concluded, "there never was a man yet who had wielded great power over his fellow man, that was not oftentime the slave of his own feelings, for to rule humanity you must be human."

He thinks me exceedingly like Lady Blessington, & so do other persons who knew her. He has asked us to make him a visit in the country, which I should love to do, of all things.

I have not yet seen Lord Brougham, but I meet his wife everywhere. She is as ugly as sin & has a face like a horse, but poor old soul, I pity her. She has been sitting about in corners, neglected & forgotten, for the last forty years . . . & seen her husband flirting with all the belles & beauties of every London season.

Yesterday we were at an afternoon party at Miss Coutts [Angela Burdett-Coutts, granddaughter of the famous banker] who very kindly loaned us her box at Drury Lane theater last week. . . . Her manners are so simple & modest & retiring, as though she were one of the most insignificant old maids in the world. She has a very good figure, & her features are excellent, . . . but unfortunately her face is covered with a sort of red eruption, which of course spoils everything.

I hope you will think I have somewhat mended my ways when I tell you that I never come home from a ball or party without putting away everything I had on before I retire.

5
LONDON: "THE SEASON" (1854)

"Exchanging your wreath for your nightcap" at dawn.

The Lawrences had been in London only a few weeks when they decided they were heartily sick of "lodgings" and rented a townhouse at 48 Upper Brook Street, two blocks from Hyde Park:

> The house is very small, but beautifully furnished. It has a dining room, . . . two small drawing-rooms with yellow satin curtains & furniture to match, the walls covered with white & gold paper; the woodwork round the door panels gilded, & five elegant mirrors, together with all sorts of lovely little tables & knicknacks innumerable; a bed room, a dressing room, & three servants' rooms.
> We keep a cook, a chamber maid, footman, a coachman, & a boy who waits on the door & is called a page, dressed in black roundabouts with a row of gilt buttons down the front; [and] Susan, who dresses me when I go out.
> The little page, called Charles, I fear will not live long. He was nearly starved to death before he came here—poor little soul, he seems to be perfectly meek & broken-spirited, & I pity him from the very bottom of my heart. He has a very pretty face—if it was not so pale.

She thought the house "the most cheerful, cosiest-looking place," and the servants all excellent and honest. Fortunately, they had worked for her mother-in-law when Abbott Lawrence had been Minister, so they had some familiarity with American ways.

She found keeping house in England ever so much easier than at home. For one thing, in addition to their wages, servants were also given "board wages"—generally about twelve shillings a week—with which to buy their own food, since their table had nothing to do with the master's. It was the cook's job not only to know how to cook, but also to buy all the provisions and to reckon the quantity required for each meal.

Such a thing as a servant forgetting to obey an order was simply unheard of, for they were all so "admirably drilled," they not only never forgot, they scarcely ever required any instruction. Of course there were occasional slips. Never the domestic type, the lady of the house had difficulty, albeit infrequent, in communicating with Emma the cook. Early on she bought a cookbook, and after assiduously studying it, she gave Emma instructions on the making of custard puddings. If she had not known better, she would have thought the results were "mush—like which they both looked and tasted."

When they first set up their own housekeeping arrangements, Bigelow wrote his father asking for the loan of "some silver forks and knives." To Elizabeth's astonishment, the return steamer brought a present to *her* of two thousand dollars with which to purchase her own silver in London. In the meantime his mother sent Bigelow a dozen silver forks, "pie knives," and pearl-handled fruit knives to tide them over, along with an assortment of tongs and ladles. When Elizabeth went to "bespeak" her tableware—augmented by a handsome tea service—she was quite sure she and her husband would be able to open a "private mint."

Usually they breakfasted about half-past ten, after which Bigelow took off for the Legation, returning about three, when they drove forth to call. They dined at seven, then adjourned to the parlor for a cup of tea and a chat—generally about home and family. At nine they retired to dress, being "obliged to go somewhere every evening."

One of her favorite sights was Hyde Park on a fine spring afternoon when it was filled with all the splendid carriages and liveries. She especially enjoyed Rotten Row, which was reserved for horseback riders. No one was permitted to drive down it but the Queen, who occasionally dashed into the park "in an open carriage & four, followed & preceded by two out-riders in flaming red livery."

In spite of an outbreak of cholera, causing some streets to be closed off with black flags flying at either end, she thought London a "wonderful" city. No matter whether day or night, there was such a "rolling" of carriages in the streets, one heard a "continual roar—like the fall of water at Niagara":

EL had never seen such "beauty & rank & diamonds" as were displayed at the Queen's ball at Buckingham Palace. *The Illustrated London News*, April 1855.

At this season of the year coachmen, footmen, & horses are nearly worn to death with the London season. Night after night these poor wretches have to wait until their masters & mistresses are ready to drive home from the ball or party, which is often not until daylight streams in through the windows, & the consequence is that they are perfectly overcome for loss of sleep the next day, & wherever you see a fine carriage stopping, you may be sure to see the liveried coachman sound asleep on the box. They are paid enormous wages, however, which I suppose they think compensates for everything.

A typical day brought forth eight or nine invitations, two or three of which they would accept. The others had to be regretted by note, and she was learning to make a "first-rate seal." One of the invitations accepted was to another ball at the palace, at which they were treated to a most unusual sight. The Queen's hair started to fall down, and the lovely Duchess of Sutherland, Mistress of the Robes, stepped up and rearranged it:

It was all done in the most solemn manner, the Duchess putting in the hairpins, smoothing the Queen's hair with her hand, & then drawing off to see how it looked, just as a dressing-maid might do, although I scarcely imagine there was ever a dressing-maid that appeared in such elegant apparel. Her dress was of gold moiré antique embroidered all over the bosom & down the skirt with diamonds & emeralds.

She has the reputation for being terribly extravagant, even with such a fortune as her husband's, & certainly judging from her dress, I should think that the report was a true one. In America we consider it something very elegant to have dresses embroidered with silk, but what is that to precious stones?

The young king of Portugal & his brother, the little Duke of Oporto, graced the ball with their presence. The latter, thinking, I suppose, that he was in one of his royal palaces at home, was constantly standing in front of the Queen, while she was just as constantly motioning him to stand to one side. Had anyone else done such a thing, the gentlemen ushers would soon have put them out of the way, but of course, they can give no orders to a royal Duke.

The King of Portugal was presented to Sir Edwin Landseer the other night—the artist, you remember, who is so famous for painting animals. His salutation was: "Good evening, Sir Edward [sic]—I'm most happy to make your acquaintance; I am very fond of beasts!"

The Lord Mayor's banquet was another subject for her caustic pen:

The guests were two hundred in number, & were received in an immense drawing room. You were first presented to the Lord Mayor & then to the Lady Mayoress, who was seated on a chair of state & never rose to anyone under a Duke or a Foreign Minister! It was quite rich to see the grand airs of the wife of a retired tallow chandler.

His Honor the Mayor is a little paunchy man, & was covered with gold lace & almost bursting with self-importance. The dinner was about as stupid a thing as I ever sat down to, & after consuming our turtle & punch we both nearly fell asleep. Warlike speeches, which certainly had enough lead, if there was no fire in them; toasts & doleful dirge-like soup constituted the feast of reason & the flow of soul, & I was obliged to keep myself busily employed in the graceful occupation of eating oranges, or I should have fallen asleep & probably been carried out as intoxicated.

The peculiar feature of the dinner was the passing round the "loving cup," which is a golden tankard with handles on either side, covered with a golden lid & filled with a spiced wine. The drinking of it is quite a conspicuous thing: when it comes to you, you rise, take the cup by the handles, turn to your partner, who also rises, takes off the lid & holds it while you bow, drink his health, then wipe the lip of the cup, & he replaces the lid & you hand it to him, & then take off the lid & he does just as you have done, & then passes it in the same way to the next.

All this health-drinking before two hundred people is, I can tell you, quite confusing, but I like the custom on account of its antiquity. It has been handed down from Lord Mayor to Lord Mayor for centuries, the Lord Mayor always drinking first to show that there is no poison in the cup, so you may imagine how barbarous the age was in which the "loving cup" was first introduced.

On the Fourth of July Bigelow was invited to a "gentlemen's dinner," so Elizabeth decided to celebrate the "glorious Fourth" in her own special way. She took a cab to Westminster Abbey where she stood contemplatively before the memorial to Major John André in the nave. She studied the figure of young André stalking off to his execution as a spy captured in civilian clothes, while in the foreground Washington receives a petition beseeching a soldier's death. Forty years later, at the request of the Duke of York, André's remains had been transported to Westminster Abbey, his monument paid for by George III. As Elizabeth studied it, she reflected on how near John André and Benedict Arnold had come to "destroying our Independence Day." With a pang of homesickness, she realized that the closest she would come to a fireworks celebration was "an astral lamp & a sperm candle."

* * *

One day she and Bigelow went down to Greenwich to see the observatory, then wandered around the grounds of the naval hospital. Just as she had asked the French soldiers about Napoleon during her trip to Paris the previous year, she now elicited tales of Nelson's battles from the British veterans.

Later they strolled through a street fair, watching the "common people" play games like "blind-man's buff" and "kiss-in-the-ring." Most of the fair-goers were armed with a little wooden toy which they slyly rubbed on the backs of those they passed, producing a noise that sounded exactly like the tearing of cloth. After her back had been scratched by the toy a number of times, she decided her little half-sister and brother would have fun with it in Doylestown and bought two to send home.

* * *

Another fine day they drove to Ascot. She was astonished to find that the course was grass-covered—instead of being "completely bare," as it was at home—to give added spring to the horses' hooves. As the jockeys urged their mounts over the course full speed, fifty thousand people, she estimated, shouted and cheered in tremendous excitement.

They watched from their open barouche, listening to the bets being made all around them. A lunch of "chickens & pigeon-pies & champagne & straw-berries & all sorts of good things" had been packed in a hamper, and they devoured it sitting in their carriage. During the intervals between races, gypsies told their fortunes.

* * *

One evening they dined with the Archbishop of Canterbury at Lambeth Palace. As the guests returned to the drawing room after dinner, Elizabeth spotted one of the Archbishop's grandchildren sitting in a corner working a sampler. The girl looked so much like Fanny, Elizabeth's little half-sister, she could not resist walking over and speaking to her, though the child was shy and replied only in monosyllables. She then sought out the girl's mother and commented on the resemblance to Fanny, which seemed to please her, "for, said she, the Americans are so famous for their beauty."

* * *

At a ball at the French Embassy, Elizabeth had a long talk with the Duchess of Sutherland. Amazingly enough, the Duchess's gown was almost exactly like hers—hardly cause for lamentation, at least on *Elizabeth's* part! They were both in "illusion embroidered in silver & floss over white satin." The headdresses, however, were rather different. The American attaché's wife wore "merely a wreath of summer flowers." Her Grace's consisted of "white May blossoms studded with diamonds that lay among the flowers like immense dew drops with the sun shining on them."

* * *

At Lord Granville's dinner, her partner was the architect of the Crystal Palace, Sir Joseph Paxton. Since he was also a landscape designer, interested in plant material, she entertained him with a litany of American flora. To her chagrin he was entirely familiar with all of them, pronouncing the poppy his favorite. Elizabeth found him "not in the least degree affected by the wonderful rise that his fortunes have met with" since construction of the renowned showpiece.

* * *

The leaders of London fashion, Elizabeth reported, were the Duchess of Sutherland and the Marchioness of Ailesbury:

> I imagine Fanny [her half-sister] would think Lady Ailesbury perfectly superb. Ne'er did you see such a profusion of diamonds, feathers & flowers—she would almost fill up the folding doors at home, & has a great quantity of fair hair frizzled out on either side of her face. I think I won her heart entirely by taking her for twenty-five, when she is nearly fifty.
>
> You ask me to give you some of the conversation that I have with great people. Let me assure you, you can imagine nothing more commonplace, but I will nevertheless repeat to you the remarks that the Duchess of Sutherland made to me the other night.
>
> "How do you do, Mrs. Lawrence," (shaking me very warmly by the hand). "I hope you are very well, with all this dyspepsia."
>
> "Very well, thank you."
>
> "And how do you like England?"
>
> "I am delighted with it, & very much pleased to have met your Grace. Mr. Prescott told me that the first thing I did after my arrival in England must be to catch a glimpse of the Duchess of Sutherland."
>
> "Indeed" (looking exceedingly pleased), "& how is Mr. Prescott, for we were all in love with him when he was in London."

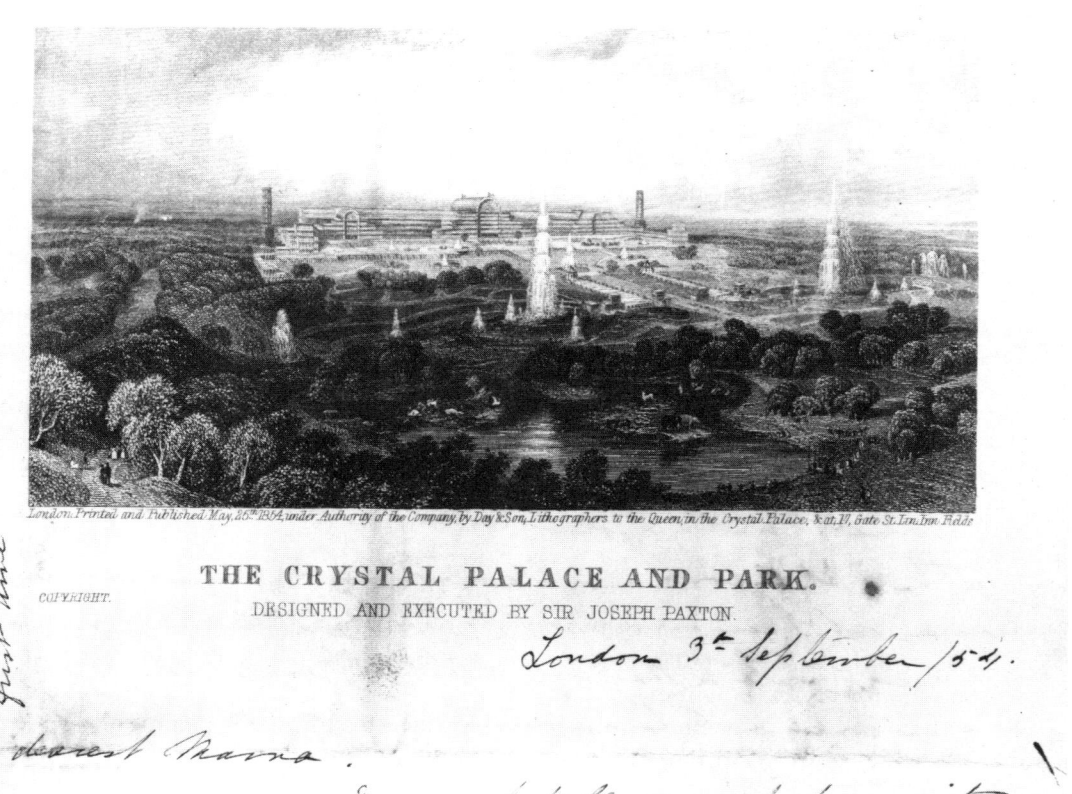

Portion of a letter to Mama, written on stationery showing the Crystal Palace reconstructed south of the Thames. EL was introduced to Sir Joseph Paxton, designer of this "fairy-like structure," at a dinner party.

"Very well, thank you, & I assure you the love was reciprocal."
"He used to tell me that my daughter Constance was like his daughter. Do you think so?"
"Yes, there is a resemblance."
Just as she was about leaving me, she turned & said, "Mrs. Lawrence, I am going to have a little dancing after dinner on Friday, & would be delighted if Col. Lawrence & yourself would come."
The next day we received a printed invitation from her Grace, & "the dancing after dinner" proved to be a splendid ball.

Elizabeth felt highly flattered when, the night of the ball, the Duchess led her to the supper table, offered her an ice, and then took her on a tour of the beautiful house. Her Grace's taste was "exquisite." Imagine a marble vase filled with a pyramid of pink and white roses arranged in alternate rows!

When Elizabeth finally returned to the dance floor, she barely escaped another revealing incident. In the midst of a quadrille, one of the dancers stepped on her skirt, which was fastened to the waist by a series of hooks. Several of the fasteners broke, and if the dance had not come to an end at that moment, enabling her to beat a hasty retreat to the dressing room, she would have been caught in that "brilliant company" in her petticoats!

* * *

Elizabeth was not the only one that season to have difficulty with her dress. She attended a dinner for thirty-five at Miss Coutts's which included the Duchess of Cambridge and the poor "feather-bed," Princess Mary. After dinner, when they were assembled in the drawing room, the Princess suddenly discovered that "the smallest of small moss rose buds" had fallen off her skirt. One of her ladies-in-waiting scooped it up to keep as a memento, "but no, her Royal Highness could not afford to make so extravagant a present, but sailed out of the room with Miss Coutts to have it sewed on." Elizabeth left no doubt about Princess Mary's attractions:

> She has a thick coarse voice, as if her fat had got into it, & is as vulgar a person in appearance & manners as you ever saw, switching herself from side to side like a great whale when she walks, & looking like anything on earth but a royal highness.

One of Elizabeth's more ardent admirers was Lord Lansdowne, the delightful old Cabinet Minister, who still retained "all the vivacity & agreeable manner" which had made him so popular. Captivated by Elizabeth's free spirit, he gave a dinner party in honor of the Lawrences, at which he piloted her to table himself. Thereafter they found themselves invited to all his "entertainments," where he made a point of introducing her to his most distinguished guests. When she confessed to him she had a great desire to meet Macaulay and Caroline Sheridan Norton, the fabled beauty and authoress, Lord Lansdowne promised to produce them, as they were "intimate friends" of his.

She loved to have him walk her around his remarkable house, telling her stories of the paintings and statuary. One evening, after such a tour, she was preparing to leave and was engaged in bundling herself up in not one, but two cloaks to ward off the chill, when Lord Lansdowne turned to Bigelow and said: "Well, she's right to take care of herself, when she knows she's valued so highly."

* * *

There were several occasions when the damp, cold English weather threatened—though never quenched—her *joie de vivre*. The fête at Ealing Park came near to being disastrous:

> The weather, which has been perfectly horrid lately, had looked very lowering before we started, but hoping that it would break away, we drove out & arrived in a drizzling rain....
> What a prospect—the sky heavy & grey seemed almost to touch the tree-tops; the fountains spouted dismally in the air; the statues gave you a shiver to look at them; & what with two or three hundred aquatic English women trailing over the lawn with muddy muslins and pink parasols pattering down gentle showers of pink rain, & with the piazzas crowded by a muddy, sneezing set who, as we got

out of our carriages with our unsoiled gowns, gloomed at us with a "you'll soon be as muddy as we are" sort of look—what with all this & the damp solemnity that seems to exist everywhere, our chances for enjoyment certainly appeared very small, & no smaller, I am sorry to say, then they actually were.

Every dry place was crowded with people, & the refreshment room was literally packed, & we felt ourselves both happy & fortunate in getting a quiet place in a sort of cellar above ground—possibly the smoke house, where in silence & darkness we consumed our chicken, & then departed, inwardly vowing that never but in the most brilliant sunshine would we go to an English fête again, especially where it was expected of each guest to do the greenhouses & the hothouses, though he died for it.

* * *

The moment came, of course, when Elizabeth had to give her first formal dinner party. She started in a small way with Miss Fitzpatrick, the actress whom she had first met singing ballads on the deck of the *Atlantic*, and several Bostonians. After consultation with Emma, the cook, the bill of fare they concocted was as follows:

1st course: pea soup
2nd course: boiled salmon with shrimp sauce
3rd course: roast chicken, stewed pigeons, boiled ham, lamb cutlets, roast wild
    ducks, peas, asparagus, French beans, cauliflower
4th course: Stilton cheese and salad
5th course: strawberries, cherries, pineapples, raspberries: French [floating?]
    island & vanilla [ice cream?] & water ice

Bigelow teased her unmercifully about the bustle in the house:

> [He] laughs at me so about my dinner that I regret to say the dignity with which I should be invested on such a distinguished occasion is entirely lost. It is my earnest prayer that I shall not ask my guests to take anything that is not on the table, as I regret to say was one striking feature of my tea-table attentions in Doylestown.
> My pride as a housekeeper received a fearful shock the other day when Mr. Gilbert was asked to dinner, & Mr. L. in a very master-of-the-house sort of manner remarked: "James, bring up the coffee," & Mrs. L. sat at the head of the table with a very smiling countenance & a perfect conviction that there was not a grain of that exhilarating beverage in the house. Fancy my disgust when James returned and announced that fact to me in a whisper that might have been heard in the third story!!!
> Just as I had commenced this letter yesterday I received a present of the most splendid pine-apple I ever beheld from no less a person than Lord Lansdowne. It is three times the size of any American one I ever saw, & Emma tells me that it brought 20 dollars in market.

* * *

Much as she enjoyed entertaining, the dinners generated a few "after-claps" in the way of bills. The Crimean War had sent prices skyrocketing, and even such a princely sum as six thousand a year was "insignificant on this side of the water."

Of great concern to everyone that summer of 1854 was the progress of the war, and beneath the surface of "gaieties" ran an undercurrent of uneasiness:

> Everyone in London looks forward with great anxiety for news from the East, & at about ten o'clock every few nights you hear a perfect outcry of "Extras!" in the streets. You cannot imagine what a terrible noise these newsmen make. They have such horribly unnatural voices, that the first time I heard them shouting out the last tidings from Turkey, I had the same feeling that I used to experience upon hearing the trumpets of the firemen in Philadelphia. While I've been writing, I have heard such an extraordinary sound in the street.... I discovered it to be a Chinese singing one of his native ballads under the window.

* * *

When "the season" was over, Elizabeth summed up her feelings about London society for her sister Mary:

> There is about as much enjoyment in it as looking at a Fireman's Parade or visiting the Franklin Institute. You may laugh at my comparisons, but I assure you the feelings that you have in looking at the above spectacles, & in going through a London season are very much the same. You begin by saying: "How very pretty," "How very amusing," & long before you close, it is your never-ceasing cry: "When will it be over?"
>
> Such a thing as loud talking or loud laughing is never heard, everyone speaks in undertones, & more than half the time the conversation is of the most formal kind. Pauses which at home are considered very awful are thought here to be very high-bred, & that sort of listless, half-asleep manner we used to see on the Eastern Shore is very high "ton" in London.
>
> It has been my good luck to know a large number of the most agreeable men in London, many of whom are entirely without the coldness of the English women, for you can imagine nothing more frigid than the manners of most of the latter not only to foreigners, but among themselves.
>
> I would not say all this to anyone but you, because people would be sure to think... I was neglected, which does not happen to be the case, for I have sometimes had an Earl, a Viscount, a Count, a Bishop & a Lord-in-waiting, all talking to me at the same time. Lady Palmerston has told me that she does not see how I could remember all the people that I know.
>
> I have seen a great deal of English society this year,... & I regret to say it presents but a melancholy picture of human nature. You may judge slightly of its heartlessness when I tell you that a person dies here & is forgotten almost as soon as he is buried. A daughter of Lady Jersey died last fall under the most distressing circumstances, & two months ago the Countess & Lady Clementine were out at all the balls & routs in black drapes & purple ornaments.
>
> The Marchioness of Westminster's son died the latter part of March; his Mother & sisters have been out everywhere for more than six weeks, & this afternoon we go to a party at their house.
>
> Nearly all the great fashionable husbands & wives seem to care no more for each other than for the dust on their feet, & nearly all of them have some scandal or other attached to their names. It costs twenty thousand pounds to get a divorce, & therefore very few people can afford to have one. Of course, there are great exceptions to this rule, for instance, Disraeli. His wife told me that they had been married for [fifteen] years & never had a difference.

. . . Don't talk of bones aching & back aching until you have gone through a regular London season. Wait until you have kept it up till daybreak for three or four weeks with scarcely an intermission, exchanging your wreath for your nightcap with the daylight streaming in through the windows, wait until then . . . & you may begin to have some idea of what it is to follow the ball of fashion.

6
THE STATELY HOMES

"This wonderful realization of my old Doylestown air-castles."

When the Lawrences were invited to visit Knebworth, the country seat of Sir Edward Bulwer-Lytton, they accepted with alacrity. There, "amid the green hills of Hertfordshire & amid the most charming & delightful society," they spent three of the "happiest days" of their lives:

> ... glad enough we were to exchange its [i.e., London's] smoke & heat & noise for the hedge-rows & hay-scented fields of old England. One hour in the train & a drive of five miles brought us at last to the princely home of the great novelist.
>
> We entered through a stone gate-way with its old porter's lodge, & found ourselves in a road which led through a thicket.... Suddenly we were in open daylight with the great park stretching on either side of us as far as the eye could see. Clumps of majestic trees studded the gentle undulations & green slopes; herds of brown deer were reposing in the shade, with a few wanderers out in the sunshine cropping the cowslips.
>
> The horses flew over the graveled carriage-way, & it was not long before the turrets of Knebworth were in sight. How can I describe to you my delight, as this feudal pile, built in the times of Henry the Seventh, first burst in view? I had expected something very grand, but nothing so princely as this....
>
> We were met on the door-step by Sir Edward, who with both hands extended, gave us a most cordial welcome, and passing immediately through the hall, we entered the flower-garden, which like the grand entrance is surrounded by a stone balustrade, each pillar of which is surmounted by a griffin rampant, the crest of the house.
>
> Gravel walks & flower-beds surrounded us on all sides. The air was perfectly fragrant with the profusion of verbenas, heliotropes, & mignonettes. Stone vases filled with crimson geraniums gave a still greater beauty & brilliance to the scene, which spread before us like a splendid Eastern carpet that combined all the gorgeous colourings of Persian looms.

On turf that felt and looked like velvet, their host led them past the bowling green to a thicket in the center of which towered an ancient elm. Supported by its branches was a giant tree house, reached by a stairway that wound around the huge trunk. Walking on beneath a green arcade, they came to an old English garden laid out in "the stiff & box-encircled fashion of bygone times." At one end stood the old bower, the interior covered with gilded and painted leather:

> I fancied the stately dames of olden times seated there with their tapestry, while their thoughts perhaps wandered to Palestine.
>
> From the gardens we returned to the house, where fresh delights awaited us....
>
> Passing through the vestibule of the garden entrance, you come to the lofty arch in the side of the hall which leads in to the grand oaken stair-case.... Upon [its]

Knebworth, the country seat of the novelist Sir Edward Bulwer-Lytton. "How can I describe to you my delight, as this feudal pile... burst into view? I had expected something very grand, but nothing so princely as this." *All photographs of Knebworth courtesy of the Honorable and Mrs. David Lytton Cobbold.*

"Each pillar is surmounted by a griffin rampant, the crest of the house."

"The splendid old dining hall" in which EL dined with Bulwer-Lytton, Maclise, and Landseer. The room, altered by the architect Sir Edwin Lutyens (who married into the family), still retains many of the features she described after her visit.

One of a pair of lamps unearthed at Pompeii. "When they were first lighted, Sir Edward invited a large company to see the first flame they had emitted for so many centuries."

lower posts stand two gilded Morish dwarfs, & on each of the others, the griffin rampant carved in oak.

At the first platform it branches off, the one side leading to the grand drawing rooms, & the other to the sleeping apartments. The whole is lighted by an immense oriel window of stained glass, & family portraits, with which the walls are covered.

On the gallery overlooking the splendid old dining hall we paused & looked down while Sir Edward pointed out to us the oaken beams of the ceiling built in the time of Henry the 7th, the oaken wainscoting from a plan of Inigo Jones, the splendid carved screen & gallery of solid oak of the time of Elizabeth, the gallery itself for the retainers of the family, & the iron lattice hole in the wall where the ladies of the house peeped down at the baronial banquet in the Hall below.

Walking to the extreme end [of the gallery] we found ourselves at the door of the haunted chamber where Queen Elizabeth slept on her way to review her troops. The walls of the haunted chamber are covered with faded tapestry, & all the furniture of oak almost black with age. The bed is hung with faded curtains of red & gold, which are the same as when the Queen slept there. Such a gloomy, ghostly old place you never saw, & I was really glad to leave it for something more cheerful. . . .

The bed in which Queen Elizabeth slept "on her way to review her troops." Hung with "curtains of red & gold," it is carved of oak "almost black with age."

We crossed to the grand drawing room, . . . its ceilings painted with the quarterings of the house, the old velvet curtains, the walls of green with golden bitterns, the beautiful Italian pictures & family portraits, . . . the mosaic tables of black & white marble, . . . the superb Buhl cabinets of tortoise shell & brass, the portrait of Sir Philip Sidney given to the Lytton of that time by the splendid soldier himself, the original portrait of the great Earl of Strafford in a coat of mail, ... the ancient look that everything wore having all the charm of antiquity without any of its decay or gloom.

My own recollections & love for the olden times, freshened & enhanced by the family legends & old traditions narrated to me by the novelist at my side, all served to throw me into a state of excitement & delight at this wonderful realization of my old Doylestown air-castles.

[Then] we descended to the splendid library. . . . At one end of it stand two iron pillars supporting small brass lamps which were found underground at Pompeii. When they were first lighted Sir Edward invited a large company to see the first flame they had emitted for so many centuries, certainly not since that night which he describes in his novel *[The Last Days of Pompeii]* "when the last arrow quivered upon the dialplate of its doom."

I was the only lady guest at Knebworth, for which (& I hope my sex will excuse me) I was very thankful, as I am sorry to say that I think the English women are both very stiff & very stupid. The other guests beside ourselves were Mr. Maclise, the great portrait painter, Sir Edwin Landseer, Mr. Foster, the editor of the *Examiner* and the intimate friend of Hood, Lamb, & also of Bulwer, Mr. Elwyn, the editor of the *Quarterly Review* . . . . Never was I in such a delightful, such a witty, such an amusing society—I was sometimes thrown into perfect convulsions of laughter.

The day after our arrival we all went fishing. Mr. Lawrence, Landseer & young Lytton, Sir Edward's son, sat on the bank, Sir Edward, Elwyn & Foster under the trees, & Maclise & I in a boat in the middle of the pond.

The sun was boiling, & do what we would the fish would not bite. Landseer, who prides himself on his luck as a fisherman, after watching his cork with intense interest for three quarters of an hour, imploring us at the same time to be still, at length pulled up his line with a triumphant flourish & discovered that he had caught a leech! I laughed until it was perfect agony.

Jokes, stories, & puns on the heat & our luck flew about in every direction, & Maclise, as we were leaving, remarked that after fishing for two hours, the only thing he had caught was a freckle!

Upon our return to the house we lunched, & then got into carriages & took a drive of 16 miles over the exquisite country of Hertfordshire. Sir Edward, Landseer, Foster & myself occupied the inside of the barouche, Mr. Lawrence & young Lytton behind.

As we drove along we had an immense quantity of conundrums, & among others I asked the party the one about a person going down the street, met a little boy coming up & said: "I am not your Father, but you're my son," & wished to know what relation they were. There they all sat, puzzling their wits & giving all sorts of absurd answers. When I announced that it was the boy's mother, you should have heard how they all laughed!

Among other things we talked about Bulwer's novels, & he said the best ones he ever wrote was *[sic] Eugene Aram* & *Godolphin*. I mentioned the scene in *Paul Clifford* between the Father & son at the trial, & he said he never had written

This portrait of the popular novelist, Sir Edward Bulwer-Lytton, by his friend Daniel Maclise, still hangs at Knebworth.

anything better than that. I told him of that night when you were reading aloud to Mary the first chapter, & I jumped from the sofa with a mouse running down my hair, & you both—with your nerves excited over the book—were frightened half out of your wits. He was highly amused....

Foster had given him his name for *Night and Morning*, "but," said Sir Edward with a sigh, "I shall never write another novel."

"I have rarely had such good reason for believing that you have one just ready for the press," replied Mr. Foster....

Upon arriving at the graveyard we descended from the carriages & walked to the grave of Lady Ann Warlock, who had been a dreadfully wicked woman in her time, & said on one occasion that the Bible was a lie, & if her words were not true, she hoped her tomb stone might be rent asunder—& it is so!

Immediately out of the grave has grown a mighty elm, whose roots have shattered the marble slab to fragments, broken down the brick work, ... & grown straight through the iron railing, the spikes sticking out of the wood in every direction.

As we looked at the tomb with its gloomy legend, & then turned to the tree that seemed to grow with almost fiendish energy, rending the marble, crumbling the foundation, splintering & twisting the iron work in its growth—shivering, scattering, swallowing up marble, brick work, iron, everything that came in its way, I thought I had never seen a more awful spectacle, & Sir Edward told me that often as he had looked upon this tomb, he never saw it again without horror.

I cannot tell you how sorry we were to leave [Knebworth] at the end of three days. Sir Edward begged us to stay longer, but we could not. Upon leaving, he came to the carriage door, & taking my hands in both his, said, "Mrs. Lawrence, I have just been congratulating your husband upon his marriage to you, & I cannot tell you how much pleasure your visit has given me, & how much I have been charmed with you."

* * *

Shortly after the Lawrences returned to London, they received an invitation from Lord Lansdowne "to take a sociable dinner with him at his Richmond villa to meet Mr. Macaulay," a meeting which Elizabeth had long been anticipating:

There was no other lady but Lady Duff Gordon, & no other gentleman but Mr. Taylor & Mr. Phillips, the latter a very fine artist, & the former one of the wittiest writers for *Punch*. Lord L. took me to table. Macaulay was in his most agreeable mood, telling a thousand anecdotes—talking about the Arabian Nights & the last new novel one minute, & a tragedy of Aeschuylus the next.

I had heard he was dying—what was my surprise to see a stout, hale looking man with grey hair, a splendid forehead, light grey eyes, that lit up with a wonderful intelligence every time he spoke....

* * *

Another spectacle Elizabeth attended was the Queen's dissolving of Parliament in the House of Lords, with the ladies of the diplomatic corps seated in the galleries, and "the Peers and Peeresses resplendent in diamonds & feathers" below. Immediately opposite the throne sat the Indian Rajah who had once owned the "Mountain of Light," the Koh-i-Noor diamond which Victoria wore that day on her bosom. How must he have felt, Elizabeth wondered. He gave no clue, sitting impassively, looking straight ahead, his "splendid golden dress" glittering with precious stones.

Victoria, trailing a red velvet train trimmed with ermine, bowed gravely as she progressed to the throne, and "without a single change in her attitude," she awaited the coming of the House of Commons:

I had an excellent opportunity of seeing her as she sat holding her speech, with her cold blue eyes fixed on vacancy. On one side of her stood the Prince & Lord Aberdeen, & on the other the Duke of Wellington with the sword of state, while behind the throne was the Duchess of Wellington & the Marchioness of Ely, & I could not but think what a pity it was that that splendid train & gold embroidered petticoat & dazzling diamond crown could not all have been placed upon the stately & regal looking Duchess instead of that little dumpy red-faced staring queen.

At the foot of the throne stood the Cabinet Ministers in their robes of state, Lord Lansdowne carrying the crown of state upon a red velvet cushion, & the poor old gentleman looked tired enough of his burden before the ceremonies were over.

In the midst of all this stately silence... in tumbled the House of Commons, rushing, pushing, & jostling for the best places, & I must admit it reminded me much more of a bear garden than, as Englishmen love to call it, "the first assemblage of gentlemen in the world."

Immediately the speaker commenced making his speech, which he had evidently committed to memory, but unfortunately forgotten, for he repeated it exactly like a school boy would his exhibition oration—stammering, repeating, saying the sentence first that should come last, correcting himself, & altogether behaving as if the cold grey eyes at the head of the Hall & staring at him had frightened him half out of his wits.

As soon as the speaker had finished, there was a dead stillness, & then her Majesty with a "hem" commenced: "My Lords & Gentlemen." Her voice, which you know is greatly admired, certainly is wonderfully clear—every word is perfectly distinct, & she trills her r's in a way that would give credit to any Irishman. Indeed, she has quite an Irish accent—but when you say this, you say all, for it sounded to me cold & like a person's with a sore throat, & as if she did not feel the importance of what she was saying.

As soon as her speech was read she rose, the audience rising also, & descending from the Throne the splendid pageant swept out of the room.

I went in Mr. Buchanan's carriage, Mr. L. taking Lizzie West in our brougham, & upon our return we saw the Queen's coach literally covered with gold—& drawn by eight cream-coloured horses, each horse led by a groom in splendid livery. It was a most inappropriate thing, I must admit, but I could not help thinking of our gilded orchestral menagerie wagons at home, & the little boys cheering at them.

There sat the Queen with both windows open, the wind blowing a perfect gale (she never can endure an atmosphere warmer than sixty-five), & there was the poor Duchess of Wellington, crouched up in one corner, vainly endeavoring to keep herself warm by holding her opera cloak tight round her throat.

I am at present sitting to Phillips the artist[1] for a picture he is painting of music—what could have got into the man I do not know, but I met him at Lord Lansdowne's dinner at Richmond, & he asked Mr. L. if it would be too great a favour for me to give him a few sittings. I enjoy going to his studio very much, for he is extremely clever, & the intimate friend of Doyle & Landseer & all the first literary people in London. I am to go to him this afternoon at five.

* * *

The last two weeks of August, Elizabeth and Bigelow traveled around the English countryside. They followed the valley of the Wye, visiting Tintern Abbey and Raglan Castle, then Goodrich Court, "a modern imitation of a Gothic Castle." With their predilection for "feudal times," they enjoyed seeing "in its perfection" what they had so often admired "in ruin." Bigelow was especially interested, because this "modern" castle contained one of the finest collections of armor in the world.

Typical of the era was Elizabeth's reprehensible desire for a souvenir. She managed to tear out a small piece of the "tattered lining" from one of the boots of Charles I. Fortunately, as she says, she was not detected!

The travelers proceeded on to Ross, then took the train to Shrewsbury:

"At three in the afternoon by Shrewsbury clock," says Falstaff, & to the old abbey we went. Mr. L. set his *watch* by the famous clock—when for the sake of the sentiment, I regret to say, it instantly stopped!

They moved on to Hereford and its cathedral and the birthplace of Nell Gwyn. At the foot of an "obscure" lane they found the "miserable uninhabited old hovel, about one story high, & very much such a looking place as some of our Irish cabins in America."

From Chester they drove out to Eton Hall, the residence of Lord Westminster, with its gardens laid out "somewhat in the style of the gardens at Versailles." Elizabeth decided she would just as soon live in Girard College in Philadelphia. Everything seemed too vast for comfort.

In the north of Wales they were joined by Bigelow's sister Annie and her husband, Benjamin Rotch, and together they visited Caernarvon. While there Elizabeth bought some "Welsh airs" to send to her sister. (She tried them first on her own piano and found them very "hum-drum.")

Another hard day's travel by rail brought them to Lake Windermere, where, during their rambles, they visited Wordsworth's house. Covered as it was with roses and honeysuckle, and with an unbroken view of the lake, the abode was "eminently fitting for a poet." Wordsworth had died only four years before, and as they were leaving, they caught a glimpse "through the lattice" of a "mild-looking old lady in a white cap," presumably his widow, who lived there with his "crazy sister—the same one whose 'wild eyes' he alludes to in his lines to Tintern."

After Fountains Abbey, they headed for Liverpool, where they saw the Rotches off for America on the *Niagara*. Even that whiff of sea air made Elizabeth feel nauseated, and she decided then and there she would cross the ocean only once more—going home! Therefore it behooved her to see all she could on that side of the Atlantic while she had a chance.

* * *

In early September they spent two days at Maresfield Park with Lady Shelley, a cousin of the poet. Among the guests was Mrs. L—— [illegible], "the English wife of an Indian Prince, who died mad & left her enormous wealth." After dinner she sang *Old Robin Grey* so movingly, she was asked to repeat it. Several of the ladies begged her not to, however, for they could not "bear to hear it again." It reminded Elizabeth of the time her sister Mary had refused to listen to *Uncle Tom's Cabin* a second time.

Another guest was a Miss Bickersleth, worth fifty thousand a year, who wore a black velvet jacket embroidered with steel beads to *breakfast!* When Lord George Beauclerk departed very early one morning, it was assumed she had "given him his walking papers" the night before.

Breakfast was served from nine till twelve, luncheon at two, and dinner at eight, at which time they all appeared "in full dress just as we would at a party." After dinner the guests played games, retiring about one in the morning.

On the last afternoon, they had a "pic-nic" in a neighboring grove, making their own tea and luncheon "all seated on cushions among the fern leaves." Several of the gentlemen sang, as well as the moving Mrs. L——, though this time it was "most merry":

> As we sat there with the tea-kettle bubbling over the embers, the horses & carriages in the distance, & wine & cake & sandwiches all spread on the ground, we looked much more like a party of gypsies "all under the green wood tree" than London ladies & gentlemen.

The Lawrences went on to Brighton for the weekend, exploring the famous Oriental palace which was built as the residence of the Prince Regent who later reigned as George IV. Elizabeth was disappointed. Whatever it may have been like in its prime, its "dark &

bare & dismantled rooms have certainly small vestiges either of comfort or magnificence" to commend them now.

* * *

Back in London once again, Bigelow found himself plunged into the middle of a contretemps at the Legation:

> There has been the most jolly awful row about Mr. Peabody's dinner that you can possibly imagine. Mr. Buchanan was raging because the reporters made him say what he didn't say & Sickles [the Secretary] was raging because they made him do what he didn't do. Mr. Lawrence was mad at Peabody, Saunders was mad at Peabody, & Peabody was mad at the whole party including Mr. Sturgis, who was mad at being accused of refusing to loan a picture of Washington for which he was never asked.
> The quarrel, I am happy to say, now rests alone between Mr. Peabody & Sickles, & they must fight it out the best way they can.
> Please do not breathe this to anyone, as it would never do to get out that I had written home about it!

7

MORE STATELY HOMES

The "domestic arrangements" were on a very large scale.

News came from Doylestown that the Navy ship on which Mary's husband, Willie Mercer, served—the *San Jacinto*—would be stopping over in England en route to the Baltic. The vessel, plagued with mechanical difficulties, finally docked in Southampton the end of September. The Lawrences took the train down to see Willie and found him more handsome than ever, his face suntanned beneath his "glazed cap," and sporting a new "pair of moustaches."

Willie showed them the most recent "daguerros" of the family, then took them aboard his ship, where they had a glass of champagne together with the Captain and some of the officers in the wardroom. When the *San Jacinto* sailed a day or two later, Elizabeth and Bigelow took a steamer bound for the Isle of Wight, and passing so close they could "recognize Willie with the naked eye," they all waved handkerchiefs till he was out of sight.

No sooner were they back in London than they were invited to spend a few days with the banker Mr. Bates and his amusing wife, coming away with "a Dresden China pitcher, a bottle of ginger, a Dutch cheese, & the sword of William the Conqueror —a strange combination, you may say."

Several days later Elizabeth was seated at breakfast when she heard a cab stop at the door. She remarked to her husband: "There is another of those wretches coming to spoil our breakfast with their passport!" Glancing around, she was astonished to see her brother-in-law standing in the doorway. Willie explained that the *San Jacinto* had suffered another catastrophe—its propeller had broken "short off in a smooth sea" only two days out. The ship had managed to return to Southampton for repairs, and the crew had been given several weeks' leave. Elizabeth thought it ridiculous that the Navy would send such an "old hulk" to sea—and to England, of all places, "among the splendid English fleet!"

For the next few days, guidebook in hand, she enthusiastically conducted Willie on a tour of the city in their blue brougham. Into one of the carriage pockets she tucked a box of macaroons, and when they were exhausted from their "labours," they had a go at the box.

Bigelow secured special permits so that they could go behind the scenes at such places as the Tower of London. Elizabeth could hardly keep a straight face when the warden intoned: "This is the harmour hof 'Enry the Heighth," before leading them to the record office. Her fingers "fairly burnt" for some of the manuscripts they were shown, and she was amused to discover that the old kings always used the Cockney "h," writing *hit* for *it*.

In the evenings, joined by Bigelow, they continued their exploration of the city with such amusements as Madame Tussaud's Exhibition (where Elizabeth happily scampered in and out of Napoleon's carriages), and the Turkish Exhibition, another wax display featuring slaves dancing before "beautiful Sultanas" in a harem. One night she invited the officers of the *San Jacinto* to dinner, and they regaled her with tales of their ill-fated voyage.

In between bouts of sightseeing, Elizabeth had long discussions with Willie about the possibility of his resigning from the Navy and getting a job on land so that he did not have to be separated from his wife for months at a time. Bigelow mentioned the fact that at Lowell, and many other manufacturing towns in New England, ex-Navy officers were hired to superintend the workmen, maintaining "sailor discipline." Lt. Perry, he claimed, got $6,000 a year in such a position. He volunteered to write his father and ask about the duties of such officers.

Elizabeth profoundly hoped some such arrangement could be worked out, for in her letters Mary sounded depressed from the long absences.

* * *

When Willie finally left to rejoin his ship, life in London settled down into its typical slow November pace. Elizabeth persuaded Mr. Buchanan to procure for her a ticket to the banquet at Guildhall. She turned out to be the only "foreign lady" present, and even the cabinet members' wives had not been asked.

About fifteen thousand people were there, separated by a railing, on one side of which sat the friends of the Lord Mayor, "or rather the aristocracy of the city," and on the other side sat the ladies and gentlemen of "the second circles"—and how they ate! She saw thousands of faces that reminded her of "Dickens characters drawn from that class." Two hundred and fifty tureens of turtle were passed, and a number of speeches were made, all short and all inaudible, except for Lord Palmerston's.

The hall's impressive illumination compensated somewhat for the lackluster oratory. At one end, against a "perfectly black ground," an enormous twinkling star lit up the motto of the Order of the Garter, the other walls were "illuminated in squares with innumerable jets of gas," and the chandeliers could only be compared to "showers of opals."

* * *

She continued to follow with "an immense interest" the progress of the Crimean War, which had reached "a most critical period," and "pumped everybody I can get hold of in my old-fashioned manner." Lord Cardigan's "deadly charge" was the talk of the town:

> Until the charge, the light cavalry had been very much abused by the rest of the army, & they gave Lord Lucan the nick-name of Lord Look-on....
>
> I am decidedly for the Russians, not but that the Allies are in the right, but who can help siding with the glorious doomed defenders of Sebastopol? I, however, keep my predilections *very private* in this country. There is scarcely a family of any note that has not lost friends or relatives in the War.

In spite of the war, life in the upper echelons continued to produce what Elizabeth sarcastically referred to as an occasional "pleasing little anecdote":

> I heard the other day that a lady in the country, who has a beautiful lap-dog, gave a dinner to the dogs of the neighborhood. [The dogs] all came, were announced by name, & seated around a table, each with a plate which was changed for every course. There were fourteen courses!
>
> In Petersburg everything is gayer than ever, never were known such brilliant balls, & the Emperor by his manner inspires all his subjects with confidence.

* * *

The foibles and eccentricities of the nobility never ceased to fascinate her. One of her primary sources of such information was Sir Edward Cust, the handsome Master of Ceremonies:

[He] was telling me yesterday of one of Mrs. Norton's *bon mots* as Miss Sheridan, when it was all the rage to praise her beauty & repeat her witty sayings.

There was a great Fair in London, at which Mrs. Norton (then Miss Caroline Sheridan) acted as one of the saleswomen. While standing behind her table, the present Marquis of Bath passed by, famous for his fat purse & fat person.

"Come, my Lord," said Miss Sheridan, "buy something, we want eldest sons here."

"Although I am an eldest son, I'm not a prodigal one," replied his lordship.

"No, you are more like the fatted calf," retorted the lady.

* * *

The end of November the Lawrences were invited to Cadlands, the country seat near Southampton of Lady Elizabeth Drummond, the daughter of the Duke of Rutland. To their delight, the grass of the "pleasure gardens" was still a brilliant green, and the chrysanthemums still bright, not "faded & forlorn & frost-bitten" as they always were at that time of year in Pennsylvania and Massachusetts.

Footmen in scarlet-and-fawn livery ushered them to their rooms, where they found a fire blazing, a teakettle bubbling on the hearth, and "every comfort that curtains & lights & pictures & books & writing desk & sofa & arm-chairs could possibly bring" on such a dark evening. As the clock had just struck seven, and dinner was to be served in half an hour, she "plunged" into her trunk and "primped" into her green moiré, rather in the "harum-scarum" manner in which she used to array herself "for the Doylestown stage," while Susan, her maid, in a state of nervous excitement, "endeavored to arrange my hair & flowers & bertha."

Breathlessly they descended to the library, where they were introduced to the other guests, before filing in to dinner according to rank, & then commenced "the business of the hour":

> Grace was said & then... we were waited on by the butler, who never wears livery, & is always dressed like a gentleman & only passes the wine, & six or seven footmen in scarlet & buff, who moved about as noiselessly as so many mice.
>
> After dinner we all went into the drawing room, & I had a long talk with His Grace [the Duke of Rutland], who is nearly seventy-[seven] & one of the greatest Dukes in the kingdom. Papa will remember that Haddon Hall belonged to him....
>
> He had asked Col. L. to visit him at Belvoir Castle, but it was a long time ago, & he had specified no time, & fearing that his memory was treacherous, I had little hopes of ever seeing his princely mansion; so to tell the honest truth, I implored Mr. L. to go to Cadlands in order that the Duke, whom I had never seen, should give us a definite invitation.
>
> So in this first conversation I tried the agreeable on the old man, who converses remarkably well, & told me a thousand anecdotes about his old crony, the Duke of Wellington, & many a famous contemporary now dead & buried.
>
> The Star of the Garter glittered on his breast, & the George hung from his buttonhole, he had lived among kings & queens & the great people of the earth all his days, & was one of them himself, so you may think I gave his remarks no small attention....
>
> That night after leaving the drawing room, Mr. L.'s first question was, "Well, did the Duke ask you to Belvoir?"

"No," said I with a very sheepish expression, whereupon my unfeeling husband laughed at me in the most heartless manner, & spoke of my playing the agreeable to the Duke in terms to which I shall not allude.

The next day being Sunday, we all went to church, some driving, some walking, & listened to service in a chapel that was built before the Conquest....

As we drove to it through the park, I could not but think of the bridal processions I had read of as winding from the great house over the park hills to the church....

After luncheon (another dinner, with the exception of the soup & fish, & that everyone waited on themselves), Lady Elizabeth, Mr. Drummond & myself walked over the farmyard & buildings, & I only wish Papa could have been with us to enjoy a sight of the perfect order & arrangement of an English farm. The cattle live quite as well as their masters.

From the farmyard we went to a long row of cottages with a long piazza entering in front & covered with vines in which is the dairy, & where live the dairy maid, the farmer & some of the grooms.

We first went into the dairy-maid's parlour & upon my word, it had all the look of a dressing-room in some of our gentlemen's country seats at home! A table covered with fancy annuals, pictures, pretty bits of china, armchairs & sofas gave it a look of actual elegance.

From the parlour we went to the dairy, & could you but have seen it! You passed down two or three steps & found yourself in a very light room. The walls, ceiling & floor were as white as snow. A broad white wooden shelf extended around the walls, on which were placed white oval china pans of milk & Alderny cream. In the centre of the room stood a white marble table on which were white china jars of beautiful little pats of potted butter, jars of thick cream, & pounds of butter that looked all the more yellow from contrast with the marble table.

There was no other hue in this delicious-looking apartment but the purest white & the richest cream colour, with the exception of a superb bouquet of flowers... in a white china vase.

The dairy-maid herself was exceedingly pretty, & with her white cap & white apron & pink cheeks, looked as fresh as a rose.

I told Lady Elizabeth that some fearfully hot day in America I should think of this dairy room, & I was sure it would refresh me.

From the farm yard we took a long walk through the park of four miles, & I saw for the first time the gorse with its yellow flowers.

That evening I again had a long talk with his Grace, & exerted myself within an inch of my life. The old Duke listened & laughed—but oh! most mortifying conclusion, when my unfeeling husband asked me again his most unnecessary question, I was obliged to make the same painful response. The laughter with which it was followed was uncalled for, if not to say ill-bred.

The next day all the gentlemen went out shooting, & tell Papa, as I saw them start in their dog-carts with their hounds & shooting jackets & splendid guns, I wished for him from the very bottom of my heart.

They returned in the evening laden with game—[including] eighty pheasants! Mr. Stanley, one of the sportsmen, is nearly eighty years old, & although he has given up following the hounds as much as he used to, still carries his gun with any man, but generally for one day's shooting has two days' gout. He is a perfect old character—one of the few remaining specimens of an old fox-hunting Tory.

After dinner the old Duke took his usual seat by my side, & as this was our last evening at Cadlands, I trembled with anxiety as I thought of the life-long laugh a

Portrait of EL, a pastel by James R. Swinton, dated London, 1854. "I am taken with a green wreath in my hair, & dressed exactly as I used to be as Miss Chapman at the balls in Philadelphia." *Courtesy of EL's great-great nephew, Baron Bernard von Friesen.*

certain person would have against me if the sole wish I had in coming to Cadlands was a failure.

Imagine my relief when almost the first words his Grace addressed to me were: "Mrs. Lawrence, I shall hope to see yourself & the Col. at my castle at Belvoir during the Winter. Which would be the most convenient time for you? I am always at home from January until March."

I named February, & could scarcely keep from crowing over Mr. L. in the drawing-room. I will leave you to imagine my triumph when we retired....

Let me give you a never failing cure for fever blisters on one's mouth: rub them constantly with laudanum.

* * *

On December 14 Elizabeth dispatched a box of Christmas presents to Doylestown. For her sister Mary she sent a pattern and "matched worsted" for a fire screen; for Mama there was a series of Leech's best sketches and a box of turtle-oil soap—the kind used by the Queen; brother Tom got *Punch's Almanack;* and little Fanny and Arthur, a couple of books. For the whole family she included Dickens's "new Christmas story." At the last minute she added a "surprise" to the box of presents: two lithographs of her portrait by James Rannie Swinton, which her father-in-law had commissioned:

> For the last two weeks I have been going every day at eleven o'clock to sit for my portrait to Swinton, the great coloured crayon artist. I am taken with a green wreath in my hair, & dressed exactly as I used to be as Miss Chapman at the balls in Philadelphia. You can imagine nothing more disagreeable than starting out these misty November mornings in full party dress & looking much more like a frosted turnip with my green topnot than a dame in all her elegance on her way to sit for her portrait!

She reminded her family that they had a copy of a portrait by Swinton of Lady Jocelyn, and that he had "taken all the great people in the land!"

Excitement mounted when she discovered that Richard Lane, the lithographer, intended sending a copy of her portrait, along with eleven others, to the Industrial Fair in Paris that summer. "In very grand company" she would certainly be, for she was the only sitter "untitled."

* * *

Christmas was spent at The Grange, Lord Ashburton's country seat in Hampshire. (The friendship between the Ashburton and Lawrence families went back to 1842, when Bigelow's father and the present Lord A.'s father had negotiated the northeastern boundary between the United States and Canada.)

As the Lawrences approached the imposing Greek-porticoed mansion through an avenue of old elms overgrown with ivy and mistletoe, Elizabeth decided that the English style of landscaping was the most beautiful in the world. The formal gardens nearest the house were cultivated to perfection (here it was in the Italian style, with a marble fountain in the center), while the surrounding areas were left in all their original "wildness," forming a "most pleasing contrast." Stepping into the great hall, she nearly took a tumble—so smooth was the floor from centuries of waxing—and regained her balance only through the dexterity acquired years ago sliding on the frozen brick-kiln pond near home.

Once again they were woefully late dressing for dinner, and on descending the great staircase, hung with old masters, they were horror-struck to discover the guests already seated in the dining room. English people never wait for anyone, she lamented, and even if Mr. L. had been a Duke, Lord and Lady Ashburton would have proceeded without them.

The Grange, Lord Ashburton's country seat. The "domestic arrangements" included "a house physician, a groom of the chambers, an upper butler, an under butler, two French cooks, a baker, a housekeeper," plus a retinue of "maidservants and footmen." J.P. Neale, *Views of the Seats of Noblemen and Gentlemen*, London, 1823.

Lady A. spent the next day—Saturday—distributing clothing to "the poor." The houseguests all watched from the drawing room windows as the local folk wended their way back over the park hills, carrying their bundles of Christmas gifts. At church the next morning they were all turned out in their "new bonnets & cloaks," looking "smiling & happy."

Christmas night was especially gala:

> The chandeliers in the hall & drawing rooms were hung with mistletoe—you know of course, the penalty of being caught under its dangerous branches—& gentlemen were constantly lurking about in dark & secret corners & wrapped up in mysterious curtains, all lying in wait for any poor victim who might accidentally pass beneath the branching evergreens. Fortunately I escaped by dint of a series of the profoundest stratagems, but Lady Ashburton was one of the earliest victims.
>
> The same night we had charades, & I think you would have been amused could you have seen them. The word was "courtship," & the first part of the charade was a court room with a judge & jury, before whom was being argued an important case between Susan Primrose (alias myself) vs. Patrick O'Donohue (alias Mr. Corie).
>
> Patrick O'Don was charged with having stolen the bracelet of Susan Primrose, a maid servant at the Grange, while she was in the act of dusting one of the drawing-rooms, & I wish you could have heard the speeches. The audience screamed with laughter.
>
> Mr. Brookfield, in his defence to prove that Patrick was too fervent an admirer to commit a theft on a person whom he quite adored, read a few verses which he

said had been written by the defendant [Patrick] to the plaintiff [the maid Susan, alias Elizabeth] in happier days & fairer fortunes. Could you but have heard the shouts with which the following lines were received:

> Most transcendant Transatlantic!
> Ne'er did passion so romantic
> Animate the breast of man!
> Oh! most fair American!
> Wilt thou daily add, oh cruel!
> To the fire within me, fuel?
> Wilt, oh wilt thou drive me frantic?
> Oh! hard-hearted Transatlantic!
> Canst thou daily see me kneeling,
> Yet display no fellow feeling?
> Canst thou hear my plaintive ditty
> All without one spark of pity
> For the love the most romantic
> (Most transcendant Transatlantic)
> Ever filled the breast of man?
> Barbarous American!

Mr. Brookfield closed his defence with the hope that if his client was not found guiltless of the charge, he would at least be acquitted on the plea of insanity.

I was a witness in my own case, & I will not pretend to tell you all the compliments that my acting & answers in the cross-examination elicited. I was dreadfully saucy to the opposite counsel's questions, & they shouted at everything I said whether I deserved it or not.

Patrick was convicted & condemned to transportation to Norfolk Island for seven years. The judge, after delivering his charge, which was one of the wittiest things I ever listened to, asked Patrick if he had anything to say for himself.... I positively laughed at Patrick's defence until I found it decidedly prudent to stop.

The next scene was on board ship [the second syllable of the word being acted out] on the way back to Norfolk Island. Susan, who has all along had a sneaking tenderness for Patrick, follows him on ship-board, & the charade closes with Patrick offering her a convict's heart.

Charades were followed by Christmas dinner, the delicious highlight of which was roast turkey stuffed with truffles. The entire dinner service, including the plates (which were changed frequently during the course of the meal) was of silver. Only dessert was served on china dishes.

Throughout their stay two kinds of soup were served each day, along with two kinds of fish. Every morning at breakfast the boiled eggs were marked with the day of the month on which they had been laid—an "admirable plan," she thought. Dessert always included pears, white and purple Hamburg grapes, and "pine-apples." The bill of fare, which was written out in a fine hand and set before the master of the house, reminded her of the bills of fare at some of America's grander hotels. The cooking, she was happy to report, did not.

Obviously the "domestic arrangements" at The Grange were on a very large scale. There was a house physician, a groom of the chambers, an upper butler, an under butler, two French cooks, a baker, a housekeeper, in addition to a retinue of maid servants and footmen.

Gloom was cast over the gaiety one day by the arrival of a letter for Lady Ashburton from the Crimea describing the terrible conditions. Even high-ranking officers had worn the same clothes for so long, they were "covered with vermin." Lord Raglan's ability as chief of the Army was questioned. "Is it not dreadful?"

Along with this letter to Doylestown Elizabeth sent "some bunches of the mistletoe bough."

* * *

On New Year's Day, 1855, the Lawrences left London for Elvaston Castle, the Earl of Harrington's estate near Derby, noted for its extraordinary variety and quantity of evergreens. After passing through gates that were "one blaze of gilding"—formerly the outer gates to Versailles—they found themselves in a "wilderness" of spruce and cedar. In the former Earl's time, a hundred gardeners had been employed to keep the grounds in order. Many of the trees had been pruned into shapes such as peacocks and pyramids and coronets, which looked very strange to an American's eye.

Elvaston Castle, seat of the Earl of Harrington. "In the former earl's time, a hundred gardeners had been employed.... Many of the trees had been pruned into shapes such as peacocks and pyramids and coronets." F.O. Morris, *A Series of Picturesque Views of the Seats of the Noblemen and Gentlemen of Great Britain and Ireland*, London, 188–.

On one side of the castle stretched a "wandering covered way" of cedars through which they walked, marveling at the Gothic-shaped windows that had been cut out in the branches to give light. Gazing down on this curiosity from her bedroom, however, Elizabeth thought the "fairy-land" anything but attractive, looking for all the world like a "gigantic green caterpillar writhing about on the grass!"

She felt transported to Baghdad, for the castle had an Oriental feeling that reminded her of the descriptions in the *Arabian Nights*. On either side of the great chimney in the hall stood two golden chairs that had belonged to the last Doge of Venice. There seemed to be no end to the paintings and portraits.

In spite of all the grandeur, she felt a "kind of melancholy," as she lay in her satin-draped bed at night and watched the firelight dance over the stern portraits of "mailed warriors & courtly dames," who had long since "mouldered away to dust & ashes," and watched the moonlight silhouette the dark cedar trees that were waving and "sighing" to and fro. She wanted to hide her head under the bedclothes, as she had when she was a little girl.

The garden at Elvaston. A "wandering covered way" of pruned cedars looked "for all the world like a gigantic green caterpillar writhing about on the grass." *Harper's New Monthly Magazine*, March 1881.

Their host, Lord Harrington, was the brother of the last Earl, who was responsible for the present decorations at Elvaston. He had married an actress, a woman "of very doubtful character," who had "won his heart" in her famous character of "Fair Star." After their marriage society had shunned them; so the Earl had taken his Countess to Elvaston, which he had spent the rest of his life "beautifying." All the ceilings he had painted with golden stars in honor of his wife's stellar role.

Among the profusion of pictures Elizabeth spotted a large miniature of the poet Byron. On inquiring, she was told by Lord Harrington that Byron had been an intimate friend, and that he had been with him during his last illness. He added that the poet had a habit of walking to the nearest mirror and looking at his teeth—which were "remarkably fine!"

He then proceeded to recount a "perfectly shocking story" about Byron's daughter Ada, Lady Lovelace. Not long before her death she visited Newstead Abbey, totally unaware that it had been her father's boyhood home, and that he was buried there. (Since she was in "perfect ignorance" of most things that related to him, his "last resting place" was not quite "so sacred to her as the grave of a favourite spaniel.") After Lady Lovelace had been shown the ruins of the abbey by the present owner, Col. Wildman (a great friend of her father's), he said that with her permission he would repeat some lines that had been written on Newstead, and recited Byron's description of his old home. She was impressed:

"Dear me, how pretty," exclaimed Lady Lovelace. "Who can they be written by, Col. Wildman?"

"Your father composed them, madam."

"My father!" continued her Ladyship. "I really had no idea he could write anything so good as that. Why, they really are very clever. Upon my word, I believe I shall begin to read some of my father's poetry. I always thought he had written nothing but trash."

The next day Col. Wildman drove her to the spot where her father was buried, & when they arrived there he said, "Lady Lovelace, I wish to show you the grave of someone."

"Whose can it be?" cried her Ladyship.

"I wish to show you the grave of your father."

"My father!" she exclaimed. "Why, you don't tell me he's buried here! How funny that I shouldn't know it!"

... I think I have given you enough to show you what a perfectly heartless creature she was. A short time before her death she lost 2,000 pounds in betting at the St. Leger Races.

* * *

Among the guests at Elvaston were Lady Constable and her son, one of the "stupidest, most disagreeable flabby-looking young men" Elizabeth had ever seen, with a "weakly moustache and an immense fortune," which the present French Empress's mother "tried in vain to capture for her daughter." Although Mr. Constable did not take to the future sovereign of France, Lady Constable was still very intimate with the Empress and confided to Elizabeth that Louis Napoleon was so devoted to his wife that whenever she was ill, he never left her bedside and insisted on giving her her medicine himself.

* * *

Before returning to London they spent a few days with Lord Lansdowne at Bowood Park, where their accommodations were less awesome and more charming. Here their bedroom was draped in violet-colored silk scattered with gold palm leaves, and they each had a cozy dressing room. Elizabeth was particularly taken by her "toilette table." It was draped with white muslin, which fell from a blue-and-gold cockade above the oval mirror. At least a dozen toilet articles were arranged on its surface, the uses of which she had not the faintest idea! Instead of being against the wall, this white-curtained delight stood in the middle of the room and looked far more "stylish" than any of "those great mahogany things we pay so much for." She added, "Behold an idea for housekeeping!"

Bowood Park, Lord Lansdowne's country seat. The night the Lawrences arrived, the servants' ball was "started up" by Lord Lansdowne's eldest son, who "led out the housekeeper." Morris, *A Series of Picturesque Views*....

The room also contained a large folding screen to ward off draughts, a small wheeled screen to deflect heat from the fire, chintz-covered furniture, a Dresden bowl filled with flowers, and a pink muslin basket for caps and headdresses. With its bright wallpaper depicting tropical birds in golden cages, she thought it one of the most inviting rooms she had ever seen.

But the art! Elizabeth was totally captivated. Lord Lansdowne told her it was the rule of the house for every gentleman visiting Bowood to "lose his heart" to the black eyes sparkling with "fun and frolic" of Peg Woffington, painted so entrancingly by Hogarth.

The other picture she had to mention was "Sir Joshua's idea of Dr. Jonson when a baby." She thought it extremely funny that the baby face bore a "wonderful likeness to the great philosopher"—although it was hard to believe that "anything infantile could look like the coarse, scowling, intellectual peevish face of Boswell's adoration."

The night they arrived there was a Twelfth Night ball in the servants' hall. It was the custom, she was told, that one night a year the master of the house gave a ball to his servants which he opened in person. That night the dance was started up by Lord Shelburne, Lord Lansdowne's eldest son, who led out the housekeeper. In spite of her "republican" principles, Elizabeth was amused at the spectacle of ladies' maids and countesses "figuring in the same quadrille."

Just before they left they were treated to a highly unusual dish: birds'-nest soup! It had been sent to Lord Lansdowne from China, but it was not cooked in the Chinese fashion, and Elizabeth was disappointed, for it tasted like an "ordinary gravy soup with sprigs of Iceland moss in it!"

"May God bless you, my dear Mrs. Lawrence," said the old gentleman as he bade her good-bye, his eyes filling with tears.

* * *

Not long after their return to town, Elizabeth found herself the subject of another poem. Sir Henry Taylor, the politician–poet–playwright, sent her the following:

> Astronomers of various schools—
> Of various theories and rules—
> Agree, at least,
> 'Tis in the East
> The heav'nly bodies rise—
> And yet the Star,
> More bright by far
> Than all that gem the skies,
> (As is by one consent confest)
> Dawn'd on admiring Nations from the *West!*

She could not resist telling Mama something Bigelow had heard the other day that pleased him very much: His wife was considered "the most popular American woman that e'er was in England." She begged Mama not to read that sentence to *anyone.*

8

A COLD ENGLISH WINTER

The most stately "feudal pile."

The Crimean War continued to be the chief topic of conversation, and everyone was "on tiptoe" waiting for the resignation of the cabinet. Elizabeth sent her father a copy of *The Times* containing a long account of the disasters in the East, which had been posted and read by crowds at street corners. The aristocracy hated *The Times*, she told him, and "revile it in unbounded terms," but they all take it anyway.

The reports were fearful. The soldiers were dying in the trenches from cold and hunger, and no one would be surprised if the high command were recalled:

> The Earl of Cardigan, of whom you have heard so much on account of his charge at Balaclava, is one of the worst men living. A few years ago he was tried for the murder of his own valet. His Countess left her husband to run away with him, & the only good thing I know of him is that, after the divorce from her first husband consequent upon her behaviour, he married her...
> However, his conduct at Balaclava was something very grand, & upon his return he said to the handful of his regiment that survived: "My men, this charge was not the folly of my mad brain, I but obeyed orders."

Everyone agreed that Lord John Russell would be the next Premier and Lord Palmerston the Minister for Foreign Affairs. "Lord Palm" was undoubtedly the frontrunner among the English people, as well as a favorite of Louis Napoleon, but the Queen was another matter. She "positively hated" him because he had sent a state paper to France without consulting her—or even worse, Prince Albert—about it.

Determined to be present the night the House of Commons debated the conduct of the war, Elizabeth and Bigelow arrived at six in the evening and stayed until one-thirty the next morning. During the course of the long debate, she heard the finest speeches she had ever listened to: Bulwer, Disraeli, Gladstone, Palmerston, Lord John Russell, and Sir Francis Baring all spoke "amidst thunder of applause":

> Lord Derby's recall has surprised everyone, for people hoped & expected that Palmerston was to be Premier. I think it is very little in the Queen to allow her personal dislike to come in on such an occasion as this.
> ...If ever there was an angel on earth it is Miss Nightingale. She moves among the very highest in the land, & was born & brought up with the aristocracy, has refused many offers, among them Monckton Milnes the poet, & yet leaves rank, wealth & friends all behind her to be a slave & a drudge in those Crimean hospitals. They say that when [she was] a little girl, she used... to be breaking her dolls' legs & then binding them up with lint & splints.

Elizabeth was fascinated to see in *The Illustrated London News* a sketch of a "drying closet"[1] that her friend Miss Burdett-Coutts had sent out to Miss Nightingale. The philanthropic lady, who had worked with Dickens for social reform, had persuaded him to help her design this strange-looking "centrifugal machine," which was capable of drying one thousand articles of linen in twenty-five minutes—a tremendous boon to the filthy camps. Though Elizabeth could fault the lady's blotchy complexion, she had to applaud her pure heart.

Punch's view of "the Nightingale."

After nearly ten months, Elizabeth was beginning to feel more at home, for she had missed the presence of friends "of her own kind" more than she cared to admit. She chafed under the formal etiquette that revolved around the leaving of cards and hated large parties, preferring informal, friendly visits. The apathy of the women particularly bothered her, and their "heartlessness" appalled her. With the new year, however, she began to receive notes from several ladies inviting her to "drink tea at five o'clock" whenever she so desired, or to stop by in the evening. She considered herself lucky, for it was a "rare thing" to be on "social terms" with anyone in London.

That winter the city saw one of its rare snows, and Elizabeth was amused to see how the people rushed to the doors and windows whenever a sleigh passed. One afternoon as she stomped through the snow in Hyde Park she heard a tinkle, and turning around, saw a "miserable sledge" coming down the drive with more people following it than usually followed the Queen in her coach-and-four!

Even the Serpentine was frozen over, bringing out skaters who waltzed and formed quadrilles on the ice. Guards were stationed along the banks with dragnets and ropes, but even so, many of the skaters drowned. Elizabeth found the weather mild compared to what she was accustomed to at home, and thought a "good stiff breeze from the Bucks County hills would freeze off an Englishman's nose at the first whiff."

One icy afternoon she sallied forth to an afternoon reception. Just as she was mounting the steps, in full panoply of hat, feathers, cloak, and furs, she slipped and both feet flew out from under her. Footmen in red breeches with powdered heads rushed to her assistance so quickly, the powder swirled around their heads "like a snow-storm." She managed to get up before they reached her, and she was grateful no other guests had witnessed her "wonderful performance."

Though Elizabeth thought the winter mild, it was cold enough that her footman's canary almost froze to death. So he moved the bird cage down to the pantry, where he played his accordion—which, to the mistress of the house, frequently sounded more like a *dis*cordion. And Charles, the little page, was too delicate to man the door in such weather. So he was found a home in the country, "which is the best place for him, poor little thing."

"Even the Serpentine was frozen over...." *The Illustrated London News*, February 1855.

To add to the miseries of the weather, Elizabeth was suffering from a "face ache" caused by a tooth that had been giving her intermittent trouble for years. After enduring "perfect agonies" for nearly a week, she sent for Ballard, the only American dentist in London. He finally pulled the tooth, and five minutes later her "old enemy" was lying before her on the table.

At first she thought of sending it home—along with some verses she had composed—to be burnt in the parlor fire before which "it had made me utter so many weary moans." She changed her mind, however, and contented herself by sending just these lines:

> Oh ruthless tormentor, what have I not tried?
> What acres of poppies & camomiles dried?
> What lotions & potions
> And old women's notions
> That thou in thy malice hast always defied,
> And only thumped harder, when to close the disaster
> I've spent my last six-pence in buying a plaster.
> And oh! then to think of the tears thou hast cost me,
> Of the pleasures, bouquets, & the balls thou hast lost me,
> Of those nights when each belle all her beaux was entrancing
> While I stayed at home, and my tooth did the dancing!

* * *

Early in February Elizabeth and her husband took off for the Duke of Rutland's "princely residence," the invitation for which she had angled so expertly the previous fall. All the other "stately piles" paled before Belvoir. Built before the Norman Conquest, it had been in the Duke's family for seven hundred years, and many of the British monarchs, including Victoria, had been entertained there. It had the aura of a royal palace:

Belvoir, seat of the Duke of Rutland. The Lawrences walked into dinner "to the music of a full band," and the silver wine coolers were so enormous they looked "large enough to bathe in." Neale, *Views of the Seats....*

> Every day at dinner an entirely new set of ornaments stood on the table. One day it would be a succession of silver vases & gigantic silver candelabra, bearing a multitude of wax lights & surrounded by silver salt-cellars in the form of shells & mermaids & numberless nautical devices. The next day the ornaments would be of gold, lofty golden flagons & a candelabra supported by golden dancing girls..., the costly ornaments varying as we would bouquets of flowers.

They walked into dinner every night to the music of a full band which played until the dessert was served, at which time several of the musicians sang quartets or solos. For the first few days Elizabeth could hardly keep her eyes off the servants. The old butler, who stood at the head of the table, was seventy-three and had been with the family for half a century. All the footmen appeared to have "grown grey" in the service of this splendid castle, and only their liveries distinguished the "gentleman who sat in the chair from the gentleman who stood behind it."

Every room was breathtaking: the ballroom; the chapel with a Murillo over the altar; the dining room surrounded by immense mirrors, and solid silver wine coolers "large enough to bathe in"; and finally the vast wine and beer cellars where, the previous winter, when the castle was full of guests, seventy gallons of ale were drunk by the retainers every day!

In spite of all this splendor, she found Belvoir to be the least formal of all the stately houses, surprisingly enough, and she enjoyed herself enormously. Customarily the shake of the hand and the formal bow are "quite as ceremonious at parting as at meeting"; not so at Belvoir—which she informed her family, incidentally, is pronounced "beaver."

A fox hunt had been planned, for the Duke was the head of the Belvoir hunt and had the largest pack of hounds in the country. All the members of the hunt wore dress coats of red when they dined at the castle, and Elizabeth would have loved to have seen such a spectacle. Unfortunately the snow was too deep; so instead the guests took sleigh rides in a "Hamburg sledge," accompanied by a footman behind and a groom on horseback in the Rutland livery.

When the Duke learned of her interest in "olden times," he took her into his library and showed her some of his priceless ancestral manuscripts: a letter of Sir Philip Sidney's, a permit from King John to build a stone wall around Haddon Hall, and a papal bull from "one of the Gregories" permitting a chapel to be built.

One of the castle's towers contained the apartments of the beautiful Duchess of Rutland, who had died twenty-seven years ago. The rooms were locked, and not a thing had been touched in all that time. Once a year the Duke and his housekeeper went in and looked over the clothes of the "long-departed" Duchess.

At Belvoir Elizabeth learned another housekeeping trick:

> Tell Mary that after she finishes her [fire] screen, I will send her two or three patterns with which she can work the edge to a large table-cover. After the border is finished it is sewn on to a coloured cloth, say dark blue, to fit the table, & makes the handsomest & most stylish looking cover I ever saw... far prettier than any marble top, which I think looks cold & unsociable.
>
> I got the idea from..., a lady I met at Belvoir. She has any quantity of squares of canvas all worked with the same bunch of flowers, but in different colours, & she gives one to each of her friends to work, so that the border when finished is a souvenir of them. I think it an excellent idea.

On leaving, the old Duke made them promise to visit again and see a fox hunt.

* * *

On their return to London they found the city suffering from the most severe winter in seventeen years. Thousands of dockmen, boatmen on the Thames, and gardeners were out of work. Newspapers reported increasing bread riots. Coupled with the depressing war news—the military strength of the nation was exhausted, and Lord Raglan was rumored to have resigned—nothing but "misfortune and calamities" stared one in the face on every side:

> I wish you could take a look out on Upper Brook Street at this moment. A sort of yellow snow lies on the ground & housetops, over which hangs a bilious-looking fog of so penetrating a nature that the atmosphere of this room is almost as thick as that in the street. Out of the mist rises the dismal cry: "Frozen-out gardeners, frozen-out boat-men! Pray aid the frozen-out poor boatmen!", & an old Jew is passing beneath the windows with a greasy towel hanging over his arm, & utterng with the most sepulchral accent the one word: "Lamp!"

Prices were astronomical. Imagine paying twelve-and-a-half cents for a single egg! She had just been fitted for a pink silk dress "with alternate flounces of silk & tulle," and it was going to cost forty dollars at the very least. Her dressmaker's bill for the previous season was three hundred sixty dollars! What the nation was coming to "would puzzle the wisest to foresee!"

"The Streets and the Weather." *The Illustrated London News*, February 1855.

One bright spot in the gloom was a dinner at Ham House with the banker-philanthropist, Samuel Gurney. It really did her good "to see the Quaker coat again!":

> I told him my grandfather belonged to the Society of Friends, which pleased him extremely. He lives like a patriarch surrounded by an immense family, & with all that comfort about him for which his sect are so famous.... He spends an immense portion of his vast fortune in charity, distributing it among the poor of his Parish.

* * *

Influenza was prevalent, and Harriet Lane was one of her many friends who contracted it. Elizabeth called on her while she was still confined to her bed, and was treated to a full account of a dinner Harriet and her uncle had attended with the Queen just before she fell ill:

> She [Harriet] was obliged to go in black, as the court & all the fashionables are in mourning for the Duke of Genoa. Upon their arriving at the palace, they were ushered into a large drawing-room where several guests were assembled, & after waiting for some minutes the doors were thrown open, & the Queen & Prince entered.
> Her Majesty first shook hands with the ladies, & then with the gentlemen. Then taking the Prince's arm, they all followed her into dinner, Mr. Buchanan having a seat by her side, being the first in rank of the gentlemen present. The Prince sat on the other side of the Queen.
> Her Majesty talked & laughed in the most affable manner during the dinner, & ate more than Mr. Buchanan, although she only drank one glass of wine. She rose to leave the table just as Miss Lane was in the midst of a bunch of grapes, which she was obliged to leave, & follow the royal lady.
> Upon reaching the drawing-room the Queen & the ladies-in-waiting proceeded to the fireplace, while all the others stood off at the door by which they had entered, until the lady-in-waiting advanced & said that Her Majesty desired them

to draw nearer the fire, as it was very cold. Upon doing so, the Queen stepped up to Miss Lane & remarked: "I think you must have a very bad cold, for I heard you coughing at dinner."

Miss Lane said that she had. The Queen then asked if her uncle was married, & if she had any other uncles, & from what part of America she came. Upon Miss Lane's saying "Pennsylvania," Her Majesty asked if it was a slave state, & whether they had not great difficulty in keeping maids there, on account of the free institutions.

Miss Lane answered that we had most excellent servants, & that the coloured ones were the best. She also asked the Queen if she had ever seen Mrs. Stowe, who had given everyone in this country such a very wrong idea of our domestic arrangements in America. Her Majesty said she had never seen her.

After a while the Queen sent for the gentlemen, & then the Princess Royal came in, a lively little girl of twelve or thirteen years of age, who talked away to Miss Lane at a great rate, & taking off her gloves, showed her a ring. "This stone has a scratch on it," she said, "and they tell me I can have it taken off, but it was always there when the lady who gave it to me wore it, & I love her so much that I like to wear it just as she did."

She asked Miss Lane how old she was, & upon Miss Lane's telling her she exclaimed: "Why, I have a cousin just that age, but she looks a great deal older than you—but then she's so enormously fat! Dear me, what is her name? I have so many cousins, I can't remember the names of half of them. I have cousins all over the world, & there's no end to my German cousins, but I have very few in England," & so she ran on in the most unaffected & simplest manner....

After the gentlemen entered the Queen approached each one & made some remarks, & then they all seated themselves around two tables—the Queen & the maids of honour—where they remained conversing until about eleven, when the Queen rose, shook hands with the ladies & gentlemen, bowed, & then taking the Prince's arm, left the apartment, & the dinner was over.

Both Miss Lane & Mr. Buchanan were very much pleased with Her Majesty. Dining at the Palace is one of the honours I shall never enjoy, as it is only accorded to the highest of the English nobility & their wives, or the heads of their establishment, but we have the satisfaction of feeling that whatever honours we do receive are paid to ourselves, & not to our positions; that last remark is *entre nous*.

It never does to give an inch to anyone in this country, & if anybody gives you the cold shoulder, give it back to them, which I have always done, & it has delighted me sometimes beyond measure to give certain persons a very cold stare or a supercilious nod, who never could see Mrs. Lawrence when they thought she was nobody, but who were only too ready to be sociable with her when they saw her talking on the most sociable terms with people they would give their eyes & nose, too, to be intimate with.

I know this is a very unamiable feeling, but it is impossible not to have it in a society so swarming with snobs & worshippers of rank as this in London, & I can tell you, these are ladies with great blood in their veins, as well as among little people.

* * *

The end of February Bigelow also developed a bad cold, which the doctor finally diagnosed as whooping cough, recommending that he get out of smoky London.[2] So the first two weeks of March the Lawrences spent at the seaside resort of Torquay. Elizabeth attributed her own good health to the fact that she took cold sponge baths every morning, using "flesh brushes," then put on a silk shirt before donning the rest of her clothing.

From Torquay Elizabeth dispatched to Doylestown *Punch, The Times,* and *The Illustrated London News,* all of which contained accounts of the death of the Czar. Two years before, the Grand Duchesses Marie and Olga had spent the summer in Torquay, and the local people were still talking about it: The Grand Duchesses had been accompanied by two London policemen who never left them, sleeping in the same house, and even riding on the box of the carriage with them.

While at Torquay, Elizabeth and Bigelow celebrated their first wedding anniversary. He presented her with a red-velvet jewel casket with brass ornaments; a gold-filigree brooch, bracelet, and earrings; two Venetian bracelets; and "an exquisite apple green silk with flounces with stamped borders." Not long before he had given her a lace "point" collar and "undersleeves." He was constantly "presenting her with something or other," and she was touched.

* * *

Bigelow recovered from the whooping cough in time to accept a second invitation to Belvoir. On arrival they found forty guests in the castle, all of the "highest nobility," including the Queen's aunt, the Duchess of Cambridge, and her daughter, the ample Princess Mary. In spite of her unprepossessing looks, the Princess turned out to be one of the "nicest" people Elizabeth had ever met. Especially endearing was the fact that she quickly caught the point of a joke.

One afternoon the Princess, the Countess of Wilton, and her daughter Lady Catharine drove over with Elizabeth to the Croxton Park races. On the way the ebullient American entertained them by repeating the tongue twister, "Theophilus Thistle the Thistle-Sifter," causing the English nobility to "nearly expire laughing."

When they got to the races, the Princess, Lady Catharine, and Elizabeth bet on Lord Wilton's horses (not money—heavens, no!—just a verbal bet), and as they rode past, she showed them the American trick of crossing the feet and twisting the thumbs together for luck. Lord Wilton rode one of the heats himself, much to the "mortification" of his wife and daughter, who looked as though they wanted to sink into the earth as he galloped by in a red jockey cap and blue and white satin waistcoat. Poor Lady Wilton always had a wretched look on her face, and Elizabeth was convinced people in America had not the "slightest conception" of what an unhappy marriage was *really* like.

Driving home, all once again in the "merriest mood," the poor Princess sighed, "Ah, how different this is from sitting bolt upright in a carriage by Mama with all the windows down, & keeping my merry thoughts, if I happen to have any, all to myself."

That night there was a ball.

The next day the Lawrences, accompanied by the Princess and Col. MacDonald, a "Crimean hero," drove out to see the fox hunt:

> Imagine an immense pack of beautifully spotted hounds all in full cry through a beautiful valley, & followed at full speed by a hundred persons on horseback, the gentlemen in crimson coats & the ladies with riding habits & waving plumes, & each putting their horses to the fullest speed to be in at the death, & bounding over the hedges & ditches with as much indifference as if they had been so many plough furroughs *[sic]*.

During the drive home the Princess confided that she could not "endure her house," that Henry VIII was her favorite ancestor, and that she would have been a Jacobite, had she lived "a century before." Consequently, as their carriage entered the park, Col. MacDonald started singing Jacobite songs at the top of his lungs. All in all, it was "a most amusing day."

* * *

Princess Mary of Cambridge, granddaughter of George III, and first cousin of Queen Victoria. Though she looked "more like one's ideal of a butcher's daughter than the scion of a Royal Duke," she turned out to be one of the "nicest" people EL had ever met. Calotype, dated April 1854. *Reproduced by gracious permission of Her Majesty Queen Elizabeth II.*

Surely no American ever saw Royalty—with a capital R—"in such a familiar manner" as the Lawrences did that night.

The Duchess, the Princess, Lady Suffield, and Lady Sandwich sat down to a game of whist after dinner. Before long the Princess looked up and called Elizabeth over to sit beside her on the sofa, behind which stood a tall marble pillar topped by a large brass lamp with a glass globe. No sooner had she deposited herself next to the Princess than a servant accidentally struck the pillar with his tray and over went the lamp, "shivering into atoms" at their feet. How it missed their heads they could not imagine, until they discovered that Bigelow had lunged forward in the nick of time and knocked it off course. Had he not, everyone loudly agreed, the two ladies would unquestionably have been killed.

The Princess was wearing a pink silk dress covered with lace—a present from the Queen. Saturated with oil, it was completely ruined. Elizabeth escaped untouched. "Her Royal Highness," she reported, "considers that Mr. L. saved our lives."

Afterwards the Duchess presented Elizabeth with her bouquet, while the Princess was "most marked" in her kindness to them.

* * *

Among the guests at Belvoir was the Earl of Cardigan, who had led the "famous charge" at Balaclava. Elizabeth took a long walk with him one afternoon and lost no time in eliciting a description of the battle. How did he feel, she asked, when he "rode towards the Russians"? "As if he was riding straight to Eternity," he replied, and continued:

> ... he did not see the slightest chance for life, as they were all surrounded by a perfect shower of balls & shells not only from the twenty cannons before them, but from the cross-fire on both sides of them. He thinks now that Sebastopol will never be taken. There were two chances... when the allies first landed in the Crimea, but they were allowed to slip, & they will never return.

The Lawrences left Belvoir the same day as the Royal Highnesses, who were escorted to the door by the Duke and his entire family. As the Duchess and the Princess walked down the great hall, they passed between two rows of musicians attired in the Rutland colors, playing *God Save the Queen*. How astonished Elizabeth would have been could she have foreseen that, a little more than a decade later, the friendly Princess would marry the Duke of Teck and produce a daughter, Princess Mary of Teck, who would one day wed her second cousin (Victoria's grandson) and become Queen Mary to his King George V. With the providential rescue by Bigelow, God had indeed saved a Queen.

On their arrival back in London, they read in the paper that Miss Brontë, the authoress of *Jane Eyre*, was dead. "It does not mention what she died of."

* * *

April's high point was the visit of Emperor Napoleon III and his elegant Empress Eugénie to London. Wherever they went, they were greeted with "perfect thunders" of applause. The day before they were scheduled to pass along the Strand, the police, wary of an assassination attempt, visited every shop and requested the shopkeepers not to admit any Frenchmen to their windows except the ones they knew.

The Lawrences were presented to the Emperor and Empress, along with the other members of the *corps diplomatique*, at the French Embassy. As she was introduced in the imperial salon, Elizabeth found herself wondering if it were true that in Paris the American Minister presented his compatriots to the Court "in divisions of fifties," merely announcing with a wave of his hand, "Emperor, these are Americans!"

Instead of the "melancholy" man she had been led to expect, she found the Emperor—though short—both "handsome & fascinating," his face "beaming with smiles."

The Empress Eugénie, world-renowned leader of fashion, was wearing a green-silk ensemble "with a profusion of snow-white lace flounces," a lace mantilla, and a "fancy" white bonnet, saucily perched over hair "thrown back as you see it in her portraits." By delightful coincidence, Elizabeth was also in green-flounced silk, a white-embroidered mantle, and a straw bonnet with a white Brussels-lace veil looped back with bunches of apricot blossoms, which Bigelow had recently given her. The similarity of costume was assuredly a *coup*.

Wherever Eugénie and Napoleon III went they were greeted with "perfect thunders" of applause. *The Illustrated London News*, April 1855.

The Empress's features were "delicate & regular," her eyes a deep bluish-grey with "drooping lids" which gave them a "melancholy & most interesting expression." Certainly she must once have been very beautiful, but her "extreme palor," and the deep circles under her eyes showed that her beauty had faded. As a result of an ill-fated romance, her smile was "the saddest thing you ever saw":

> The Empress was once very much in love with her cousin, who pretended to return her affections, but she suddenly discovered that he was having an intrigue with her sister the Duchess of Alba, & so intense was her grief at the double deception that she took poison & they say has never recovered from the effects of it.

Elizabeth had heard that "the formality of court etiquette" bothered Eugénie, and watching her at the reception concluded that "indeed her manners are much more those of a very fascinating young lady than of a great Empress."

According to the amusing Mrs. Bates, the banker's wife, when Louis Napoleon had been in exile in England, Mr. Bates used to "lecture him on his wild doings." Once Louis got so angry he did not visit the Bates's house for days. Mrs. Bates—a forthright Yankee—ran into him by chance one day and said: "Now, Prince, I know why you don't come to see us, it's because Mr. Bates has been lecturing you, & you know you deserve it; so come & dine with us tomorrow & don't be so foolish any longer." With a shout of laughter, the Prince had accepted the invitation.

Added the irrespressible Mrs. Bates: When Louis first showed up at their home with his moustache shaved off, she had informed him that he "looked just like a little apothecary." One day he had walked from their home all the way into London for a pack of cards!

On hearing Mrs. Bates's stories, Bigelow confided to Elizabeth that when Louis was still President of France, before becoming Emperor, his "cousin Napoleon" was "very anxious to marry Kitty Lawrence [Bigelow's sister], but her parents would not hear of it."

The Empress's features were "delicate & regular;" the Emperor was "handsome & fascinating." *The Illustrated London News*, April 1855.

Everyone from cabinet minister to policeman breathed a sigh of relief when the Emperor's visit to London came to an end. The French Ambassador's wife had been "perfectly sick with anxiety" for fear he "would be shot at." Indeed, the only person who had seemed unconcerned was the Emperor himself, who "has no fear of anything."

An "eye-witness" told Elizabeth that the parting scene between the royal families was very "affecting." The Empress wept and kissed Victoria over and over again. The Emperor's eyes were moist as the Queen kissed him three times, "when twice was all that was necessary."

The royal children clung to the Empress and begged her not to leave, and there was simply no consoling the Princess Royal. They all used to spend hours in her room, and

Elizabeth supposed her "warm-hearted manner" was a delightful change from the "stately German visitors" with whom they usually were saddled.

* * *

Soon after the Emperor's departure, another invitation was forthcoming to the Queen's Drawing Room. The dress Elizabeth ordered was cut low off the shoulders and dragged behind "like the tail of a peacock."

The new London "season" was accelerating into high gear. They had already been invited to Lord Palmerston's, followed the next night by dinner at Lord Lansdowne's. An invitation to the Mansion House they promptly declined. One Lord Mayor's dinner was "enough for a life time!"

9
THE SECOND "SEASON" (1855)

"The everlasting roll of the wheels of fashion."

Elizabeth's second London "season" began with an unusual addition to the household. One day as Emma the cook was fussing about in the kitchen, she heard "a kind of cluck," and there in the doorway stood a "great Pekin China hen!" Mr. L. insisted on keeping it in the backyard, which his wife now called "the farm," inquiring if he didn't think they had better keep a cow too? With a straight face she asked if he planned to take the hen along when they journeyed to the Continent.

After much discussion it was decided they would not go to Paris until after "the season." Originally Bigelow had planned to give up his post in early spring, then make an extensive "grand tour," but his father had been "exceedingly anxious" that he remain at the Legation at least until Buchanan's projected return home in the fall. So Bigelow had agreed to stay. He and Elizabeth got on well with the Minister, who had developed into "an immense friend." During the winter she had sent him a pheasant, a brace of which she had just received from Lord Lansdowne, with the hope that he would find it "as palatable as we did your kind present of the grouse...."

Again the attaché's wife found herself turning on "the everlasting roll of the wheels of fashion," out all day long leaving cards, and out all night long at dinners and concerts and balls. It lacked some of the excitement of the first time around. However, there was a new entertainment that suddenly became all the rage: spiritualism. A medium, David Home, arrived in London from Boston, and the Lawrences were among the first to watch him perform at a friend's house. Elizabeth couldn't decide whether it was wonderful or "awful":

> I had my feet on his feet, his hands were on the table, and yet there were knocks all over the room, & presently the room shook at my bidding three times, just as you might suppose it would in an earthquake.
>
> The table, at our command, became so light that I could lift it with three fingers, & then so heavy that I could not budge it.
>
> A bell was stood between Mr. L. & our friend Mr. Jarvis, a little under the table, & in the midst of our conversations [it] commenced to ring, & then what do you think? came across under the table & was put into my hand.
>
> I then said, "Will the spirit take it to Mr. L?" and in another instant Mr. L. said, "The bell is in my hand," & placed it on the table.
>
> The hand, or whatever it was, came & laid in my lap, wrestled my dress, & pulled it until I thought it would tear it, & touched everyone at the table, & at each touch everyone sprang back as if from the shock of an electric machine.
>
> The other night *here*, Mr. Home, the medium, sat in the window, Mr. L. on a chair, & upon the latter's saying: "Will the table move across the room?", the table walked across the room to him & made a bow! & became as light as a feather, & then again so heavy that he could not move it with all his strength!
>
> Mr. Rotch [Bigelow's brother-in-law] wrote us word from Boston that he saw the table rise up from the floor & remain suspended in the air! & what do you think, the hand sometimes comes out & lies on the table! Home said it was coming

Tuesday Morning,

Dear Mr Buchanan.

I send you the number of the Court Journal you alluded to last evening; & also a pheasant, a brace of which I have just received from Lord Lansdowne. Hoping that you may find it as palatable as we did your kind present of the grouse last autumn, I remain dear Mr Buchanan.

your very sincere friend.
Elizabeth Lawrence

The Hon James Buchanan.

EL's note to the U.S. Minister, James Buchanan, which accompanied a pheasant, "a brace of which [she had] just received from Lord Lansdowne." *Courtesy of the Historical Society of Pennsylvania.*

out the other night—when it tossed up the table cover. Everybody is talking about it here, & parties forming to see him. What it is I cannot imagine. Sir E. L. Bulwer thinks it fairies.

The other night when I saw the medium, it rapped out this sentence (you take the alphabet & say the letters slowly, until you hear three raps, & then begin again, & so on): "Elizabeth, my child, I wish you to believe in the reality of these things."

REMARKABLE CASE OF TABLE TALKING.

Table (loquitur). "DON'T YOU BELIEVE HIM, MUM—I'M NOT MAHOGANY, BUT I'M VENEERED AND SECOND-HAND." [*Table dances about on its legs for a considerable time and vanishes in a blue flame.*

Punch ridicules the craze for spiritualism.

So Elizabeth decided to test it. She rapped out a name—Rebecca Chapman—and the answer rapped back: "Your mother." Astonished, she said to herself "without change of countenance or moving of lips, I will not believe it unless it gives the maiden name." And what did it do but rap "Rebecca Stewart," which was indeed the name of Judge Chapman's first wife, who had died in 1837!

Elizabeth was nonplused.

Not long afterwards she and Bigelow dined *"en famille"* with Lady Ashburton, the only other guests being Thackeray, Thomas Carlyle, and Mr. and Mrs. Brookfield. The conversation inevitably got around to the "table-movings," and Elizabeth recounted what had happened a few nights before. Neither Thackeray nor Lord Ashburton had yet been exposed to the medium and were in "a state of amazement," declaring they would go see him at the first opportunity. Carlyle, on the other hand, "railed" against the whole thing "with might and main." Elizabeth suggested he go see for himself:

"What do I want to see a table move for?" was his answer. "If my life was as long as Methusela's, perhaps I might, but I have no time for such tomfooleries as that, & I cannot understand how people can spend their time in running after such nonsense."

I told him he ought to investigate a thing so mysterious, for no one knew why tables turned.

"There are a great many things in the world that I can't explain," he replied. "I can go into a carpenter's shop & be surrounded by mysteries on every side," & so he went on until he quite nettled me, & at length I said: "Well, Mr. Carlyle, if the philosophers had treated the bubbling of a tea-kettle lid with the same contempt that you treat the table-turnings, it is very probable we would now be without the locomotive engine."

My remark nettled him in turn, & a few minutes afterwards, when I was describing to Lord Ashburton the wonderful gravity of the North American Indians, & how they would come from the Rocky Mountains & walk through a great city without the slightest expression of surprise, & without looking either to the right side or the left, Carlyle (who I had not addressed in the least) chimed in with: "Once upon a time when I first came to London I was walking in the Strand, & I saw a butcher come riding along with a calf tied round the neck of his horse, & the calf did not look to the right side or the left either."

"Well," said I, "Mr. Carlyle, I think if you or I were to ride into a city for the first time tied to a horse's neck, we should have been so busy with our position that we would very probably have done as the calf did."

After this little spat, you would have thought the great philosopher would never have spoken to me again. Judge, then, of my surprise when, upon coming in from dinner, he sat down by my side & talked to me all the evening with a power & eloquence such as I have never seen equalled.

It was like one of his most splendid essays—the subject, Louis Napoleon, whom he hates....

He speaks with a broad Scotch accent, which adds a great deal to the drollery of his remarks. His eyes are grey & very sad, & he wears a moustache & whiskers, because he has no time to shave!

Several nights later they dined with Thackeray, who placed Elizabeth next to him. Charles Dickens sat across the table, and a "very merry time" was had. During the course of the dinner she regaled the two novelists with a description of the table walking across her dining rooom floor:

"You depend upon it, that Home is a cheat," said Thackeray.
"But it was an honest table," chimed in Dickens.

At the conclusion of one of the most delightful evenings she had had in England, Thackeray insisted upon rushing out in the pouring rain to hand her into her carriage.

Within a day or two a note was delivered to her which was bound to be "very valuable" because of its *two* autographs on the same piece of paper:

Tavistock House,
Saturday, Second June 1855

My dear Thackeray,
    A friend of mine wants the address of the man who makes the bells leap into people's hands, & does all those ticklish things with the extensive skirts of the ladies' dresses. Will you get it for me? That little Darling who sat opposite to me at dinner *must* know where he lives.

Very faithfully yours,
Charles Dickens

36 Onslow Square

My dear Mrs. Lawrence,
   Whom *can* Dickens mean by that little etc.?—But I dare say you know the Ghost seer's address & will send it to yours very truly,

W.M. Thackeray

Elizabeth promptly replied:

Dear Mr. Thackeray:
   The Weird Man's address is 8 Jermyn St. & I could almost forgive him his cloven foot (or laizy tongs*, O Sceptic) for procuring me two *such* autographs as I received last evening.

Most truly yours,
Elizabeth Lawrence

In copying the correspondence for Mama's benefit, she asterisked "laizy tongs," and described them as "a kind of long scissors the English ladies use to pick up anything they've dropped on the floor." Thackeray had suggested that the medium concealed one of these useful implements in his trousers!

(Left) Charles Dickens sat across the table from EL at Thackeray's dinner, and later referred to her as "that little Darling." *Harper's New Monthly Magazine*, February 1856. (Right) One of four likenesses of Thackeray found among the Chapman-Mercer family papers. The novelist, who said he "had lost his heart" to EL in Philadelphia, placed her next to him at his dinner party.

Although the medium continued to astonish all who watched him perform, Elizabeth finally decided never to see him again; it was just "too shocking." Imagine "feeling touches from invisible hands, & sometimes you see them—it's awful." Bigelow, however, agreed to go with a group of "scientific men" and interview the man. She strongly suspected nothing would come of it.

* * *

At Lady Palmerston's (where she was seated between Lord P. and Lord Shaftesbury) the subject of the medium did not come up. However, after dinner a guest confided a story about Lady Palmerston "which is really true":

> Before her last marriage, & when she was the Countess Cowper, Lord Palmerston was supposed to be deeply in love with her, & her youngest son, the Hon. Mr. Cowper, was always supposed to be his [i.e., Lord Palmerston's] child.
> A short time after Earl Cowper's death, she became Lady Palmerston.
> When Mr. [George] Bancroft [the Minister who preceded Abbott Lawrence] first arrived in this country, of course he did not know of this scandal. (Indeed, so many years had passed since it was talked about that it was quite forgotten).
> However, Mr. Bancroft was dining with Lord Palmerston one evening, when young Cowper came into the room, and Lady P. presented him as her son.
> "Ah, my Lord," said Mr. B. in the blandest manner, turning to Lord Palmerston, "one could tell that he belonged to you."

One of the "most agreeable people" in London paid a long visit one afternoon: the Countess Dowager of Morley, conceded to be the "wittiest woman in society."

She recounted a story about Carlyle, who was staying with Lady Ashburton in Scotland. It was the cholera season, and the philosopher, feeling under the weather, shut himself up in his room, and no amount of coaxing could get him out. Lady Ashburton sent for a doctor, who had not been in the patient's room more than a few minutes when he came flying out looking perfectly furious. Carlyle, he announced, had informed him that "of all the sons of Adam, there isn't a set that imposes more upon the weakness of poor human credulity than yours, sir, & for all the good you [doctors] do, a man might as well pour his sorrows into the long hairy ear of a jackass!"

Elizabeth encountered Lady Morley later that week at a dinner given by Lord Lansdowne, at which the ex-Prime Minister, Lord Russell, was the only other guest. The witty lady entertained the group with epigrams, Elizabeth's favorite being "on the occasion of a gentleman's showing his portrait to his wife":

> " 'Tis my portrait, my dear, don't it strike you?"
> "Not at present, my love, but it certainly will,
>   It's so like you."

It is likely that Elizabeth rejoined with an epitaph she had heard recently at one of her own dinner parties:

> "Here lies the body of W. W.—
> "No longer able to trouble you trouble you."

* * *

The first week in June the Lawrences were invited by the Duke of Rutland not to Belvoir, but to "The Wood House," his "little retreat" near Haddon Hall in Derbyshire, for trout fishing. The place had only seven rooms, and His Grace had once been heard to say to the Duke of Devonshire, who was visiting at the time, "Well, what a comfort it is to get out of our great troublesome houses."

Since the catch of trout is noticeably unrecorded, one can only assume that the same luck prevailed as at Bulwer-Lytton's, when the only thing caught was a freckle!

* * *

During the year in England, Bigelow had succeeded in amassing a remarkable number of items to add to his collection of arms and armor. In one week alone he bought:

> ...a headsman's sword which has been used many times & is very old; the sword of a Malay Pirate adorned with bunches of human hair!; an exquisite silver gilt Damoscene sword; a Russian bayonet picked up at the Battle of the Alma; & a powder flask taken from the dead body of a Cossack.
>
> A gun mounted in silver such as are only carried by the chiefs in Indian battles, axes, cross-bows, guns, daggers & swords innumerable & the most awful *savage-* looking weapons from the East strew the house in every direction, & I am in momently terror that the *Times* will announce some fine morning that one of the inmates of 48 Upper Brook St. came to their death in a frightful manner from a deadly weapon, "name unknown, & of which the coroner, a profoundly scientific man, has not yet discovered the use."

One night Elizabeth went into the dining room in the dark and was "half frightened out of my senses" by what she supposed was a "gigantic house-breaker lurking in the corner," but which she discovered to be Bigelow's latest acquisition: a complete suit of link armor, the helmet mounted on a pole!

* * *

The lease on their Brook Street house ran out and could not be extended; so in the middle of June the American attaché went house hunting again. A much larger residence was found at 8 Hertford Street, in Mayfair, that had belonged to Sir William Hamilton, and Elizabeth's ever-fertile imagination immediately conjured up thoughts of "the lovely Emma" carrying on her "flirtation" with Lord Nelson within those very walls. They rented the house rather cheaply, because it was so late in the season, and in they moved, hen and all.

Elizabeth continued to give small, intimate dinner parties, which on the whole she thoroughly enjoyed, in spite of an occasional *faux pas* on the part of her staff. The night James forgot to pass the sauce, when ex-President Martin Van Buren was a guest, was a case in point:

> Martin... was extremely affable & pleasant, but I regret to say that I came within an ace of losing the points of three of my stories on account of the idiotic James forgetting to hand the cucumber sauce with the salmon.
>
> It was in vain that between my most impressive smiles to my guests I sent glares to him, but it was of no avail, my eyes in spite of their color could not look like cucumbers, & therefore the intelligent footman could not tell what I meant.

Nevertheless the conversation over the unsauced salmon would have been stimulating, for Van Buren, who had been Minister to England back in 1831, must have reminisced about the challenges of his job before railroads and steamships and the telegraph revolutionized travel and communications.

* * *

In the company of a more recent ex-President, Millard Fillmore, the Lawrences visited Windsor Castle. After being shown the private apartments and some "remarkable curiosities," they were taken to see Prince Albert's farm, where they drank milk fresh from the cows. Whether by coincidence or design, they watched the sheepshearing, which must have held special interest for Fillmore, who at fifteen had been apprenticed to learn how to dress wool. Since he was out of office only two years, (and soon to run again on the Know-Nothing ticket), the royal wool could not have failed to conjure up his American rags-to-riches background.

Elizabeth borrowed a pair of scissors and cut herself a souvenir of Prince Albert's wool, which she intended to send home to little Fanny. Somehow it got lost on the return journey to London.

* * *

During the course of one of her tea parties, Elizabeth was asked by a guest if she had received an invitation to Dickens's "private theatricals," where he and a number of literary luminaries were to perform. Even at home in Doylestown she had heard of these "celebrated performances," and to be in London and not see one was almost more than she could bear. In fact she was so exercised, she spilled her tea over her new pink silk dress, and the color came off on her gloves, her arms, and her handkerchief, which she had quickly but unsuccessfully brought into play. Although she suddenly saw everything about her turn literally *"couleur de rose,"* the sight made her "none the happier."

The next day, to her surprise, she received a note from Mrs. Dickens saying that her husband had discovered "in a very mysterious manner" that she was eager to "witness their little theatricals," and he had managed to find two more seats for the Lawrences in their "limited apartments." The "printer's bill," which Mrs. Dickens had enclosed, gave the full particulars. The play was to be a new one, written by Dickens and entitled *The Light House*, and the actors were to be the "principal literary people" in London. Willingly would she have sacrificed her new silk dress for such an invitation!

The following Tuesday they took off for Tavistock House in a high state of excitement. Ushered into the drawing room, they found themselves surrounded by "a company of wits and celebrities." Mrs. Dickens rushed up and expressed her pleasure at seeing them, then introduced them around:

> ... Then came Tom Taylor with his bride, & an invitation to their little Brompton Cottage to hear Viardot sing; then Mrs. Carlyle with her plain face & broad Scotch & Thomas with his solemn eyes...
>
> Old Braham had crowded himself up in a corner & looked like a cross between a baboon & a mummy.... I made the acquaintance of Douglas Jerrold [playwright and humorist], a little old man very much bent with long white hair thrown back from his forehead, & a pair of light, wild-looking grey eyes that gave him all the look of a crazy man just about to spring on you.
>
> At precisely 8 o'clock Foster of the *Examiner* took his stand at the door, calling out the names of the guests, & we all passed out two by two to a little temporary edifice built at the side of the house. It was a perfect theatre in miniature.

The first piece was a melodrama by Wilkie Collins, the second a farce by Dickens. The actors were Dickens, Mark Lemon, Wilkie Collins, Augustus Egg, R. A., Miss Hogarth, Miss Dickens, etc. etc.

The highlight of the evening was Dickens's acting. Elizabeth was certain that if he were on the stage, he would be considered the equal of Garrick. When she suggested this to Jerrold, he agreed with her, "but," said he, "it's better as it is."

In the farce the novelist played half a dozen different roles, all with equal competence. Many of Dickens's lines were "the wit of the moment," causing the other actors on stage, who ought to have been "gravity personified," to collapse in convulsions of laughter. Elizabeth laughed till she cried. Mrs. Dickens seemed particularly pleased with her delight and confided to her afterwards that she had made "a conquest" of the novelist.

* * *

The end of June, news came from Boston that old Abbott Lawrence's health, which had been deteriorating, was now fast reaching a critical stage. As a result, they gave up their social activities, and Elizabeth canceled her appearance as Belinda in a tableau, *The Rape of the Lock*, in which she was to have been the principal figure. The charitable entertainment was sponsored by London's social leaders, and she had been scheduled to wear a magnificent costume: a blue brocade gown that opened in front revealing a crimson satin petticoat covered with lace, and a stomacher blazing with jewels.

When the next steamer brought word of the Bostonian's recovery, the social round resumed:

> The other day I had the pleasure of breakfasting with my pet poetess, Mrs. Browning. She sat next to me at table, & we had a long conversation on Spirit rappings. She, I think, is a decided believer.
>
> She is a small woman with a broad intellectual-looking forehead, very calm, dark, clear grey eyes, dark brown hair curling on either side of her face, & would, I think, be pretty were it not for a projecting mouth which, without being disagreeable looking, of course spoils the regularity of her face.
>
> She has a very placid expression, a low voice, & manners extremely modest & retiring—so much so that when in an argument we were all having upon the Spirits, she found everyone listening to her, she became so confused that she could scarcely go on, & when I brought to her mind some fact upon the subject, she commenced telling it across the table, & then stopped, & with a very modest manner said: "You tell it, Mrs. Lawrence."
>
> She was very neatly & plainly dressed, & neither by appearance or words reminded you of an authoress.

* * *

Tea at Lord Westminster's was an experience worth writing home about, for he was the "richest & meanest" peer in England. What was served? That "economical beverage," *milk!*:

> Fancy the thing, with the hostess beside you covered with old lace & diamonds, & the walls adorned with some of the grandest pictures the world ever saw.... We expect to dine there next Wednesday. I am already fancying the puddings *a la pauvre homme*, game *a la ragged urchin*, etc. etc., with which we will be regaled.

* * *

Dinner at Monckton Milne's produced a fascinating conversation with a French refugee who, prodded by the ever-curious Elizabeth, described Mme. George Sand. The novelist, he told her, had once been "extremely handsome," but she had a quiet, immobile sort of face that never revealed "the fire of her genius and character" except by an occasional flash of her dark, beautiful eyes.

Elizabeth then inquired about Rachel, the famous actress, and was told the poor lady had no more feeling for her roles than "a block of marble." Her fame was entirely attributable to a little old French actor from whom she learned her parts by rote. When she played without benefit of his instruction, she made mistakes in the meaning she gave to a sentence, and even worse, in the pronunciation of words.

* * *

Most conversations at some point turned on the war, and everyone was eager to report the latest scrap of news. Elizabeth heard one day that when both armies were burying their dead after a disastrous attack, a Russian officer was heard to say to an Englishman: "We always thought you were lions, but we never knew before that you were led by asses."

At the end of July Bigelow went to Paris for a few days. Since his stay was to be brief, his wife decided not to accompany him, dreading the Channel crossing. It was the first time he had left her during their marriage, and she missed him. She found herself in complete sympathy when, on his return, he spoke of "suffering torments" at the hands of Thomas Evans, the famous American dentist then living in Paris.

She was surprised when her mother wrote that steamers had come and gone without bringing any letters from her. Elizabeth was indignant, for she had missed only one steamer in months. What had happened to all her laborious efforts? There was bound to be a delay, she acknowledged, ever since "our delightful government at Washington" enforced the "abominable rule" that the foreign dispatch bags had to be sent to Washington before being forwarded elsewhere. But that did not account for her letters not being received at all!

She decided on a strategy that involved Mama's help. She would keep a list of the dates she wrote, Mama would mention the dates of the letters she received, and with proof in hand she would march straightaway into Mr. Buchanan's office, for he would be "only too rejoiced to give the government a *dig*!"

On the whole subject of the postal service she was in "a perfect state of rage." A few weeks before, she had written a very long letter on very thick paper to her aunt in Philadelphia. As usual she had sent it via the dispatch bag to be posted by her mother-in-law in Boston. The very week it arrived in America "this sensible postal arrangement" went into operation, so that her aunt's letter went to Washington, where it was posted collect, undoubtedly causing her to pay a "pretty sum" on it! Elizabeth was mortified beyond words!

* * *

The beginning of August they were invited once again by the Duke of Rutland to Belvoir to see the castle "in its summer beauty," then accompany the Duke to Longshore for grouse shooting. Elizabeth longed to have her father along, so that she could show off "what an American shot really is!"

It was their last journey to the English countryside. On August 18 Abbott Lawrence died in Boston. As soon as the news was received on the other side of the Atlantic, Bigelow and Elizabeth began preparations to return to America. On black-bordered paper they sent out communications to wind up their affairs. Bigelow dropped a note to Buchanan, expressing a desire to see the Minister and his niece whenever they chose to call "during this hour of our affliction."²

The affliction was not so overwhelming that Bigelow was not able to give a thought to a more mundane matter: the importation of some fine wine into the United States, for use upon his return. Through the good offices of the Spanish Ambassador he tracked down a Spanish wine merchant who handled the "best Amontillado." He then wrote Buchanan, who planned to return to the States that fall, suggesting they split a cask. If the Minister ordered it and had it shipped to New York or Philadelphia under his own name, Bigelow would carry on from there. It would save him having to pay duty:

> I will, therefore, leave the matter entirely in your hands, merely adding, that if you can procure for me a choice wine of this character before you leave England, I shall feel under the greatest obligation, and shall be proud to bring out my "Buchanan wine" on grand occasions!
>
> Mrs. Lawrence joins with me in kindest regards and Adieus. Neither of us will ever forget your undeviating kindness and attention to us. . . .³

* * *

James Buchanan, an engraving by A.L. Dick, after a painting by Jacob Eicholz. An "immense friend," Buchanan was asked to ship some *good* wine to the Lawrences, before he returned to the U.S. to run for President. *Courtesy of the Historical Society of Pennsylvania.*

Elizabeth paid a parting call on the Minister. Her concern was not the wine; it was Willie Mercer. A frantic note from Mary had just arrived bemoaning the fact that her husband had been discharged from the Navy.⁴

For months Elizabeth had been trying to secure a place for her brother-in-law in the Lawrence mills. Bigelow had written enthusiastic letters about Willie to his father, and both Mary and Willie had journeyed to Boston to look over the situation and meet the Lawrence family. Abbott Lawrence had liked the young couple and held out hope that a suitable position could be found. Now Abbott was dead, and what was even worse, Willie had been discharged. So once again Elizabeth took up the cudgels for her brother-in-law. She tied on her bonnet, marched into Buchanan's office, and laid out her problem, proposing that the Minister contact his old friend, President Franklin Pierce, about Willie's dilemma. The next day—October 4—Buchanan wrote the President:

> .... Mrs. Bigelow Lawrence called to see me yesterday in deep distress on account of the discharge of Midshipman Mercer, her sister's husband, from the Navy. She informs me that he was a good officer, as is testified by the fact that Commodore Macauley appointed him to do the duties of master on board the *Princeton.*
>
> It appears that at the time of this appointment, Midshipman Mercer had received assurances from the late Mr. Lawrence that he might obtain a place at Lowell, the emoluments of which would enable him much better to support his family; and he gave this as a reason to Commmodore Macauley for declining to act as master, with which the latter appeared to be satisfied.
>
> Mrs. Lawrence believes this to have been the cause of his dismissal. When Mr. Mercer went on to Boston, Mr. [Abbott] Lawrence was no longer able to attend to business, and he did not get the place.
>
> This is certainly a hard case, and I shall be personally very much gratified should you be able to do anything for him. His father-in-law, Judge Chapman of Bucks County, Pennsylvania, is a man of great respectability and influence ....
> His wife is the daughter of the late Governor Shunk, of Pennsylvania.[5]

Two days later Elizabeth had second thoughts about "the painful subject." A letter from Mary had indicated that one of Willie's Maryland relatives, who also had access to the President, was planning to intercede on his behalf. Quickly she dropped Buchanan a note saying that she would be very sorry to have him write Washington to ask for a favor that had, perhaps, already been granted, knowing the reluctance the Minister felt to ask favors for anyone. The fact that Buchanan had offered to do so put her forever in his debt, and she would never forget his kindness "so long as memory is left me."[6]

She paid Buchanan one final visit before sailing, only to discover he had written the President anyway. She was overcome with gratitude.

To Harriet Lane, who was already back in the States, Buchanan wrote: "She [i.e., Elizabeth] appears to be much rejoiced at the prospect of getting home."[7]

He was quite right.

10
BOSTON (1856–1861)

"I am getting very shaky about honest old Abe."

Elizabeth and Bigelow arrived in Boston the last week of October, after a "very fair voyage for that season of the year!"[1]

One of the first things Bigelow did was to drop Buchanan a note, telling him that politics were in a "fearful condition":

> I do hope that when you return, you will allow your name to come before the people once more for the Presidency. Who else can we have? I am sure a great part of the Whigs will now be ready to unite upon a *Statesman* (after the little people we have had) without respect to party....[2]

He closed by reminding Buchanan about shipping a *good* Amontillado before leaving England, because he appreciated how "correct" the Minister's taste was in wine. "I know of no one else in London whom I can rely on in this *essential* point," he concluded.

After a suitable stay in Boston trying to console his inconsolable mother, Bigelow and Elizabeth headed down to Doylestown for a much more joyous family reunion. Early in the winter of 1856 they returned to Boston, where they would make their home for the next five years.

The return trip north was far from uneventful. Because of bad weather, they decided to take "the cars" instead of the boat. Six miles beyond Hartford the train was engulfed by snow drifts and came to a halt. The engine was unhitched and proceeded on a few miles for wood and water. Steaming back to the stalled cars in a blinding blizzard, the engineer could not see the train and rammed into it, damaging the baggage car, and "knocking flat" all the passengers who happened to be standing. A trainman came through and announced that they would be stuck there till daybreak; so there they sat for twelve "mortal" hours.

At the first streak of dawn a passenger in the Lawrences' car handed around "a paper of mint stick," and in mid-morning some farmers appeared with "great bushels of eatables." It was a funny sight: the hungry passengers all sitting around buttering their bread with penknives!

The train finally pulled into Boston at ten that night.

The Lawrences' new home was at 97 Beacon Street. While they awaited their crates of household goods from England, and workmen installed bookcases and made preparations for the armory, they stayed with the melancholy Mrs. Abbott Lawrence, who was in deep mourning.

The Beacon Street house was a delight to its new mistress. It was dark-red brick with an iron balcony, up which climbed a rose bush. From the upper floors one caught a glimpse of the Charles River, with Cambridge on the far bank. In another direction one could see distant hills.

The hall floor was covered with the latest "oil cloth," and featured a hat rack dominated by an antlered deer's head. The oak-paneled dining room had a round walnut table surrounded by armchairs with leather seats, an Egyptian marble mantlepiece, and a black walnut "dresser" for plates. They planned to add an oval mirror and a carved buffet and to cover the walls with pictures.

97 Beacon Street, EL's home from 1856 to 1861. It is no longer standing. *Courtesy of the Boston Athenaeum.*

Upstairs, the front drawing room, soon to be converted into a library, was done in shades of green. The sofas revealed no wood; just three large cushions piled on top of one another and cushions for backs. It was "very stylish." Under the gilt chandelier stood a table with a "very rare pale brown marble slab" (which she undoubtedly debated covering). Down the hall was a "nook supported by two imitation yellow marble pillars, ... a lovely place for flowers and pictures." The back drawing room had blue and gold satin curtains, a tapestry carpet with a "splendid border of brilliant flowers," and chairs and sofas with gilt backs covered to match the draperies.

The armory—a long room with a bay window—was all in red: the Brussels carpet, the velvet wallpaper with raised gilt panels, the curtains, and the high-backed chairs and sofas! Between the armory and the staircase was a tiny windowless room just large enough for two chairs. It reminded her of the "flirtation room" at Mrs. Rush's.

Besides all this furniture which they had "bought with the house," Elizabeth discovered Bigelow also had stored a sofa, two ottomans, and "a divan of satin patch work with gilded legs and backs."

Their bedroom was furnished in mahogany: wardrobe, tent bedstead, a table, a lounge at the foot of the bed, chairs, and a marble-topped washstand. Wallpaper and upholstery were in French blue with "great bunches of shaded red roses." Her boudoir, as yet unfurnished, led into a "wash room" with a bath, hot and cold water, and a "water closet." Bigelow's dressing room opened into an even larger room which they thought of making into a billiard room. The third story contained two guest bedrooms plus a "water closet!"

Elizabeth was relieved and delighted that her mother-in-law was taking an interest in the renovations at the Beacon Street house, sending in ten people to get the place cleaned and in shape, and even paying the expenses. The old lady also informed all the servants Elizabeth had hired that they were going to have "the best mistress that ever came to Boston," and if they did not serve her daughter-in-law well, they could expect to "hear from her on the subject."

The two women got on well, particularly under the trying circumstances. Elizabeth had "worked" a bag for her for Christmas that so pleased her, she insisted on showing it to everybody who came to the house. Even the most businesslike merchant was expected to take out his spectacles and go "into ecstasies" over it.

One night when Elizabeth was in her room writing a letter to her sister Mary, old Mrs. Lawrence appeared at the door in tears. Pressing a fifty-dollar bill into her daughter-in-law's hand, she begged her to send it to Mary to buy something for the baby she was expecting. She was *so* distressed, she sobbed, that Willie had not got the job in the mills that her late husband had promised him, and on which other members of the family had later reneged. Though *she* was not to blame, perhaps her little offering might help make it up to Mary.

As she was leaving, she cautioned Elizabeth to make no allusion to its source, but to pretend it was her own gift. Paying no attention to this latter injunction, Elizabeth told her family about the gift and added that old Mrs. L. possessed a "tenderness that cannot be surpassed."

* * *

In between bouts with the house, Elizabeth went sleighing, heading out into the country, for the Boston streets were "awful." Bigelow had a beautiful sleigh painted gold and apple-green. When he saw his wife's pleasure with it, he bought her another, a small two-seater lined in red plush.

The other great amusement among the Bostonians that winter was skating:

> Both ladies & gentlemen drive out from Boston on fine afternoons to the surrounding ponds & skate away for hours. They say these hoop petticoats aid the ladies exceedingly & act like fullspread sails, & that nothing can be more graceful than the way they skim over the ice. I am going to try it some day, although I fear I shall make but a poor hand at it.
>
> I think we shall keep a boat in summer.

* * *

Just before they were to move into their house, Bigelow developed a high fever and "pains all over his body." At first the doctor could not diagnose the illness because "typhus, lung fever, & smallpox all had about the same symptoms" at the beginning. After several days the fever began to abate, and he was considered well on the way to recovery when two spots were discovered on his face. To Elizabeth's horror the doctor pronounced them smallpox, then changed his diagnosis to "varioloid," a milder disease thought to produce the more fatal smallpox.

There was much consternation in the family when Bigelow recalled that he had had several of these same spots on his head the previous week when his sister, Annie Rotch, "just approaching her confinement," had appeared with her three children for tea. Fortunately no one else contracted the pox, and Bigelow only developed eighteen spots in all. Everyone got vaccinated—a recent innovation, but one which Elizabeth considered pointless in her case, as she had already been "so much exposed." However, she postponed writing to her family, fearing the letters might carry the "infection," and she took the precaution of "smoking" the first one she sent although she was sure there was "no danger" from it.

* * *

As soon as Bigelow recovered, they threw themselves into the preparations for the new house with "redoubled vigour." By that time Elizabeth could hardly wait, for her mother-in-law, kind as she was, "cried most of the time," and there was an all-pervasive gloom about the place. Renovations were hampered by one of the deepest snows in years, which made the roads like "the waves of the ocean," and driving in a carriage had "all the motion of a ship at sea"—a situation in which she was well versed.

Even before they moved in, a cook was installed. On one of her daily visits, Elizabeth supervised the making of a citron cake, to be presented to her mother-in-law. The cook, and the cake, proved to be disasters. The mistress of the house promptly fired her, and taking into account other problems, refused to give her a recommendation. The cook threatened to "put the law of the land" on her erstwhile employer. The threat never materialized, but Elizabeth had never heard of "such impudence!" (More than likely it was not the tartness of the cook's citron cake, but of her saucy tongue, that brought about her downfall.) A new cook was quickly hired, described as "a most excellent person."

The Lawrences moved into the house on Beacon Street on 15 March 1856, the day before their second wedding anniversary. Elizabeth was reminded of their first one, spent at Torquay while her husband recovered from whooping cough. She thought it a good omen that, as they entered their new house together, Bigelow's "first performance" was to "fall flat on the front door steps!"

* * *

The beginning of April Willie and Mary, six months pregnant, arrived for a visit. The house was far from finished, and the household still in a turmoil, but the sisters were too delighted to see each other to care. Elizabeth had asked Mary to bring along seven or eight Philadelphia cream cheeses, "provided they are not more than about two dollars."

Both Lawrences reveled in the contents of the box that came with the Mercers from Doylestown. Besides the cheeses, there was a blotter Mary had worked for Bigelow with his crest on it; little Fanny's bookmarkers and a velvet pincushion; woolen sleeves and cuffs (to combat the Boston weather); a glycerine vial; and a box of sweetmeats. The "shower of encomiums" peaked, however, with the canned tomatoes and the jellies.

Mary was positive her sister had the finest house in Boston. Some of the furnishings were completely new to her. For instance, she had never seen buhl or marquetry tables or gilded sofas or carved Numidian slaves before. She thought the bed draperies falling from the ceiling entrancing; the white muslin curtains trimmed with pink, cascading over the looking glass in the dressing room, gave "a most beautiful effect,"[3] and the little baskets lined with pink and white standing about in nooks and corners, charming. (Obviously Elizabeth had adopted some of the decorating ideas she had admired at Lord Lansdowne's estate, Bowood.)

Ensconced in the white-and-pink boudoir, the sisters had many a confidential chat. Mary was startled by Elizabeth's account of the high incidence of insanity in Boston. There was scarcely a family that did not have at least one relative in an asylum. Even a cousin of Bigelow's, who had attended Elizabeth's wedding, had gone "crazy on Spiritual Rappers," and was hospitalized. A neighbor down the street had *three* insane children!

Elizabeth also gave Mary a lengthy recital of her problems with the staff, beginning with the citron cake, and continuing with Hardy the butler, who was a "simpleton." One evening when they were entertaining Mr. Prescott, Hardy had been instructed beforehand to bring up a full decanter of wine. What did he do but bring up a decanter containing only enough for two glasses! At these tales of her sister's "domestic troubles," Mary laughed "until the tears ran down her cheeks," and it was not long before Elizabeth, too, collapsed in paroxysms of laughter.

When the bookcases for the library were finally completed, Bigelow and Willie would descend to the basement and haul books upstairs. Mary and Elizabeth would dust them and place them on the shelves, all the while admiring the beautiful Morocco bindings. The armory was progressing more slowly because the man who was helping with the arrangements appeared so infrequently.

Some evenings were spent listening to visiting lecturers: Rufus Choate ("wordy & commonplace"); Edward Everett ("spellbinding"); and an unnamed orator who spoke on "Politics and Patriotism," and inveighed against "the young men of today, . . . that their life, so full of magnified trifles, could be compared to nothing else than 'a tempest in a teapot.' "What a contrast between them and their forefathers," reflected Elizabeth, "whose teapot was Boston Harbour, & whose tempest a nation in arms!"

* * *

During the unpacking of the crates from England, it had been discovered that the porcelain dinner service they had bought was missing. So while the sisters chatted away happily in the boudoir, Bigelow sat in his new library and penned a letter to Buchanan, who, upon his return to the States, had begun campaigning for the Presidency. Bigelow wrote that he was sure the ex-Minister's reception in New York must have been "most gratifying," and that "the compliment was fully deserved."[4]

Having discharged the amenities, he then came to the point. Before leaving England, he had secured from Buchanan a letter to the customs collector requesting that his "furniture, books, and household effects" be passed by the customs officers "without examination." By accident the dinner service had not been loaded at the same time as all their other belongings and sat on the docks for two months. The vessel on which it was finally shipped took so long, it was believed lost at sea. After a voyage of 112 days, it suddenly turned up in New York. Bigelow immediately wrote the collector to inquire if his crates of porcelain could not also be "passed," as they obviously had been part of his "household effects." The collector would have been only too willing to comply, if he had not recently received instructions that "such favours are to be granted *only* by the Treasury Dept. at Washington."

Since Bigelow had no "personal acquaintance" with the Secretary of the Treasury and did not know how else to proceed, would Buchanan be so kind as to intercede for him? Had the china service been a "new importation," and not part of his "household effects" when he left England, he would not have dreamed of troubling the future President. Nevertheless, he felt it "rather hard" that he should have to pay a duty of nearly one hundred dollars because of a mere oversight.

This was the only favor he had ever asked of his government, and the only one he was "ever likely to ask." After all, he had served without remuneration at the Legation, even acting for several months as its Secretary. Though his father had urged him to "make an application" to the Secretary of State for compensation, he had never done so. The dinner service was now sitting in a bonded warehouse in barrels marked *TBL 1, 2, 3*, awaiting clearance. If Buchanan would be so kind . . . .

Finally, he reminded Buchanan of a promise to visit them in Boston. Since they were now reasonably well settled in their new home, they hoped it would not be long before they could entertain him—and toast him with "Buchanan wine."

* * *

In June 1856 James Buchanan was handily nominated in Cincinnati for the Presidency on the Democratic ticket, and Judge Chapman was nominated for a seat in Congress. Beside herself with excitement, Elizabeth begged the family to keep her posted on "exactly how things look in Bucks, as far as the election is concerned." It was her understanding that one hundred thousand dollars had been sent to Pennsylvania to secure Buchanan's election, half of it coming from Augustus Belmont, her Liverpool acquaintance with the large diamond buttons. The "same game," of course, had been tried (though unsuccessfully) by the supporters of John C. Frémont, the candidate of the newly formed Republican party.

Sister Mary's first child, Henry Chapman Mercer, dressed like a typical Victorian boy. He was then called Harry or Hal.

To top off her happiness, Mary had a son, born on June 24. He was named for his grandfather, Henry Chapman Mercer, and nicknamed Harry or Hal. The new aunt longed to head south to Pennsylvania the minute she heard the news.

There were two clouds in the otherwise clear sky: the death of her grandfather, who was buried in the Quaker cemetery not far from John Chapman the First's cave; and Willie's continuing lack of a job. In spite of the influential letters, Willie's position with the Navy was unsettled, and no other job had opened up. There were plenty of suggestions bandied about: an agent for a coal company; a summer clerk in a Philadelphia law office; an engineering assistant. When Elizabeth heard Willie was considering a job in one of the Western territories, she quickly expressed her displeasure. She had no desire to have her dear sister buried thousands of miles away in a wilderness.

As for the possibility of his finding a clerkship with a merchant or a banking house in Boston, Bigelow had been inquiring around, and it was out the question. The top clerks had all risen "step by step," commencing at sixteen, when they started as errand boys while learning bookkeeping, and progressing up the ladder to become head clerks—or sometimes partners—at forty or fifty. As soon as a vacancy occurred, it was filled by the person on the rung below who had been training for the job for years. Furthermore, Willie was not experienced in "financial affairs."

Times were bad, jobs were few, and gloomy faces abounded. Elizabeth found herself dreading the approaching winter, for everyone she knew was either in mourning or "expecting to be ill." One bright spot was the election results: Buchanan was going to Washington, and so was her father. She knew this would entail much loneliness for Mama, who would remain at home in Doylestown.

Finally out of mourning, Elizabeth was able to take part in a series of tableaux given at Chickering's Rooms for the benefit of "the Poor." At three dollars a ticket, the participants hoped to raise one thousand dollars. Elizabeth thoroughly enjoyed herself. Compensating for the aborted experience in London, this time she had two roles. First she was an angel in *The Nun's Vision*, a tableau suggested by Fanny Kemble, the actress, in which she appeared in a long white gown with wings as tall as she, and her hair streaming over her shoulders. In the second, she was Lady Jane Grey, in black velvet with high-standing collar, a Mary Stuart cap of pearls, and a long white lace veil. In this tableau she knelt beside the Queen's confessor, while the jailer, with sword and keys, stood menacingly in the background—just like a picture she remembered in a Philadelphia museum.

Ater this social highlight, everyone resumed a look of gloom.

Elizabeth continued to be plagued by servant problems. The exceptionally cold weather caused the water pipes in the house to freeze, which in turn caused the kitchen boiler to be in imminent danger of blowing up. The only way to avert the danger was to put out the fire. In spite of Elizabeth's instructions, the cook persisted in keeping the fire going in the kitchen grate, though the boiler was making the most "frightful" noises all day long.

After the cook—that "most excellent person"—refused for the third time to extinguish it, the mistress of the house ordered the butler to do it, whereupon the cook gave vent to a stream of impudence and got herself fired, just like her predecessor. All this excitement occurred just as Elizabeth was expecting guests for tea; so she had to have the tea water boiled in one of the bedrooms, and the chicken for salad "boiled out of the house."

During one of her periodic visits to Doylestown, Thomas the coachman made love to Sarah the maid, causing her to become "good for nothing." The whole time Elizabeth was away Sarah scarcely lifted a finger, so that on her return she found the house filled with moths, and many valuable things "almost ruined." Thomas was sent packing, but Sarah seemed so penitent, Elizabeth relented and let her stay.

Hardy, her ex-butler, was caught stealing from his new employer. When he defiantly told the police that the lady of the house had *given* him the alleged stolen goods, they had to release him, because she was too afraid to appear in court against him.

"Heaven defend me from a Boston-trained servant," Elizabeth wrote home. "They have as many rules & regulations of their own as Congress itself."

* * *

The cold weather made good sleighing. One day in mid-January Elizabeth and Bigelow took a sleigh ride out to Lexington:

> [There] we drank some flip, a beverage something like egg nogg made by an old farmer, seated in a farm-house kitchen round a blazing fire, with the walls around us pierced with bullet holes, the souvenirs of the battle. Afterwards we went to the hotel & took a game supper, & did not get back to Boston until twelve o'clock at night.
>
> The consequence of our spree was that the next day Mr. L. was in bed most of the time with a violent sick head-ache, the result of the flip.

Scarlet fever was prevalent. One night the Lawrences were invited to dine at the Wadsworths, but declined, having heard their laundress had the fever. Everyone thought their refusal to go was foolishness—until it developed that three of the guests at the dinner contracted it.

* * *

After much urging, Fanny came for an extended visit. At twelve, her half-sister was turning into a very pretty young lady with charming manners, and Elizabeth was proud to include her in many of their social engagements and theater parties.

Bigelow bought Fanny a pair of the new double-runner skates, on which novices could learn to perform in a mere three lessons. Elizabeth saw to it that the girl practiced on the piano at least three quarters of an hour every day, and often sat with her while she did.

* * *

At long last Willie was settled. Through a combination of a mortgage, gifts, and loans—mostly from the Lawrences—he bought a farm in Claverack, on the Husdon, for $2,700. There he started growing fruits and vegetables, primarily for the New York City market. He had always been interested in things horticultural, and with a couple of part-time helpers, he launched into his new enterprise with enthusiasm.

Since it was just a day's journey from Boston, Elizabeth went over to inspect the house, then arranged for improvements, so that the place would be in order by the time Mary arrived in the summer of 1858, after the birth of her second child. The baby, a girl, was named Elizabeth Lawrence Mercer, and nicknamed Lela. Aunt Elizabeth was beside herself with joy.

* * *

By now Elizabeth had been married nearly five years and had no children. With true Victorian reticence, only once did she drop a hint in her letters on her lack of offspring. It was not long after both she and Mary were married. Mary had apparently had a miscarriage. At first she had complained of feeling depressed, but later confided she was glad to be "free," since she was then shuttling between parents and in-laws while Willie was at sea. Elizabeth had thought her sister "most sensible":

> I, too, am entirely free, & I earnestly hope that I shall always remain so. If I were ever to find myself to the contrary, of course, I should make the best of it, & not behave like a simpleton & cry for nine months as some women do. Mr. Lawrence is of the same opinion as myself about such matters.

One deduces that at least at the beginning of her marriage, with the prospect of the London "season," Elizabeth was relieved not to have a "confinement." Once settled in Boston, however, it is hard to believe that she did not want children, knowing her strong attachment to her family and to her little niece and nephew. Possibly Bigelow was ultimately to blame. The illness that left him deaf may also have left him sterile.

He had been married to Sallie Ward for nearly nine months before she left him, and there had been no child. Shortly after the divorce, Sallie married Dr. Robert Hunt (who had told his appalled family he "would rather go to hell with Sallie Ward than to heaven without her").[5] The Hunts moved to New Orleans and proceeded to have three children (only one of whom survived infancy).

Sallie had at last found her place in the sun. Until the Civil War broke out, her elegant entertainments (which often featured the orchestra from the French opera playing in the tree-shaded courtyard), and the sumptuous furnishings of her magnificent mansion (modeled after those of the Duchess of Orléans in Paris) were unrivaled.

In 1860, while at the peak of her social career in New Orleans, Sallie had her portrait painted by one of America's most fashionable artists, G. P. A. Healy. "She was the most beautiful...the most exquisite woman I have ever painted," he is said to have told visitors to his Parisian *atelier*.[6] In fact, so captivated was he by his sitter, that shortly afterwards he painted a self-portrait "for his friends Dr. and Mrs. Hunt," and presented it to them with his compliments.[7] Healy also painted their blond, curly-haired son John, whom Sallie liked to dress in clothes like those worn by the little French Prince Imperial, son of Napoleon III and the Empress Eugénie, who was about the same age.

* * *

The dinner parties that the second Mrs. Lawrence gave in Boston were far from pedestrian affairs, though in terms of pure luxury they could not compete with the extravaganzas Sallie Ward Lawrence Hunt was staging at the same time in New Orleans. Whereas Sallie boasted a magnificent marble fountain in the middle of her statue-filled courtyard, Elizabeth surprised the Bostonians with a little portable fountain, which she set up in the center of the table. With a profusion of flowers, and "all our red glass & red wax candles in the candelabras," the guests all proclaimed these occasions the "most splendid they ever sat down to."

Often she set up her parties in the armory. Dining among the swords and suits of mail made for a dramatic evening. One night she entertained about eighty gentlemen from the 7th Regiment in New York who had come up for some Boston festivities. She had to admit the house was "so crammed with furniture," it was no small job to move things around to get ready for such a large party.

As a dinner guest, Elizabeth was as popular in Boston as she had been in London, and she continued to make interesting friends. A "beautiful fête" at Mrs. Cushing's was followed by a dinner at the Shaws, where she sat beside Louis Agassiz, the geologist, who entertained her with tales of a scientific meeting he had attended in Edinburgh in 1837.

Fanny Kemble paid her a long visit one April day:

> "We talked about Miss Brontë, & she told me that the authoress of "Jane Eyre" had literally starved to death. After her marriage she soon found herself *enceinte*, which was accompanied by a total loss of appetite, & instead of her father & husband insisting upon her taking stimulating food, she was allowed to go on from month to month totally & entirely neglected by them, until her system fell into such a state of weakness that there was no rallying it.
> This was told Mrs. K. by Mrs. Gaskell, who is about publishing her [i.e.,

Brontë's] life, but Mrs. K. says very truly that the real life cannot be given to the world now.

Fanny Kemble, the actress, dressed as Portia, one of her most famous roles. *Courtesy of the Historical Society of Pennsylvania.*

Taking tea with the actress not long afterwards, Elizabeth begged her to suggest a costume she might wear to a forthcoming fancy-dress ball. Mrs. Kemble proposed a French lady in the court of Henry IV and volunteered to help her design it. The actress loaned her the *pièce de résistance* (which she had worn on the stage): a broad girdle of different colored stones, from which was suspended a long pendant that almost reached to the feet. There was also a large ruff, which Elizabeth was sure would "rather startle" her husband.

* * *

As the rumbles of the approaching Civil War grew louder, Bigelow spent more time at the encampment of his battery, which he had helped to organize years before. He procured passes for Elizabeth, and she would occasionally invite friends like Dr. Hooper and Mrs. Shaw to go on a "pic-nic" near the campground. Once she accompanied him to a three-day encampment at Springfield.

As time went on, the city seemed more and more "Bostony." The Yankee character was a bit "shrewd" for Elizabeth's liking, and what would pass for "friendly interest" in other places was sheer "curiosity" in Massachusetts. "A bucket of cold water is nothing to it!" She was inclined to agree with a "Down Easterner" who had been heard to say that "every man seemed to think that the sun . . . riz & sot in his back-yard."

Whenever she felt a fit of depression or homesickness coming on, a short trip quickly dispelled it. One summer they journeyed to West Point, where one of Mama's relatives, Frank Shunk, taught mathematics. He took them to his quarters and treated them to sherry-cobblers and mint juleps. The view from the "back piazza" of their hotel was one of the finest she had ever seen, and the place was lively with "balls and hops all the time"; but the food was wretched. "Oh," she moaned, "that I this moment had a nice piece of shad & some Doylestown bread and butter."

En route, they had stopped over in New York where they had "breakfasted" at Delmonico's on "shad, spring chicken, green peas & omelet . . . very nice, I can assure you." They also stopped in at the studio of Frederic Church to see his huge picture *The Heart of the Andes*. There was an "Inca bird" in the studio (as well as in the picture) which Elizabeth greatly admired. On Christmas night her old friend Mr. Prescott presented her with one just like it, "the most gorgeous thing you ever beheld, with two long feathers hanging from its tail a yard & a half long, & of a brilliant green color," with breast feathers of crimson.

Mama quickly wrote back: "Is the bird alive?"

The reply: "No, stuffed. Mr. L. is in a state of enchantment over it."

When *The Heart of the Andes* was exhibited in Boston, she went again, sitting in front of it for three hours. It was "as good as a visit to South America," and she urged the family not to miss the famous painting when it came to Philadelphia.

* * *

Each August they spent a week or two at Newport, and in mid-winter they visited the Prescotts in Pepperell. The leisurely, amusing chats around the fire suddenly ended when the nearly blind historian died in 1859. Elizabeth was devastated, for he was one of her favorites. She promptly went into partial mourning.

In September there were weekends in the White Mountains, after which they usually followed the fall coloring south to the Adirondacks and Pennsylvania.

His first summer in office, President Buchanan had sent her an invitation, while she was staying in Doylestown, to visit him at his home, Wheatland, in Lancaster. Reluctantly she had had to regret "the delightful proposition":[8]

> . . . as I only see my family together once a year, & that but for a very few weeks, I feel as if I could not leave them for even so short a time . . .
>
> Otherwise, my dear Mr. Buchanan, nothing could give me more pleasure than to accept your most flattering invitation, & to renew that delightful intercourse which forms one of the most agreeable of my London reminiscences. I often think over our pleasant conversations in Harley St. & Brook St. & gloomy Hertford St., nor have I forgotten our Jacobite discussions.
>
> It was a very great relief to me to find by your letter to Mrs. Abbott Lawrence that you knew of my steadfast friendship during the last exciting campaign. I fought a great many battles for you, my dear Sir, & it was with no small triumph & gratification that I heard of your success.
>
> I was delighted to hear . . . that you are looking so remarkably well, & that the cares of your high office have left no impress on you. Mr. Lawrence is now in Boston; we often speak of your kindness to us in London which we never shall & never can forget. Pray present my best love to Miss Lane,—the echos *[sic]* of her popularity reach me from every quarter, & with my affectionate remembrances to you my dear Sir,
>
> I am
Your ever sincere friend,
Elizabeth Lawrence

* * *

In December 1858 Judge Chapman and his wife received an invitation to dine at the White House. Mama was thrown into a dither, and hastily wrote her knowledgeable daughter asking for advice on the subject of clothing, the proper form of replying to invitations, and visiting-card etiquette. Elizabeth was full of helpful hints:

> If you have your black brocade handsomely fixed, I should not get another dress, but put all my money on my cloak, bonnet & best dress. I was in New York for three weeks, & never wore anything but my black silk when I walked in the street, & my blue moiré when I paid visits in the carriage. My other dresses I never put on.
> You must be sure when you go out of an evening to get someone to dress your hair, & see that they dress it low down on the back of your head....
> You will find that if you put two pieces of elastic across the back of your hoop at some distance apart, it will improve the hang of it very much... preventing it from bulging out in front—in other words, it keeps it out below as the bustle does above.
> I should also, my dear Mama, put an extra width in two or three of the petticoats to wear when you are in full dress, & also when you are in full carriage dress, be sure to wear light gloves, & never wear any furs on such occasions, but only a handsome collar outside of my cloak, as the heat of the rooms is always very great, & besides it looks more dressy to be without them.

She then gave several examples of proper replies to invitations, for instance, to the White House:

> Willard's Hotel, Jan. 2nd.
>
> Judge and Mrs. Chapman will have the honor of dining with the President and Miss Lane on Thursday evening next.

If Mama received a card stating that "Mrs. Blank is at Home" on a certain evening, she should not answer it, but "either go, or leave your cards the next day." After every invitation, two of Papa's cards must be left—one for the gentleman of the house, one for the lady—plus one of Mama's for the lady. It went without saying that she would be expected to "call first at the White House."

Elizabeth's "point lace collar" would be loaned for the occasion. In return, would Mama please report what she thought of Miss Lane as a hostess? Reports of her "coldness" had been widely circulated.

* * *

The linkup of the trans-Atlantic cable in 1858 had enabled President Buchanan and Queen Victoria to enjoy the immediacy of telegraphic communication. Relations between the two were cordial, and when the President learned in the spring of 1860 that Albert Edward, the Prince of Wales, was being sent to Canada to lay the cornerstone of Ottawa's Parliament House, and to officiate at the opening of the railroad bridge across the St. Lawrence, he suggested to the Queen that the Prince's itinerary be extended to include the United States.

Victoria was enthusiastic about the idea, and in September the nineteen-year-old Prince arrived in the States—the first member of the royal family to set foot in the former colony since the Revolution. In a half-hearted attempt at anonymity he traveled *incognito* as Baron Renfrew, accompanied by a suite that included Lord Lyons (the British Minister in Washington), Lord Hinchinbrook (who came along for "buffalo hunting on the prairies of

Doylestown July 23d.

My dear Mr Buchanan

It is with sincere regret that I am obliged to forego the delightful proposition you a short time since made to my Father of paying you a visit this Summer, for beyond the small circle of my own family there is no one I so much desire to see as yourself.

I have however but just arrived on my annual visit home, & as I only see my family together once a year, & that but for a very few weeks, I feel as

The first and last pages (above and right) of EL's letter to President Buchanan, regretting an invitation to visit him. *Courtesy of the Historical Society of Pennsylvania.*

never can forget. Pray present my best love to Miss Lane,— the echos of her popularity reach me from every quarter, & with my affectionate remembrances to you my dear Sir,
I am
your ever sincere friend
Elizabeth Lawrence.

A painting of Harriet Lane (artist unknown), showing her serving as First Lady for her bachelor uncle, James Buchanan. *Library of Congress.*

the Far West"),[9] and an Oxford tutor. Arriving in Washington, the Prince and his entourage were escorted by the President and his First Lady, Harriet Lane, on a cruise down the Potomac to the grave of George Washington, where the great-grandson of George III planted a horse chestnut tree.[10]

Boarding a special train, the royal group worked its way north—whistle-stopping in small towns, alighting for *fêtes*, as Elizabeth called them, in larger cities. On arrival at the station in Boston, they were met by a phalanx of dignitaries, who escorted the visitors to their hotel, the Revere House. In the fifth carriage rode Bigelow, together with Lord Hinchinbrook and the Hon. Charles Eliot, son of Earl St. Germains, Lord Steward of the Queen's household.

For the military review on Boston Common next day, the newspapers reported with relish that the royal party, including the Governor and his suite, mounted "a beautiful stud of horses, the Prince riding the noble charger 'Black Prince,' the property of Col. T. Bigelow Lawrence." The horse's saddle was of "quilted buckskin, covered with blue silk velvet, bound with gold," and in each corner the royal crest gleamed. As Black Prince "pranced gracefully over the ground, he seemed to understand the precious load he was bearing." His proud owner also marched in the parade—on foot, as Adjutant of the 2nd battalion of infantry.

Visit of the Prince of Wales, President Buchanan and Dignitaries at Mount Vernon, October 1860, painted by Thomas P. Rossiter. In this portion of the painting the President is standing with the Prince to the right of the arch; Lord Lyons is to the left, next to Harriet Lane, who is under the parasol. Lord Hinchinbrook is the seventh man from the left. *National Museum of American Art, Smithsonian Institution.*

After a day that included an interview with a one-hundred-and-five-year-old veteran of the Revolution, and a "musical festival" presented by twelve hundred school children (who sang an ode by Oliver Wendell Holmes to the tune of *God Save the Queen*), the Prince was entertained at a ball at the Academy of Music. That the Lawrences are not mentioned in the accounts of the ball may be explained by the fact that Bigelow's mother had died two months before. They were both in mourning.

The Prince of Wales, traveling as "Baron Renfrew," photographed in Boston in 1860. This picture was found at Fonthill, in the Lawrences' album of *cartes de visite*.

Prominently displayed in Bigelow's photograph album is a picture of the Prince in the regulation uniform of an English Colonel: red frock coat and black *"chapeau"* with white plume. Since the press reported him dressed just so when he sat astride Bigelow's horse, this photograph may well have been sent as a royal thank-you.

* * *

Buchanan spent the first months of 1861—his last in office—hoping against hope that the first shot of the rebellion would not be fired. On March 4 he escorted President-elect Lincoln to the inauguration ceremonies with overwhelming relief.

One of the new President's first appointments was the Vice-Consul Generalship at Florence to T. Bigelow Lawrence. Elizabeth received the news with a mixture of delighted anticipation and consternation, for it entailed another long separation from her family and the agony of another ocean voyage, compounded by reluctance to leave the country on the brink of war.

Bigelow requested clarification of his duties, made affidavit as required by the State Department that he had never resided in Sardinia "or any of its dependencies," and secured a separate passport for his wife and "maid servant."[11] With the opening shot of the war, he also had misgivings about leaving for his new duties at such a time. The middle of June he wrote Secretary of State Seward asking for a leave of absence till November:

> Having been an officer in our State militia for many years, I have felt it my duty, since the commencement of the war, to devote my time and such military knowledge as I possess, to the public service. For several weeks, I have been Chief of Staff at Fort Warren in Boston Harbor, garrisoned by 2000 troops.
>
> Since being relieved from that duty, I have in connection with a brother officer, organized and commenced the drill of a Battery of Light Artillery, which is being equipped at great expense by the Government of this state. It requires a considerable length of time before a Corps of the Army can be brought into a complete state of efficiency, and having commenced the task, I am anxious not to give it up at present....
>
> It has been thought that ... I may be able to do more for the public service here than at my post abroad, during the next few months....[12]

In the meantime, anticipating the move to Florence sometime in the near future, they relinquished their Beacon Street house and took temporary quarters in the Parker House, one of Boston's best hotels.

When news of the Battle of Bull Run was received, Elizabeth termed it "most melancholy and unfortunate." She found it hard to believe that the last quadrille she ever danced was with Col. Magruder, who "has just been banging away into our flag & covering us with defeat & mortification."

After each battle communiqué she leafed through her album of *cartes de visite*, considering which photographs of military heroes to pull out. Anderson and Lee she kept in, at least for the time being, on the theory that there were some "splendid, honorable although misguided men in the Southern Army."

As for Bigelow, he was serving as Adjutant of Cobbs' Artillery, "the most splendid turn-out of military" Boston had ever seen:

> There are one hundred & fifty horses, & the train of guns & horses together is a quarter of a mile long. They turned out for the first time on Saturday, & everybody was perfectly amazed at the sight.
>
> They left Boston at half past eight in the morning.... They drilled all day in the broiling sun, never returning until ten at night, at which time Mr. L. staggered into my room so tired that he could scarcely either speak or stand, having been in the saddle all day.
>
> A body of Zouaves drill daily on the Common. Their commander dashes them through the Frog Pond up to their arm pits in water, & the other afternoon made them scale the peaked iron fence. Thirty members resigned the next day!
>
> Gen. Pierce, who seems to be blamed for it all, before he left Boston, offered Mr. Lawrence a position on his staff & begged him to go with him, if it was only for a month. Mr. L. was sorely tempted.... The aid who took [the position offered] was severely wounded....

She read all the newspapers—usually six a day—in order to keep herself "posted up." In addition, she sought out "private & reliable sources," for the newspapers only "increase instead of relieving one's ignorance." An aide to the Governor, for instance, had just given her an account of his inspection of the various encampments around Washington:

> He reached Fort Munroe the day after the battle of Great Bethel, & the accounts which he gave me of that affair were neither creditable to our forces or the rebels.
>
> Gen. Pierce stood behind a tree whittling a stick. One of the captains divided his company, ordering part of it to make a detour, & join him at a certain point,

This "daguerro" of EL, taken in Boston, is probably the one she sent her family before leaving for Florence. All her life she thought her "likenesses" turned out poorly.

These two daguerreotypes of Bigelow Lawrence were undoubtedly taken at the same time as his wife's, soon after his appointment as Consul-General to Italy.

but such was the confusion that in following out their instructions, the captain & his command mistook the advancing section for the enemy, & actually ran from his own men!

Two of Pierce's aids insisted upon being rowed across the river, one fainting on the other side. Soldiers fled like deer in squads & companies, & the story at Fort Munroe was that both sides ran at the same moment, & the rebels won the day by simply discovering first that the other side was running, when they turned & occupied the field. This latter I, however, believe to be a canard—the rest is all true.

.... There were strange rumors in Washington as to the habits of Mr. Seward, & it was said that one of the causes of the misunderstanding with Lord Lyons was that the latter had found the former in an unpresentable condition....

I feel very anxious to know which Penna. regiment contains the Bucks Co. troops.... I imagine [Mama] passing most of the summer baking sponge cakes & making jellies for the regiment.

In Boston the ladies were hard at work knitting stockings, finishing the tops with the national colors, while some knit in the words: "Guaranteed not to run!" Elizabeth's stocking, to her dismay, was "widening tremendously."

* * *

As the war escalated, Bigelow became increasingly "nervous and unhappy" at the prospect of not seeing active duty. Eager to take part in the forthcoming operations of the Army of the Potomac, he traveled to Washington, accompanied by his wife, to ask for another six-month's leave from his duties in Florence, then to join the staff of Gen. McDowell as "volunteer aide-de-camp." Anticipating the extended leave of absence, Bigelow dispatched to Florence, at his own expense, a clerk to assist the Vice-Consul General until his own arrival. If Bigelow took part in an advance across the Potomac, Elizabeth planned to stay with her family in Doylestown, concurring with the prevailing view that the war would soon be over.

While the Lawrences were in Washington they were invited to a ball at the White House. She thought President and Mrs. Lincoln "very gracious," little suspecting that before the war was over, her opinion would change. She was complimented that Mrs. Lincoln had sent her "extra cards," and was surprised to find the supper table so "elegantly arranged."

Shortly afterwards they went to the White House again for a distressingly different reason:

> On last Monday we went... to the funeral of the poor little Lincoln boy. It took place in the East Room, which a few nights before I had seen at the ball, so brilliantly lighted. Mrs. Lincoln was ill in her bed, & I really pitied poor honest old Abe, who at parts of the ceremony covered his face with his handkerchief & was dreadfully overcome!

* * *

In the meantime, they were putting their affairs in order, preparatory to sailing. Again they sat for their daguerreotypes. Elizabeth started taking French lessons, to become proficient in the language of diplomacy. Thirty years later she would still be at it, strong on determination, but weak in natural ability.

Bigelow wanted his own horses in Florence, so he shipped them ahead only to learn, to his dismay, that a fearsome storm wreaked havoc aboard ship, causing the death of big Black Prince. That was not all. The groom broke several ribs while exercising the terrified horses shortly after landing, but was reported to be recovering.

Since Willie and Mary had decided to move back to Grandpa's old farm in Doylestown, Elizabeth shipped them her best featherbed and mattress, along with a brand-new sewing machine, which she was sure Mary and Mama would enjoy mastering.

* * *

Meanwhile, Boston received a "dreadful shock": the horrible death of Mrs. Longfellow, the poet's beloved wife:

> She was amusing her little children last Wednesday afternoon by making seals for them, when the sleeve of her dress caught in the lighted wax taper, & she was almost immediately enveloped in flames.
> Her shrieks brought Mr. L[ongfellow], ... who was asleep in the library, but before he could extinguish the flames, she was so badly burned that she died the following morning. Mr. L's hands are dreadfully burned. He is still kept under the influence of chloroform, & whenever he arouses from it he exclaims: "That dreadful shriek!" & immediately his mind is gone....
> Mrs. Longfellow was the most elegant & at times the most beautiful woman in New England, & my perfect ideal of a poet's wife.

* * *

As the war showed no signs of ending, Elizabeth found herself less and less eager to embark for Florence, and there were times when she wished her husband would "throw it up altogether." In the spring of 1862 she wrote her family:

> Do you not feel terribly anxious about Richmond? The long lists of the dead & wounded with which the papers are filled make me perfectly sick & wretched, & although I read six papers daily, I have yet to find one giving me any hope that the rebels are any nearer to laying down their arms this year than they were last.
>
> The Abolitionists are doing all they can to make it a war of extermination. I fear we can no longer call this a rebellion, but a revolution.

* * *

Although Bigelow's dream of action at last materialized, it did not last very long. His deafness proved an insurmountable handicap—especially when the guns roared. Reluctantly he decided to take up his post in Florence. Staterooms were reserved on the *Asia*, and Elizabeth dispatched a final salvo on the war:

> Whatever you do, do not give up McClellan. I am getting very shaky about honest old Abe, & think he would have done much better to have turned out Stanton & put Banks in his place, than to have taken a star off of little Mars' shoulder strap by placing Halleck over him, & thereby in a covert manner laying the blame on military shoulders, instead of civilian ones, as ought to have been done.
>
> If victory is to place us still more tightly in the clutches of the black Republicans, I am ready for defeat.

* * *

She was disappointed that she could not see her family once more before sailing. It was especially trying because Mary had just had another son, named William Robert after his father, and like him, called Willie.

Her conviction that she would be seasick the entire trip proved only too true. Not exactly *"in extremis,"* nevertheless she lived through the most "stupid" ten days of her life, nearly "expiring from nausea & ennui." There was a "disgusting" set of passengers on board—"mostly Spaniards & dirty French," and the monotony was only relieved by a nice English Colonel.

The ship was late arriving because of a sad accident: A fireman fell into the machinery, stopping the engine. Everything came to a halt while they pried his body out. Afterwards, the passengers made up a purse of $250 to be presented to the poor fellow's widow. As they neared England, many ships looking like "great white tents" made a beautiful sight. But the finest sight of all was the first little bird with a bit of "greenery from land" in its beak.

11
FLORENCE (1862)
"Depravity worthy of Sodom itself."

The Adelphi Hotel at Liverpool had not changed "one jot" since she had lodged there with the Buchanan–Belmont party eight years before. Her breakfast of fried sole and muffins, though not so all-inclusive as the one she had devoured with Harriet Lane, compensated in part for the tea, toast, and porridge she had been endeavoring to swallow for ten days.

Arriving in London, the Lawrences put up at Claridge's, a new luxury hotel that had grown out of a small hostelry run by a French chef named Mivart, close by their Upper Brook Street house. Among their first callers was the Duc de Chartres, a grandson of the deposed French King, Louis Philippe. M. le Duc had recently returned from America, where he had gone the previous summer with his older brother, the Comte de Paris, to observe the modern weaponry and military tactics employed in the Civil War. The two young princes had donned the Northern uniform and joined Gen. McClellan's staff as volunteer aides, in which capacity they had undoubtedly met Bigelow during his brief stint.

M. le Duc had returned to England (his family's home in exile) in time to attend several balls at the end of "the season," at which he had ruffled English feathers by expounding on the overwhelming charms of the ladies of Boston and New York. As "revenge," he gleefully told the Lawrences, he had been accused of "talking Yankee!" An "amusing" and "animated" conversationalist, he told of visiting the America Exhibition, where he spotted a large sign advertising "American Drinks." Eagerly he had rushed in—and had ordered a "gin cocktail." Unfortunately we are left to wonder at the Frenchman's reaction.

He warned them about the strong feeling then prevailing in England against the North. When Elizabeth later drove around to all her favorite London haunts, everyone she met confessed to siding with the North at first, but had now changed, and thought "we ought to let the South go."

* * *

The first weekend was spent at Althorp, the country seat of Earl Spencer—the most interesting "stately home" Elizabeth had yet visited. Ben Jonson had written a masque for Althorp during one of the royal visits, and Charles I was playing quoits there when he heard "the Roundheads were pursuing him."

Its five-hundred-acre park was dotted with deer, sheep, and cattle. But even more impressive were the "numberless avenues" of enormous trees, some dating back to the time of Henry VII. More astonishing still was the library, reputed to be the finest private library in the world. The Earl showed her an edition of Boccaccio that had sold at auction for $2200!

The walls of the grand staircase were lined with portraits of the Spencer ancestors by "Sir Joshua, Kneller, Copley, & Lawrence." Among them were some famous beauties, such as Sarah, Duchess of Marlborough, who was painted after she had cut off "her beautiful hair, which she flung in a rage into the face of her husband the Duke."

The present Lady Spencer was a little younger than Elizabeth, and "one of the prettiest & most charming women in England." She informed her houseguest that the "tapestried

Althorp, seat of the Spencers. Here EL and Lady Spencer discussed the marriage of the Prince of Wales, and attended services in the church where the last English Washington—"the ancestor of our own"—was buried. Neale, *Views of the Seats*....

hangings" on the "old oaken bedstead" in which she and Bigelow were sleeping had been worked by "the fair fingers of the beautiful Mistress of the Poet," the distant kinsman who wrote *The Faerie Queene*.

On Sunday they all went to the little church in the chancel of which was buried the last English Washington, "the ancestor of our own." A kind of trapdoor covered the stone under which, when raised, one could read the name and dates of Lawrence Washington.

Lady Spencer also passed on a "little piece of gossip" about the Prince of Wales, who was soon to marry the Danish Princess Alexandra. When he met her the previous summer in Germany, he was asked what he thought of her. "Very pretty—for a Princess," was his reply.

The announcement of their engagement "crept out" prematurely, making the Queen, as well as the Prince of Wales, "very indignant." The young suitor was quoted as saying: "To think of such an announcement—& before I have even proposed to her!" According to Lady Spencer, it was all the more awkward in that the Crown Prince of Russia also "had his eye on Denmark," and the little Princess "had declared she would marry whichever of the two she liked the best." The Prince of Wales was "extremely fidgety & anxious" the week before he sailed for Germany, "where his proposals were to be made."

How startled the two ladies would have been, that day at Althorp, could they have known that, more than a century later, a pretty young descendant of the house—Lady Diana Spencer—would wed another Prince of Wales, the great-great grandson of the man they had been chatting about!

* * *

In mid-September the Lawrences journeyed on to Paris. The Americans in residence there were full of forebodings about the war and anxiously awaited the most recent "telegraphic dispatches."

Elizabeth was convinced that McClellan, "for the first & only time his own master," had won a decisive victory. If not, the sooner the North let the South go, the better. "Stonewall Jackson in Pennsylvania! Even now I scarcely believe it, & all the result of blundering incompetency!" In the face of the constant anxiety, even the theaters and art galleries of Paris suddenly lost their charm. The only festive undertaking the Consul-General's wife indulged in was to assemble her wardrobe for Florence, buying six gowns that had her in ecstasies.

Her old enemy, the "face ache," returned, and feeling so "blue" about the war that she was "ready for anything," she betook herself to Thomas Evans, the famous expatriate American dentist, the friend and confidant of Napoleon III. With "A sort of chisel, or elevator, I believe they call it," he literally "gouged out the roots" of a wisdom tooth that had been broken off in an attempted extraction a year before. The operation took five minutes, and she nearly fainted from pain, but she was sure it marked the end of her dental problems.

Always "on the *qui vive*" for anything relating to Napoleon Bonaparte, she urged her family to buy an English translation of Victor Hugo's new novel, *Les Misérables*, for it was considered to have "the finest account of the battle of Waterloo ever written." The battlefield as Hugo described it was just as she and her father had seen it nine years before.

As for the present war:

> I cannot tell you what an inexpressible relief it has been to me to hear of the battles of the 14th to the 18th, & that the rebels are out of Maryland, & no longer menace Pennsylvania.... I was perfectly convinced that if Lee reached Phila. his foraging parties would find their way into Bucks Co.
>
> The telegram reports a list of wounded generals on our side that is positively incredible. It is perfectly distracting waiting on this side for news. First we get a meagre telegram... & then are obliged to wait... days for the papers from home. Then I see friends of mine mentioned as killed; then it's contradicted, & then a doubt thrown over both statements. I wish I was at home again....
>
> I heard yesterday from the very best authority that the southerners in Paris say they cannot hold out much longer. Even after their victories, the Rebels here were in the greatest possible state of anxiety, & the day the news by the next steamer was expected, T—— [illegible] from Virginia was made sick, & went to his bed from pure excitement. I should think that when the news really did come, he probably stayed there.
>
> They have made every arrangement to give a great supper at the Grand Hotel on the retaking of New Orleans!
>
> The other day I bought the most beautiful spray of rose buds with one large damask rose, which is covered with dew drops, & a large "devil's darning needle" with bright blue wings—a real one—fastened on a concealed wire, seems to hover over it. The buds & leaves have three or four tiny green & gold colored bugs crawling over them. Butterflies used in this way are all the rage & extremely expensive—particularly bright blue ones, which come from S. America. The Empress has a great fancy for them.

* * *

Before they left Paris, Bigelow—increasingly worried about the war-torn economy at home—decided to make an investment abroad for his wife. Accordingly he ordered a jeweler in Paris to design a bracelet of black onyx set with three large diamond stars which could be detached and worn as hairpins, brooches, or set into a tiara. When the stars were removed, a narrow diamond band could be substituted on the bracelet. The center diamond of the biggest star cost $700; the whole bracelet would come to $5,000, an unbelievably generous gift. "Will it not be superb?"

EL's sketch of her tiara with the three diamond stars.

* * *

The beginning of October they set off by train for Florence, accompanied by a curious entourage: Ellen, her American maid, and Sarah, a Londoner, both of whom spoke nothing but English; Giuseppe, who spoke nothing but Italian; and Grouse, the Lawrences' dog, who gave vent to his feelings in this strange foreign land by a series of "despairing howls." To Elizabeth's amusement, as they passed mile after mile of vineyards in Burgundy, Sarah, a "true Britisher," thought for an entire day that they were passing through fields of beans! Her mistress, on the other hand, thought the grapes—pruned low, rather than climbing on arbors as they did at home—resembled nothing so much as raspberry bushes!

The journey through southern France was not without difficulties. They boarded the train at six in the morning, only to wait for hours while the engine was repaired. Each time their luggage was offloaded at a station to await loading on the next train, it "assumed the stately proportions of a pyramid of leather, covered with the oft-repeated inscription 'T. B. L.'" At the base of the pyramid huddled the three servants, "hapless mutes, helpless as mummies," while Grouse looked heavenward and howled.

Crossing the border, they stopped in Turin to visit the armory where Bigelow "nearly lost his mind" over a suit of inlaid armor. On they traveled to Genoa, where in the gardens of the Doria Palace Elizabeth was introduced for the first time to the vegetation of Italy—the "jessamine," roses, heliotrope, orange trees, and oleanders. From Genoa they took the boat to Leghorn (Livorno), a rough trip that produced the usual result. Leghorn proved to be a "vile" place with a "disgusting" hotel, where several of the dishes she attempted to eat "had evidently been to the barber's shop." There they were met by Bigelow's new secretary, who helped arrange transportation of the pyramid of luggage to Florence. After a quick side trip to Pisa, they reached their destination on 21 October 1862, staying temporarily at the Hotel Grande Bretagne.

The day after their arrival they drove out to see the Villa Torrigiani on the Via de' Serragli, which Bigelow had rented, furnished, from the Marchese for 8400 lire a year (roughly sixteen hundred dollars, then a tremendous sum). Elizabeth had been shown several photographs of the "villino," as she always referred to it, and had learned that the garden was a third the size of Boston Common. But nothing prepared her for the enchantment she found.

The house, though only two stories high, contained forty or so rooms, with a suite of "state apartments" that included a splendid ballroom, and another suite of rooms with two parlors, a dining room, four bedrooms, two dressing rooms, and a boudoir. All the rooms were bright and comfortable, but not ornate, "the carpets being all of ingrain." The only drawback was the lack of gas lighting—a subject on which Bigelow waxed eloquent after "clashing up" against an open door in the dark and splintering his nose.

"But now for the charm!"

The Villa Torrigiani as it looks today.

The "reading candlestick" used by EL, since the villa lacked "modern" gas lights. Identified in Henry Mercer's inventory of Fonthill, its shade is typically inscribed with a bold catalogue number.

The garden brought tears to her eyes whenever she thought about it. She could not imagine how glorious it would be come spring when the magnolias and the orange trees would be in full bloom, the lawns purple with violets, and the thickets filled with nightingales! In one portion of the grounds she discovered a part of the old wall of the city, covered with ivy, and bearing on a marble slab the name and date of Cosimo de Medici. The garden itself was laid out in "stately avenues," the entranceway lined with sycamores. It was embellished with exotic, ornamental trees, hedges of roses, and countless flower beds interspersed with marble statues. Through long green vistas one caught breathtaking glimpses of the domes of Florence.

This photograph of Florence, sent by EL to Doylestown, was inserted in a scrapbook begun by the family in 1863 to illustrate her travels. Excerpts from her letters were sometimes copied to help identify the pictures.

From the terrace, where she pictured herself taking tea and breakfast in the warm weather, there was a lovely view of the distant mountains. All the balustrades were a mass of roses and "jessamine." There was a "ruin" and a grotto and a tower, from the top of which one could see for miles over the Tuscan hills. Opposite the front door, running parallel to the house, was a vast conservatory, in which all the plants were arranged on white marble tables that stretched the entire length. When she stepped inside she was greeted by a blaze of blooming cacti. There was also an orangery, which formed a wing of the villino on a line with the entrance. Whenever you entered or left the house, you were greeted by the "delicious perfume" of the orange trees.

In her wanderings that first day she discovered a camellia tree covered with pink buds, its trunk thicker than her wrist. She assured Mama that "the delight of the Berber in the Arabian Nights on his enchanted carpet" could not equal what she felt!

* * *

On November 3 they moved in. All things considered, the domestic arrangements worked reasonably smoothly—no worse, certainly, than in Boston. There was a cook ("I wish you could taste his delicious devices—like cockscomb & truffle pie"), an indoor man, a footman, two coachmen—plus Sarah and Ellen, in addition to an unspecified number of gardeners, porters, and gatekeepers.

Delicious butter and cream were produced nearby at the Royal dairy. Every morning Elizabeth "had the honour of cutting the Royal arms" with which her butter pat was stamped.

The horses that had been shipped from Boston were finally moved into the stables. (The hoof of poor Black Prince, who had died on shipboard, was encased in a steel horsehoe and placed in a conspicuous spot on one of the drawing room tables—a fitting tribute to a steed that had borne the future King of England on his broad back.) When Elizabeth and Bigelow ventured out with the horses for the first time, the coachman headed for the Cascine, the beautiful drive that wound along the Arno, to a public square where the carriages often stopped so their occupants could listen to the music:

> We found it crowded with handsome equipages filled with gaily dressed ladies and surrounded by officers in the beautiful blue and white uniform of Sardinia. Our own carriage... was beset by flower women in straw hats about the size of doormats, who insisted on presenting Mr. L. with roses & carnations & me with large bouquets of orange flowers and tuberoses, until to save ourselves from having the air of an engine in a firemen's procession, we ordered the coachman to drive on.

* * *

They continued to devour the war news. The only bright spots appeared in the *London American*, an "otherwise trashy paper" that printed some amusing "travesties" of the dispatches:

> "A British steamer laden with iron-plated medicinal drugs was captured off Wilmington [South Carolina] by the Federal gun-boat *Seminola* on the 12th. The Captain declares that he was on his way to Greenland for whales, and that he simply looked in at Wilmington to see his wife's uncle."
> "The military hospitals continue to be deplorably neglected; eye witnesses say that the patients gnaw their own bedposts for food. The dust on the floors is so thick that the convalescents amuse themselves by planting mustard and cress in it!"
> "The expected engagement at Bagdad did not transpire; without being aware of it the rival armies passed each other at doublequick during an intensely dark night, and when last heard from, were still in hot pursuit of each other six hundred miles apart."
> "The President still continues in a most melancholy condition. He eats nothing but black walnuts which he picks with a large black pin."

When the dispatch bag brought a letter and "splendid sketches of the war" done by Mary's oldest, seven-year-old Harry, Elizabeth was overcome with pride and homesickness.

* * *

Among their first visitors was Hiram Powers, the American sculptor who had been living in Florence for years. Elizabeth could see that he had been handsome when younger, "with an eye like an eagle." She found him to be "a tremendous American, & endorses the Emancipation Proclamation up to the handle." She begged leave to differ with him—but "very good-naturedly."

When she returned his visit, the sculptor entered the room in his "white working apron and paper cap, looking for all the world like a stone mason." In his hand was nestled a tame caramel-colored dove, which he held out for her to admire.

Powers lived not far from the villino, and the Lawrences found themselves seeing him frequently. Elizabeth thought him "perfectly charming" and decided she liked him "far better than anyone" she had met so far in Florence. He had done a bust of Abbott Lawrence years before in Boston, which Elizabeth vividly remembered in the Park Street house. One evening when Powers was visiting at the villino, he told an amusing story about the Bostonian's first sitting:

> In modeling the face, upon reaching the mouth Powers discovered a peculiar lump on the left side of the lip, a little below the nose. At once he copied it in the clay.
> The next day there was another sitting, & on reaching the mouth, what was Powers' disgust to find that the lump, in place of being on the left, was on the *right* side of the nose. Amazed at his mistake, he at once corrected the model, but when at the next sitting the lump was *again* on the left side, Powers threw down his chisel in despair & informed Mr. L. at once of his difficulty, & lo & behold, the mysterious lump was a bit of cigar, & a hearty laugh they both had over it.

While Mrs. Lawrence organized the Villa Torrigiani, Mr. Lawrence organized the office of the first Consul-General in a coalescing Italy. An inventory of the "effects" was dispatched to the State Department:[1]

1 flag staff, 2 flags, large & small
1 coat of arms of U.S. on wood for within doors
1 old fashioned screw press & seal
1 modern ditto
1 desk seal
1 office stamp
1 writing board
& pamphlets, forms, books, etc.

He was delighted with his clerk, Mr. Joseph Matteini, who had lived four years in Vermont, married an American lady, and spoke English flawlessly. Furthermore, his handwriting was exemplary (as the correspondence in the National Archives proves). It was quickly apparent to Bigelow that the job was no "sinecure," as some Congressmen had been complaining, because the "labours"[2] of his post most certainly could not be accomplished in the four hours daily expected of him. However, he was quick to point out to Secretary of State Seward that for the moment he had no intention of applying for a salary.

He expressed annoyance that all private letters transmitted by the dispatch bags were ordered to be sent unsealed. And why were no Washington newspapers forthcoming? After Paris and London, Florence had the largest American population in Europe, but only New York and Boston newspapers were available in the reading rooms and clubs.

Exports had been cut in half because of the war between the States, he reported, so that the fees collected by the consulates—one of their chief sources of revenue—were correspondingly lower. Straw continued to be the chief export—usually in "braids," though sometimes made up into baskets, hats, or bonnets. The shipping of marble, statuary, paintings, frames, and mosaics had almost ceased since "the commencement of our present troubles."[3]

Passports and visas consumed a large portion of time, as did the closing of unneeded consulates, and the opening of new ones throughout the country. He thought it a waste of time, for instance, to maintain a consulate in Carrara, as the only export was marble, a commodity with little demand during a war; so he decided to close the office. It was not long, however, before irate complaints were received from the few exporters remaining,

Hiram Powers, the "perfectly charming" sculptor, looked "for all the world like a stone mason in his white working apron and paper cap." *Dictionary of American Portraits.*

fussing about the long trip to Leghorn "to obtain verifications and triplicate invoices."[4] The Carrara consulate was soon reopened.

Occasionally the daily routine was broken up by weightier issues more to the liking of a man long interested in *les affaires militaires*. At one juncture rebel privateers were believed to have been sighted in the Mediterranean. With a certain gusto Col. Lawrence informed the State Department: "The spectacle of a privateer seizing and destroying an American merchantman with impunity could not fail materially to lessen the good will which exists [towards the North]."[5] To add to his consternation, the *Constellation* was the only federal cruiser sighted in the Mediterranean, and as it was "an old-fashioned sailing sloop of war, entirely unfit to cope with modern steam vessels,"[6] he urged that steam-powered reinforcement be dispatched immediately to strengthen the Mediterranean squadron.

Such communiqués made him feel closer to the war effort and added zest to the drudgery of passports, visas, and export fees.

* * *

In spite of Elizabeth's experience at the Court in London, she had heard enough about Florentine society to be wary about the difficult path she would have to follow in this "dissipated capital." She had little doubt she would "get on," and plunged once again into French lessons, while picking up some Italian from her servants.

Every day she walked in the garden for an hour, marveling at the *allées* of cypress and the ilex and olive trees. Though it was November, the roses and camellias were still in full bloom. She had not yet set foot in the Uffizi, or any other gallery for that matter, which astonished her as much as it did her family. But she was so enraptured by the Italian landscape that she could not bring herself to go inside. And the Boboli gardens were practically next door!

Towards the end of the month the weather turned, and the chill, to her surprise, was worse than any she had ever experienced, even in the draughty English country houses. All the floors and walls of the villino were of stone, and though there were three carpets piled on top of each other in her little writing room, she still kept her feet up on a footstool whenever she sat down. Ellen and Sarah were miserable with chilblains. Fortunately, she was told, winter would be over by the middle of February.

The talk of Florence that fall was the disappearance of the three sons of a Russian Princess. When Elizabeth first arrived, the boys—aged thirteen, eleven, and eight—could be seen walking along the Arno, dressed in beautiful Russian outfits of velvet. It was thought the boys had been murdered or kidnapped, and jewels and laces were supposed to have disappeared with them.

The story had a comic dénouement. The lads, "disgusted with their tutor, and enamoured of Freedom," had run off to consult with Garibaldi at Pisa on the "propriety" of their joining his forces. "Let not the U.S. complain of Russia," wrote Elizabeth, "when even her babes are rushing to defend her."

* * *

On Christmas eve the Lawrences accompanied an American neighbor to a midnight service at the cathedral. Though she found much of the "mummery" ridiculous, the organ music was awe-inspiring.

She must have recalled Christmas at Lady Ashburton's eight years before. In Florence there were no boughs of mistletoe, no charades, no gifts for the poor villagers. But at least there was a turkey. A friend sent her one which had been fattening for the past three months at the Baths of Lucca on chestnuts—"those immense ones they use in sugar plums!"

* * *

The last week in December a fellow American secured admittance to San Donato, the legendary residence of the Russian millionaire, Prince Demidoff, and invited Elizabeth and several friends to accompany her. The palace was overwhelming. Even the conservatories were so splendid, they made those at Chatsworth look like "an ordinary greenhouse."

After clumping for hours in her heavy boots over the marquetry floors, she had to laugh when she thought of her one little table of the same fine work, on which she never permitted even a book to lie without a mat to protect it. Never again would she be able to admire a brooch of malachite, after seeing whole mantelpieces of the precious stone! And as for Venetian lace, chairs and sofas were covered with it—and her one little collar cost twenty dollars!

Although Elizabeth's group had visited most of the fine palaces of Europe, they wandered about this "*coup d'oeuil* of magnificence" with mouths and eyes open like so many "country bumpkins," exclaiming over the quantities of silver and gold, of Greuzes and Bouchers, of tapestries and velvets, of enamels and gems. It was sad to have to report that Prince Demidoff had had a severe attack of apoplexy about three years before and was now living, a lonely old man, in an apartment in Paris, his fortune having "dwindled" to a mere $100,000 a year. Only servants now lived in his extraordinary palace, and it was opened only occasionally for special visitors.

* * *

News from home cast a pall over that winter. Her brother Tom died, which gave her an excuse to steer clear of the "international set" of Florence, whose "depravity" was "worthy of Sodom itself." Although other European cities might be as "wicked," she was sure none was quite so "brazen" in its "vice."

Even their physical appearance repelled her. The men were small, thin, "leaden-eyed," and far from clean. One of the most famous "beaux" was noted for his dirty face! Bigelow attended the Prefect's annual ball at the Palazzo Vecchio and returned disgusted with the "sallow skins" and "retreating foreheads" of the various Princesses, who, in their badly fitting "modern" dresses, seemed to have "degenerated" from the "stately dames" who looked down from the canvasses of Titian and Raphael. An American girl was there, whom Bigelow pronounced "tolerably good looking," but compared to the other ladies, she stood out like a raving beauty.

The only occupation of this set was conducting "heartless intrigues." After breakfast at two in the afternoon, they "crept out" to the Cascine on horses that could do little more than creep, being allowed only three quarts of oats a day. There they remained till dusk, when they dragged themselves to dinner and a "wretched" opera, then to some "stupid" reception where they drank tea and smoked until seven in the morning.

One of the most prominent groups of this international society was the Russian one, and smoking played a featured role in any of their entertainments. The ladies all showed up with cigar cases in their pockets, and often the "additional charm" of an amber mouthpiece. When they "lit up," a volume of smoke could be seen to issue from "the lips of a fair Russian Countess that would do honour to the funnel of the Great Eastern itself."

* * *

Another piece of bad news was the defeat at Fredericksburg. Elizabeth expected "nothing better," and felt the government did not deserve a victory, after its "black ingratitude" to Gen. McClellan in dismissing him from his post! At such a moment, to think that "our only great man" should be without a command was incredible! She intended writing her friend Mrs. McClellan and "expressing her mind—or rather, relieving it."

The Rev. Hall, a New England clergyman, planned to open a church in the basement of Wilson Eyre's house. (The latter, a Philadelphian and father of the architect, was also in the diplomatic service.) The clergyman was "a good man," but Elizabeth would have liked him better if he were not quite so "radical" in his "sentiments about the War, & the President's vile policy of Emancipation."

How she detested the present government! How she longed to have a talk with Papa! To think they would "disgrace us" by turning to "the black men of the North to do what the white men have failed to accomplish!" The American colony in Florence was heartily sick of the war and furious because all the issues had become "nothing more than an instrument in the hands of the rank Abolitionists." "To think that it should come to Horace Greeley's dictating our National Policy is," she fumed, "a little too bad!"

As Lent approached, the carnival season grew more "fast and furious." She relayed the story making the rounds of the former Grand Duke, who was a noted bigot:

> On a certain day of Lent, it was always the custom [for the Duke] and his Duchess to wash the feet of twelve old men & women in one of the great salons of the Pitti [Palace]. Each old man & woman had to number over eighty years before they could enjoy this royal favour.
> Two or three days before the great ceremony a chiropodist was sent to each of them, who got their feet into the most faultless condition, & on the day itself one of the royal carriages carried them to the Pitti, & as they were always chosen from

the very poorest of the lower classes, their royal transit from a hovel to a palace was probably their first and last drive.

The washing of the feet was a very nominal performance, the Grand Duchess, followed by her lady-in-waiting, merely trailing a napkin over the feet on which the latter had already poured the water.

* * *

The other story that Florentine society was chuckling over concerned the shooting excursion the French Emperor made to the Rothschild estate near Paris, where he spent the day and was entertained with "great magnificence":

> It is said that the Emperor, being very short-sighted, at the first shot brought down Rothschild's favorite parrot. On discovering his mistake His Majesty rushed up to the wounded bird, who pluckily exclaimed: *"Vive l'Empéreur!"*—& expired.
>
> Rothschild's French is very bad; to understand the following you must remember that *le mémoire* means "the bill," and *la mémoire*, "the memory." Upon the Emperor's departure Rothschild exclaimed with much feeling: *"Je garderai toujours le mémoire de cette visite!"*

* * *

For several days at the end of the carnival, just before Lent, came the Corso, an ancient custom that involved a parade of carriages passing along a designated route—the carriages, the riders, and the horses in "gala attire." As one line of equipages descending the hill passed the other line coming up—many drawn by four horses, with postilions in powdered wigs—bouquets of flowers were tossed from one to the other. With the sun turning the Arno to a sheet of gold, and the distant Apennines to white-capped purple, Elizabeth thought it one of the loveliest sights she had ever seen.

All the festivities were climaxed by a "grand masked ball" at the Pergola. Sarah, Ellen, and all the other servants were given permission by their mistress to attend, for it was the "great holiday night for all classes."

Whenever she drove out with Mr. L.'s horses, they produced a "sensation." One day when Bigelow was trotting his white horse in a secluded area of the Cascine, he was suddenly surrounded by "all the first people" of Florence, who had deserted their "usual rendezvous" on the piazza to watch the "wonderful American horse" perform. No one had ever seen anything like it, and one enthusiast offered Bigelow $2,000 for his mount!

* * *

In March Elizabeth undertook a series of weekly receptions for the Americans in Florence. According to an unidentified American gentleman "taking the year" in Italy, her "reunions" were "particularly pleasant for our artists," who found many new friends who were valuable "not for their social qualities, but for the interests of art."[7]

The author of this account was also impressed with Col. Lawrence's "refinement" and "culture," which belied the customary impression of the raw, "uncouth" American. It had been a frequent complaint that the new nation had been poorly represented abroad. But with Charles Francis Adams in London and Col. Lawrence in Florence—two Bostonians whose "dignified politeness bore ample testimony to the accomplishments of the American gentleman"—the country could rest assured that it was indeed "worthily represented."

By the end of her second reception, Mrs. L. realized that many of the Americans, too, could be added to her tales of "amusing Florentine experiences." She had quickly discovered that one set of her countrymen and women "turned up its nose" at the other set, so that when they happened to be together in one drawing room, there was little "amalgamation."

At one of these early receptions she "had the honour of receiving" a dentist from one of the western states, along with his wife and son, a youth of twenty clad in "a frock coat & light brown trousers," and hair like a "hay mow." As she was leaving, the wife was effusive in her thanks and pressed her hostess to "be sociable & drop in" whenever she had a hankering.

A few mornings later the western trio showed up at the villino again. Elizabeth's only other visitor happened to be Lord Hinchinbrook, who had ridden with Bigelow during the Prince of Wales's visit to Boston, and who was now en route back to England for the Prince's wedding. Poor Lord Hinchinbrook—who was inclined to stammer a bit anyway—could not get a word in edgewise. Elizabeth did her best to talk her other visitors down, but her efforts were unavailing. The West won the day.

That same evening another countryman called, this one from Kentucky. Towards the end of his visit she had difficulty extinguishing the fire under the teakettle.

"Let me assist you, Madam," said her Kentucky friend. "Allow me to prevent the egress of any oxygen."

Before she could say a word, he took out an enormous "old red silk pocket handkerchief, and entirely enveloped the silver tea-kettle with it!"

Her next reception was a notable success. Not only was there "dancing to the piano," but several "dreary old women in highneck dark silks" stayed away, so that the general appearance of the party was much improved.

* * *

With spring came a profusion of wild crocuses and anemones covering the hillsides. Elizabeth gathered quantities, pressed them, and then sent them on to Doylestown. Even some of the more interesting weeds were carefully placed between the pages of the heaviest tomes, for she was determined to collect all the specimens in Tuscany for Mama and Mary, both flower enthusiasts.

The Boboli gardens never ceased to enthrall her, and often during her rambles she would sit for a while on one of the stone benches and look up at "the ilex trees cut over my head in shapes that reminded me of the jutting eaves over the old stoops in Germantown." An ilex leaf crossed the Atlantic to join the other specimens which the family pasted into a scrapbook devoted to Elizabeth's travels.

With spring also came a steady stream of old friends, for whom she gave dinner parties. The Comte de Paris and the Duc de Chartres, the exiled French princes who had been on McClellan's staff, were entertained one evening. The latter reported that the Prince of Wales was "tremendously" in love with his fiancée, the lovely Alexandra, who was due to arrive in England the following Saturday for her wedding.

Elizabeth accompanied the Comte de Paris to San Donato, feasting her eyes for the second time on Prince Demidoff's sumptuous villa. The poor Comte came to a sudden stop before one of the paintings, and after staring at it for a long time, turned to Elizabeth and said with an expression she would never forget: "That picture [once] belonged to me."

* * *

Her Victorian sensibilities were frequently outraged. She had always understood Florentine society was "corrupt and depraved," but she had expected that at least there would be the fascinations of "wit & grace & agreeability" to throw a veil over the flagrant debauchery. On the contrary, instead of enlivening wit and laughter, no Boston tea party she had ever attended produced a duller time for the participants, who looked bored to death as they rode the treadmill from villa to villa.

One day at the Cascine one of the "beaux" of society walked around her carriage five times, impudently peering in the window. The sixth time he circled, she favored him with a glare which she was sure had been inherited from Papa—and off he scampered. She had been told she was the only woman they ever saw who looked "too proud to flirt." She was immensely relieved that they thought so, but it didn't seem to stop some from trying anyway.

Portion of a page in the family scrapbook, showing two pressed flowers—a purple anemone and a buttercup—picked by EL in Florence in the spring of 1863 and enclosed in a letter to Mama. They are pasted above a view of the Boboli Gardens.

12

EXCURSIONS AND ALARMS (1863–1865)

"Singing mice" and "frantic Abolitionists."

The Lawrences traveled to Rome for Holy Week. To Elizabeth's delight, they stayed with an American banker who occupied a floor of the Palazzo Buonaparte, where "Madame Mère," Napoleon's mother, had died.

As soon as dinner was over the first night, she donned her bonnet and set off with Bigelow to view the Coliseum by moonlight. They circled the walls, then went inside the arena, where they perched on a broken column for an hour, imagining all that had transpired in that historic setting over the centuries. The sounds that permeated the darkness heightened the sense of romance. A party of young Frenchmen were "making merry in the sacred gallery of the Vestal Virgins," owls hooted in the palace of the Caesars, and dogs barked across the Tiber.

The following day she immersed herself in sightseeing. Nothing gave her a better idea of the antiquity of Rome than the way "the dust and débris of modern centuries" had "choked up & buried" most of the monuments. Driving past the ancient temples, she often found herself on a level with the acanthus leaves at the top of the Corinthian columns! On the other hand, the excavations around the Forum resembled nothing so much as "the foundations of a house." Modern Rome had "literally grown out of the ancient one, but what a feeble offspring of that mighty root!"

The art galleries enthralled her as much as the ancient monuments. Guidebooks and art history books in hand, she spent hours devouring the old masters and the statuary. Whenever possible she bought photographs and sent them to Doylestown, complete with captions. Of da Vinci's *Last Supper* she wrote that the fresco in Milan was reported to be "almost entirely faded.... This is the last generation that will see even the lingering traces of this once marvelous picture."

As for the statuary, she was spellbound by "those pale Greek dreamy faces!" There was no need to be told they were antique, one knew it at once by "their happy, lost look of Arcady" that had "left this earth with the Fauns & Dryads!"

She went to hear the Holy Week music, sung in the Sistine Chapel at twilight, with the Pope and his Court kneeling beneath the Michelangelo frescoes. She had wanted to hear it ever since she was a little girl and had read of it in a biography of Mozart. As she listened to the wailing music, sometimes scarcely louder "than the note of a mourning dove," she thought of her "dear far-off country with its bloody battlefields & desolate hearthstones." Suddenly she buried her face in her hands and "sobbed like a child."

* * *

After Easter she and Bigelow were invited to several splendid parties. The Portuguese Ambassador gave a ball in honor of the Infanta. At midnight Elizabeth happened to walk past an open doorway, and peeping in, saw the Infanta sitting at supper, surrounded by a dozen cardinals in their scarlet caps and gowns. The Ambassador himself, moving slowly around the table, poured the wine for each guest, followed by a liveried servant bearing decanter and glasses.

At the ball she also saw Liszt, the great composer and pianist, by far "the most striking looking person" present. She had wondered who he was, this man with the "classic face"

Two photographs sent to Doylestown by EL from Italy. (Above) The Coliseum in Rome, in the center of which "a simple cross of stone rose on the spot where a thousand martyrs had been butchered." (Below) A ruined temple in the vale of Tivoli. "Beneath its marble Corinthian columns we dined on the fairest April day, . . . quaffing our champagne."

147

framed with iron-grey hair parted in the middle and hanging down over his shoulders. She was told that in his "grand days," the ladies of the Court of Berlin went "so mad" over him that they would "eat the grounds out of his coffee cup!"

One night they dined at the home of the poet–sculptor William Wetmore Story (son of the renowned Supreme Court Justice), who had left Massachusetts to live permanently in Italy. At the dinner they were introduced to Mrs. Elizabeth Gaskell, who had published *The Life of Charlotte Brontë.* The authoress proved to be a "very ladylike" person, with a soft voice and a gentle manner, which did not inhibit her from being a "capital" storyteller. For example:

> Sometime in the last century there lived in England a gentleman by the name of Harry Vernon, who acquired for himself the flattering distinction of being the greatest liar of his day, & although no one in London believed a word that he said, he told his lies so well, they were so startling & original, & he had apparently such a faith in them himself, that he was asked everywhere, both in town & country, & the wonderful lies of Harry Vernon afforded amusement to everybody.
>
> One of his favorite adventures was a day's shooting in South Africa, where in the midst of great success with his rifle he brought down something which, on examination, proved to be a Cherubim, & unique as this style of game might appear to his hearers, he had others to match it equally remarkable.
>
> But the greatest lion will grow old, & even Harry Vernon had his day, & repeated himself, & went out of fashion, & a more youthful aspirant usurped his métier & filled his place at country house & dinner table.
>
> They came, & Harry Vernon sat quiet & attentive while his rival, with thrilling effect, gave an account of a remarkable adventure on shipboard off the Cape of Good Hope, where, when about three days out, what was the astonishment of passengers & crew to perceive a black object on the waters, which on examination proved to be a man holding an umbrella & seated on a hen-coop.
>
> At once, conjecturing that he had lately been wrecked, the vessel was immediately stopped to take the unfortunate wretch on board, but upon a nearer approach they found that he was nothing of the kind, being on the contrary quite at his ease, & tranquilly steering for the island of Jamaica.
>
> He had one little trouble, the loss of his cask of fresh water, & replied to their many inquiries that if they could supply him with another, it was all that he wanted.
>
> "We did so," continued the narrator, "and then set sail again."
>
> At these words, the countenance of Harry Vernon underwent a most astonishing change. He jumped up from his chair, rushed to the other side, & seizing both hands of his rival, exclaimed: "What, Sir? Were you one of that generous & noble-hearted crew who saved my life at that fearful moment? How, how can I ever be sufficiently grateful for having spared me to thank you for it!"

In addition to Mrs. Gaskell, Elizabeth also made the acquaintance of Charlotte Cushman, the actress she was denied the pleasure of meeting long ago on a Sunday night at Mrs. Rush's in Philadelphia. Miss Cushman invited her to breakfast in her apartment near the top of the Spanish Steps, and served "Philadelphia waffles & stewed chicken cooked by an old Philadelphia black woman." It was such a treat, Elizabeth consumed enough waffles to rival the buckwheat-cake record set by a certain Doylestown gentleman.

Miss Cushman, too, told a funny story, which gained in the telling by the "expressive" face and the dramatic tones of the actress's voice:

A party of strangers were travelling one night in a stage coach. The hours were long, & each agreed to while away the time by telling a story. Everyone had fulfilled their promise, & it came the turn of the last one, a mysterious individual who had sat perfectly silent in one corner of the stage coach, . . .

At first he refused to speak, but after persuasion he at last assented, & in a deep sepulchral voice, told the most frightful tale of an encounter with a savage beast in the depths of a forest. The whole company was roused to the highest pitch of excitement, as he described the terrible roarings of the unknown beast, & his frightful mane & claws.

"Suddenly," he continued, "the monster opened his red jaws, raised himself on his hind legs, & made a fearful spring"—here the narrator stopped.

"Well," exclaimed the passengers, "Did you kill him?"

"No," replied the deep sepulchral voice, "He killed me!"

* * *

Before leaving Rome, Bigelow presented Elizabeth with an antique scarab bracelet. The fifteen scarabs, each over three thousand years old, were joined by links of old gold. No doubt the gift was intended for her thirty-fourth birthday.

They returned to Florence by way of the vale of Tivoli. En route they lunched beneath the Corinthian columns of a ruined temple, and as they quaffed champagne and looked at the blooming Judas trees, she was once again overpowered by the loveliness of the Italian landscape.

During her absence, spring had indeed come to Florence. She found the air heavy with the fragrance of roses, and her own garden a paradise. She changed the household schedule so that she could enjoy the longer evenings. Now they dined at five, and when Bigelow returned to his office, Elizabeth drove out in the barouche, the "handsomest in Florence." She always picked up a friend, then headed for the Cascine to watch the setting sun. They returned by way of Doney's, "the great café," where they ordered an ice and ate it sitting in the carriage in the moonlight.

At last she was beginning to enjoy her new home. The death of her brother and the dispiriting war news soon after her arrival had dampened her ebullient nature and made her desperately homesick. Now she was beginning to understand the "charm" of Italian life, and she was enjoying the delightful people who were passing through.

The war news continued to be frustrating. They received a telegram that Hooker was locked in battle—but with no mention of the outcome. The Radicals still seemed to be "having it all their own way," and she came close to having a pitched fight with the Rev. Mr. Hall, when he told her he had just read the War Committee's report, and that McClellan "appeared like a school boy, & the excellent Abe a great military strategist!" She wondered what Papa thought of that report. As for herself, she would stand up for McClellan "through thick & thin!"

* * *

A memorable evening was spent at Mme. Drontzkoy's palace. Thanks to Dumas' novel, the Russian Princess was known as "*la dame aux perles*," and Elizabeth had never encountered such a "mélange of refinement, and the want of it, & of elegance & shabbiness." In spite of the Princess's reputed wealth, the vestibule was paved with "common red brick," and the "ingrain" carpet of her drawing room had a large hole in the center. On the other hand, gold tankards and "ancient drinking cups" overflowed one of the mantelpieces, and her boudoir contained the entire "toilette service" of Marie Antoinette: gold mirror, gold pitcher and bowl, gold brushes and combs, and powderboxes and trinket cases—all marked with the cipher of the unfortunate Queen.

Supper was served at three round tables. As Elizabeth sat down and regarded her hostess draped in one of her famous ropes of pearls, and listened to the Italian and French songs "being trilled from the piano," she was suddenly struck by this scene of "continental society," so similar to those depicted in a "clever novel."

* * *

One fine spring day Mr. and Mrs. L. organized an excursion to Vallombrosa, the celebrated "leafy dale" high in the Apennines in which nestled an ancient monastery. Several other American couples, as well as a Russian and an Italian gentleman, were invited to join them.

For the first time since their arrival, the "drag" was brought out—their smart sporting coach with seats on top, drawn by four horses. Seven of the nine travelers promptly clambered to the top, but Elizabeth and another lady grew "faint-hearted" at the height and timidly climbed down inside with the footman. Such an "ignominious" move was loudly jeered by the others, so the two ladies crept back up to the top of the coach and deposited themselves gingerly on the back seat, with the "somewhat ostrich-like reflection" that at least there they could not see the horses. Off they rattled over the stone roads of Florence, and as they began to ascend into the mountains, the invigorating air restored Elizabeth's courage, and she was able to revel in the spectacular scenery.

About six-thirty they reached a little inn at the foot of the mountain, where, after light refreshments, they transferred to sledges. Each sledge was drawn by a pair of milk-white oxen and contained two chairs tightly strapped into large baskets woven of grapevines. At first the ascent was comparatively smooth. The sledges slid over a road that gradually rose overlooking a lovely valley. But as they went higher, the road became steeper and rougher, and the baskets—alas!—"pitched & tossed like a boat at sea."

At last they reached the chestnut forests, and it was nearly dark when they were drawn into the pine groves of Vallombrosa. At times the forest was so dense, not even a star could be seen, let alone the outlines of the white oxen. When a few drops of rain fell, they only added to the "ghostly charm," heightened by the lateness of the hour and the stillness of the forest.

After nearly two hours they emerged suddenly into a large plain, in the center of which gleamed the welcoming lights of the monastery. They were ushered into an adjacent building which the monks had built to entertain travelers, where they were greeted by the superior of the order, who was attired in a "strange-looking cap" and a long black robe. As the famished group huddled around the blazing fire, and the monks glided in and out of the room "bearing platters of meat & pastry," Elizabeth "fancied ourselves a party of cavaliers enjoying the hospitality of some godly abbot," and she half expected to hear Friar Tuck intone *pax vobiscum* any minute.

The next morning they wandered through the pine groves, admiring the distant view of Florence with its domes, and beyond to the sea. They met only one other person: a man in a coarse brown suit, with bare feet, who had "fled from the world," and had been "doing penance" for eighteen months for some "deadly sin."

After listening to the chapel organ, "so impressive in the wilderness," the group remounted the sledges and descended to the drag, which brought them "back under the gaslights of Florence" at ten that evening.

* * *

One nice day they went on a "pic-nic" to Pratolino. The repast was spread out on the lawn of one of the Grand Duke's villas. Though the meal was "sumptuous," the guests amusing, and the weather intoxicating, it was all spoiled by a cat, which persisted in prowling about among the crockery in spite of everyone's best efforts to chase it away.

Another annoyance, which she had forgotten to mention during her first six months in residence, was the fleas:

> They do not bite me much, but take it out in crawling over me. But then, the delight & luxury, after having been tormented by a flea the whole evening long, of getting off your clothes, laying them on the floor, & then with candle in hand, commencing a thorough search, & at last capturing & crushing the wretch in one of the folds of your flannel petticoat!
>
> At this moment I feel one walking slowly & heavily down my back! You should see Mr. L. in a flea agony. He won't crush them, preferring to pierce them with a large white-headed scarf pin!

* * *

Bigelow asked Hiram Powers to do a bust of his wife. Elizabeth looked forward to the sittings, for she found the sculptor not only "quaint & old-fashioned," but highly amusing, with an endless store of anecdotes and conundrums. Often when she arrived at his studio she found the old gentleman standing at the door in his "working cap & apron," on the watch for her.

At the second sitting he suddenly asked her, without interrupting his work: "When & how may a ship be said to be three times in love?"

The sitter had a hard time retaining her stiff pose when he provided the answer: "*ridiculously*, when she is attached to a buoy: *dangerously*, when she is tender to a Man of War; and *desperately*, when she hankers after a swell."

When they were not exchanging jokes, they discussed the war, in which he had an absorbing interest. She told him Bigelow was growing increasingly disenchanted with the present government, and was convinced the South would secede, in which event she intended calling herself a German "on the same principle that Powers proposes proclaiming himself an Italian." Indeed, she wondered who would wish to claim a nationality "made up only of Greeleyites & nigger worshippers!"

* * *

Late one Friday evening they drove out to Pisa for the famous "illumination" that took place every third year. As they traversed the main street of the town they could see that the façade of every building was outlined by a wooden superstructure decorated with quantities of tiny oil lamps. Where the outlines of the old palaces and churches were architecturally pleasing, the wooden latticework conformed; where they were not so attractive, a more graceful design was substituted.

When night fell, and all the tiny lamps were lit, Elizabeth and Bigelow stood on the porch of their hotel overlooking the river, spellbound at the two "dazzling walls of fire" that stretched along both banks. Corinthian capital, Gothic arch, tall column, and long colonnade glittered before them in a great sweep of light, reflected in the Arno. Barges floated by, decorated with flags and festooned with colored lanterns, some bearing bands of music, others alive with gay champagne supper parties.

It was a sight never to be forgotten.

* * *

When the weather turned hot, the city was considered "unhealthy." Accompanied by two Boston friends, Mrs. Dexter and Mrs. Wadsworth, Elizabeth spent part of the summer in Switzerland, leaving poor Bigelow to swelter at his desk in Florence. Not long after her return in early fall, he applied for a three-month leave of absence to attend to some urgent personal business in the States. Since it was to be a "flying" trip, with nearly as much time spent on water as on land, Elizabeth—homesick though she was—reluctantly decided not to accompany him, and settled in to await his return.

Just as Bigelow was packing up in Boston for a quick visit to the State Department before sailing back, he was struck by a "severe" but unnamed illness—possibly a "rheumatic attack," about which he had complained some months before. He was forced to ask for an additional three-month extension of his leave.

Never one to mope about, Elizabeth determined to make the best of what promised to be a long, dreary winter alone in the damp, chilly villino. However, she was not alone for long. Two days before Christmas Bigelow's clerk, Mr. Matteini (temporarily acting as Vice-Consul), informed her that the widow of a recently deceased U.S. Navy lieutenant, with two young daughters, had suddenly taken ill in Florence. Without a moment's hesitation Elizabeth took command, and Mr. Matteini was able to report in his next dispatch to the State Department that the poor lady's "closing hours . . . were consoled and comforted by Mrs. T. Bigelow Lawrence."[1]

The two orphaned daughters were briskly packed up and whisked off to the villino, where they were bedded down in rooms adjacent to Elizabeth's, until relatives from the States could come for them—a matter of at least six weeks. Try as she would, it was hard to make that Christmas season a merry one. Even a theater party—for which she took a box and invited a neighbor's children to accompany her two sad little charges—cast only a feeble ray of sunshine into the gray winter.

To add to her woes, the villino was assaulted by a sudden invasion of mice—"& not only nibbling mice but singing mice." For two nights neither the mistress of the house nor the two little girls caught a wink of sleep, while a creature "no bigger than a thumbnail" pattered from chair back to bureau, "chanting away." In the morning from downstairs in the servants' quarters came the same tale of woe.

Traps baited with toasted cheese were of no avail; the culprits skittered over and around them as if to say, "We know a trick worth two of that!" In desperation Elizabeth decided to move to a guest room so that the servants could install in her bedroom "an ancient Italian trap . . . that looked as though it might have caught mice for old Cosimo de Medici." Getting ready for bed that night, she heard a "tremendous drop" in her room. She ran in, and there was the singing mouse, caught at last.

Also upsetting was the matter of the mad dog. The two children of Princess Drontzkoy were walking in the Cascine, when suddenly a dog with tongue hanging out leaped up and bit both of them so near the eyes the wounds could not be "burned" for fear the children would lose their eyesight. Though no one could be sure the dog was mad, he was killed immediately, and it would be forty days before it was known whether the children had been "poisoned." Elizabeth considered it almost "a judgment" on the Princess, who was known as "one of the worst women in Europe."

Most disquieting of all was the discovery that one of her servants, Augusto, had stolen a diamond-and-enamel watch and pawned it for $14. When Augusto was brought onto the mat, he sorrowfully confessed his crime, but claimed the bailiff forced him into it by threatening to "seize the bed from under his wife," along with the rest of his furniture. At first Elizabeth believed him and was ready to forgive and forget, until further investigation among the other servants convinced her the man was lying. She was obliged to dismiss him, and only hoped Bigelow would not get wind of it in America.

In need of a "great recompense" for all the lonely months, she was overjoyed when

Fanny. The original pastel (artist unknown), probably done in Florence, is now in the possession of Elizabeth's and Fanny's great-great nephew, Baron Bernard von Friesen. *Photograph courtesy of the National Carl Schurz Association.*

Bigelow finally returned, bringing Fanny with him. About to turn eighteen, her half-sister had developed into an extremely pretty young lady, and Elizabeth was determined that she should be the most stylish member of the younger set in Florence. Not only did she plunge into a buying spree for the girl, but she also hired a singing master and a language teacher, and launched her on an intensive tour of the galleries and monuments, equipped with all the appropriate reading material.

* * *

Telegrams about the war worsened. Even Mama, who had occasionally demonstrated Republican sympathies, had given up calling "the excellent Abe 'Mr. Lincoln'!" Elizabeth doubted the North would ever conquer the South, and thought it would be better to separate and "leave it to future generations to make up the quarrel," which would never be done by fighting. She would "a thousand times" rather have Lee in the White House ruling the North, than the "frantic Abolitionists" then in power.

Elizabeth wasn't sure whether it was the dismal war news, or the eating of too much chocolate that caused it, but she was increasingly troubled by dyspepsia. As an antidote she took up horseback riding. Every fine morning at seven-thirty she and Fanny drove down to the Cascine, where she rode and Fanny walked. To her surprise, she thoroughly enjoyed it. She was convinced that it was the "going round & round" in a miserable ring that had blunted her enthusiasm when she had tried it before.

During the warmest part of the summer, the sisters departed for Switzerland, where Bigelow would join them later. He had bought a new horse when he was in the States, and he planned to head north when he heard the animal had arrived in Paris. Joined by another couple, the Arthur Dexters from Boston, Elizabeth and Fanny took off, accompanied by two servants and the usual mound of luggage. They traveled by way of Milan, where Elizabeth played the tour guide, leading the way to the Cathedral, then on to Lake Como, which they all thought looked like a "drop curtain in an opera."

Crossing the mountain passes in a carriage, they gathered alpine roses and forget-me-nots near the snow fields, which they proceeded to press in a book—and then, to their disgust, forgot at the next stopping place. On the other side they boarded a train for Zurich, where Elizabeth dispatched Fanny to see a curiosity that Papa would remember from that first trip: William Tell's crossbow with which he shot the apple from his son's head. The following day they settled into Baden, a "quiet little spot" more German than Swiss, with a band of music at the hotel every afternoon, which one listened to from "vine-covered piazzas."

Among the guests at the hotel was an attractive young Russian lady, Madame Olga, who soon became friendly with the sisters and often dined with them. She was *au courant* with all the "little tattle & quarrels" that took place between the Countesses and Baronesses with which the hotel was filled, and enlivened dinner with her running commentary. Often they found at their places a beautifully decorated little box of almonds or sugar biscuits provided by Madame Olga.

One afternoon the three decided to take a walk in the country. Elizabeth descended to the lobby in her "traveling dress" of black and white foulard—to be met by Madame Olga in an astonishing costume: a white alpaca Louis Quinze coat with tails, braided in black, opening in front to reveal a cherry-and-black bodice worn over a lace chemise, and a white petticoat trimmed with black ribbons looped up over a short crimson one! High Balmoral boots peeped out below, and crowning all was a helmet-shaped cherry and white "chapeau" with streaming white ribbons! With this flamboyant companion they set forth through the peaceful town—it was Sunday afternoon—and everyone they passed stared as though "turned to stone!"

When they reached the countryside, Elizabeth reveled in the gardens, for they reminded her of home. Lovely as the Italian gardens were with their terraces and orange trees and statues, these homely little kitchen patches suddenly made her nostalgic, with their bright flower beds down the middle, and beets and cabbages and potatoes down either side. This landscape looked like "Nature's own"; the other, a scene from opera, or "classic literature." Even the old men and women reminded her of those she had seen as a child, walking past the courthouse to a midday meal at the nearby tavern. The thought struck her that this was only natural, since many "upper" Bucks Countians were descended from émigrés who had lived in Switzerland just two or three generations before.

* * *

One of the new arrivals at the hotel in Baden was a Mrs. Gilman from Baltimore, who was traveling with an English party. The Dexters, Fanny, and Elizabeth had many a discussion about whether or not the lady was a "Secesher" (the nickname for a Secessionist). Mrs. Gilman approached them one day in the reading room and politely introduced herself, adding that she came from Baltimore. Mrs. Dexter announced with some asperity that *she* came from Boston, at which Fanny jumped in with the fact that *she and her sister* came from "near Philadelphia," skipping all mention of Bigelow's origin.

The Dexters had a "holy horror" of Secessionists, so they kept "rather shy" of the lady from Baltimore. Fanny and Elizabeth, on the other hand, always gave her a "most radiant smile" whenever they met, and thought it sad she looked a bit shabby. They privately agreed Mrs. Gilman was the kind who "would wear rags & be proud of them." In subsequent conversations they discovered many mutual acquaintances in Annapolis, as well as among the Mercers on West River. While quietly befriending Mrs. Gilman, the sisters concluded it was only sensible to "never talk politics" with the Dexters, for such talk would obviously only end in disagreement.

* * *

With the coming of fall they returned to Florence, accompanied by Bigelow and his new horse. Elizabeth promptly plunged into a series of dinner parties for a friend who arrived from England. One night sixteen guests came at nine and left at three-thirty the next morning. Fanny had never stayed up so late before!

Four A.M. was the retiring hour after another party, when a pupil of Liszt's performed on their American piano and pronounced it *"magnifique!"*

To insure the parties' liveliness, raconteurs and wits were included, along with artists and poets, whenever possible. Charles James Lever, the Irish novelist, was invited one evening and kept the company in stitches with his caustic commentaries. To the hostess's delight, his critique of a recent theatrical production concluded with the pronouncement that "the best part of the performance was the prompter, for though you always heard him, at least you never saw him!"

Someone at table complained that the Irishman had *laughed* all through the melodrama. "But, Madam," he protested, "I was perfectly grave all through the farce!"

Guests who performed like *that* made a *succès fou* of one's dinner party!

* * *

Elizabeth and her English guest breakfasted one morning with the evicted royalties, the Comte de Paris and his Countess—an "amiable little thing" barely seventeen years old—and his uncle, the Duc de Montpensier (son of Louis Philippe) and his Duchess. The Count took Elizabeth to table, and she was charmed to find that the whole family breakfasted together, including the children of the Montpensiers. One of the little dukes behaved like "less royal children," marching into the room in a sulky humor, then jumping up from the table in tears and running to bury his head in his mother's dress.

Inevitably the conversation turned to the war and the approaching election. Needless to say, Elizabeth, if she had been home, would have been prepared to "stump the whole North" to put the Democratic nominee, McClellan, in office, and defeat the "vile Radicals," who were boosting Lincoln for reelection. Most people in Florence, both friend and foe, were convinced that McClellan would be defeated, and her letters from home had the same "dreary echo."

She was surprised—and not a little disappointed—to learn that even the Comte de Paris, who had so often expressed admiration for her hero, was now actually for Lincoln!

He softened the blow somewhat by conceding that he would like to "see McClellan in the White House, but after the War was over."

Her blood boiled when she read in the letters from home about the "unjust" elections. She was resigning herself to the fact that if Lincoln won, the Radicals would be more "intolerant" than ever, "beasts" that they were!

* * *

Fanny continued to cut a wide swath. Charley Morgan (who was painting Elizabeth's portrait) told her that several Italians had been raving to him about *"la carissima sorella de la Lawrence,"* which translated into "the lovely little sister of the Lawrence." Even Fanny's nose, which the family had deprecated, was thought beguiling—*"un nose capricioso"*—and a number of portrait painters were begging to have her sit for them.

Several Italian noblemen were also captivated by Fanny, but things were certainly done differently here than at home. An intermediary appeared at the villino one morning bearing a message from the young Marquis Strozzi, scion of one of the oldest families in the country. He was reputed to have $15,000 a year, in addition to a palace at Ferrara. The Marquis had fallen in love with Fanny, had confided this fact to an intimate friend, and requested that he contact a friend of Elizabeth's, conveying the message that he, the Marquis, was very desirous of wedding the *bellissima* American.

Elizabeth did not even know "this sighing young Roman" by sight, and Fanny only knew him because she had inquired in the Corso one day about the ownership of the scarlet livery. Any American would have been properly horrified at such a proposition. The lady had not even met the gentleman, and here he was asking her hand in marriage!

Elizabeth had not been the wife of a diplomat all these years for nothing. Swallowing her amazement, she quickly resumed her composure and replied to the friend of the friend that she was "much flattered" by the Marquis Strozzi's admiration of her sister, but that Fanny was far too young to be thinking of matrimony. Indeed, she would not be thinking of it "for a *long time* to come."

Afterwards she and Fanny had a good laugh over it and declared the whole business "too comical."

* * *

Mme. Malaret, the wife of the French Minister, sent word that she would like Fanny to meet her daughters. Accordingly Elizabeth and her beautiful *sorella* went calling and received an invitation to a ball at the Ministry the following week as they made their "adieux."

The home folks were also apprised that Fanny had been a great success at the Maquay ball, where three hundred guests had singled her out for special notice. She had worn her old black velvet jacket, which had been so skillfully rearranged with little touches of gold here and there, that Mrs. Wilson Eyre had said: "Ah, there's no mistaking *that* basque—it's from Gupin's," naming the famous French *modiste* of Florence. How the sisters laughed when they got back to the villino!

* * *

Winter set in. To combat the chill, they put on not one but two flannel shirts and donned "colored worsted stockings."

Bigelow, in the course of his duties, made a "quick" trip to Naples, where the weather was "cold & disgusting," and to Palermo, which was a forty-hour journey from Leghorn.

He returned in time for Christmas, which was not a very merry affair in the American community, nor was there much "interchange" of gifts. Fanny and Elizabeth thought longingly of the scene at home, with Mary's three children playing with the gifts in their stockings and the parlor aglow with the Christmas tree candles.

The sisters spent hours each day with their French and Italian tutors. Elizabeth had a burning desire to learn enough to read Dante in the original. Fanny's singing master pronounced her voice worthy of his talents, but he hoped to increase her volume.

* * *

The Ingersolls and the Wisters from Philadelphia came to town for a few days en route to Rome. Then the Hoopers from Boston "popped through," along with Gen. Francis Barlow, "fresh from our battles & travelling for his health." Elizabeth gathered them up and led them on a tour of the art-filled palace of San Donato, which was bound to impress visiting Americans. Gen. Barlow, she discovered, was only twenty-seven, and she so respected his courage and bravery on the battlefield that she "forgave him his Republican principles" and took him "everywhere."

Two gentlemen called at the villino one evening, and to her relief and joy, they proved to be Democrats who had voted for McClellan—rare birds indeed! It was the first "satisfactory political conversation" she had had with anybody for over a year, and she pumped the subject dry.

Then a Congressman from the Confederacy, who claimed to have known Bigelow's father, wangled an invitation to dinner. The garrulous Southerner was violently anti-Jefferson Davis, and discoursed *ad nauseam* on "that scoundrel" who wanted to make himself "emperor," and whose "jealousy & mismanagement" were bringing about the collapse of the Rebellion. He told his spellbound audience that he had been paying fifty dollars a day for board in Richmond during the past year, and that Gen. Lee's hair and beard had turned "white as snow." By the time her long-winded guest departed, Elizabeth felt "numb with information."

* * *

Florence continued to be one of the stopovers for "broken-down" Americans who had fled because of the war. One evening a gentleman came to dinner whose nerves were so shattered by a forced disposal of "$90,000,000 of Government bonds," he was on the brink of insanity. Elizabeth happened to be wearing a pair of long, dangling earrings, and the gentleman was so beguiled by them, he leaned across the table and began swinging them back and forth as though they were playthings.

Several of the Secessionists who had all their property in the South had taken to their beds on hearing the news from America. One was a poor harmless lady from Charleston who had never offended a soul. It would certainly be an "outrage" if the government refused to give back what belonged to her!

* * *

Hiram Powers sent word that he had finished Elizabeth's bust. Quickly she drove over to see it and liked it far better than before. Now that it was mounted on a pedestal, she thought it made her look younger and "not nearly so matronly."

The sculptor then dropped Bigelow a note enclosing his bill. Bigelow returned only partial payment, occasioning this reply from Powers:

Florence
Feb. 16th, 1865

My dear sir:
You will find enclosed a receipt for 1250 Italian Lire (£50) [the equivalent of $250] on the bust of your lady. I duly appreciate the justness of your remarks and shall not call on you for further payments soon unless compelled to do so by the same reasons you have given—viz., the high rates of exchange, which press more heavily on a weak back than on a strong one. But happily for me, I have not had to draw on America for the last 18 months and I hope to tide over the present hard times, but to do so I must put in practice all the economical rules I know of.

I shall send the bust over in a few days. The spindle of the column is fastened with plaster and wants a little more drying.

> With sincere regard, I am truly yours,
> H. Powers[2]

In the meantime, Elizabeth had been asked to sit for another sculptor, a young American named Pierce Francis (Frank) Connelly. Though she felt guilty about it, she had to acknowledge that she preferred his bust of her to that of Powers. The former showed her as she would like to be; the latter was "me as I am." Furthermore, the price was only twenty-five lire more than the down payment on the Powers bust.[3]

* * *

(Left) Bust of EL by P. F. Connelly. She preferred it to the one done by Hiram Powers (now lost). *Courtesy of Baron Bernard von Friesen.* (Right) Bust of Bigelow, also by Connelly. Though the original is now lost, this photograph was found at Fonthill.

The other "great event" of February was the establishment of Italy's capital in Florence and the subsequent arrival of King Victor Emmanuel II. When the King passed the Club House, the city's "principal gentlemen" rushed out, seized torches, and lighted his way to the Pitti Palace.

The following evening His Majesty attended the opera. The opera house blazed with candles, and all Florentine society—"in stars & decorations & feathers & diamonds"—rose *en masse* to welcome him. The ladies carried bouquets of red and white flowers, the center forming the cross of Savoy. In spite of the gala atmosphere, Elizabeth thought His Majesty looked "very grave & melancholy," contemplating the past rather than the present.

She was told he hated courts and ceremonies and balls, preferring his gun and his dog and a day's shoot in his old woods in Savoy. On returning to the palace after the opera, he sent for his head gamekeeper, and the two sat in front of the fire and chatted about pheasants and woodcock for more than an hour.

* * *

Of course Fanny had to attend the Corso. Elizabeth had the open barouche and the horses decorated with flowers; they each flourished in a new bonnet; and with a "splendid skin of white & fawn colored eiderdown" spread over their knees, the whole effect was sensational. The younger girl was enraptured by the "shower" of bonbons and bouquets that were tossed between carriages and by the gaily dressed ladies and gentlemen, some of whom were masked.

A few days later Elizabeth sent Fanny forth to a Corso escorted by Bigelow. The girl wore a blue bonnet with a white lace bow under her chin, a black velvet cloak, and furs. The two footmen and the coachman up on the box had camellias in their buttonholes; the horses, shining like satin, had tricolor ribbons flying from their brass harness. As the "turn-out" trotted down the carriageway between the rows of sycamores, Elizabeth said to herself, "There'll be nothing better than *that* on the Corso today."

* * *

A masked ball at the opera was also not to be missed. The Lawrences took a box one evening, and had a supper served in it about two in the morning. During the course of the festivities, Elizabeth descended to the main floor of the theater, "all covered up in a black mask & domino." She caught sight of her husband, walked over to him, and linking her arm through his, proceeded to "intrigue" him for half an hour. Mr. L. had "not the faintest idea" who she was.

When they had made their separate ways back to the box, and Elizabeth had carefully concealed her mask and cloak once again, Bigelow consulted everyone in their party—including his straight-faced wife—about the mysterious lady's identity, even repeating some of their conversation. When Elizabeth finally confessed it was she, he rushed out of the box "in perfect disgust," followed by shouts of laughter. Bigelow was not amused. He had been suffering lately from "nervous depression," which he feared was "a chronic malady." A masked wife playing the coquette only added to his depression.

Perhaps fifteen-year-old memories were revived, for Sallie, too, had loved masked balls. But Sallie was certainly having none of that now. Her second husband Dr. Hunt had joined the Confederate Army, and she had returned to Louisville with her son. Gone was the magnificent courtyard and the luxurious house in New Orleans. Gone with the war was the family's wealth.

13

ITALY AND SWITZERLAND (1865–1869)

"The Gineral who beat 'em so completely at Antietam."

When the "glorious" news of Lee's surrender at Appomattox was finally received in Florence, the American flag was ordered to be flown from every consulate in Italy for three days. Elizabeth prayed that the government would "know how to use the victory that our generals have won for us," and deplored "this ridiculous adulation" of Lincoln—as though he and his Cabinet had a single thing to do with ending the hostilities! It was due entirely to two West Point soldiers, McClellan and Grant. The "glorification" of the Republicans and their leaders reminded her of the fly on the carriage wheel who proudly proclaimed: "What a dust *we* do make!"

As for Lincoln, his first step was not "a shining one," either as an example of his "good sense," or for "our national dignity." Imagine sending Henry Ward Beecher to Charleston to "inaugurate the ceremonies" at Fort Sumter! But then, she reflected, "what can you expect from a pig but a grunt!" And as for that "beastly Andy Johnson...!"

* * *

News of Lincoln's assassination reached the Lawrences in Bologna. They had gone there for a short visit, after dispatching Fanny (with an escort) to Rome, armed with an imposing list of sights not to be missed, and an invitation to dine with William Wetmore Story (the sculptor) and his wife, and Gen. and Mrs. McClellan, who had come to Europe shortly after he lost the election to Lincoln.

Elizabeth and Bigelow hurriedly returned to Florence, where they found all the American ladies in mourning for the "slain" President, and the men with "crêpes" on their sleeves. She was not only horrified at this sudden, tragic turn of events, just when peace was "at hand," but also contrite. "Abe" was suddenly transformed into "Mr. Lincoln." The "dastardly deed" was particularly untimely, because every word he had recently uttered had been full of "kindness & forgiveness" towards the South.

Bigelow assembled a hundred American residents (all men) in his office and worked up two unanimous resolutions, "deeply deploring the appalling event," and maintaining "entire confidence in the ability of his [Lincoln's] successor to direct the destinies of the nation."[1] He also transmitted the dismay of the "native population, who had considered Abraham Lincoln as the foremost leader of the century in the cause of human progress and liberty."[2] Translations of speeches of condolence were sent to the State Department from such organizations as the Society of Artisans of Italy, and Bigelow was pleased to report that the Masonic Lodge had "taken the mourning for nine days."[3]

When the newspapers arrived, Elizabeth devoted hours to reading the evidence at the trial of the murderer, John Wilkes Booth. She was eager to know her father's opinon as to the conduct of the trial, since it struck her as "most illegal."

Soon afterwards the McClellans came on to Florence. The General told her he believed that if Jeff Davis "was not convicted of having a hand in Mr. Lincoln's murder, he would cause the Government a great deal of embarrassment." Before the assassination the General had thought the best thing that could be done with Jeff was to "leave him to the South," where he was bitterly hated, and they would "take care of him." One thing was certain: If the U.S.A. should see fit to hang Davis, the members of "the Club" in Florence had announced they would exclude every American—beginning with the Minister!

When a dispatch arrived saying Lee had been accused of treason, Elizabeth prayed it was merely a rumor. If true, the effect abroad was bound to be catastrophic, and she would "blush" to have her husband hold office under such a "despicable" government.

* * *

Mourning for Lincoln coincided with the 400th anniversary of Dante's birth, observed in May with a month-long celebration. Evincing a proper Victorian preoccupation with bits and pieces of memorabilia, Bigelow acquired several fragments of the poet's exhumed coffin. He carefully packed them up and sent them off to Henry Wadsworth Longfellow, who was working on a translation of Dante. When this lugubrious gift was received in Boston, Longfellow's brother-in-law, Thomas Gold Appleton, (a friend of the Lawrences and a noted wit) wondered what would be done with the pieces of coffin. Would one "leave them as they are, or imprison them in gold and precious stones?"[4]

* * *

With the first onslaught of summer heat the sisters again went north to Switzerland. Just before leaving Elizabeth gave a dinner that included a couple of artists, "our Minister in Rome," Gen. King, his wife and daughter, and two gentlemen who represented a new line of steamships soon to be established between New York and Genoa. To them she was prepared to be especially "amiable," since it would be convenient and sensible to have "friends in court" in a line of ships that promised to make the journey in only twelve days.

Promptly at six the footman ushered in a "solemn-looking Yankee," followed by a "dapper little fellow" in a frock coat and white waistcoat across which dangled a gold watch chain "the thickness of a rope cable," who had the air of "having passed most of his life mixing sherry cobblers & mint juleps behind a tavern bar." Determined not to be put off by appearances, she seated Gen. King to her right and Gold Watch Chain to her left.

Scarcely had the soup been served when the latter began talking, and he showed no signs of stopping when the dessert appeared. Comparing notes afterwards with Gen. King, she agreed with him that the man was a "consummate liar." Not only had he owned the London *Times* for a couple of months when he was only twenty-one, but he had had a "very interesting conversation" with John Wilkes Booth just a few days before Lincoln's assassination—claims difficult to swallow.

In vain did the accomplished hostess attempt to divert the conversation. When she ran her old hero Kossuth up the pole, her guest informed her of a speech he had made on behalf of that great Hungarian that had elicited the most enthusiastic compliments. When she tried Macaulay, she was told the author was "good-hearted but without education," and that his history was "thought nothing of in England." The artist Raphael she presumed a relatively safe subject, only to be met with such an absurd observation that she and Gen. King quickly retired behind their napkins.

It was altogether disgraceful that an enterprise as important as a steamship line should be entrusted to such a representative!

* * *

The end of June she received a note from Ellen McClellan, the General's wife, from the Hotel Byron at Villeneuve, suggesting she and Fanny join them there. Mrs. McC. was finding the hotel very "compatable *[sic]*, though there was nothing in the way of society or

Maj. Gen. G. B. McCLELLAN & LADY.

General McClellan and his wife. Vacationing in Switzerland with them, EL was able to "pump" her "favorite hero" about his bitter experiences in the war, and the recent election. *Courtesy of the Historical Society of Pennsylvania.*

gayety [sic]," which was why she and the General were enjoying it so much. If the sisters did not think the atmosphere "*ennuyant*," the General would be pleased to engage rooms for them, or even arrange to meet them somewhere.[5]

Two weeks later the sisters left for Switzerland, where Elizabeth reveled in being once again with her "favorite hero." Not only did he share her politics, but also her background, for he had spent his youth in Philadelphia. To her surprise she discovered that his mother-in-law, Mrs. Marcy, recalled having a delicious tea with Mama's family many years before.

There were many long, intimate chats with the General at the Hotel Byron, during which the inveterate "pumper" had ample opportunity to ply him with questions. Was it true, she asked, that after the battle of Antietam, Lincoln toured the battlefield in an ambulance and asked someone to sing "Jim Crow?" It was, replied the General.

What was the situation when he took command of the Army after the first Battle of Bull Run? Washington was so poorly defended it could have been "taken by a cavalry regiment," said the General.

And what about the state of affairs after the "2nd Bull Run?" Was the President really preparing to evacuate? Yes, a gunboat was "puffing away" on the river near the White House, ready to take Lincoln and his Cabinet north out of danger. When the General had applied to the arsenal for supplies, he had been told that "an order had been received (which he countermanded at once) to transport everything to New York." You never saw such "consternation" in your life!

When did McClellan's troubles begin? Well, he had the President's ear up until the "great review" of the troops in Washington. Shortly thereafter he became gravely ill, and opposing "factions" took advantage of his absence, trying to poison the President against him.

One morning very early—it was only seven o'clock—the President sent for him and said: "General McClellan, they tell me you are a traitor."

"I won't permit that to be said by any man, not even the President," exclaimed the General, jumping up from his seat.

Lincoln turned "as pale as ashes" and replied that "he only repeated what had been told him, but that he did not believe it for a moment."

Elizabeth undoubtedly expressed her indignation before continuing her interrogation. Who were the best officers? That was easy to answer: those one heard least about. The officers who were "written up as heroes" were the ones who had invited the newspaper reporters to their mess and to headquarters.

Could the war have been ended sooner? It would have been over in a month, if McDowell's division had "not been taken from him at Yorktown."

When Elizabeth broached the subject of the "Seven Days' Battle," it was so painful to him, he pulled out his watch, stared at it for a long moment, and said: "Don't you think we'd better go to tea?"

A few days later the inquisition continued. Did the General have any hint of his removal? Not the slightest. After Antietam the President had expressed his "high admiration, confidence, & regard," and maintained he never had had any fault to find—unless it was "his being a little slow sometimes in getting ready."

Then, the General said, he learned by telegram that a certain Colonel had left Washington with sealed orders, bound for army headquarters. When the Colonel, on arrival, had headed straight for Gen. Burnside's quarters, McClellan "foresaw what was coming" and prepared himself, determined that no one should carry an account of his "crestfallen looks" back to Washington. Accordingly, when the Colonel and Gen. Burnside were announced at eleven-thirty on that bitter cold night, they found McClellan calmly seated in his tent writing to his wife. The Colonel, looking pale and embarrassed, delivered the sealed packet to McClellan, who broke it open, read it, and with a smile handed it to Burnside, saying: "Well, Burnside, here's the Army of the Potomac. I hand it over to you." He then proceeded to change the subject.

Elizabeth probed further: What did he really think of Burnside? To her surprise she learned that McClellan had once numbered him among his best friends. At one time they had even shared lodgings. When McClellan had first met him out west, Burnside was down to his last dollar, through "bad habits & dissipation." He had befriended the poor man, and even found him a job. When Burnside turned against him and testified before the War Committee to things that were patently untrue, McClellan, far from blaming the man, had become convinced that all the "cares & anxieties" had affected his mind.

Turning from the war, Elizabeth brought up the recent election. She was told that the General had been approached by both Mr. Francis Blair and his son (very influential Republicans), who promised him any civil or military job he wanted (Grant had agreed to this), if he would withdraw his name from nomination for the Presidency. Naturally he refused. He had always thought that Mr. Lincoln had "a very kind feeling" towards him, but that Secretary of War Stanton hated him, and Lincoln, unfortunately, was "afraid" of Stanton.

How did he first hear of his defeat? He and his wife were seated in their library when a messenger brought in the newspaper. She tore it open, read the headlines, and exclaimed: "Oh, George, you are defeated." He continued to concentrate for a few minutes on the book he had been reading, then put it down and walked into the next room and played a game of billiards. Yes, he had been sure he would win.

Elizabeth maintained with considerable spirit that her friend's defeat could be ascribed to a dearth of "adroit politicians" to "pull wires" for him. She declared he had relied too heavily on his own integrity, "after the foolish fashion of an honest man."

She prodded him about some of his other recollections. He talked of Stonewall Jackson, who had been a classmate at West Point, and at that time remarkable only for his "rough manners, his slowness, & his perseverance." The cadets found it amusing to watch "the old fellow," as they called him, when he studied. First there would come "a big bead of perspiration on his nose, then his whole face would be streaming," and finally his linen jacket would be "perfectly wet from the tremendous effort he was evidently making to master his task." Stonewall Jackson was a man "of fixed ideas," and once out west he "got the singular one that everything he ate went into his right leg!"

McClellan also recalled a trip down the Mississippi that he had made with Richard Cobden (noted British statesman and economist) and Jeff Davis. One day when the three of them were seated on deck, the conversation turned to chain-wheel pumps. Cobden said he had never heard of them. Later that day just such a pump was discovered on board, addressed to "John Ross of the Cherokee Nation." McClellan thought it curious that here was "a famous mechanical invention on its way to an Indian Chief, and one of the greatest of English statesmen had never even heard of it!"

As for Jeff Davis, it was he who, as Secretary of War, had proposed to McClellan that he visit the Crimean battlefields as an observer, convinced that this "foreign experience" would be of great service to a young officer destined to receive a high command. It was obvious that Davis at the time had no thought of breaking up the government or of heading the Confederacy, or he would have given such an important foreign mission to a Southerner.

These conversations were faithfully reported by Elizabeth for the benefit of her father. Usually, she wrote the Judge, the General was "reticent." Among "warm & devoted" friends, he had opened up, and she was not only surprised but "flattered."

* * *

The Chapman and McClellan parties, along with several other guests at the hotel, decided one day to organize an excursion to Chamonix. Someone suggested they equip themselves with "Alpine chamois horns," and off they set, blowing their horns "in full chorus." Elizabeth would never forget the sight of their merry little band, "the sturdy figure" of the General in the lead, clutching an Alpine stock and furiously blowing his horn, followed by a long procession of "mules, *chaises à porteurs*, & guides." This time she was prepared for the dizzying heights—nor did she have need of her umbrella.

After several weeks it came time for the travelers to go their separate ways. As Elizabeth and Fanny were about to head for the Hotel Gibbon at Lausanne, Mrs. McClellan bade them a fond farewell and told them that "our all being together had been both to herself & to the General as great a pleasure if not the greatest that they had experienced since arriving in Europe." For her part, Elizabeth would never forget for an instant that she had been "in the presence of the man who saved Pennsylvania."

* * *

Moving on to St. Moritz, the sisters quickly became convinced they had arrived at gastronomical heaven. During the course of their daily wanderings over the hills, they would stop at "some rude hut" to rest. Invariably cakes and tarts and puffs were set before them that would have made the pastry cook in the most sophisticated hotel blush for shame, so delicious were these rural concoctions:

> This valley of the Engadine, being higher up in the world than most its inhabited quarters, has but two staple productions, viz., barley & pastry cooks, of which the latter are to be found in every capital in Europe.
> After making their fortunes, these *chefs de cuisine* generally return to their native valley, & building themselves a snug little cottage, end their days among the hills amid which they were born.
> One of these old fellows, not content with having his roof scalloped until it resembles one of his own pie crusts, has had himself imaged in the wooden weather-cock that surmounts it, & there he stands—or rather, whirls—in the act of shoveling a pie at the four winds of heaven.

Although the canton was Protestant, at that season the Italian shepherds herded their flocks on the mountainsides; so every Sunday a Catholic priest arrived to conduct service in the square in front of the hotel. It made an impressive sight from the hotel window to see the white-robed old monk "hypnotizing his black-haired & weather-worn audience" with his account of "the delights of Paradiso."

As Elizabeth watched the sunburnt faces of the shepherds quivering with emotion, she was certain there was as much "real piety" in their hearts as in those of the "High Church English" who were chanting their service in the chapel down below. Only in these mountain valleys did one find Catholicism "in its purity"; in Italy proper it was "corrupt beyond all language to describe."

Bigelow joined them the end of August. It was so hot in Florence, he reported, that even the sealing wax in his desk melted out of shape, and some lozenges he bought during his journey oozed all over the lining of his pocket.

His wife and sister-in-law had thought it exceedingly hot in St. Moritz, rising at seven, when the air was still bracing, and covering several miles before breakfast, which they then tackled with appetites of "harvesters." Later in the day their walks were more leisurely (sometimes they totted up eleven miles), with periodic rests on the heather-covered hillsides to recover from the heat.

To their surprise, Bigelow thought St. Moritz so cold he promptly bundled up in his thickest winter overcoat and ordered a large fire built in the stove. The rest of the group nearly suffocated.

They journeyed on to Zurich, then Geneva, where they all visited the dentist, and returned to Florence by way of the Simplon Pass and Lake Maggiore. If Mama was curious to know what the lake looked like, she had only to refer to "the Portfolio" on the parlor table.

* * *

Once again the sisters got on with their French and Italian tutoring, but Fanny's singing lessons were postponed till spring because head and throat colds were practically "universal" in the damp winter weather. During dinner it was disconcerting to have Giovanni and Giuseppe suddenly retire to the china closet for nose blows that sounded rather like gunpowder blasts!

An assortment of Kings and Queens visited the city in November, and the Lawrences were kept in a "perfect whirl." Adelina Patti also arrived, and Bigelow took a box to hear the diva for the "absurd" price of $40.

One night at the opera, when Fanny was looking especially lovely (white illusion trimmed with blue silk, pink roses, and blue forget-me-nots in her hair), and Elizabeth wore her grey moiré with cherry velvet bands, and the diamond "stars" from her bracelet in her hair, the opera glasses of two Kings, a Queen, and a Prince Royal were trained simultaneously on the Lawrence box—the only box in the theater to be "so honored."

Reluctantly the sisters had to forego Patti's last performance. The Captain of the *Frolic*, who was visiting in Florence, and whom Elizabeth had entertained along with some of his officers, invited them to accompany him when his ship rejoined the rest of the squadron in Nice. Elizabeth realized she would have "a pretty tough time of it," but Fanny was so excited at the prospect, she overcame her misgivings and accepted.

They departed from Leghorn one evening at six and arrived at Nice the next day at four in the afternoon. The return trip overland along the Corniche road which bordered the Mediterranean produced some of the most fabled scenery in the world and canceled out all the nautical malaise.

The winter wore on. The French Minister gave a ball for Grand Duchess Marie of Russia—"very grand, very select, & very stupid." Blumenthal, the composer, called and sent them into convulsions of laughter over the various mishaps that had occurred to him in getting from Florence to Palermo.

An American gentleman and his daughter arrived for lunch and were shown through the garden to the top of the tower, from which vantage point, as he surveyed the towers and domes of the city, he lost the enormous diamond out of his cravat pin. No amount of searching in the garden below turned up the missing stone (estimated to be worth about one thousand dollars). The distraught gentleman offered a reward of ten dollars, hoping a gardener would find it—all to no avail. Since he was the inventor of "The Balm of a Thousand Flowers," Elizabeth was afraid he would require "a long & steady application" of his product.

* * *

One of Elizabeth's favorite Americans was Mrs. Marsh, the wife of the Minister, who was "very pretty, lady-like, & intellectual." However, she was in poor health, and Elizabeth went each Wednesday to help her "receive." Her own reception day was Monday, and "glad enough" she was when it was over, for she was beginning to tire of having to attend to all the Americans who were streaming through town.

Sometimes when she contemplated the sobering fact that there were five thousand Americans in Rome, and that in a few weeks they would all be in Florence, she felt depressed. Not that she didn't think her countrymen "the most charming in the world when they are of the right sort, but that sort, alas! rarely make their appearance"—an opinion to be kept, of course, strictly *"entre nous."*

* * *

A Mrs. Wild from California was ushered in early one Monday before her hostess had quite finished dressing. When Elizabeth dashed into the drawing room, she found her countrywoman encased in an enormous white "canton crepe" shawl, which she evidently thought remarkable enough to show off in a "sort of parade" around the room. In the midst of this performance, Gen. Thun, the Hungarian, stomped in, then came to a full stop, taken aback and utterly at a loss as to what to make of this "exotic" visitor. To cover the awkward moment, Elizabeth launched into a steady stream of chatter.

The foreign callers were exhausting because they required her to run on and on in French. The American ones were exhausting because they were so demanding. No one had any idea of the "nuisance" and "annoyance" when an "unprotected American female" came to town, claiming the undivided attention of the Consul-General's wife.

Furthermore, diplomacy had to be practiced constantly. What *did* one say, when a story was told to an assorted company about a "pompous Kentuckian" who was taken by some ladies in New York to see the famous Siamese twins? Feeling that some remark was expected of him upon beholding them, the Kentuckian hid his hands in his waistcoat pockets, made a magnificent bow, and observed: "Brothers, I presume!"

* * *

The chill of winter was dispelled slightly when several barrels of oysters arrived from home—"pickled & for stewing." How she longed to taste some fresh ones "on the shell!" Several boxes also arrived filled with edibles from Mama's kitchen in Doylestown. The peaches and pickles arrived intact, but the preserves had obviously spent most of their sea voyage standing on their heads, for all the juice had leaked out.

Poor old Grouse also succumbed. Though she had never seen much of the dog (who had come over with the horses and had always lived in the stable after his harrowing train journey), his departure was mourned like that of an old friend.

The Marquis Strozzi continued in a "desperate state" over Fanny, and Elizabeth was beginning to pity him. Whenever they drove out, there he was, hovering about, visibly thinner and paler. On Sundays he haunted the American chapel area. Recently it was reported that he had put his palace in Ferrara "in order," and had enlisted "as a common soldier in the regular army." He was heard to say that he expected to be killed, "& didn't care much if he was."

There was a considerable flurry when Alexandre Dumas arrived in Florence and proved himself to be "as famous a cook as a novelist." One evening he cooked a dinner at Mme. Rattazzi's (the wife of the ex-Prime Minister), jumping up from the table between courses to give "the last touch" to each dish. The menu struck Elizabeth as being a "very simple" one: "Julien & cabbage soup, boiled fish with sauce *à la Dumas*, some little trifles that I forget, & then roast chicken & salad." To her mind this was a "limited allowance" for eighteen people, but she understood that "very simple cooking is now the fashion in Paris."

* * *

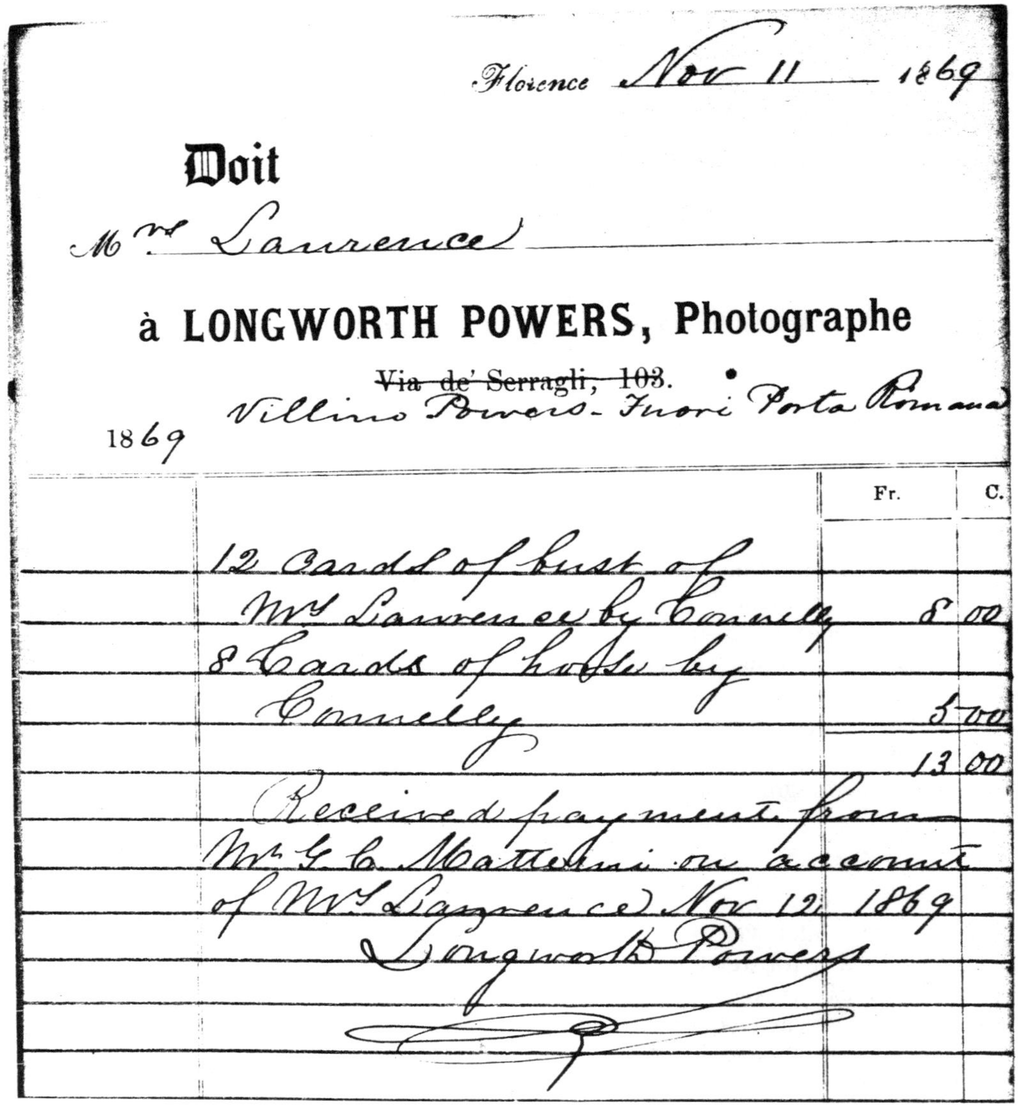

Florence Nov 11 — 1869

Doit

M.rs Laurence

à LONGWORTH POWERS, Photographe

~~Via de' Serragli, 103.~~ Villino Powers — Fuori Porta Romana

1869

	Fr.	C.
12 Cards of bust of M.rs Laurence by Connelly	8	00
8 Cards of horse by Connelly	5	00
	13	00
Received payment from M.r G. C. Matteini on account of M.rs Laurence Nov 12, 1869 Longworth Powers		

The bill submitted by Longworth Powers for photographs he took of EL's bust and Bigelow's horse. Both pieces of sculpture had been done—not by his father Hiram—but by another American sculptor, P. F. Connelly.

Frank Connelly, the young sculptor who had done her bust, was at work on a small marble cast of Marengo, Mr. L.'s handsome black horse, and had asked if he could "take the model" of Fanny's hand. So pleased was she, in fact, with Connelly's work, she later had twelve photographic "cards" taken of her bust, and eight of the statue of Marengo. Oblivious to the ironic nuances, she chose for the photographer Longworth Powers, son of the rival sculptor—who sent his bill from the "Villino Powers!"

Having lived with the Powers bust for a while, Elizabeth was more convinced than ever that *"entre nous"* she would not regret to hear that it had been "lost overboard on its way home to America." Never in her life had she seen anything "more self-satisfied or more strong-minded."

* * *

She was astonished to learn, that winter of 1865-'66, that one of John Wilkes Booth's "supposed accomplices," John Surratt, had turned up in the Pope's Guard in Rome. Surratt's mother ran the boarding house where the Lincoln assassination plot was hatched—and now, here was son John in Italy! She had it on the best authority, although it was being kept a secret.

Equally bizarre was the sudden reemergence, also in Italy, of "Mrs. Eaton of Gen'l Jackson memory." Bigelow received a letter from her in a "very tremulous & aged hand." Papa would surely remember the uproar back in 1829, when Secretary of War John Eaton (a long-time friend of President Jackson's) married the pretty daughter of a Washington tavern keeper and widow of a Navy purser, who had allegedly been driven to suicide by her infidelities.

Washington society had boycotted the wedding, and the Vice-President's wife, Mrs. John C. Calhoun—emulated by the other Cabinet wives—refused to call on the notorious Peggy. President Jackson was furious. With the flames of *l'affaire* Eaton fanned by Secretary of State Martin Van Buren (a widower with no wife to contend with, and an eye on the Presidency), the reeling Cabinet resigned.

It was nearly forty years later, and "Mrs. Eaton of Gen'l Jackson memory" was still making news. Her present husband, an Italian dancing master, had just eloped with all her money "& her youthful granddaughter beside." She demanded that the Consul-General "in his official capacity" write to the town in which the dancing master and his *inamorata* were now residing, to "warn the people against harbouring them."

It is safe to surmise that the Consul-General's wife applauded her husband's decision "to have nothing to do with the matter."

* * *

In the spring of 1866 Bigelow again planned a trip back to the States, but this time he would be accompanied by his wife and Fanny. The sisters were beside themselves with excitement. Trunks and portmanteaux were hauled out of storerooms and set up in the sewing room. Gifts were purchased and packed. The ladies waited impatiently for Bigelow to announce the date of departure. One maid, Ellen, was to accompany them; Sarah was to be left in charge at the villino.

Eager as they were to get home, they all agreed stopovers should be made in Paris and London for Fanny's sake, for the girl had seen almost nothing on her way over. In Paris they would visit the couturiers, buy gloves for Mama and Mary, and attend the Emperor's fête. It was not until the middle of September that they finally took off.

One presumes that Elizabeth's ecstatic predictions of the reunion came true: that they were met at the Doylestown railroad station by a family that looked exactly the same, in spite of the four years' separation; that everyone exclaimed in delight over the sisters' new French traveling outfits; that there were quantities of the requested bread, butter, and vegetables from the farm for the homecoming dinner, and plenty of "frizzled beef" on hand; that Mama was impressed with Fanny's linguistic abilities, her well-trained voice, her poise, her style, and that Papa was impressed by her knowledge of "pictures & statues," which surely exceeded that of "any girl her age in America."

In her mind's eye Elizabeth could see them all walking down the hill to the farm, where Mary and Willie would proudly show off the sheep and the dairy cows, and the gardens where the Italian seeds she had been sending were planted. In London, she planned to buy him seeds of rare evergreens, so that he could start a "pinarium" like those in "English pleasure grounds." Above all, Elizabeth looked forward to getting to know her nephews and niece: Willie, four, whom she had never seen; Lela, her namesake, a dainty child of eight; and especially Harry, who at ten was already showing promise as a scholar and an artist. It was high time the boy be sent to boarding school; Bigelow had agreed to pay the tuition.

* * *

After a visit to Boston so that Bigelow could attend to his business affairs, the Lawrences returned to Florence the following May, without Fanny. Elizabeth wrote the girl that *"Firenza la bella"* had changed very little. The same little woman opened the gate at the villino, the same pink roses lined the carriageway, and the same servants were inside and outside, she was happy to say, though Bigelow planned to add another stable boy to exercise the horses.

Mrs. Marsh, the American Minister's wife, had recovered, and now gave both day and evening receptions. Elizabeth's assistance, therefore, was no longer required.

On Washington's birthday a group of patriotic Americans had concocted an evening of entertainment that included "Bryant the poet."

A man and wife whom Fanny had met had lost all their money through the "rascality" of their son. So the Americans in Florence, Elizabeth reported, had made up a purse for them. The impoverished couple were in the throes of deciding whether to return to America (where the lady proposed giving music lessons), or to remain in Florence (where she could earn some money writing for the home newspapers).

It was rumored that the new Spanish Minister spent most of the winter in Nice, where he lost heavily at cards. Blumenthal, the composer, had lost everything "through the failure of a musical house in Paris."

A Cabinet Minister's wife had just published a book in which half the people they knew in Florence were shockingly caricatured. Elizabeth was thankful that she and Fanny had never frequented certain salons, for the authoress would very likely "have had a glance at us!" The Cabinet Minister, meanwhile, had received several "challenges to a duel," and it had been decided by a "council of honor" that as soon as he was out of office, he would have to accept them.

Mrs. Wilson Eyre had been to Rome, where she dined with Liszt. He had served "apple fritters" especially fried for her benefit!

Mrs. Maquay was ill. It was attributed to the fact that at a ball she had danced twelve hours "without cessation."

Mr. Trollope had married his daughter's governess. They were both "very happy & domestic."

Just outside the Porta Romana, the new stables of the King were finished at last and looked very imposing.

The gardener was outdoing himself in the baskets of roses he arranged for Elizabeth to send to her friends.

Mr. K—— [illegible] had acquired a fresh barrel of whiskey, and his "specific gravity is even less than when we parted."

Mrs. Eliot paid a long visit. They sympathized with each other on the "vague condition" produced in them by the climate in Florence. A few days before, someone had asked Mrs. Eliot the age of her daughter, and she had replied: *"Onze heures!"* Fanny could be sure that Elizabeth had never done "worse than that," even in her "vaguest moments!"

* * *

On her return to Florence from the States, she was determined not to let the "silly people" annoy her. Though the arrival of Americans *en masse* she still found "wearisome & confusing," she planned to "take to her beloved Giottos" as soon as they departed and immerse herself in the beautiful things with which she was surrounded. She was becoming a "near maniac" about pictures and frescoes, and spent most of her mornings in the old churches, where the sentries were beginning to know her so well, they greeted her by name.

She was also reading a great deal, and if she kept on at her present rate, few people would ever "know old Florence" better than she!

* * *

Her enthusiasm was not reserved for the ancients. The studio of Holman Hunt, the English Pre-Raphaelite, was also on her agenda. The artist had intended to paint Biblical scenes in Egypt, but was prevented by an outbreak of cholera, which had forced France and Italy to close their ports to all vessels sailing to or from the disease-ridden country. Unable to proceed, Hunt had settled in Florence instead.

Isabella and the Pot of Basil, by W. Holman Hunt. The Pre-Raphaelite artist was urged to paint into the unfinished picture EL's favorite "terrace rose." *Courtesy of the Laing Art Gallery, Newcastle-upon-Tyne.*

When Elizabeth visited his studio, she found him at work on *The Pot of Basil*, based on a poem by Keats from a story by Boccaccio. The unfinished painting depicted the heroine

Isabella mourning over a large urn planted with sweet basil, her tears keeping it watered. In the bottom of the urn she had buried her lover's head, which she had cut off after he was murdered by her brothers. The artist thought it "a delicious subject,"[6] and it is likely Elizabeth concurred with him. Since his previous painting had brought "a reported $50,000," this one was bound to produce "a great sensation."

Hunt had painted several flowers lying loose around the urn, and Elizabeth hoped to persuade him to include the "terrace rose," the name she had bestowed upon her favorite at the Villa Torrigiani.

* * *

Salvini, the celebrated Italian tragedian, opened in *Othello*. He had toured America the year before, winning acclaim playing Othello to Edwin Booth's Iago, and Elizabeth was wild to see it. Unfortunately the night she went, the huge theater was so packed, the heat and smell were almost more than she could bear, and only Salvini's sublime performance induced her to stay.

Near the end of one of the scenes she suddenly heard "terrible cries" outside. Thinking the theater was on fire, the audience rushed pell-mell for the doors. Elizabeth sat perfectly still, fearing she would be crushed to death by the hysterical mob. The dénouement was anticlimactic: The uproar had been caused—not by fire—but by a noisy quarrel among the drivers of the waiting cabs.

* * *

Once again Elizabeth joined the McClellans in midsummer, this time in St. Moritz. The General she found "more charming than ever." The town was so stuffed with Grand Dukes and royalty, she had to share her room with her maid for a short time, and heartily wished that all the "great people" would pack up and go back to their own kingdoms.

Staying in a town close by was a lady Elizabeth had first met in England years before, Mme. Usedom, and her husband, a Prussian diplomat. Not long after Elizabeth's arrival, poor Madame U. had a dreadful accident when her horses ran away, plunging the whole equipage—and Madame—over an embankment.

Oddly enough, Count Usedom, galloping out to meet his wife, was also run away with by *his* horse, adding to the commotion. Another carriage was dispatched to pick them both up, and the rescuers found the Count only a little shaken up, but his wife bloodied and in a "frightful state" of hysterics.

Elizabeth and the McClellans were seated at dinner when in rushed the disheveled Count. His wife refused to let the carriage proceed to their hotel unless the General came along. McClellan forthwith abandoned his dinner and gallantly climbed up on the box with the Count, Madame U. all the while screaming at the top of her lungs inside.

After a short distance the Count muttered *sotto voce:* "Now, General, you can slip away, I think, without my wife seeing you."

Not a bit of it. At that moment the lady stopped shrieking and cried out from the depths: "Is Gen. McClellan still there?" The rest of the journey was accomplished to alternate shrieks and inquiries.

Arriving at their hotel, Madame was carried through the lobby, creating a scene the likes of which the General, accustomed to a battlefield, had never seen before. Only when a doctor appeared was he able to steal away.

* * *

The end of August Elizabeth hosted an intimate little dinner party for her friends at the hotel. In addition to the McClellans she invited William Wetmore Story, his wife and daughter, and a couple of painter–poets from Florence.

The dinner was held in the McClellans' sitting room, and during the course of an evening noted for its profuse laughter, one of the poets recited in a broad brogue a poem purporting to be an Irish bumpkin's description of the Queen's coronation. Everyone was convulsed, and the next day Story wrote a parody, substituting Elizabeth's party for the coronation.

It was titled *The Grate Larrance Trate* ("The Great Lawrence Treat" in brogue), and Elizabeth knew, even as she copied the long poem for her family's delectation, that it had to be read aloud to be appreciated:

> At the top of the table sat majestical the Gineral
> A-servin' the broiled chicken in such illegant style,
> And our hostess she poured off the delicious tay & coffee
> A-swatinin' 'em both with her sugar & her smile.
> Such a laughin' & a winkin' & an eatin' & a drinkin'
> That the Gineral who beat 'em so completely at Antietam
> He declared the Larrance tea-fight beat Antietam all to pot . . . .

* * *

William Wetmore Story. Invited to EL's party, the poet–sculptor thanked her with a hilarious poem in Irish brogue. *Archives of American Art, Smithsonian Institution.*

Bigelow joined her the beginning of September in Lausanne, and they went on to Paris.

The Exposition was in full swing, and Elizabeth was so enthralled she spent every morning there. The building itself she thought hideous—rather like a large "gasometer"—but the exhibits and their unique arrangement were fascinating. On her first visit she headed straight for the American paintings, but the only one that her critical eye found pleasing was Bierstadt's *Rocky Mountains*, which she considered "superb." Frederic Church's *Niagara* and a "queer cloud-colored picture that he calls *A Storm in the Tropics*" left her unimpressed, though she could not explain why, and certainly the former was well-executed.

In the French section Meissonier was the only artist whose work she admired. The statue of Napoleon at St. Helena was a disappointment for the face was too young and "too French," and lacked the "solid massiveness" of her hero's head.

As for the English section, she liked a painting by Millais—the parting of a British woman from her lover, a Roman soldier—though the woman was "ugly & had a slight moustache." Another by her friend Landseer of a lady in a riding habit lying beside a prostrate bay horse reminded her of the clown in the circus who goes to sleep in exactly that same position, after requesting the audience to "wake him up when supper's ready."

Finished with the art exhibits, she moved on to native habitats. In a hut transported from Abyssinia, a little fellow "black as the ace of spades" pounded out gold rings, and Elizabeth bought one. The boy wrapped it up in a scrap of paper covered with hieroglyphics "from which faint effort at civilization the ring rolled out" almost immediately.

Not far away two Japanese girls, who looked as though they had stepped off a fan, were painting rice paper. Elizabeth purchased a cup of Japanese tea ("delicious!"), and some tiny sugarplums, then sipped a glass of Japanese liqueur.

* * *

Shortly after their return to Florence, Bigelow bought some Majolica plates, a few costing up to $400 a piece, and a painting by Dürer for $500. The villino was steadily acquiring the beauty inside that it had outside. Elizabeth contemplated sending home several terra cotta pots like those in which the orange trees were planted in the garden.

14

DOYLESTOWN, PENNSYLVANIA (1869–1872)

"Our bright comfortable cottage."

The summer of 1868, Mr. Marsh, the American Minister, took a leave of absence, and Bigelow filled his place, with the rank of Chargé d'Affaires. On the Minister's return, Bigelow again brought his wife back to the States, after stopping over for a month in England. It was the last time. He died in Washington, shortly after Grant's inauguration.

The obituaries in the Boston papers were fulsome, underscoring his "Puritan ancestry," and his "liberal hospitality."[1] Only one mentioned his first marriage "in early life to Miss Ward of Louisville, and subsequent separation,...one of the misfortunes of his career, which he supported with manly dignity and soon overcame." The second Mrs. Lawrence was termed "a most accomplished lady."

His will had been executed in Boston on 26 April 1864,[2] just before he sailed back with Fanny to Florence. The bulk of the estate, valued at well over a million dollars, was left to his "beloved wife, Elizabeth." In addition, there were provisions for each of the Doylestown in-laws. Mary was to receive the income from $30,000 for life, the principal to be directed by her at her death; Judge Chapman inherited $10,000 outright, and Fanny and Arthur $5,000 each.

To his wife Bigelow bequeathed all his "wearing apparel, watches, jewelry, ornaments, household furniture and effects, paintings, engravings, plate, books, horses, carriages, wines, provisions,..." His "valuable collection of ancient armor" was left to "the Proprietors of the Boston Athenaeum, but upon the express condition, that a suitable apartment shall be provided by them for the care and preservation and for the exhibition of the same to the public."

* * *

Elizabeth was not one to gloom about for long. She launched into a frenzy of activity. After the estate settlement was under way, one of her first moves was to publish in Boston a compilation of the obituaries. Although the book was anonymous, one can imagine who was responsible for the elegant, gilt-edged, leather-bound volume. It rang with Victorian fervor:

> ....His infirmity of deafness prevented his entering upon the active service for which he had a desire, and would otherwise have had brilliant opportunities....His faithful administration of that office [Consul-General for Italy], his attention to the interests of his countrymen, and his elegant hospitalities, have been the subject of general praise and of the high commendation of his government....[3]

Sallie Ward was given short shrift. "...his second wife, Miss Elizabeth Chapman of Pennsylvania, surviving him."[4]

A copy of this memorial volume may be found, among other places, in the British Library. There can be little question about who saw to its deposit there.

* * *

Without hesitation Elizabeth began spending her suddenly-acquired fortune. She went about it like one to the manor born.

She returned to Doylestown and activated a long-time dream to build a proper, comfortable home for Mary and Willie and their three children. Although they had made improvements to Grandpa's old farm on the edge of Doylestown, where they had been living since 1862, it lacked the Victorians' idea of comfort. Like most early Bucks County farmhouses, its two-foot thick stone walls, large fireplaces, and low ceilings were considered neither picturesque nor historic, but rather a reminder of an embarrassingly primitive existence. With the Civil War in the past, and the Centennial in the near future, the spirit of the times favored new construction.

It probably never crossed Elizabeth's mind to update and enlarge Grandpa's farmhouse. What she wanted was a much more monumental, yet intimate, building in the European style. Of course there would be a vestibule, a conservatory, a library, a pantry, a "modern" kitchen, and bathrooms—the whole complemented by lofty ceilings, stained glass, and elaborate woodwork.

Pursuing her dream, she purchased a twenty-nine acre tract adjacent to "the Farm," and had the existing buildings on the property demolished. Samuel Sloan, one of Philadelphia's leading architects, was hired. Acclaimed nationally for his courthouses, schools, hospitals, and churches, he was also known for his "villas" in the Italianate style. Elizabeth visualized an amalgam of an English "stately home" and an Italian villa, scaled down to a cozy "cottage" size. The house was to be called "Aldie," after the Mercer ancestral home in Scotland, and it would contain a suite for herself, to serve as a *pied-à-terre* for the few months a year she planned to be in Doylestown.

About the same time Judge Chapman, now sixty-seven and buttressed by Bigelow's bequest, retired from the bench and decided to devote himself to "literary pursuits." The handsome house he had built in 1845 across the street from the courthouse was by now too close for comfort to the expanding town's bustle. He sold it and built a mansard-roofed "mansion" on a portion of "the Farm" property which he called "Willowmere."

A formidable family compound was in the making. On one side of the road were Mary and Willie Mercer and their three children, whose Aunt Elizabeth (they called her "Aunt Lela") was in residence at intervals. Across the way were Judge and Mrs. Chapman, with Fanny and Arthur. She had always wanted her family tucked up close by, and now she had achieved it.

* * *

With all these plans under way, the widow returned to Florence in the spring of 1870 to oversee the packing and shipping of the Lawrence possessions left in the villino. Another long-time dream was realized: Her sister Mary would at last see "the Old World." Along with Mary she took Harry (now fourteen), Fanny (now twenty-four), and Ellen, the "faithful domestic." Willie would join them later.

Arriving first in London, Elizabeth settled her entourage into a hotel and saw to it that they dined on all the "great English dishes: salmon, turbot, white bait, cutlets, muffins, & last but not least, frozen pudding."

Harry proved himself a "most appreciative little sight-seer," invariably admiring all the right things, while his mother was in one "perpetual state of excitement & exclamation." At Westminster Abbey Elizabeth was at last able to prove a point she had been making for years. She had her sister place her head in the same attitude as that of the Mary Queen of Scots effigy and found the resemblance "between the marble head & the living one positively startling."

At the stopover in Paris, consideration was given to enrolling Harry in a French boarding school for the coming winter. The plan was dropped, however, when Mary was told by one of Elizabeth's friends that along with the language the boy would "undoubtedly acquire French morals."[5] (Even if Harry never spoke a word of French, that was too steep a price to be paid, and he was later sent to the Mohegan Lake School in Peekskill, New York.) While the highlight of the Paris stay for the ladies was a visit to Worth, the couturier *par excellence,* for Harry it was a ride around the city on a new contraption, the bicycle.

The three Chapman sisters, (left to right): Fanny, EL, and Mary. This photograph may have been taken when they were all together in Europe, judging from their apparent ages, and from the fact that EL is attired in a high-necked gown, while her sisters are preening in formal regalia—perhaps purchases from Worth.

Arriving in Florence, the little band of travelers occupied a commodious hotel suite which the staff at the villino had filled with flowers. The following morning Elizabeth took them out to see the beautiful house and garden they had heard so much about. It was a "dreadful ordeal" for her at first, as Mary put it in a letter to Willie, and she was "dreadfully overcome." She "recovered herself at last,"[6] however, and led them through every nook and cranny of the villa, while Fanny bubbled with reminiscences. Mary was awed by the painted ceilings and marble floors.

For the occasion the gardener had decked out the villino with a lavish hand. Mary was particularly impressed by the arrangement of orchids in the library, which she described raceme by raceme to her horticulturally-oriented husband.

A surprise awaited them in the ballroom. There stood a knight on horseback! Elizabeth had recently bought it, sight unseen, in Bigelow's honor, to be added to his armor collection. The horse was only "wood painted white," but it was due to be covered with brown horse skin, and the tail, still to be attached, had belonged to the noble Black Prince.

The horse was superbly caparisoned. Its armor was bordered with a deep green velvet ruffle trimmed with gold braid, and its gold-fringed saddle cloth was of matching velvet embroidered with the former owner's coat-of-arms. The knight's helmet was topped off with a burst of blue and white plumes, and his lance was aimed between the horse's ears. Elizabeth pronounced it "magnificent and unique of its kind," and thought it was "worth what she had paid for it"—presumably a handsome sum.

The packing was already well under way. The carriages, the marble busts, the piano, and the paintings had been crated by "the best packer Europe can afford." Mary estimated there were at least a hundred and fifty boxes of different sizes, all "beautifully lined with paper," awaiting their contents. She doubted there was a vessel large enough to transport them all across the Atlantic! Although she and Fanny were prepared to roll up their sleeves and help, the servants and packers had already made such inroads, the only task remaining was to "wrap" the books.

While they were still in Florence a letter arrived from the architect about the plans for Aldie, suggesting that the house be made higher, with a "French roof," and that it be built entirely of stone. This was not what the two sisters had in mind, and, as Mary wrote Willie, they planned to send the architect a telegram the next day in which "we will just say we prefer the old plan (the villa or cottage) raised as much as is practicable." Neither sister could bear to give up "what we see in our mind's eye as our bright, comfortable cottage in exchange for anything else, be it ever so much better." The money, of course, was "not the consideration," for "that dear Liz would never tire of spending on that place." The only regret was that they felt obliged to "differ with such acknowledged superiority as possessed by Mr. Sloan...."[7]

In a letter to Mama (written on black-bordered paper) Elizabeth explained her decision:

> I suppose you were greatly surprised at the telegram we sent about the house—but I am quite certain, & so is Mary, that while of course, the house would have been much handsomer with the stone walls & French roof, it would not have comported with the limited grounds that surround it.
>
> My object from the first was *not* to make the house the prominent object, but to have it & the lawns & trees & flowers all blend together as you see them in England & in this country [i.e., Italy] when the house is not surrounded by a park....
>
> I do wish you could see Mary in her Worth dress. She is really superb, & in place of being lost in it, seems to be as much at home with that & the titled people she meets as though she never had been used to anything else.

* * *

Often she dispatched her family on sightseeing expeditions while she went calling on old friends. She delivered a copy of the memorial volume on Bigelow to Hiram Powers, who dropped her a note acclaiming "the simple, modest form of this memoir, so unpretentious and yet so true."[8] He thought it "contrasted charmingly" with the "ostentatious display" usually associated with such undertakings.

* * *

The packing was finally completed, and the hundred and fifty cases dispatched to be loaded on the *Emma F. Harriman*. They were insured for $50,000—excluding all the large pieces and the silver plate, which was to be shipped separately.

Just before their departure, Mr. Matteini turned over to "Sig. Colonella Lawrence" a list in his elegant hand of the bills he had paid over the past year, along with their receipted vouchers. Besides the rent to Marchese Torrigiani, he figured board and wages for the butler, coachman, and porter, to which were added the extra costs of wine, coffee, sugar, and milk. Sundries included wicks for house lamps, sacks of sawdust for the stables, a broom, and a "woman for iron linen."

There were a number of bills from the veterinarian, one from the druggist, and one "for send Joseph['s] boy at Viarraggio Bath," presumably for his health. "To feed cat" cost 5/100 lire a day. The brougham was revarnished and relined, and the landau received the attentions of a "bronzist."

The expenses in connection with the armor were considerable. Spurs, "gantlets," harness, "gold trimming," velvet, "feathers, dying, and arranging the same," "making of mankin," "paint the head of mankin," "blacksmith for armour," and gilder all were listed with great exactness. So was the packing, freight, and "porterage."

Elizabeth's final orders to Mr. Matteini concerned the distribution of cash "presents" to the porter and his wife, to the gardener and his men, and to the offfice boy. Another 2500 lire was to be sent to Mr. Marsh, the U.S. Minister, for the "Orphans' Asylum."

* * *

The band of travelers journeyed by train, gondola, diligence, rowboat, and steamer to Venice, Trieste, Vienna, Munich, Nuremberg, Berlin, Cologne, Frankfurt, and Wiesbaden. Elizabeth found that at last she felt more like "enjoying things," and happily explored caverns and grottos with her "indefatigable" nephew.

In Venice they conversed with an Armenian monk who had known Byron. In Cologne they tracked down the "true place" where *eau de cologne* could be purchased. It was hard to find "nowadays"; three times they had been tricked into buying inferior imitations. In Vienna they sat for four hours at a stretch under the linden trees, sipping coffee, and listening to the "world renowned" band of Strauss, who seemed to be the "very soul of the waltz." As he led his orchestra, the music seemed "to flow from his very finger ends."

* * *

Trans-Atlantic communication about the new house had its drawbacks:

> I hope Metcalf [the landscape gardener] is going on as well as he promised at first. I agree that his estimate for the cost of the ram & water pipes is very large—much larger than Mr. Sloan's. If I am not mistaken in this conclusion, I think it would be best to let the above work alone until Metcalf has finished, & then have the water pipes & ram put in by a plumber recommended by Mr. Sloan.
>
> Of course it is *most important* that the work should be *well done*, & that *the best materials should be used*—the slow poisoning process not being a desirable one.

1870				£	63,022	85
		Brought forward				
May	7"	To Dr. Guastalla for stirrups & bit (Voucher No. 62.)			47	
"	10"	" purchase of spurs			10	
"	12"	" " gantlets, (Voucher No. 63.)			150	
"	20"	" Mr. Connelly £50 for Mrs. L. bust, (Voucher No. 64.)			1275	
"		" Harnesses maker for repair of Mrs. L.'s harnesses (Voucher No. 65.)			20	40
"	25"	" Mr. Trollope for sword			100	
"	30"	" purchase of feathers, dying, and arranging the same			85	
"		" " 16½ braccia Velvet at £9 for armour			148	50
June	1"	" making of mankin, (Voucher No. 66.)			180	
"		" paint the head of mankin			6	
"		" shoemaker for boots, (Voucher No. 67.)			85	
"		" Wages of servants etc. (Voucher No. 68.)			176	77
"		" One month of my salary gold at 2½ per %			427	06
"		" Corsellini for gold trimming (Voucher No. 69.)			78	
"	4"	" bill for saddle, bridles etc. (Voucher No. 70.)			150	
"		" " of blacksmith for armour, (Voucher No. 71.)			245	
"		" " gilder (Voucher No. 72.)			75	
"		" purchase of 86 braccia gold trimming			45	70
"		" Carriage-hire to go to Mr. Stibbert several times			25	00
"	8"	" frontist for repairs of Landeau & Brougham, (Voucher No. 73.)			30	
"		" G. Almenara for Expenses of Armour (Voucher No. __)			52	53
"	13"	" telegram to Mr. Stevens			62	25
"	24"	" Balance.			112	41
			Total	£	66609	47

Florence, Ju

E. D

Record of expenses for the armor bought by EL.

A page in an 1870 account book of Baring Brothers bank in London. The family's European itinerary can be traced through the bank draft records, on deposit at the Guildhall Library. *Courtesy of Baring Brothers & Co., Ltd.*

Her sense of humor was returning. She promised the family at home not to lead her little group into any "dangerous localities in the way of brigands," and to avoid those parts of the Alps that might be "break-neck."

She was still collecting furnishings for the projected "armour room" in Boston, but it was not till she reached The Hague that she found just the wallcovering she had been looking for: old leather hangings, fawn-colored with gold arabesques, which produced a "fine effect."

She decided not to return to Paris as planned because of a smallpox epidemic, but to sail from Belgium to England. There Willie joined them for the final leg through England to Scotland.

* * *

By the time they returned to the States in late summer, the house was under way, and by March of the next year (1871) the local newspapers were awestruck at the new "cottage":

> A very large and elegant residence built after designs by Samuel Sloan, of Philadelphia, has been erected, and is now far advanced toward completion. This is probably the most spacious and elaborately finished private dwelling in Bucks County, some of the single rooms being as large as the entire ground floor of an ordinary house.
>
> Every possible comfort and convenience are inside the walls, and gas and water are to be supplied from private works. The external appearance is pleasing.... The surrounding grounds have been laid out, graded, drained, and planted under the direction of Mr. Metcalf, a landscape gardener of Germantown, and already presents an attractive aspect. Improvements in extent and cost far surpass anything of the kind we have about Doylestown.[9]

Aldie, the "cosy cottage" near Doylestown designed by the Philadelphia architect Samuel Sloan for EL and her sister's family.

Indeed the house was the epitome of late nineteenth-century elegance. Although generally referred to as "English cottage style,"[10] there were elements of the Italian villa in its balustrades and pillars. The ceilings were high. The library, for instance, measured 11′3″, and the conservatory 13′8″.[11] The rooms were spacious, and even Harry had a "study."

Certainly the garden was inspired by the one at the villino. A half-century later, when it had reached maturity, it was considered one of the showplaces of the Philadelphia area. One entered through a huge wrought-iron gate, over which two arborvitae arched. A path led to a large lily pond, past a "grotto," then on to the more formal area through an arbor of grapevines. An *allée* of pleached evergreens converged on a fountain of Italian Renaissance design.

The loggia overlooking the garden.

St. Martin Dividing his Cloak, of Carrara marble, bought by EL from the sculptor Connelly in Florence and installed in the garden of Aldie. In 1876 she loaned it for the Centennial Exposition in Philadelphia.

Flower beds were punctuated by stone columns topped by marble heads. At the far end another gate opened into a more intimate garden, the focal point of which was a large antique grain jar from Ostia. Groined arches, decorated with mosaics, were patterned after those of fifteenth-century Italian pavilions and formed a "loggia" which provided "a pleasant resting place."[12] Very likely Elizabeth had imported a "terrace rose."

* * *

Guests at the house party at Aldie. They were identified in 1920 by Henry Mercer (after consulting with his Aunt Fanny) as follows: "(1) Amy Shaw, Boston (Mrs. John C. Warren); (2) Martin Brimmer, Boston; (3) Thomas Gold Appleton, Boston; (4) Charles S. Sargent, Boston; (5) Miss Fanny Chapman, Doylestown (sister of hostess); (6) Miss Alice Parker, Boston; (7) Henry Chapman, Doylestown (father of hostess); (8) Mr. Hoppin, New York and Providence, R.I., diplomat; (9) William R. Mercer, Jr., Doylestown; (10) William R. Mercer, Sr., Doylestown; (11) Mrs. T. B. Lawrence, Doylestown; (12) Mrs. Howland Shaw, Boston (née Cora Lyman); (13) Mrs. Martin Brimmer, Boston; (14) Miss Susan Williams, Baltimore; (15) Major George Douglas Mercer, C. S. A., Maryland (brother of no. 10); (16) Mrs. W. R. Mercer, Doylestown (née Mary Rebecca Chapman)."

When the house was furnished to her liking and the grounds planted, Elizabeth gave a house party and invited some of her Boston friends. Among the guests was the witty raconteur, Thomas Gold Appleton, who kept the company in a constant state of amusement with his stories—notably the "celebrated" one about "wollaping [sic] an impudent Turk with his boots, when followed by the man [as] he was walking through the Mosque of St. Sophia in his stocking feet."[13]

Another guest was Martin Brimmer, president of the fledgling Boston Museum of Fine Arts. One of the chief topics of conversation at the house party must have been the proposed building of the new museum, which had been triggered by Bigelow's armor collection. Since no "suitable apartment" had been available at the Athenaeum as his will had stipulated, nor was there space on the property to add a new gallery (which Elizabeth had offered to finance), the trustees had decided instead to encourage the founding of a new museum for the city, in which would be housed, along with other works of art, Bigelow's armor collection.

Enthusiastic about the new Museum of Fine Arts, in which the hangings and other artifacts she had collected in Europe would be installed, Elizabeth agreed to donate twenty-five thousand dollars, "provided the sum of seventy-five thousand dollars in addition thereto should be raised from other sources."[14] Since hers was the largest single gift, and the second largest was that of Thomas Gold Appleton, the Doylestown house party had overtones that transcended mere sociability.

Like all her entertainments, the weekend was a gala one. To add to the celebration, she allowed the servants to help themselves to the beer. One old fellow, an ex-sailor, who was employed in the gas house to "keep things going" day and night, took full advantage of the free beer. When Elizabeth and some of the Boston ladies walked by him in the garden one afternoon, he attempted an "Oriental salaam," bowed too low, and losing his balance, plunged head foremost into the gas tank![15]

* * *

The old Museum of Fine Arts, Copley Square, Boston. When it was built in the 1870's, Elizabeth was the largest contributor. *Courtesy of the Museum of Fine Arts, Boston.*

The Lawrence Room, Museum of Fine Arts, Boston, 1879, an oil painting by Enrico Meneghelli. Since EL gave the room in memory of her husband, presumably she is the lady inspecting the collection. *Courtesy of the Museum of Fine Arts, Boston.*

Who could have imagined, that gay summer weekend in 1872, that within a few months the warehouse in which Bigelow's collection was stored would be destroyed in the great fire that devastated central Boston? The loss was considered "irreparable." The collection was "as perfect for its size as any now known, either in England or upon the continent... on account of its extreme variety and its great intrinsic value."[16]

Even the catalogue—the only one—went up in flames. Someone remembered glimpsing "long bows, cross bows, halberts, poleaxes, lances, spears, maces, targets, shields, and buckles...." There were also finely worked swords, rapiers, dirks, pistols, and "slender daggers of mercy intended to be thrust through the bars of helmets," as well as medieval instruments of torture, arms from the East "inlaid with cornelian, turquoise and silver," and executioners' swords.

At least seven suits of plate armor were consumed by the fire, along with several of chain mail, and some horse armor. Undoubtedly the latter was Elizabeth's purchase, complete with Black Prince's tail. The collection also included tapestries from Holland, a library of several thousand choice books collected in England on "ancient and modern arms, treatises on heraldry, and manuscripts relating to the Lawrence family history." Some "superb leather" unquestionably included the gold-embossed hangings Elizabeth had found in The Hague.

Finally, the statue of Marengo, Bigelow's other beautiful horse, done by Frank Connelly, was a victim of the holocaust, as were two marble busts by Hiram Powers. One was

This sketch of the Lawrence Room appeared in the May 1879 issue of *Harper's New Monthly Magazine*, along with a description of its contents. The room contained sixteenth century carved oak paneling from England, antique Italian furniture and decorations, and Renaissance bronzes from the famous Castellani collection.

probably that of Elizabeth, which *"entre nous"* she had hoped would sink crossing the Atlantic!

Ultimately the insurance was collected, Elizabeth's cash gift was more than matched, and when the Boston Museum of Fine Arts opened in 1876, a room was dedicated in Col. Lawrence's name. To replace the leather hangings that had burned, Elizabeth purchased antique paneling out of an old English castle.[17]

15

EUROPE (1874–1875)

"The courtly splendors of other days."

Now that Aldie was completed and her sister's family installed, and the Boston museum under way, Elizabeth turned her attention in a new direction: Washington. At intervals over the years she had visited the capital, and although the swampy little town could not hold a candle to London or Paris or Florence, it was nevertheless the seat of power and attracted some of the world's most influential people. Still fascinated by the milieu of politics and diplomacy, she decided to establish a small ménage there for use during the winter season. When the Potomac heat descended and everyone fled the sweltering town, she would return to her suite in Aldie, or travel.

As Grant's first term neared an end, it was inconceivable that the electorate would vote for his scandal-rocked administration again. It would be interesting to be in Washington when a new administration—hopefully Democratic—took over. When her hopes were dashed and Grant was returned to the White House for a second term, Elizabeth gathered up Fanny, and in disgust hurried back to Europe, temporarily postponing her plan to settle in Washington.

The two ladies sailed away in August 1874, accompanied by two new servants, Rose and Ferdinando. (Ellen had found herself a husband, thanks undoubtedly to a bequest of a thousand dollars left her by Bigelow.)

* * *

Ensconced in a London hotel, in a chintz-covered armchair in an upstairs parlor, served cold roast beef and a tankard of ale by a waiter in dress coat and white tie, Elizabeth felt at home once again. Aside from a visit to Baring Brothers (the banking house) and a stop at Poole's to order the Judge a suit of clothes, the sisters devoted their days to the picture galleries. American art Elizabeth considered vastly inferior, and she "fairly pined to see a good picture once more!"

En route to Paris, the Channel crossing was made bearable by the foresight of Ferdinando, who produced a flask of brandy, and even wine glasses! Everybody took a generous "preparatory quaff." Later, settled in a bright little salon awash with blue silk portières and ormolu, Elizabeth would have known she was in Paris, with no other hint than the aroma of chicken *à la Demidoff*, her favorite green beans stewed with cream, a frozen Charlotte Russe flavored with strawberries—and a fine bottle of claret.

* * *

After a week they headed south to the château country of the Loire, stopping on the way to explore the forest and palace at Fontainebleau. While Rose and Ferdinando wandered around in a daze, Elizabeth and Fanny tried to decipher some of the emblazoned initials and were fascinated to discover that those of "Henry the 2nd" were intertwined with the mark of his mistress—"a combination which modern propriety would scarcely have permitted, even to a king."

In the midst of all the magnificence, Elizabeth was struck by the "plainest object of all":

a round mahogany pedestal table, about a third the size of the one in Papa's library, on which Napoleon signed his abdication. "Many an old-fashioned sitting-room in Pennsylvania has a similar one," she noted.

They rolled on through Barbizon, a little town "greatly frequented by artists," to Blois. No sooner had they arrived than a French tutor was hired to come to their hotel every morning. In the afternoons the tutor's wife and her friend, the wife of a bank clerk, arrived and, bending over their pieces of handiwork, engaged the Americans in several hours of conversation *en français*.

Except for the Prussians in the recent war, the two French women had never met any foreigners before. As far as "progress of ideas" was concerned, Blois seemed to be "one of the least advanced quarters" of France.

One day they made an excursion out into the countryside with the tutor and the two French women to visit one of their brothers. It was the vintage season, and as their carriage lumbered down the poplar-lined lanes, the white caps and blue blouses of the "peasant men and women" who were gathering grapes made a colorful scene. Coming to a high white-washed wall, they were directed through an archway into an enclosure filled with poultry, on one side of which were the stables, on the other the farmhouse. At the door they were met by a lady with a white muslin cap tied under her chin, who welcomed them into a "great big kitchen with a large old chimney place," and an alcove containing two large beds with "blue hangings & coverlets to match."

With the exception of the beds, it was "just such a kitchen as you would find in any farmhouse in America," even to the bright-colored prints on the walls and "the little framed photos of different members of the family which hung beneath them." A braid of onions hung from the rafters, and several bunches of "remarkably fine" white and purple grapes hung in the windows.

Elizabeth admired the lady's composure and "quiet good breeding"—no fluster, no apologies, in the presence of these *"grandes dames,"* as she surely characterized her high-style American guests.

Presently the bank clerk appeared wearing a blue blouse, for he had been grape-harvesting. Apologizing for his appearance, he asked if they would like to taste some of the new wine. When they quickly accepted, the little white-capped lady disappeared and came back with wine glasses, wine, and a *"galette,"* a large cake baked especially for the *fêtes* and the vintage season.

It was all very "jolly," with everyone laughing and joking and devouring a second portion of the cake. One of the ladies suddenly remembered the coachman outside, and he was invited into the kitchen to try the new wine.

Promising to come back later, when the sun was not so hot, to "assist at the grape harvest, & also to see the process of making the wine," they went on to the château of Chambord. Just outside its walls they found a "pretty little inn," where they ordered dinner to be ready when they had finished their tour. Then they drove into the royal château. For Elizabeth's part, she was "glad to have republican France shut out for a time."

She was enthralled by this "poem in stone," this "inspired relic of the courtly splendors of other days." She could imagine it as it must have been when its gilding and colors were still fresh. Now it stood lonely and deserted, "its lofty galleries & winding staircases too vast to be thought habitable by modern efficiency."

In one of the apartments they were startled to come upon a portrait of George Washington, which they were told had been brought back by a Frenchman who had been in America during the Revolutionary War and was a "great friend" of both Washington and Franklin. Elizabeth was disappointed, for it showed the first President as a young man, a "rather ordinary looking individual with a somewhat weak expression of countenance, and no grandeur or majesty about it."

She bought photographs for "the album," and wrote Mary to be sure to instruct her children on the historical points of interest their aunts were seeing. For Papa's benefit she attempted to explain the complicated political situation in France. There were Orléanists, Legitimists, Imperialists, and Republicans—and no one strong enough to "get the entire control." Discouragement about the future and bitterness about the past were rampant. Even the two ladies who came every afternoon grew "perfectly furious" when they talked of the Prussians and the indignities they had endured during the three-month occupation of Blois.

The bank clerk's wife had had several Prussians quartered with her, and she had been forced to rise at all hours to make their coffee and to sleep on the floor while they commandeered the beds. Once she had two soldier–tailors, who filled one of her rooms with the dirty uniforms they were mending, and the smell made her deathly sick. She had to admit the Prussians never committed any violence, but the rumor that preceded their march through France had it that every woman would "lose her right hand, and have her child killed before her eyes."

* * *

Certainly the most excellent products of the countryside—in addition to the wine and the grapes—were the pears and the game. Dinner invariably included red or grey partridge, and occasionally snipe or quail, "always served with a silver skewer run through each."

Among the new arrivals at the hotel was an English family with a maid who all the world could see was not "respectable." But not so Ferdinando, who promptly fell head-over-heels in love. Each evening the maid came to Rose's room and made such a racket "coquetting" with Ferdinando that Elizabeth finally gave him "a tremendous talking to."

She explained that if he expected to stay in her employment, he could not "carry on with that sort of woman," of which they would meet many during their travels. Ferdinando burst into tears, and his mistress said she was sorry if she hurt his feelings, but she really could not have him "flirting with every young maid that came along." She truly believed he "had done no wrong," but in future he must be "as careful to *appear* to do right as to *do* it, for people nowadays were judged very much by appearances."

She gave him her hand—which he kissed! (Though this was an "Italian fashion among servants," it was the first time Ferdinando had ever done it.) All next day his eyes looked as though he had been crying—something he had never done before. Elizabeth and Fanny inferred that "once fairly started, he liked crying so well he concluded not to stop."

* * *

Another visitor at the hotel was the Duc de la Rochefoucauld, a gentleman of such immense proportions Elizabeth had to step aside on the staircase to let him pass. The headwaiter told the sisters many funny stories about *Monsieur le Duc*, who lived in a château about thirty miles away. Whenever he came to the hotel, he had post horses for his carriage stationed along the way, traveling at *"grand galop"* at twelve miles an hour.

Once, when he was elected a Consul-General of that Department, he arrived with thirty-six horses and eighteen servants and spent money like water. On the day of his departure he paid his bill to Alexander (the headwaiter), who brought him change amounting to several thousand francs. The Duke looked at his change, picked out one franc, and with a wave of his hand presented the rest to Alexander. On another occasion his valet took sick, and Alexander had to attend to him, even to pulling on his stockings, for His Grace was so fat he could not possibly do it himself.

Alexander also regaled them with anecdotes about Prince Bismarck, who had stayed there a few years before the Franco–Prussian War. The Prince spent two days visiting the neighboring châteaux, and in that time he drank two bottles of Cognac—verifying the rumor that Bismarck drank a bottle of brandy every day. "After all," wrote Elizabeth, "he is not a man, but a steam locomotive, & requires more fuel than ordinary humanity."

* * *

For their expedition to the château of Cheverny the sisters decided to invite their two French ladies to go along. They accepted with alacrity, for a drive in a carriage was a rare treat.

Although the château was not nearly so fine as some of the others they had visited, it was especially enjoyable because it was still lived in by family descendants. As they were wandering through the public section, they ran into a "whole nursery-full" of children—nine altogether, with two babies in nurses' arms, and a battery of governesses.

Later while walking in the park they saw them all again, some on swings, some on "jumping boards," while two little brothers galloped down the *allées*, one on a pony, the other on a little donkey, blowing horns that swung around their necks. In the distance a benevolent-looking priest in black gown and hat was sunning himself. The whole scene made a delightful picture of "domestic high life in France." Obviously they were in the domain of a "thorough Legitimist," whose family "lived the lives of their forefathers," which was easily believed, for everything had "the flavor of at least a hundred years ago."

On the way back to the hotel they stopped for dinner, which again they had ordered on the way to the château. The little country inn served as good a repast as one could find at Delmonico's, and the bottle of old Bordeaux was probably better. And all this without a tablecloth, on a brick floor without a carpet!

The next day, en route to Amboise, they stopped at Chenonceaux. Resting on arches that spanned the river Cher, the château resembled a "lovely barge." Since the present owner, a wealthy Countess, was not in residence, Elizabeth had a chance to peep at her "magnificent grand piano," strewn with music by Mozart and Beethoven.

Separated from her husband, the Countess was apparently no happier than her royal predecessors, because of a devastating quarrel with the Count on the subject of alterations to the château. Among her other extravagances, the willful lady had ordered an ancient oak, planted by Diane de Poitiers, to be transplanted across the river—at a cost of $7,000! It interfered with her view, she said!

* * *

Back in Paris again, Elizabeth and Fanny plunged into another round of dining, shopping, and theater. They heard Offenbach's latest ("very poor!") and Mozart's *Don Juan* ("perfectly marvelous!"). They dined with friends in the café at the Palais-Royal, then went around the corner to the Théâtre Français to see Dumas' "famous piece on the Demi-Monde." Many theatergoers thought "the home of Molière" lowered its dignity with such plays, which depicted "the least respectable portion of Parisian life." The popular *"opéra bouffe"* which "ran through everything" she found "dreadfully tiresome" and French theater in general "very much run down."

Considerable time was spent with an old Florence friend, Lady Paget, who was determined to find good "paste jewels" to go with her real ones. During the shopping expeditions, Worth was assiduously avoided. Elizabeth's occasional burst of Pennsylvania thrift asserted itself, and she told Fanny she "could do almost as well elsewhere," for the famous couturier's clothes were "dearer than ever." She had to admit, however, that Worth's gowns were "always the thing," and "never seem to go out" of fashion.

One day the ladies all went to the Conciergerie, where they were dumbfounded by the miserable cell once occupied by Marie Antoinette. Even Elizabeth's fertile imagination had never conjured it up so dark and small—only half the size of her new dressing room at Aldie! Nor could she take her eyes off the door that had been so cruelly lowered, after the prisoner had told her "persecutors" that they could kill her, but "they could never lower her spirit." Passing through the shortened doorway on the way to her trial, the defiant lady was forced to "bend almost double."

Lord Lyons, the British Ambassador, invited them all to dinner one night. As Elizabeth expected, it was a "very formal & stiff" affair. They were the only females; the other guests were "solemn secretaries & attachés, & all with the air of incipient Talleyrands & Metternichs!"

Chatting with Lord Lyons after dinner, Elizabeth was told that the Embassy had once been Pauline Borghese's palace, and that he slept in the bed once occupied by the Princess. His avid listener had difficulty keeping silent. How she longed to see the very bed in which Napoleon's sister had once slept!

* * *

The day Lady Paget left Paris the Richard Morris Hunts and entourage arrived. Hunt, the distinguished American architect, was an old friend of Bigelow's family.[1] Already to his credit were his Beaux-Arts mansions on Fifth Avenue, as well as a number of palatial "cottages" in Newport.

Elizabeth could hardly believe all the troubles that had befallen the Hunts during the last six months. First, they told her, Mrs. Hunt had been dangerously ill, then Mr. Hunt had nearly died. No sooner had the family finally sailed for London than their children's nurse developed a "fatal disease" and had to be sent home. Then the maid Mrs. Hunt had hired suddenly went insane. Finally off to Switzerland, "Dody" (Joseph, a son) came down with scarlet fever, and they were detained for a month.

They had just settled down in Como when a telegram summoned them back to London. Mrs. Hunt's sister was ill, and her husband "in a strange state that resembled insanity." Arriving to take charge, poor Mrs. H. was run away with in an open carriage. In the midst of this turmoil Richard Hunt was summoned to Paris. His brother, "swamped with debt" and encumbered by a mistress of twenty years' standing and an insane daughter, had committed suicide. (The folks at home were not to mention the mistress, as it was a "profound secret)." As if all this were not enough, the architect was facing a lawsuit over the Stevens building, a large apartment house he had designed in New York.

As soon as Mrs. Hunt recovered from an "agonizing attack of neuralgia," they hoped to "have a good time!" To celebrate her recovery a few days later, the sisters and the Hunts went to the circus. The funniest act of all was billed as "The First Skating Lesson," and featured two splendid young skaters from Chicago who bumbled around the rink so hilariously, they all laughed harder than they had in years.

Several nights later they all went to the Opéra Comique to hear a "lovely opera by Gounod." Among the guests in their box was General Boucher of the French army, a commander to be reckoned with. During one of the *entr'actes* the General, noticing his friends' discomfort from the stifling heat, slipped out and returned with "the latest *nouveauté* in Paris "partly frozen sugar plums!"

Misfortune, however, was still dogging Richard Hunt.

After the performance, just as the architect and the General were stepping into their carriage (the door of which was held open by an attentive Ferdinando), a one-horse brougham galloped up so close that Elizabeth was sure they would all be crushed to death on the spot. Fortunately, Mrs. Hunt was already inside, and Elizabeth and Fanny were

Richard Morris Hunt, by John Singer Sargent. The noted architect, touring Europe with his family, made an amusing traveling companion. *Courtesy of The Biltmore Company.*

safely ensconced in another carriage, from which they could see that the General's face, illuminated by the gaslights, was white with rage. They heard him shout "in a voice of thunder" to the brougham driver, then saw him seize the oncoming horse by the bridle and thrust him away from the carriage just in the nick of time. Whereupon the "impudent varlet" on the box screamed at the General, calling him, among other things, an *"insolent."*

When the driver's anger finally subsided and he trotted away, the Hunts and the General proceeded unscathed to their hotel, the latter convinced that it had been no accident and that the "varlet", spotting the military uniform, had fully intended to run him down. Elizabeth had no doubt the General would see to it that the fellow was "well punished" for his insolence. Poor Richard Hunt—an innocent bystander—had narrowly escaped another disaster!

* * *

To avoid the bitter weather prevailing over most of Europe, the sisters and the Hunts left for the south of France the beginning of December. Counting children and servants, they made a party of ten.

The first night was spent in Dijon, "the headquarters of Burgundy, the monarch of wine." The following morning they drove around the town to see the sights. Guided through the palace of the Dukes of Burgundy, they came to its "ancient" kitchen. Of all the "dream castles" Elizabeth had ever imagined or seen, never had she got such a "forcible idea" of the "prodigal festivities of other days":

> We fancied what a scene this kitchen must have presented on some great festival night, with a wild boar roasting in one chimney, a whole sheep in another, an ox in another, & so on . . . & the sculleries turning the enormous spits & the cooks beating with their carving knives their orders on the trenchers.
>
> Fancy what a sizzling there must have been, what rivers of juice & gravy—what a smoke, requiring not only the mouths of the six great chimneys to carry it off, but the aperture in the roof beside.
>
> And then imagine it, if in those days cooks were as they are at present—just imagine the squabbling, the din, the uproar! I have rarely seen anything that gave me such an idea of medieval revelry.

That afternoon the children, their parents, the sisters, assorted servants, and luggage piled onto the train. As it rumbled southward, Elizabeth struck up a conversation with an Englishman and his wife, who were on their way to visit her sister in Ceylon. They told their probing interrogator they planned to sail from Marseilles, go through the Suez Canal, and arrive in Ceylon in twenty days—a voyage they apparently thought nothing of, having done it several times before. The lady gave an enraptured account of the flowers of Ceylon, but then described for Elizabeth the island's "drawback":

> . . . . the serpents, which make such a noise rattling about on the thin roofs of the houses at night that sometimes it is impossible to sleep. The natives make a hole in the roof for, strange to say, if the serpents can look down into the rooms beneath, it quiets them.
>
> I asked if the serpents ever entered by these holes & was told "occasionally but very rarely!" Imagine yourself in bed with a hole over your head & an enormous black serpent as thick round as your wrist glancing at you through it, & "occasionally" descending & making you a visit!

*   *   *

On reaching Marseilles they registered into the most enormous hotel Elizabeth had ever seen—the Fifth Avenue in New York was a "pygmy" beside it. After washing up, they descended to the *table d'hôte* dinner, and what a "dreary spectacle" they found! The room looked like the "Hall of Spectres," for all the diners appeared to be in the "last stages of consumption." She would long remember the gloomy sight.

On arrival in Nice, they were surprised to find the town filled with Americans—"& nice ones," she was glad to say. It was interesting to observe the servants' reaction to the Mediterranean ambiance. Ferdinando, finding himself in "home-like surroundings," underwent a change of facial expression that was "wonderful to behold." Suddenly he looked "so Italian." Rose was "nearly wild" with delight at the palm trees, and the Hunt's servant, a French-Canadian, was completely overcome by the colorful, luxuriant vegetation.

A faded photograph of Nice from the family scrapbook of EL's travels.

The tree that most impressed Elizabeth was the eucalyptus, which she was informed was a rapid-growing native of Australia. As tall as "the tallest forest oak in America," it was said to have the property of "disinfecting a malarious district." She was curious to know if Willie was familiar with this wonderful tree, for she was told it would grow very well in the Pennsylvania climate.

She never ceased to marvel at the flowers:

> When on our long walks we find ourselves in some neglected, apparently forgotten, spot where the roses seem to bloom unplucked & the oranges are let to rot on the trees, I can't but think what a poor affair man is, with his spade & hoe & fertilizers, compared to Dame Nature, when she chooses to smile on some such a favored spot as Nice.
>
> Away from this enchanting shore we plant & transplant, water, weed, hoe, & even grub in order to give our little starveling of a rose slip or heliotrope the proper soil to flourish in, & we are filled with delight if by the time the autumn frost has killed it, it has grown a foot or two above the ground.
>
> Here, on the contrary, the heliotropes & geraniums cover the walls just as the most ordinary vine does at home, & as for the rose trees, I send you a piece of *bark* that I picked off a stalk as thick as my two wrists the other day....

Among the specialities of the place, she discovered, were candied fruits and candied *violets!* The former were delicious, but as for the latter—the first mouthful was delectable, tasting "like the flower itself." But subsequent mouthfuls proved a disappointment: Chewing flowers seemed "not a very agreeable idea."

This was "the moment" for Mandarin oranges. When a great cargo of them arrived from Sicily, together with some fresh dates, Ferdinando quickly acquired "a paper full of both" at the local market, and everyone reveled in them.

Compared with Paris, there was little to do at night. To entertain his fellow travelers one evening, Richard Hunt recalled his journey up the Nile some years before. After three months in Egypt, he had traveled on to Syria, where a singular mishap had befallen him. One day, as he was riding along with a friend, their horses suddenly got into a furious fight, which ended by horses and men falling on top of one another in a "terrible mêlée." Hunt's horse extricated itself from the heap, picked its master up by the shoulder, and carried him some distance. There he swung, suspended in the beast's mouth. Suddenly the horse gave him a "terrible bite & a terrible shake," and let him drop.

"The consequence was," Hunt concluded, "I entered Jerusalem next day on a camel!" He had hated horses ever since, and Elizabeth could imagine how unpleasant the one-horse brougham business must have been in Paris.

Sometimes she found the architect "very funny." One night when they were dining together in a café in Nice, he found a hair in his roll. "How I do wish they would comb their bread!" he exclaimed.

Again bad luck overtook the Hunts. Their little daughter Kitty contracted a bad case of scarlet fever (the same disease which had struck her brother Dody) and everyone worried about her for days. When she finally recovered, they all moved to another hotel, a little farther back from the sea, to escape the "constant beat" of the waves, which sounded particularly unpleasant at night.

The new hotel was "not much fancied," either. It was expensive, and the landlord tried "in every way to make on his guests." When Elizabeth complained to the hotel's servant about the firewood, which seemed to "consist of old stumps, & burnt up in no time," he shortly returned with a basket of splendid wood. When asked why he had not brought it in the first place, he replied that he had orders to "use the poor wood first."

While Richard Hunt made "some lovely sketches" on the hills around Nice, the ladies took long walks among the orange groves and olive orchards and Roman ruins. Elizabeth wished Harry were there, so they could indulge their common love for "historical antiquity" together. She found few people who sympathized "nowadays" with her "romantic feeling" about the past, and it gave her great "pleasure & comfort" to find it in her elder nephew.

EL's nephew, Harry Mercer, at sixteen, photographed in Philadelphia by Gutekunst.

Among the Americans at the hotel was Mrs. Gibbs, Mrs. Astor's mother, who proved to be "very sociable & friendly." When Elizabeth ventured to show her a photograph of Harry, which she had just received, Mrs. Gibbs remarked: "What a charming boy," immediately confirming Elizabeth's warm feelings about her. She anticipated some pleasant talks with the lady about "New York society in olden times when Washington Irving, etc., adorned it."

On Christmas day the hotel served an "elegant banquet." The tables were decorated with "great pyramids of fruit & candied baskets," and the centerpiece was a Christmas tree, covered with lighted candles. Unfortunately, the tree caught fire early in the dinner, & had to be "wafted out of the room one blazing mass."

Mrs. Hunt presented the sisters with some lovely Christmas gifts. Elizabeth received a "cross of different stones—a rococo ornament to wear around the neck," and Fanny got a "velvet pocket covered with lace to wear at her belt." There were other "pretty things" from the children.

Elizabeth's present to Fanny was a necklace of amber beads, to be bought in Florence, and to Rose, "Frs. 60" to buy herself a brooch and earrings in Rome. Ferdinando's gift was "Frs. 100"—unrestricted.

Soon after Christmas, Elizabeth and Fanny made a quick "excursion" to Monaco with Richard Hunt and Joe Peabody, an old friend from her London days. Having heard it was "the loveliest spot on this coast," they were all in agreement, as they rode through the little principality, that it lived up to its reputation. Later, however, the "grimy tables" on which they were served breakfast, and the "bad-looking lot of both men & women," induced them to change their minds. As for the gambling:

> Monaco, fortunately, is the only place in Europe where gambling is permitted. I heard the other day from some people in this hotel that last week while they were looking at the gambling going on at one of the tables, they saw quite a young man who had just lost everything he possessed in the world. He was pale as a sheet, & trembling all over, & they led him away in order to sign a paper making over his possessions to his successful antagonist at the gambling table.
>
> One of the sights at Monaco until quite recently was an old woman who did nothing but gamble. Her children allowed her a certain sum every year, & she spent it this way. She is now 79 years old, & has just signed a paper promising them that she will gamble no longer.
>
> I trust that even at Monaco this scourge will not be permitted much longer. Public opinion is against it everywhere, & it will have to fall before it ere long.

* * *

Among the arrivals at Nice were Prince Pandolfino and his wife, who had been one of Elizabeth's close friends in Florence. Though past fifty, the Prince was a "perfect boy in his feelings," and played the flute and violin beautifully, while his wife accompanied him on the piano. The Pandolfinos were engaged in furnishing the Prince's old palace in Sicily and had come to Nice to buy "the greatest quantity of Turkish rugs" for it.

One evening, when they were expected for a visit, they did not appear. By nine-thirty Elizabeth was convinced they were not coming, and she felt relieved, being so "dead beat" from her walk that day, she wanted only to climb into bed. Just then there was a tap on the door, and in they came, the Princess claiming it was all the Prince's fault. He had gone to the club, and she had been waiting for him to return all evening. The Prince was "very contrite," told the sisters he had been "scolded all the way down the street, & that he deserved it," and then proceeded to make himself "so charming" that they soon forgot the lateness of the visit, and the "peccadillo" that had caused it.

He talked away in accented English so fast that the sisters only caught one sentence in six, but his voice and animated manner were so ingratiating, they hardly cared. "There is nothing like the charm of the Italian manner, & on this occasion we had it in its perfection."

Ferdinando had brought along with him a volume of *The American Kitchen*, a Baltimore "receipt" book. With its help he concocted an "egg nogg" that had the Pandolfinos in ecstasies. While "quaffing" it they discussed the latest news from Spain:

To think of there once more being a King of Spain. What a change for Queen Isabella, to have her son on the throne of her native land.

She had about struck bottom when we were in Paris, having been obliged to sell her jewels. We saw her one night at the opera in the third tier, & afterwards she & her ugly daughter, sitting all by themselves on a bench downstairs while waiting for their carriage, & we left them there as forlorn a looking pair as you would find on a day's ride.

Now, however, all Paris is calling on the ex-Queen, & the whole world sending her telegrams. The excitement & change has been too much for her, & I see she is sick in bed.

* * *

When Elizabeth heard a day or two later that the Princess Pandolfino had a bad cold and was confined to her room, she sent her "such a pretty thing here in the way of flowers": a ball of violets, "about the size of a large football." Usually suspended to the chandelier at a dinner party, the one Elizabeth sent the Princess was hung near a window in her bedroom so that the air blowing through "filled the whole room with perfume."

* * *

On 23 January 1875, at ten o'clock at night, Elizabeth and Fanny arrived in Florence, after traveling all day with nothing to eat since breakfast. No sooner had they checked into the Hotel Grande Bretagne than Ferdinando announced his intention of going to see his father. He had been "affecting the indifferent" about returning to his native city, but once there, it was too much for him, and he became highly emotional. He told Elizabeth he was going to his father's shop and ask for a glass of wine, under the firm conviction that his father would not recognize him. He arrived there just before the shop closed, and the minute he crossed the threshold his father greeted him with: "Oh, it's you!" On his return he told Mrs. L. that everyone thought he had been "so much improved by his visit to America."

During the next few days a "continuous ovation of flowers" poured into their hotel rooms from the "domestics about the villino in other days." Giuseppe, grown very old, came to call and burst into tears on seeing his former mistress. She also had a visit from the son of the porter, now a handsome youth of twenty, with a "Raphael face," who told her he was studying to be an artist. On learning that the boy often lived on dry bread in order to afford pencils and paper and paints, she left "a little sum" with a local agent to be dispensed at intervals.

Florentine society had changed not a whit since she had lived there:

> Mrs. Von Schaik gives a ball tonight, in which all the costumes are to be of calico—a calico ball. Some of the ladies sent to Paris for their costumes, & Worth charged them $160 (dollars!)! Fancy giving that much for a cotton dress! The lady herself is an American, but has been living in a most disreputable way with a man of fashion here.... But all the world goes tonight to her ball, & the Grand Duchess Marie has also sent for an invitation.
>
> Lady Orford's daughter died about six months ago of diphtheria. All the ladies of Florence assisted [at the funeral], & all sat out in the grounds during the service, fearing to enter the house and catch the disease. My friend, not seeing Lady Orford, asked where she was, & was told that she & the husband had driven out into the country. She afterwards learned that they had gone to Ouida's villa. [Ouida was a notorious authoress].

I see Lady Orford going about in society. They say she is broken hearted, & perhaps so, but it is hard to believe it. These people are so light that one cannot judge them by any standard that one really knows much about.

Fanny is at present sitting at the other end of this table painting a photograph....

* * *

Once again the sisters went to Rome for several weeks over Easter. One of their friends, a Mrs. M—— [illegible], showed up one day in great perplexity. She was to be presented to Princess Margaret, and she had nothing to wear, as black was not permitted.

Fanny offered her a costume, almost new, which she had bought in Paris, and which was still "very fresh." It was a dove-colored polonaise with a garnet velvet petticoat. Mrs. M. retired and tried it on, and when she emerged for the sisters' comments, they assured her it fit "like wax":

So yesterday she came here with her maid, we arrayed her in the above, & she drove away to the Quirinal Palace looking as radiant as the day.

She had a most successful visit. The Princess talked with her for nearly an hour, they were quite alone, & among other things admired Mrs. M.'s costume extremely, & asked where she had got it.

Imagine Mrs. M.—& how she was put to the turnscrews at this!

However, she at once replied: "Mme. Marguerite" (one of the great dressmakers of Paris), "& all I could hope," she continued when telling it to us, "was that I was not telling a story."

Don't mention the fact of F.'s having lent the dress, as Mrs. M. might not like it known that she wore borrowed finery. On her return she gave Fanny the loveliest old Norman locket nearly two hundred years old....

* * *

It was just like old times. The sisters called on the Marquise de Noailles, who took them to see Castellani's collection ("not the Roman but the Naples one") of jewelry and art.[2] This "first connoisseur living" brought out his finest pieces for their delectation, paid them many compliments, and said that there was nothing in his collection "so charming as Mademoiselle's [Fanny's] expression." After lunch the Marquise presented the two ladies with photographs of her husband and son, promising to play a Chopin mazurka for them one day soon.

Another morning they visited a flower show and were astonished to find that the star of the show was a *grey* lily with white spots.

On the Via Appia Elizabeth purchased a Corinthian capital—part of a broken column that had stood there "in the days when St. Paul passed along that famous highway." She planned to put it near the old apple tree on the front drive at Aldie—and hoped to have a "bunch of acanthus" growing alongside.

She thought it would be a "very good lesson in Roman history" for Mary's children to look at it and imagine all the events and all the personages it had once looked down upon. She could just see Harry gazing at the column fragment "fixedly" for hours, Lela writing an ode, and Willie, Jr. listening to long stories about it.

The great difficulty was going to be transporting it into Rome, as it was pronounced too heavy for a carriage. But Ferdinando, now that he was back in his native land, was equal to any task. He told her not to worry, just let him manage it.

* * *

One Friday the sisters made an excursion with Sir Augustus and Lady Paget to Bracciano, a four-hour drive from Rome. Fresh horses awaited them midway, and as a compliment to Sir A. from the prefect, mounted escorts were stationed at intervals all along the route. They stopped at one point to pick up one of the young English secretaries, who was on foot. Sir A. insisted on his getting into the carriage, as it was a "dangerous thing" to take such a long walk in the hot Italian sun.

Two hours more brought them to Bracciano, "the one place that Sir W. Scott asked to be taken to on reaching Rome." The half-ruined castle, built centuries before for the Orsinis, was "so far away removed from all modern investigations" that Elizabeth had yet to find anyone who could tell her anything about its history.

Two hours were spent wandering through the salons and up and down the staircase, into the towers, and onto the battlements, which were riotously overgrown with wallflowers, and aflutter with snow-white pigeons. The lunch they had brought along was then spread out in the deserted old dining room.

On the return trip they told ghost stories, and Sir A. "bore off the palm" by telling the scariest. As they neared Rome that evening, Sir A. changed the subject to "the famous American drinks." Since he was longing to taste them, Elizabeth promised to have a book sent over from Doylestown, titled *How to Mix Drinks*, to get him started.

* * *

Urgent pleas to Judge Chapman to join his daughters in England eventually bore fruit. (Mama refused to budge; she was not a sea voyager.) Elizabeth baited the hook with mention of genealogical researches, and of "having a bang at the grouse in the blue hills of Scotland," and added that $200 would be waiting for him on arrival in Liverpool.

He sailed the middle of June, accompanied by Willie. They were met in London by Elizabeth and Fanny, who promptly saw to it that Papa was re-outfitted, even down to new nightshirts and slippers. Every afternoon they took him on a drive in Hyde Park in one of the new hansoms.

During extensive shopping expeditions, Elizabeth ordered enough writing paper imprinted with "Aldie" to last "for all time." She also ordered the three "crack" roses of the season: a pale pink, a white, and "as near as possible" a black rose, which were to be ready in pots by the time they sailed for home in September. Two specimens of each would challenge Mary and Mama "to run a race" to see who could grow the best one.

She had been reading a book on "rose pot" culture, a subject which fired her interest to the point where she thought of taking it up when she got home. It would give her a hobby, and with such "learned cooperators" as her sister and brother-in-law, great things might be achieved. She was also considering a strawberry bed, for she had always been a "good weeder."

It was a "great thing to have as many interests as possible," and people who worked with plants and flowers always seemed so happy and healthy. When in Paris, she had dined with Lord Lytton, the novelist's son, who had been a member of the fishing party at Knebworth twenty years before. She had loaned him a volume of poetry, and in his thank-you note he had complained of being "shut up" in his sickroom with rheumatism for weeks on end. In spite of his "wealth & position & talent," he apparently suffered from "two of the greatest evils in life: ill health and ennui." Elizabeth was determined not to succumb.

* * *

On the agenda for the Judge and Willie was a visit to the Garrick Club to see a fine collection of portraits of English actors and actresses. Interesting though the paintings

Two photographs from the family scrapbook: the Houses of Parliament (above) and the Tower of London (below).

were, Elizabeth's pleasure was spoiled by the appearance of an immense grey cat, which persisted in following them, notwithstanding the efforts of the servant to "shew" [sic] it away.

The next day at Swann and Edgar's, one of the imposing new mercantile establishments on Regent Street, her eyes lighted on a grey fur tippet. Stroking its soft, fine fur, she inquired of the "shopman" what kind it was.

"That, Madam," said he with apparent pride, "is the fur of the Angora cat."

Her sensations were "indescribable!"

* * *

No matter how often she visited London, she continued to be enthralled by the great city:

> The Haymarket Theatre is now closed, but its private entrance still affords amusement, for the theatre is doing its house cleaning, & I should like you to see the carpets on their way to be cleaned. When they throw them on the cart, a cloud of dust arises like a small simoom [a desert wind].
>
> We have just discovered that the door next to the stage entrance is the royal entrance. A few weeks ago the Prince of W[ales] arrived one night rather late with his children. The servants knocked & rang, but no one answered. At last the Prince, in a fit of impatience, jumped out himself & began to rap. Fancy the consternation of the servant on opening the door to find the "Heir Apparent" standing before him!

* * *

After a week, they all headed north to Yorkshire, the county from which the Chapman ancestors had come. They were amazed to discover that on most of the old cottages in the area grew the same white vine that at one time had covered the first little stone house of the Chapmans in Doylestown. Excitedly they played with the possibility that the custom had come down in the family ever since John Chapman the First's wife, Jane, had transplanted a living piece of home. "Poor Jane," Elizabeth wrote with her usual romantic zest, "torn from her peaceful vale to live in the wild western forests filled with naked Indians!"

After checking into the inn at Stanhope, Elizabeth looked up the sexton, who lived "hard by," and who was only too pleased to lead them into the graveyard and show them the Chapman tombstones. Shepherding them into the church, the sexton pointed out a stained-glass window that had been there when John Chapman left for America, and the stone font in which he and his forebears and his first children had been baptized. Presently the parish clerk arrived with the key to the vestry. Eagerly they gathered around the vestry table, and "concentrating all our energies," deciphered the old English handwriting in the ancient parish registry of births and deaths, while Papa took voluminous notes.

What a host of Chapmans had been baptized in that old church! They found the name on the first page of the oldest register—1575—and were convinced it would go much further back had an older registry existed. When they came to their direct ancestor John, "son of Lancelot & Isabella Chapman of Frosterly," a tiny village nearby, and knew "beyond all peradventure" that this "God-fearing man had been a baby in arms" in the very vestry in which they were seated, and that his baptism had been entered in the old book they were at that moment deciphering, it was "something quite startling."

Throughout these exciting revelations they refrained from mentioning to the sexton or the clerk that they were Chapmans, "not knowing how the name might stand there." Instead, they claimed their research was undertaken because "the gentleman of the party wished to collect information as to the Quaker families who had left...for America about the same time with W. Penn."

The old church near Frosterly, where the Chapmans researched their ancestry.

Back at the inn, Papa was beside himself. The name of his new house, "Willowmere," was to be changed immediately to "Frosterly." Fanny announced her intention of buying notepaper stamped with the new name as soon as they returned to London.

* * *

They continued on to the Trossachs in Scotland, where Willie left them briefly to visit a Mercer relative, before heading back to the States alone on the *Russia*. The last stop was Paris, where the Judge and his daughters indulged in epicurean meals and rode nightly along the Champs-Elysées and into the Bois to admire the spectacular lighting.

One afternoon Elizabeth went alone to the cemetery of Montparnasse, where she placed a wreath of flowers on the grave of Sainte-Beuve, the French poet who had died just six years before, to whom she felt she owed a "debt of gratitude" (after Scott and Byron) for helping to "chase away many a sad reflection." Even as she wrote about her lonely expedition, she thought it sounded faintly absurd, but realized it would give her pleasure to contemplate after she got home.

Before they left, she treated Ferdinando to a new suit of clothes. She thought he looked "really stunning" in them.

* * *

Back in the States that fall, she took Harry to Boston and settled him in at Harvard. They arrived a few days early and stayed at the Tremont House so that she could introduce him to some of her old friends. After Christmas she took Fanny with her to Washington. It was high time she got on with her new life.

16

WASHINGTON (1875–1881)

"If Blaine were a widower...."

Washington was an exciting place to be in the late 1870's. Suddenly conscious of its inferiority to other world capitals, the city was determined to become more civilized. Though still a muddy, provincial backwater, it showed signs of better things to come. Furthermore, the disruptive wounds of the Civil War had been mitigated by the optimistic mood resulting from the nation's Centennial celebration.

Returning to the world of diplomacy, Elizabeth took a little townhouse on "I" Street and settled in with Fanny each winter. In effect, she continued in Washington what she had been doing in Florence. She entertained and was entertained by all the important people—the Congressmen, the diplomats, the literati—at elegant parties that bubbled with good talk. A wealthy widow, still handsome, vivacious, and terribly *au courant*, she was bound to be popular.

In place of her beloved art galleries, she substituted the visitors' galleries of the House and Senate. Oblivious to the poor ventilation, she spent hours listening to the speeches, fascinated by the workings and—as she soon discovered to her dismay—the machinations of government.

At last the corrupt Grant administration was on its way out. The Democrats had nominated Samuel Tilden, the Governor of New York, who had destroyed the "Tweed gang." After a narrow defeat for Sen. James G. Blaine of Maine, who had been Speaker of the House for seven years, the Republicans were backing Rutherford B. Hayes, Governor of Ohio. The close contest between Tilden and Hayes kept Elizabeth in a state of suspense:

> The Democrats are very hopeful, & there is no question about it that there is a serious breaking away among the Republicans—like ice in a spring thaw. Everyone remarks it, & it is a thing one *feels* rather than sees. I believe Blaine attributes it all to Grant, who, he said the other night, has dragged the party down "with their heads in their hands & their hands in the dust."
>
> I asked Mr. Bayard [the Democratic Senator from Delaware] how he would feel after all these years of Republican tyranny & usurpation, to find himself once more in power. He answered: "Great happiness always makes me very quiet. I have such feeling of content that it effaces every other."
>
> Blaine, too, is tired out, & said to me confidentially the other day: "The fact is, I am tired of lugging a big load"—which meant the Republican party. Please don't repeat this, as everything gets into the papers nowadays. I intend this for the *home circle solely*.

* * *

When the votes were contested in South Carolina, Florida, Oregon, and Louisiana, and Congress created an Electoral Commission to sort them out, Elizabeth kept her father informed on the latest developments with hasty scribbles. One member of the Commission, she reported, came home one night in February "so discouraged and cross that he laid on the sofa the whole evening & no one dared to speak to him."

Cheered by an editorial in one newspaper that gave Tilden the edge, she had her hopes dashed when she read in another of the cross-examination of the Florida elector, which persuaded her that "the only hope ahead, dear Papa, is Oregon, & the fact that there are *two* electors there." Her quick letter closed with the news that, because of a bad cold, she was sending Fanny in her place to a dinner "given for Grant & all the grandees (!)." Although it was February, the weather was lovely, and she hoped it would stay that way for their projected excursion to Mount Vernon.

A friend urged Elizabeth not to despair about the outcome of the Electoral Commission's vote—"even if the iron has entered your soul & turned round & round like a corkscrew therein." One can imagine the shattered state of said soul when the final vote of the Electoral Commission came in: 8 for Hayes, 7 for Tilden. To Elizabeth's disgust, a Republican would continue to occupy the White House—albeit on a shaky footing.

* * *

James G. Blaine quickly became one of her closest friends. In spite of his Republicanism, the magnetic Senator from Maine was a native Pennsylvanian who as a young man had taught at a school for the blind in Philadelphia. How could she, of all people, resist his soubriquet, "The Plumed Knight"?

One Sunday he appeared on her doorstep bearing two books of poetry, and when settled in her cheerful parlor, proceeded to read selections to the two sisters. Elizabeth thought he had "beautiful taste" and "reads very well." When he had finished, he paid Fanny a number of compliments on her appearance at the Cadwaladers, and wound up by saying, "Miss Chapman, you ought never to wear but two colors—either black or white." Strangely enough, the sisters had recently come to the same conclusion.

He then turned the conversation to another favorite topic in Washington circles: poker! Now, a "full house" meant something other than a well-attended session of Congress:

> Blaine was in great excitement over an invitation he had received a day or two before to dine with the Plunketts—Mrs. P. ending her note with: "& perhaps you would not object to a little poker after dinner."
>
> "The idea of a public man playing poker here in Washington on Sunday," said Blaine, "Why, it would ruin him, & it will ruin their house if they attempt such a thing! I have written her two notes on the subject, & tonight I shall leave if they attempt it, but not before giving them some plain talk."
>
> He wound up with: "Just think of me doing regular missionary work in Washington!" The idea seemed to amuse him immensely.
>
> He then explained to us the game of "poker," & said it was one that no woman ought to soil her fingers by playing, & described a game of it he had once seen played in New York in which the stakes were $5,000 & even higher (I don't mean the stake but every throw or bet).
>
> He added that if it had not been for poker & the Emma mine, Schenck would very probably now occupy the place of Hayes. [Gen. Robert Schenck, Minister to the Court of St. James from 1871 to '76, had allowed his name to be used, for a consideration, to promote stock in the Emma silver mine, which proved to be fraudulent.]
>
> I never heard of *General Schenck's Rules of Poker* until Blaine told us of them on Sunday. He had the story from Schenck himself, who, it seems, had introduced the game one night at Lady Waldegrave's, who was perfectly delighted with it. At once it became the fashion & still is so among the fast-betting set in London.
>
> Lady W. asked General Schenck to write down the rules of the game, which he

did. They were handed about among her friends, a few copies were printed, & suddenly one fine morning London was full of *General Schenck's Rules of Poker*, which you can now buy everywhere.

It has about finished poor Schenck. I think he was played a very shabby trick by Lady W. I used to know him quite well, but he does not have much to say to me now, & I think feels shy of people.

The other night he came up, & apropos of something I have now forgotten, remarked that the line in Shakespeare which we now read: "Grapple him to thy heart with hooks of steel" was never printed so until this century, & that always before it was "hoops of steel." Did you know this? We both agreed that it must be a misprint in the early editions.

* * *

Various members of the family came to visit the Lawrence mènage, Lela, Mary's daughter, staying for weeks at a time. At eighteen her niece and namesake was about the same age as Fanny had been on her first trip to Florence, and according to the girl's not-unprejudiced aunt, she created an equal sensation in the capital's social circles:

Fanny (left) and EL (right, from a miniature now lost) in the 1870's. Marian Adams called them "jolly and handsome as ever."

Lela & Fanny went to the German Ambassador's Ball last night & had a perfect time.... [Lela] was taken out oftener than any girl in the room—excepting one [i.e., Fanny, who at thirty-two was still pretty and popular].

Fanny danced the Lancers with Hegermann [the Danish Minister], the Lascelles, etc. They all got it wrong, having forgotten the figures, & had a very amusing time. Hegermann says that at no time in his life could he learn the figures of the Lancers, & that long ago in Copenhagen the Queen, who loves a laugh, used always to send for him to make one in her quadrille just to laugh at his mistakes.

[Hiester] Clymer [a "staunch" Pennsylvania Democrat in the House] asked us yesterday, when leaving the House, to go into the Botanical Gardens. The palms & ferns there are beautiful. I told him of Willie's & Mary's love of trees & plants, which, it seems, he shares. He is on the Committe that attends to that department.

I asked him if he could show me the place where you [i.e., Papa] used to sit in the House, but he told me it was in the other House—the old one.

They are going to have [the Capitol] splendidly decorated—the dome gilded & the walls lined with Tennessee & black marble. I urged upon him taking away the bad pictures—he is on the Committee for decoration, & I think it will be done—not all, but three of them—the worst, for all are bad.

Tomorrow F. & I expect to be the entire day at the House. We enjoy this Winter even more than the last. It is perfectly delightful here. Lela has gone out to walk, Fanny to a breakfast at the Frelinghuysens, & when they return we are all going to the Fish's.

* * *

One of Elizabeth's many friends then living in Washington was the wife of the Danish Minister, Lillie de Hegermann (née Lillie Greenough of Boston). Though Elizabeth was a romantic, and Lillie a pragmatist, the two friends saw eye-to-eye on a number of subjects. They continually bemoaned the lack of theaters and other "public entertainments" which were to be found in such profusion in other capitals, leaving them with only their "social pleasures" to fall back upon.

The two irrepressible ladies therefore organized a club: "The National Rational International Dining Club" (N.R.I. for short). Lillie was its president; Elizabeth, vice-president; Carl Schurz (Secretary of the Interior) was treasurer; Kurt von Schlözer (the German Minister) was sergeant-at-arms; and Johan de Hegermann (Lillie's husband) had the difficult (Schurz called it "onerous") job of "recognizing and calling attention to the jokes, which in his conscientious attempts to seize, he often loses entirely"![1] The other members of the N.R.I. Dining Club, without official duties, were Fanny, Count Dönhoff (Secretary to the German Legation), and Aristarchi Bey (the Turkish Minister), who was an exceedingly popular man-about-town.

The purpose of the club was a simple one: When the members discovered they had a free evening, they would congregate at one another's houses for a dinner governed by a strict set of rules. The "rational" part of the exercise was the menu. They were permitted one soup, one roast, one vegetable, and one dessert. Even that much food was hardly needed, for there was generally more laughing than eating. The meal was always to be accompanied by two wines, one of which, according to the rules, had to be *"good."* The centerpiece for the table was invariably a stuffed goose from the Smithsonian Institution, sent over on the day of the dinner to the person who was hosting it. After the repast there was always music. Schurz and von Schlözer took turns at the piano, and Lillie sang. The audience never failed to be highly appreciative.

The club's laws and by-laws were inscribed on large sheets of "foolscap," with a huge, official-looking seal. Carl Schurz, as treasurer, had possession of the impressive document. Sometimes at non-N.R.I. dinner parties, if a few club members happened to be present, he would produce it from an inside pocket and peruse it "with the greatest attention," causing the uninitiated at table to speculate about "what important matter was going on in politics." The club members present had a hard time keeping a straight face. Then, when he had every eye "fastened on him," Schurz would put the paper back in his pocket with great deliberation, bestowing upon his fellow members a "sly wink." According to Lillie, it was a masterful performance.

* * *

Always on the *qui vive* for a new experience, one night at an N.R.I. Club dinner Elizabeth, Fanny, and Lillie cornered Carl Schurz and begged permission to sit in on a "conclave of Indians"[2] he, as Secretary of the Interior, was scheduled to conduct the following day. With some reluctance he gave his consent.

When the interpreter was told the next morning that ladies were to be present, he ordered the Indians to don striped shirts, which they insisted on wearing—not over their bare torsos—but over their buckskin trousers! As they filed out of the "clothes shop," they caused a sensation.

Their bare arms were rimmed with bracelets, colorful blankets were slung from their shoulders, braids of black hair hung down on either side of their faces, topped by huge feather headdresses, and each clutched a tomahawk. The three ladies were agog as the Indians filed into Schurz's office.

Sitting in a semicircle around the Secretary, tomahawks on the floor by their sides, they remained silent while their interpreter spoke. Then Schurz engaged the other members of his committee (the so-called "Under-Shirts") in earnest discussion. While this was going on, the Chief, suddenly aware of Fanny's good looks and sparkling jewelry, stared at her between outspread fingers.

Finally Schurz turned back to the interpreter and said, "I cannot accept." When this was translated, there was a "burst of wild Indian," with the Chief holding forth in a "deep bass voice." The fascinated ladies presumed he was "giving pieces of his mind" to the Secretary, which were translated in a "milder form."

Lillie de Hegermann, "prosaic to her fingertips," thought the Indians looked "conceited, brutal, and obstinate." Elizabeth, on the other hand, thought they looked "high-spirited and noble"—further proof to Lillie that her friend "looked at everything in a rosy, sentimental light." Although the three ladies were glad to get away from the "barbarous-looking people," they agreed they had had a "very interesting" time of it.

* * *

Among the new arrivals in Washington in the late 1870's were Marian and Henry Adams. The son of Charles Francis Adams (who had been Minister in London when Bigelow was in Florence), Henry had been assistant professor of history at Harvard, but left to resume his writing career. The paths of the two families, the Adamses and the Lawrences, had crisscrossed for years.

Taking up residence on Lafayette Square, the Adamses established a "salon." Their "little breakfasts," teas, and "intimate dinners," as the "feminine correspondents"[3] called them, were the envy of all who were not included. In the select inner circle were Elizabeth and Fanny.

Although Marian Adams refused to give interviews and was fairly successful at dodging the society columnists, they concocted such statements as: "The twenty wax tapers of the chandelier would light up to advantage the superb oriental Worth gown of Mrs. Bigelow Lawrence" or "their glow would fall upon the peripatetic Jack Gardners of Boston."[4]

Henry Adams, photographed by his wife, Marian, on the garden steps at 1607 H Street, Washington. Adams used EL (who lived nearby) as the model of the heroine in *Democracy*, his best-selling novel. *Courtesy of the Massachusetts Historical Society.*

In the spring of 1879 the Adamses went to Europe to research a book Henry was writing and rented their country house at Beverly Farms (just north of Boston) to Elizabeth for the summer. Marian Adams (letter writer *par excellence*, as well as an amateur photographer) begged Elizabeth to help herself to their woodpile, for unless she burned it, it would only "decay and go to waste."[5]

Before leaving for Europe, Henry Adams turned over to his publisher a novel he had just completed titled *Democracy*. The book instantly became a best-seller and was destined to become a classic, considered by many to be one of the most authentic novels of Washington politics ever written. Since it was first published anonymously in 1880, guessing the identity of the author and of the real-life counterparts of the fictional characters quickly became a favorite Washington pastime.

Adams, who thoroughly enjoyed the brouhaha, refused to divulge his authorship until very late in life because, as his publisher finally revealed in the 1925 edition, "some of his characters were carefully drawn from prominent living persons who were friends, and some of these he touched humorously and ironically. The principal characters represented were Mrs. Bigelow Lawrence and her sister, Miss Fanny Chapman, Miss Emily Beale, James Lowndes, and James G. Blaine."[6]

That Mrs. Bigelow Lawrence immediately recognized herself there can be no doubt. *Democracy* is the story of a sophisticated, wealthy, well-traveled widow named Madeleine Lee [i.e., Elizabeth], who takes a house in Washington for the winter to learn how democracy and the American system of government really work. She is accompanied by Sybil Ross [i.e., Fanny], her pretty, extroverted sister, who is considerably younger. The witty, *soignée* Mrs. Lee makes a point of being *au courant*, reading all the newspapers, Congressional speeches, and books on political philosophy. When she entertains Congressmen, cabinet ministers, and ambassadors at her elegant teas and dinner parties, she takes an intense interest in her guests' conversation. An idealist who finds the political skulduggery pervading the government abhorrent, the heroine desires to use her wealth to achieve power and influence—and thereby generate reforms.

In one scene she attends a reception at the White House, where she is horrified by the lack of culture and refinement. The President (thought to be a composite of the uncouth Lincoln, the earthy Grant, and the indifferent Hayes), was depicted by Adams as a bumbling bumpkin. Even more stinging was the satire on the President's wife. On becoming mistress of the White House, Mrs. Hayes had cast out the wine, billiards, and cards enjoyed by its previous occupant and had required the ladies to wear high necks and long sleeves. At the fictional reception in *Democracy* Madeleine Lee, accustomed to the worldly courts of Europe, finds all this "provincial morality" highly amusing.

Other characters in the book could be recognized as belonging to the Lawrence–Adams circle. Victoria Dare, for instance, was spotted as Emily Beale, the unconventional daughter of Gen. Beale, who lived in the Decatur house on Lafayette Square, where she could often be seen leading an enormous staghound on a leash. Baron Jacobi was patterned after the popular Aristarchi Bey. He was depicted as an old-world cynic, who thought that Americans considered themselves beyond the scope of universal laws, and that given another hundred years, the United States would be more corrupt than Rome under Caligula.

Above all there was Senator Ratcliffe, a thin disguise for James G. Blaine, with his steely eyes and magnetic personality. In Adams's novel the Senator courts the attractive Madeleine Lee, who nearly marries him. When she discovers that he has used questionable means to achieve his political ends, she sends him packing. On her front doorstep the Senator is given a caning by Baron Jacobi.

Democracy ends with Madeleine Lee taking off in disgust for an extended stay in Europe, accompanied by her sister.

The love story in the novel—the Senator's courtship of the heroine—must have caused a stir, for Blaine's frequent appearances at the little house on "I" Street had not gone unnoticed. Marian Adams wrote her father: "Simple Mrs. Bigelow Lawrence! I'm curious to see her course as to Blaine; it was thought last spring here that if Blaine were a widower, she would not long be a widow."[7]

Far from being a widower, Blaine had a devoted wife who, understandably, spent her time running households in Maine and Washington, teeming with six children, assorted servants, and a demanding husband. Harriet Blaine once wrote a daughter that she was "never intended for anything but an old-fashioned woman, all hands; the modern idea, and the better, is to be the head, and let others serve for hands."[8] Whether or not she had Elizabeth in mind, Harriet's hands continued to smoothe the wrinkles of the Blaine household, while the master thereof turned to Elizabeth's head for advice and understanding:

> The morning after the [Bayards'] party, Nichols [her houseman] came into the parlor to say that Mr. Blaine was below & wished to speak with me.
>
> I went down & found the Senator, who said he wanted to speak with me on some private business of his own. It was to ask me to listen to his speech on Zac[k] Chandler, which he was to deliver in the Senate that morning, & which he held in manuscript in his hand.
>
> We sat down, & he at once commenced reading it. I really think I never heard anything finer. I never expected to shed a tear over Zac[k] Chandler [Senator from

Senator James G. Blaine. EL liked him "better & better,..." as she saw "from year to year how firm his friendship continues...." *Library of Congress.*

Michigan, a radical Republican and Abolitionist who had recently died], but I was forced to, while listening to Mr. Blaine's eloquent words. It made, I hear, a profound impression in the Senate, & is thought to be one of the finest addresses ever delivered there.

As soon as he finished he put on his hat & left. I think he has very nearly forgotten the Maine trouble—all he said about it was that they threatened to burn his house & shoot him, etc., but that he had gone about all the same & unconcerned, being quite convinced that "the way to meet danger was to face it."

He is a tremendously big man, & as John Hay [Undersecretary of State] was saying last night, there is no one in this country who has so many warm devoted friends as he has. If it were not for his ambition [to be President], he would be a great man, but I am afraid that both head & heart are more or less subject to that. He asked after yourself [Papa] and all at home.

Blaine's apparent respect for Elizabeth's keenness, and his pleasure in her company could not fail to cause Harriet an occasional pang. In August 1879, she wrote a daughter from Augusta, Maine:

I am just through with a great scare, it is this, it is this! Your Father had a note from Mrs. L this morning, to the intent that she and Mrs. F [undoubtedly meant to be Miss F] would pass through town on their way from Mt Desert and would be glad to see him at the station.

Of course he went down all prepared to bring them back with him, but luckily for me, Mr. C, Mrs. L's father, is due this morning, so I had the satisfaction inexpressible, as I was watching stealthily from the sitting room window, to see your Father driven up in state by Frederick, but no lovely bonnets or feminine hats brightening the void at his side.

For the heat is intense, and to sit through all the hours of this scorching day, in one of my many black dresses, not thoroughly interested for one moment, but wearisomely polite in every one, seems, now that I know it will not have to be, more than I could bear.[9]

Even more dismaying was Harriet's discovery on Christmas Eve that her husband had expected to spend the next day "with Mrs. Lawrence at Doylestown," but one of the Blaine children "made such a fuss about his leaving our already diminished family for Christmas, that he gave it up, so now we have all to make an effort to keep him in good humor.[10]

Blaine's wife was not Elizabeth's idea of a scintillating dinner guest. One night when Harriet "fell off" [i.e., "fell off the roof," indicating the onset of the menstrual period, when Victorian ladies usually stayed home], she had to regret a dinner party at the last minute. "In despair," the hostess asked Elizabeth to bring Lela, who was visiting, to fill the empty place at table. Observing her niece chatting merrily away with Sir Edward Thornton, the English Minister who took her in to dinner, she had no doubt Sir E. was "very glad" to have Lela as a "substitute" for poor Harriet.

* * *

Visiting family were kept busy:

> .... last evening Mr. Pendleton [the Senator from Ohio who had served with Papa in the House] took me to table.... The French Minister sat on the other side of me, & Gen. Sherman on the other side of Fanny. We came home afterwards & took Lela to a young party at Mrs. Berry's. Each girl was to wear white muslin & some particular flower. Lela wore some beautiful water lillies, which we found yesterday on the Avenue....
>
> We are trying to get Willie to go with Harry to the tavern where the Indians are staying & see them, but he does not seem to care to do it.

After graduating from Harvard, Harry followed in his grandfather's footsteps by reading law, in Philadelphia. Often his holidays were spent in Washington with his aunt, who procured for him invitations to the important social and diplomatic functions. As she watched him maneuver his way around, singling out the prettiest girls in the capital's drawing rooms and ballrooms, she was convinced he was not only extraordinarily handsome, but had a "marked aristocratic look."

* * *

Elizabeth was continually shocked by the straitened circumstances of the Southerners she encountered, though the Civil War had been over for fifteen years:

> F. & I dined at the Pendletons on Tuesday. A delicious dinner—Gen. Butler of S. Carolina took me to table. He is a very agreeable man, & a very handsome one. He spoke of the poverty of the Southern members of Congress, & said that he did not believe there was one of them [who] could afford to give a dinner.

Gen. Butler said the happiest time of his life was during the War, & although he lost his leg in it, & all his fortune, yet he did not seem to regard it as an unmixed evil, & among other things he said it taught each man who was in it "just how much he really amounted to."

He said that if he could have just enough to live comfortably in the country with a good library & secure from the harrassments of debt, that was all he would ask of fortune.

As he said this, I thought with pleasure of Frosterly & Aldie.

* * *

Although Elizabeth put her usual effort into making her own dinner parties a success, there were occasional snags. At one elaborate affair, for instance, there were several bad moments, the first occurring just before the guests arrived. At five minutes of seven she and Fanny went "nearly wild" over a pair of Argand lamps, both of which looked as though they were on the verge of going out. Fortunately the houseman remedied the trouble, and the lamps glowed through the evening with a lovely effect under their rose-colored shades, which Fanny had bought in Paris.

Then Gen. Sherman was ten minutes late, due to a business engagement, he said as he rushed in out of breath. He was so charming, "almost boyish with his stern war-worn face," she quickly forgave him.

Once again there was a difficulty with the fish course, just as there had been in London nearly thirty years before, at her first formal dinner party:

> The dinner was deliciously cooked. I really think I never ate a better one. One of the dishes was some fresh mushrooms from New York.... There was but one *contre-temps:* Sammy, the head waiter, forgot the cucumbers with the fish—a dish which cost $4.50, & there they still stand in the ice chest.
>
> Fortunately, however, there was so much else with the fish that they were not missed, but his forgetfulness nearly finished Sammy, I hear, who could eat no supper in consequence, & said to Julia that he would not have had it happen for $100.
>
> I don't intend to scold the old fellow, as all the rest passed off so well, but if it had been boiled salmon in place of filet of rock fish, I think there would have been an explosion on my part.
>
> I am so thankful to have had the Outreys (the French Minister and his wife) here to a dinner that I think was as good as the one I ate in their house, for last Winter I was far from satisfied with the one I gave them, & this last night has wiped the other out.

Even Lady Thornton, the wife of the English Minister, thanked her for a "charming evening." She had never been heard to do such a thing before.

After dinner Elizabeth had a long talk with Sen. Pendleton, who told her some "very astonishing things" about the Lincoln regime. The conversation turned up a curious coincidence, which she relayed to Papa with considerable relish:

> Do you remember an old servant I once had in Boston, that I used to call Edward the Martyr because his wife once came to my house drunk, & threw flat irons at him in the kitchen, & he rushed to me in the drawing room for protection?
>
> Well, this same man afterwards lived with Mrs. Lincoln at the White House, &

I once saw him there on the occasion of a very select ball, & he got me into the supper room, when all the rest of the world had to wait outside until their turn came.

Mr. Pendleton told me last night the following fact, in which the above named Edward was involved.

A very important message of Mr. Lincoln to Congress found itself in the *N.Y. Tribune* before it reached the latter body [i.e., Congress] & a committee was called to investigate the matter, of which Mr. Pendleton was one.

While they were one day in session, there was a knock at the door, & who should appear but Mr. Lincoln himself, who addressed the committee in these words: "I am told that Mrs. Lincoln is suspected of having sold my message to the *N.Y. Tribune*. She tells me that she did not do it. I believe her—but *I do not know!*"

After saying this, the President retired, leaving the committee rooted to the spot with astonishment.

The following day the butler at the White House (none else than Edward the Martyr) appeared before the committee & avowing to his confession, which he made then & there, acknowledged that it was *he* who had sold the message (or rather, that portion of the message about Slavery which had appeared in the *N.Y. Tribune*).

[He said] that Mr. Lincoln had come down one morning very early, & had told him to go back & get a paper which he had left in his bedroom & bring it to him— that he had done so, *had read the slavery portion on his way to Mr. Lincoln's room*—wrote it down, & sold *it to the Tribune!*

This likely story the committee were called upon to swallow, & a short time afterwards Mr. Edward was given a captaincy in the army!!

When Mr. Pendleton had finished, I exclaimed: "Why, that Edward was once a servant of mine, & once flew to me for protection from his wife!"

"Why," said Mr. Pendleton, "I now remember the day he appeared before the committee, he had a black eye, which we were told had been given him by his wife!"

* * *

Washington social circles were continually enlivened by distinguished visitors, who poured into the new station near the Capitol:

Last night I dined at Mrs. Bancroft's. The dinner was given to Mrs. [John Jacob] Astor, & it was a very distinguished party. Gen. Sherman took me to table, & I sat between him & Mr. Bayard.

The dinner was at $1/2$ [after] six o'clock, & the Blaines... never arrived until ten minutes past seven. They had made a mistake, thinking the dinner was at seven, & felt awfully when they found it out.

Blaine said he would not apologize just then, but write a note after he got home, which he doubtless did, & one that smoothed down Mrs. Bancroft's feathers entirely, although they were considerably ruffled, as she came up to me after we had been waiting for half an hour & said, "Well, I certainly shall not vote for Mr. Blaine for President."

I think Blaine was a good deal quenched by the above circumstance, & although he sat between Mrs. Astor & Mrs. Morton, I never heard his laugh once.

Gen. Sherman was very agreeable. He spoke about War & its horrors, & how sad it made him to think that loads of young fellows today in the South were being brought up with the burning desire to one day emulate Stonewall Jackson, etc., & all the troubles it might lead to in the next generation.

After the dinner I stopped at home for the girls [Fanny & Lela], & we went to the Evarts [he was Secretary of State], where there was a brilliant reception. I had a long talk with Mr. Astor. He goes every summer to Carlsbad to get rid of his propensity for gaining flesh. He was there last summer, but has now lost all the good he gained there, having steadily gained a pound a week since his return, & now weighs 24 lbs. more than he did when he arrived.

We spoke of the Emperor of Russia. He said he thought he was broken down by the tremendous strain of responsibility—that few men ever lived who could sustain it. As he said this, I thought of the millions that were weighing on Mr. Astor's own shoulders, & what a burden it must be to *him*.

At the Legation on Thursday night Mrs. Astor wore a tremendous display of diamonds. They say she carried $300,000 about her person, & most of them as large as ten cent pieces; string upon string surrounded her neck & were strung across her corsage. She was one tremendous blaze. They say Wormley [a Washington hotel owner] is in a great state of anxiety at having such a load of jewels in his house.

Mr. Bayard was quite disgusted by the display, but I told him that was only one side of Mrs. Astor, & that there was another side, which was equally blazing, in charitable works & goodness of heart. Last night he told me he had met Mrs. Astor at dinner the night before, & was entirely of my opinion about her, & that she might wear just as many diamonds as she pleased.

* * *

A young ladies' luncheon, which Elizabeth gave for Fanny's and Lela's friends was "an immense success." It began at ten-thirty. The bill of fare included "oysters on the shell, bouillon, patés of chicken, lobsters on the silver shells, croquettes & green peas, asparagus, quails, & salad, & ice cream in the form of 14 little swans."

At each plate there was a bunch of roses tied with alternate pink and blue ribbons. And instead of place cards, the girls had bought fourteen little fans with "cane sticks," on which they painted the guests' names.

The girls laughed from beginning to end, and after lunch trooped upstairs to the parlor, sat in a circle, and told stories for an hour.

* * *

Witticisms, anecdotes, and amusing stories circulated as freely in Washington as they had in Florence:

We see a good deal of Jenny McLane, our next-door neighbor. She told such a funny story the other day of one of her friends in Paris, who one day bought in the street the tiniest dog she had ever seen, carried it home, & was sitting with it in her lap, when it suddenly jumped away from her &—ran up the curtain! It turned out to be a *cat*, made by some French ingenuity to look like a little dog.

* * *

There were two topics of dinner-table conversation on which Elizabeth discovered she could not trust herself to speak. One was the "*Memoires* of Mme. de Remusat," which was causing a great outcry, especially among the French in Washington, and which belittled her hero Napoleon:

> I have just finished the 2nd volume, & I am more disgusted than with the first one. You would think she was writing about some petty, cruel little scoundrel, in place of the greatest genius of modern times. Talleyrand seems to have been her guide, & the one man she trusted. This fact does not speak very well for her discrimination of character.
> Mr. Outrey [the French Minister] does not believe them & while he admits Bonaparte's great faults, yet thinks it absurd to draw him as a villain & omit his genius entirely.
> .... Doubtless if there had been such a woman at the Courts either of Caesar or Alexander, she would have written just such a book. Barring the beautiful style, don't you think, dear Papa, that the undercurrent of the book is much the same as you find in the evidence of servants when they come to testify in court about their lords & masters?

She agreed with her father that Metternich's memoirs were also disappointing, and that he "gave a false impression of his conversations with Napoleon." Why did people persist in ignoring the great man's abilities?

* * *

The other topic on which she tried, with difficulty, to remain silent was the Fitz-John Porter case. After the second Battle of Bull Run, Col. Porter had been accused of refusal to obey orders. Tried by court-marital, he had been cashiered. Now seventeen years later, Porter's friends, believing he had been made a scapegoat of the defeat, had procured a new hearing of his case in Congress.

He had been a staunch supporter of McClellan's, and any friend of the General's was *ipso facto* a friend of Elizabeth's. Daily she sat for hours in the gallery of the Senate listening to the testimony. One day as she was coming down the steps of the Capitol, she saw Porter nearby, looking "so old & grey & pale." Impulsively she rushed up to him, introduced herself as a friend of McClellan's, and told him she wished him success from the bottom of her heart. He grasped her hand "most warmly," thanked her for her interest, and said he thought he would succeed in proving his innocence.

Elizabeth scrutinized every shred of evidence with the shrewdness of a trial lawyer, one day sitting in bed from 10 A.M. to 5 P.M. in order to familiarize herself with every detail. The more she read, the more convinced she became that Porter was the victim of "lies," and that a "flagrant" wrong had been done to him—although his letters criticizing "that jackass Pope," his superior officer, were not going to help.

Everyone was talking about it, she fumed, but "not one soul is informing themselves by reading about it." She vowed they wouldn't "throw dust" in her eyes! She would be ready to "answer some of these lies." But not at the dinner table. Seated near Gen. Burnside and Gen. Devens one night, she was told that Porter had been "scared by the dust of ambulance wagons"—when she knew for a fact that Gen. Lee himself had testified that "he was in front of Porter with his full command."

Swallowing her retort with difficulty, she deftly switched the conversation to Shakespeare's "borrowing of phrases" in order to avoid what she was sure would have escalated into a "disagreeable scene." In all her life Elizabeth had never "come in contact with such audacious lying," and it made her "blood boil." Whenever she sat in the Senate gallery, she felt as though "Justice & Truth were being dragged through the mire."

One day Porter came to call on her and poured out his story to his sympathetic listener. By the time he took his leave, he and his hostess had also enjoyed airing their mutual admiration for Gen. McClellan.

Congress adjourned without acting on Porter's case. It was not until a much later session that he was finally restored to the Army and placed on the retired list—without compensation.

"I still continue to be disgusted with politics," Elizabeth sputtered, adding in mixed syntax, "Every man, or nearly all, seem to be busy grinding his own axe—nothing seems to be decided on its own merits." Echoes of Madeleine Lee, Henry Adams's disillusioned heroine!

* * *

Another of her friends—Carl Schurz—was having his troubles, too, involving the Indian Commissioner. Though he told Elizabeth at one of the N. R. I. Dining Club affairs that he had been "laying [sic] awake at nights," yet she watched him "going about in society as bright & agreeable as ever." The fact is, she was forced to conclude, that "no public man in the country can get on at all without great nerve."

Carl Schurz's informal pose emphasizes the long legs frequently featured in political cartoons. This photograph of the colorful German-American who became Secretary of the Interior—and member of EL's gala "National Rational International Dining Club"—was discovered among the papers at Fonthill.

When it was Elizabeth's turn to entertain the club that spring, the evening lived up to expectations, in spite of the fact that Lillie de Hegermann had a cold and could not sing.

To compensate, Schurz and von Schlözer played the piano more delightfully than usual, and Mama's recipe for white sauce with the pheasants was greatly admired.

Schurz kept his audience spellbound with the story of a Ute chief whose young son had been stolen from him while he was "in battle" nearly twenty years before. During his conversation with the chief, Schurz suddenly remembered having heard of a young Ute who was living with one of the tribes in the Indian reservation, and telegraphed for a description. It fitted the chief's description of his long-lost son—with one exception: The young man had no dimples! Schurz and the Ute chief decided that he might have outgrown them, so a telegram was sent summoning him to Washington. In a few days the chief and the boy would meet. "Is it not Charley Ross over again?" she asked, referring to a famous case of a boy's disappearance back in 1874.

When it was Schurz's turn to entertain the club, the "good" wine specified by the rules turned out to be a Johannesburger. Without question it was the best wine Elizabeth had ever drunk, and the other revelers agreed with her. It seemed as though "all the flavor & strength of an entire vineyard" had been concentrated in it. Whereupon their host informed them that he had had three bottles of it orignally, but imagine his disgust when he discovered that two of those "precious" bottles had been served by mistake one evening to a gathering of "rough westerners!"

* * *

When Aristarchi Bey, the "nice & gentlemanly" Turkish Minister, entertained the club, he brought out after dinner a number of "curious things" to show them. There was a photograph of his grandfather, with a "great high turban" like the one worn by the Grand Vizier in the *Arabian Nights*; and the handle of his father's sword—a white sapphire, for which Aristarchi had been offered a large sum of money by a well-known Paris jeweler.

It was rumored that his brother ("who we all know quite intimately") was in "great trouble & disgrace" in Constantinople. Since he held a high office under the Sultan, he was in danger of "losing his head."

* * *

Thomas Gold Appleton put in an appearance. Since the Aldie housewarming party, he had injured both legs and had shocked some proper Bostonians by receiving callers stretched out on a mattress in his library, his shirt open in Byronesque fashion almost to his navel.

He told Elizabeth that someone at the hotel had just asked him if he had ever been told he looked like Daniel Webster.

"No," said Tom, "I have been thought to resemble Napoleon Bonaparte, Lord Byron, & the Virgin Mary, but never Daniel Webster."

Going upstairs after dinner, they discovered that one of the new lamps had been smoking for at least an hour, and the front parlor was so black with smoke they could not sit in it. "Fancy if there had been a dinner party!"

Appleton stopped a few days later to say good-bye, and to ask if the sisters would accompany him to California in May. "We declined, & he at once abandoned the project."

* * *

It was becoming increasingly difficult to find anyone who remembered George Washington. General Joe Johnston told the sisters one evening that when he was a boy, he spent considerable time in Alexandria, Virginia, where he talked with a number of people who distinctly remembered the great man. One of them recalled a meeting at which General Washington spoke. Feeling was running high, and one of the crowd interrupted the speech to call out, "That is a lie." There was an immediate uproar:

> In an instant the friends of Washington threw themselves on the wretch, & would have torn him to pieces, when Washington himself jumped down from the platform, seized the fellow, drew him to him, & held him there with his arm around him until the tumult ceased. Was not this great?

* * *

Blaine stopped by one evening, "pleasant & friendly as ever." Again he was seeking the Presidential nomination, but he seemed not to have much hope. Elizabeth was convinced Grant would be back in the White House for a third term: "You should see the Grant wire-pullers, grouped together in knots on the floor of the Senate!" She wanted to throw her boot at them! Everyone foresaw "tremendous times" at the coming Presidential election. Elizabeth was concerned, for she thought Blaine looked "far from well":

> . . . . it is really astonishing how much he has aged since last November, when I saw him in N. York. Added to his worn look, one of his eyes has been blood-shot for more than three months, & I really think he is very much out of health.
>
> His spirits, too, are poor, & he often sits & listens in place of leading the conversation, as he always used to do. I would not be at all surprised if he had had quite a serious attack last December in Augusta, which was at first telegraphed, & afterwards hushed up in the papers. I wish he could get away & have a rest, for he seems to be literally worn out.
>
> I do not think it is the Presidential contest that disquiets him so much as his own health. One night at his own house I saw him fall asleep for two or three minutes in the midst of a very interesting conversation that was going on around him.

When the dust of the 1880 election subsided, and Garfield won the Presidency, Blaine was named Secretary of State. Elizabeth asked Carl Schurz what he thought of the selection:

> He said he thought Blaine, if he kept clear of Presidential aspirations, might make a first-rate Secretary, but that otherwise he might make a great deal of trouble, & it might be very bad.
>
> I agree with Mr. S., Mr. Blaine is very strong, with great courage & a great deal of ability. Personally I like him better & better as I see from year to year how firm his friendship continues to me & mine, but he loves to make a sensation, & like the petrel, his element is in the storm—so when the Treaty of Washington & other international matters come up, there is no betting how he will deal with them.

17

CAPITAL ENTERTAINING (1881–1884)

"As age steals on, one can do nothing except to keep many interests."

In January 1881 a Washington newspaper, *Capital*, reported that "Mrs. Sallie Ward Armstrong is coming here with a superb wardrobe and is expected to make a sensation."[1] Marian Adams's reaction to Sallie's heralded arrival was succinct: "A curious juxtaposition for Mrs. Bigelow Lawrence!" In a letter to her father, she wondered if "the Kentucky lady" would " put up at Wormley's," (the same hotel in which Mrs. Astor had stayed).

There had been lean times for Sallie after the Civil War, living with her son in an apartment over her husband's office in a dreary, war-straitened Louisville. Within a few years her second husband, Dr. Hunt, died. Somehow Sallie managed to hang on to her diamonds. She also managed an occasional trip to New York, where she was spotted at the splendid Fifth Avenue Hotel, paying $12.50 a day for herself and a maid, and a dollar a day extra for tea and toast in her room! It was thought highly indiscreet of her to be seen in a hotel wearing ten to twenty thousand dollars worth of diamonds!

When she was nearly fifty, in June 1876, she married again. Her third husband was Venerando Politza Armstrong, generally called Vene. Apparently the marriage caught Louisville by surprise, for the papers referred to it as a "Sensation in Society." The groom—"kind, clever, jovial, and warm-hearted"[2]—was a member of a firm of pork packers. The newlyweds went to the Centennial Exposition in Philadelphia on their wedding trip.

Less than a year later, Armstrong died, leaving most of his fortune to Sallie. Now, here was Sallie Ward Lawrence Hunt Armstrong, widow, in the capital, "with a superb wardrobe." Inevitably, in a town like Washington, the paths of the first and second Mrs. Lawrence must have crossed, try as they might to avoid it. However, no mention has come to light of such a potentially dramatic meeting between two ladies hardly noted for their diffidence. Furthermore, there is only one mention by Elizabeth (after her marriage) to the Sallie era in her husband's life: discreet and properly oblique, it is a glancing reference to "Bigelow's trouble."

Even Marian Adams, in her chatty letters, skips further comment, adding only that "Mrs. Lawrence and Miss Chapman are jolly and handsome as ever, and drop in a good deal at tea time."[3] At least one concludes that the sisters had forgiven Henry Adams for putting them into his wickedly satirical novel.

* * *

Another object of lively gossip that winter was "Hosscar" Wilde, as Washingtonians referred to the flamboyant playwright. Marian Adams passed him one day on Pennsylvania Avenue, his long hair flowing, dressed in stockings and tights, wearing "a brown plush tunic, a big yellow sunflower pinned above his heart, a queer cap on his head, . . . [and] a large blue card on his back [saying] 'Oscar on a wild toot.' "[4]

* * *

An invitation to dine at Col. Jerome Bonaparte's was accepted enthusiastically by Elizabeth. He was the grandson of Napoleon's brother, the King of Westphalia, whose first marriage to Elizabeth Patterson of Baltimore had been annulled after the birth of a child.

The Colonel's house was huge, and impossible to keep warm, until he "sent to Baltimore for a furnace man," who said the trouble was that the servants had been "putting on too much coal," burning at the rate of a ton every four days! This had, indeed, proved to be the problem, and since then the house had been "very comfortable."

In the center of the table was a large silver eagle, which the imaginative Elizabeth presumed was the centerpiece motif for the dinner tables of the entire Bonaparte family throughout the world. While she devoured the best food she had ever eaten in Washington, her host told her he had "great dread" of communism in France.

"The sorriest thing" he had to do in life, Col. Bonaparte continued over the delectable dessert, was to write to the Empress Eugénie, still living in exile in England. Seeing her in person was even worse. The Emperor had died in 1873, and her only son had been killed over a year ago fighting with the British army in Zululand. For a long time the bereaved lady would see no one except her maid and the sympathetic Queen Victoria. Her friends had urged the poor Empress to go to Zululand, "hoping it might rouse her." When she returned, bringing with her her son's body, she had been "somewhat better, but still very, very wretched." She had left Chislehurst, the Colonel reported, and "gone to another country house in England to live."

Remembering Eugénie's eyes at the French Embassy reception in London more than twenty-five years before, Elizabeth was sure they were even sadder now.

* * *

Following the inauguration of Garfield on March 4, Elizabeth sailed back to Europe, accompanied this time not only by Fanny, Rose, and Ferdinando's successor, but also by her niece Lela, who was to be treated to the same deep immersion into history and art to which Fanny had been subjected.

From London they all went to Paris in time to see the horse chestnut trees in bloom, staying as usual at the Hotel Meurice. Naturally there was shopping at Worth; *The Magic Flute* and *Les Contes d'Hoffman* at the Opéra Comique; the circus at the Hippodrome. Driving through the disreputable old Latin Quarter one afternoon, they found it patrolled by police five abreast. Lela was impressed that her Aunt Lela was totally unafraid, even enjoying the potentially dangerous situation.

Another day the three ladies walked across the Rue Royale to the terrace of the Tuileries gardens, where a "charity fair" was in progress. The booths were all manned by prominent actresses and "fashionable beauties." Quite the most picturesque sight was the celebrity in red stockings and yellow shoes who led a donkey with two paniers on his back, one overflowing with cherries, the other with red roses, which she was selling with notable success. She was rivaled as a saleslady only by the Princess Metternich, who looked like an elegantly attired monkey. Elizabeth bought quantities of spring flowers from her.

On the travelers journeyed to Schwabach, near Nuremberg, where they found only one other American, a Mrs. Westinghouse, whose husband "invented the air-break *[sic]*." Her blond wig of tight little curls captured all eyes, as did her low-cut pale silks. Even more startling were the two ladies-in-waiting she had in tow. It was said that whenever she entered the main salon, she tipped the band to serenade her!

Shortly after their arrival, Elizabeth had a pleasant surprise. Gen. McClellan and his wife appeared and persuaded her to continue on with them, while Fanny and Lela returned to tour England and Scotland with friends.

Elizabeth spent some time in Rome, then of course in Florence, where she "had her fill for a long while of the old pictures & places." Suddenly she was beset by a desire to "settle down at Aldie & my little house in Washington," having "embraced every chance to see on this side [of the ocean] what cannot be seen on the other."

One factor in her sharp attack of homesickness was the death on September 19 of President Garfield, who had lingered all summer from his wound. Recollections of another President's death from an assassin's bullet, when she had also been in Italy, must have come flooding back.

She had been startled to read that it was Secretary of State Blaine who had driven the President to the railway station in his carriage the day of the shooting, and Harriet Blaine who, on hearing the awful news, had rushed to the station, then gone with the stricken President to the White House, where she remained for hours.

"What a summer of anxiety & mourning it has been all over the world for the poor President," Elizabeth wrote her father. "And now he has gone & Arthur is in his place! to be followed who can say by what!"

Little consolation was to be found in "the disgusting *N.Y. Herald.*" She wanted to go home and see for herself what was happening in the capital.

* * *

The eulogy on Garfield was delivered to Congress by Secretary of State Blaine on 27 February 1882. For the occasion eight tickets to the Executive Gallery were issued to Harriet Blaine, who invited Elizabeth and Fanny, among others, to accompany her. There was an uncomfortable moment soon after they sat down, when a doorkeeper approached to turn them out. On recognizing Mrs. Blaine, however, he "beat a retreat."[5]

Blaine had worked on the eulogy for weeks, tapping a pile of reference books that "freighted" every table and chair in his study.[6] Whether or not he tried it out on his longtime critic is not known, but judging from the reaction of his listeners that day, his magnetism was still forceful.

* * *

Elizabeth and Marian Adams had much in common, in addition to being letter-writers: They adored their fathers; they enjoyed arranging houses; they thrived in an artistic milieu; and they loved to sharpen their wits at their little "salons" with the leaders of the day. Even on less important matters they were frequently in agreement. Endorsing the new look of black silk stockings, Marian wrote her father that "Mrs. Bigelow Lawrence and I have agreed that one should dress better as age steals on... and that one can do nothing except to keep many interests and keep very clean."[7]

When the two ladies heard that Washington was scheduled for a week of opera in the spring of 1883, they were elated. The stars were to be Adelina Patti and Dame Emma Albani Gye, a celebrated Canadian singer noted for her pleasant personality as well as her art. The American Minister in London, Mr. Lowell, had sent a note suggesting that the Adamses might like to entertain Mme. Gye; so a small breakfast was arranged for her. Elizabeth was included among the guests.

At the breakfast it was discovered that the diva would be performing in Boston the following week. Accordingly, Marian and Elizabeth decided to work up "a little social attention" there. Marian promised to drop a note to Mrs. Jack Gardner, while Elizabeth was to "drum up" Mrs. Winthrop. "We do our share of social work here," Marian wrote her father, "and you may as well toil too."[8]

At a small dinner at the Adamses not long afterwards, the conversation centered not on politics (sometimes *that* went on from seven till twelve), but on the exciting new explorations of the West. Among the guests were Othniel Marsh, a paleontologist who had accompanied a number of scientific expeditions to the Rocky Mountains, and Raphael Pumpelly, who was working for Henry Villard on the Northern Transcontinental Survey. To round out the group, the other male guest was Henry James, the novelist. He told his hostess afterwards that he was "charmed" with Elizabeth, "whom he had never met before."[9]

When the Adamses were entertained at Elizabeth's house, they found her parties invariably "jolly." There was much hilarity one night when a guest recounted a story about Mr. Bancroft [the historian], who sent Mr. Evarts [Secretary of State] one of his recent books on the United States. As a sort of "graceful return," Mr. Evarts sent the historian a *pig*—which he accompanied by a note, saying that he begged to offer Mr. Bancroft "the product of his *pen*."

Then there was the one about the "Western Yankee" who was in Europe, visiting a shrine where a lamp was burning. " 'This lamp,' said the priest, 'has burned here for three hundred years, & will burn as long again in the future.' 'No, it won't,' said the Yankee, & straightway blew it out."

At one of Elizabeth's "big" parties, Marian was "taken in" to dinner by the Russian Minister. Among the guests were the Minister from Sweden and Aristarchi Bey. The conversation turned to a recent "diplomatic scrimmage" involving the French Minister, and a U.S. treaty recognizing the Queen of Madagascar, on the subject of which a New York newspaper had written an editorial "not in very good taste."[10] Opinions were aired, and Marian Adams denounced the editorial as "impertinent to the French Republic and quite unworthy of the paper." Whether the hostess steered the heated talk toward Shakespearean phraseology is not recorded.

Marian Adams and Elizabeth Lawrence did not always see eye to eye on their guests. The German Minister, for instance, was considered by the former to be "a noisy buffoon,"[11] while the latter thought him "profound & delightful."

* * *

> The President requests the honour of the company of Mrs. Lawrence at dinner, on Saturday January 27th at 7½ o'clock. To meet H.E. The Govr. Genl. of Canada &c. &c. &c.

Elizabeth's invitation to dinner at the White House.

The East Room of the White House, where diplomatic receptions took place. *Harper's New Monthly Magazine*, March 1878.

Occasionally tidbits of Mrs. L.'s social activities were gleaned by the Doylestown newspaper. She was "seen at Mrs. Frelinghuysen's reception dressed in white satin and brocade, with point lace...."[12] Again, she was "a guest at the dinner the President gave to the Marquis of Lorne" [Governor-General of Canada, who had married Queen Victoria's daughter, Princess Louise]. "Thirty-six were present."[13]

On 22 May 1883, the *Doylestown Democrat* announced that "Mrs. T. B. Lawrence, of Doylestown, now living in Washington, gave an elegant entertainment on Wednesday evening of last week, to the Turkish Minister, who has been recalled."[14]

Elizabeth's farewell party for Aristarchi Bey was described by Marian Adams as "a large dinner with speech making, etc. Col. Bonaparte took me in, had Count Leydon, a new German Secretary of Legation, on left."[15] Perhaps this was the occasion on which the Turkish Minister presented his old N. R. I. Dining Club friend with a parting gift: a Dürer woodcut, *The Betrayal of Christ*. (Years later she would present it to her nephew Harry, who duly noted down its provenance.)

* * *

The dinner for Aristarchi Bey was the climax of a particularly active social season that had begun in January with a dinner party Elizabeth gave for eighteen people, among whom were the McClellans and Mr. Bancroft, the historian. The latter held the guests spellbound, speaking with eloquence of Shakespeare's "prophetic allusion to America," when he makes Cromwell refer to "the future King James," who "wherever the bright suns of Heaven shall shine," will "make new nations."

Shakespeare was the center of conversation that week, for Salvini was in town, and Elizabeth and Fanny devoted three nights to seeing the great actor perform. She recalled the last time she had seen him in Florence, when the audience had panicked at a suspected fire. Though she thought his supporting actors were poor, Salvini himself outshone even the great Garrick—especially in his *King Lear*. When he came to the famous passage; "Aye, every inch a king," he broke off the branch of a dead oak tree under which he was standing, and held it in his outstretched arm "like a sceptre." The effect was "tremendous!"

* * *

Another engrossing subject was "Telephone Bell," as Marian Adams referred to the inventor, who was then living in Washington. He was making experiments from the roof of a large building "to Columbia College on a hill a few miles off; light is flashed from a reflector and the voice rides on the ray," she recounted with awe.[16]

Lela and Harry visited once again. By this time Elizabeth's nephew had decided the law was not his métier; his interest had always been in history and archeology. The summer before he went to Harvard he had unearthed some interesting Indian relics, and his aunt had announced then that she would not be surprised if "Hal had always great success in such researches. Bucks Co. is an almost unexplored region thus far, & Hal the very fellow to explore it." It was a "great pleasure to spend money on such a satisfactory child as he is." The past year he had spent traveling in Europe and the Middle East. On his return he tried his hand at etching some of the scenes he had sketched in Egypt, and his aunt was "glad to hear he was so encouraged" with this new experiment.

Often Lela, Harry, and Willie, Jr. were included in their aunt's activities, at other times they were on their own. They went along, for instance, to the wedding of Senator Bayard's daughter, where they all ate "so much terrapin" and drank "so much champagne in healths with old friends," that she was in "anything but a state to write a letter."

Never had Washington been so gay. One night, for instance, Elizabeth whirled from a dinner party to a reception to a ball at Miss Coleman's, from which she brought Lela home at 1 A.M. Harry got in even later and announced the next morning that he was having such a good time, he had decided to postpone his departure, and wanted his violin sent down from Doylestown. They all agreed to stay home the next evening and rest "in order to get ready for the ball at the British Legation."

On reaching home one night after a late party, Elizabeth discovered to her horror that she had lost one of the diamond stars that Bigelow had bought for her in Paris. Though it was well after midnight, she rushed downstairs, roused her houseman, and together they searched the drawing room. No luck. In a near panic she asked him to take some matches and scour the pavement between the front door and the carriage block. To her immeasurable relief, there it was, lying in the gutter!

Blaine called one day to escort the sisters out to see his new house. They were amazed to see how beautifully it was furnished. Even the servants' rooms were as "tasteful & as comfortable as the master's." Although they were tucked away in the attic, of course, they were large and airy, with magnificent views of the countryside.

An ingenious invention had just been installed: a trapdoor in one of the servants' attic closets which, when lifted, revealed a ladder fastened to the wall, descending to a closet on the floor below. Down this the maids could "scramble" in case of an emergency. Blaine had conceived this idea after the "Milwalkie" *[sic]* fire, "for," said he, "I should never get over it if we were so unfortunate as to have a fire & 5 poor maids perished in the flames for want of means to escape, while we on the second floor had the broad double staircase to get out by."

Senator Blaine's house, near the present Dupont Circle. He was concerned about the maids' escape route from the top floor in case of fire. H. J. Ramsdell, *Life and Public Service of Hon. James G. Blaine*, Philadelphia, 1884.

A noble sentiment indeed from her "knight," whose plumes were looking slightly bedraggled as he began his third try for the Presidential nomination. Marian Adams referred to "Jim" Blaine as a "shining light or pretentious blatherskite, according to the point of view.... So is Jesse James [the outlaw who had been killed the previous year]...."[17]

* * *

Mary, Willie, and Willie, Jr. also came to Washington that spring, and their energetic hostess kept them busy: an exhibition of "Life Saving Machines" at the Treasury; the "Star Route Trial" (involving fraud in rural post offices); and a play starring Lily Langtry. Elizabeth and the two Willies were "ecstatic"[18] over the lovely Lily. Mary thought she wore too much eye makeup and looked too artificial for the simple country-girl role she was playing.

Willie was propelled to gardens and greenhouses, where "no end of plants, cuttings, lily roots, etc." were inspected and arrangements made to carry them back to Aldie. On she led him to the Smithsonian to see all sorts of "curious things":

> .... ancient relics found in Arizona & New Mexico, but the most curious of all was the photograph, of which they have promised me a copy, of a vast crag of rocks, which rises from the midst of the sandy plains of Arizona, with a sort of table land on the top, on either end of which are two villages, each of them speaking a different dialect.
>
> A most remarkable religious rite takes place [there] every other year—a snake dance, the snakes being rattle-snakes! Chosen men of the tribe descend into the sandy plain & catch the snakes, & when the dance begins, the dancers seize these reptiles, twist them round their bodies, & dance with them, the snakes' tails in their mouths, their heads standing out with their jaws open, & their stings darting out....
>
> A gentleman who has lived near this tribe for several years was at the Smithsonian yesterday, & described this dance to me in a most graphic way. It seems that the dancers control the snakes simply by waving a feather in front of them. That is explained by the fact of the snakes being kept in great awe by the hawks, who chase them on the plains. The snakes vainly try to strike them, which the hawks return by beating the snakes with their great wings—& eventually get the victory.
>
> The photos they showed us yesterday show regions of country far beyond anything in Europe for grandeur & variety of scenery, & when that wonderful land of Arizona & the Yellowstone is once opened up by railways, we will have far more to show on this continent than on any other.
>
> Politics are very quiet here since Congress adjourned. Mr. Blaine is very busy with his book, & is now riding on horseback. I am now reading the last days of Napoleon... which enters into most thrilling particulars of his last hours in France after Waterloo. Bonaparte is a subject that I cannot exhaust.

* * *

Blaine's capture of the Republican party's nomination embroiled him in one of the "dirtiest" elections ever held: that of 1884. His opponent in the race for the long-coveted position was the Governor of New York, Grover Cleveland.

Cleveland's campaign touted his honesty in public office—in the face of clamorous questions about his private morality. (He had seduced the directress of the cloak and lace department of a Buffalo dry goods store, then fathered her child. Cartoons showing a babe in mother's arms were captioned "Ma, Ma, where's my Pa?" This quickly became the Republicans' chant.)

Cartoons like this one by William A. Rogers doomed Blaine's bid for the Presidency. It is titled "Spurned," and viciously underscores his dealings with the Little Rock Railroad. *Library of Congress.*

Blaine, on the other hand, relied on his record of an unimpeachable family life to offset the irreparable damage of the famous "Mulligan letters." (He had dictated an alibi for his lucrative connection with the Little Rock and Fort Smith Railroad ruling, then scrawled on the bottom: "Burn this letter." This became a potent chant for the Democrats, since the recipient of the letter, bookkeeper Mulligan, failed to do just that.) Further damage was done by Thomas Nast's vicious cartoons, which showed the plumes of the knight sprouting from a top hat and looking much the worse for the wear, above a face that looked suspiciously like Boss Tweed's.

In essence, the campaign was a contest between the drunken seducer of a poor widow, and the wily corrupter of high public office. The election was close. When the votes were counted, Blaine lost by some 63,000, out of 10,000,000 cast.

Elizabeth must have had mixed emotions. By now she was convinced that politics was inherently a dirty business, and that public and private morality were considered to be on different planes. Senator Bayard had once loaned her a book about England at the turn of the century, and she had taken comfort in the thought that Congress did not "begin to be as corrupt as was the English Parliament of that time." When one considered how "comparatively pure & honorable is the English administration of today," it gave her hope that "we too may arise from the depredation of the present hour."

At least there was some joy in the fact that for the first time since the Civil War, there was a Democrat in the White House.

* * *

As a further lift to her spirits, six weeks later she received a particularly precious gift: a lock of Napoleon's hair. It was given to her by Col. Pierre Solidor Milon, one of her many French tutors.[19]

Born in 1787, Milon was then ninety-seven, the only one of the seven remaining survivors of Napoleon's army living in America. Over the years Elizabeth had frequently visited him in Philadelphia, listening for hours on end to his reminiscences about the Emperor, and about his own imprisonment in a freezing cell in Wilna, in Poland, and his escape through a snowstorm back to France.

Milon confided to Elizabeth that he had gone to Elba and had lost all his money trying to help Napoleon escape from St. Helena. Forced to leave France, he fled to the United States, where he sought out Joseph Bonaparte, then living in Bordentown, New Jersey, who sent him on a secret mission to Mexico. Imprisoned, then released, he settled in Philadelphia in 1859, where he taught music and languages, and played first violin at the Walnut and Arch Street Theaters.

During one of her visits to Col. Milon, Elizabeth suggested he go see Napoleon's death mask at the Historical Society of Pennsylvania. He did so, then wrote her in his unique and misspelled English that on beholding it he had "droped a tear." Later he sent her Thiers' history of "the greatest man that lieved during this and many old ages," together with some maps pertaining to the Napoleonic campaigns.

The old man was having a struggle making ends meet; so for some years "Lady Lawrence," as he called her, had been helping out. Since his "existance at any moment may vanish," Milon decided to part with his most precious possessions: his Legion of Honor ribbon; a cut-out silhouette of Princess Pauline Borghese, Napoleon's sister; and a

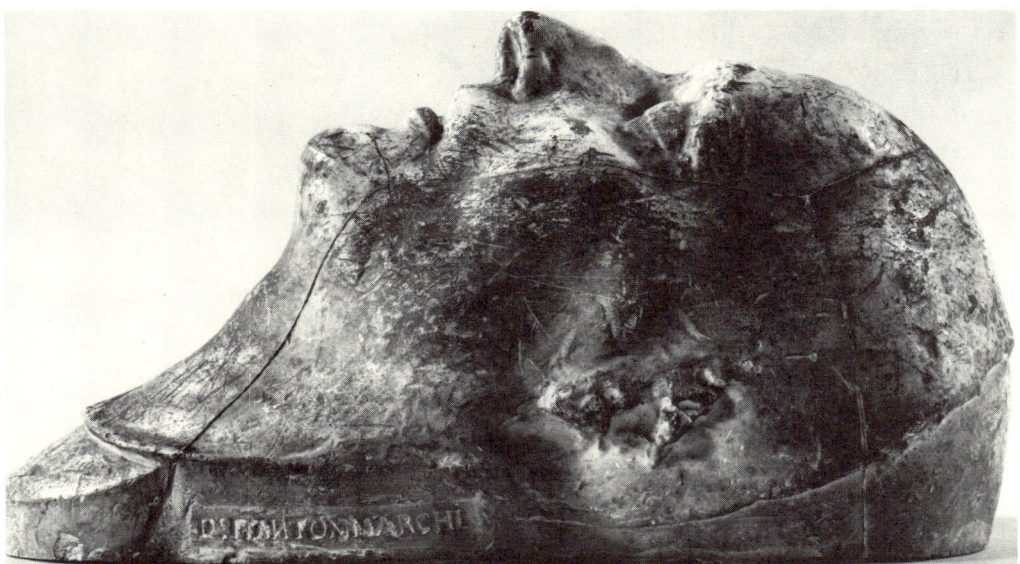

Plaster death mask of Napoleon, made by an attending physician, Dr. Francesco Antommarchi (whose name appears on the side). The mask, at one time on loan to the Historical Society of Pennsylvania, where EL sent Colonel Milon to see it, is now in the collection of the Athenaeum in Philadelphia. *Courtesy of the Athenaeum.*

lock of the Emperor's hair, encased in a locket which never left Milon's person. Who would appreciate them more than his "most cherished Lady Lawrence," his benefactress?

On 14 December 1884, he wrote her a letter, explaining exactly how he had acquired the lock of hair. After Napoleon's death the Princess Borghese, who had met Milon on Elba, had invited him to a luncheon at her "palas." When he had inquired about "a locket anging on her neck," she had told him it contained a lock of her brother's hair which she "cot herself." She had then opened it and gave him "a very few," which he placed in a case "with veneration." Enclosed in the case with the lock of hair, Elizabeth found a slip of yellowed paper on which, in the Colonel's spidery handwriting, were the names of the people who had lunched together that day and had witnessed the Princess's gift to him.

As for the silhouette of the Princess, he wrote to Elizabeth:

> Madame Wanamaker [wife of the Philadelphia merchant], a pupil of mine for music and french language, many years ago offered me, at my choice, a greatcoat of Brown or Black cloith, if I would geve her *this cot* of the Princess Borghese.

Much as the old man needed the greatcoat, he preferred to give the silhouette to Elizabeth, rather than to Madame Wanamaker.

Col. Milon lived three more years, dying on 16 March 1888, aged one hundred and one.[30] One of his proudest moments was marching in Pennsylvania's Bicentennial parade in 1882. Curiously, the obituaries in the Philadelphia papers mentioned the fact that several years before he died he had presented "to Mrs. Elizabeth Lawrence of Doylestown" a lock of Napoleon's hair. Nevertheless they had part of the story wrong. They claimed the old soldier had cut it off the famous head himself, while with his commander on Elba.

Elizabeth's generosity enabled his family to give Col. Milon "a resting place befitting an old veteran of the Empire," as one of his daughters gratefully wrote her. In the letter Milon's daughter enclosed a lock of *his* hair, very curly and very grey.

18

NORTHEASTERN U.S. AND EUROPE (1885–1899)

"Out of mantel decoration" and "knee-deep in science."

Throughout the rest of the 1880's and '90's Elizabeth continued to indulge her wanderlust. When she was not in Washington or Doylestown, or traveling in Europe, she was visiting in Boston, Newport, or New York, or summering at a cottage in York Harbor, Maine, with various members of her family in tow.

The Maplewood Inn at Bethlehem, New Hampshire. The air was "delicious," and "the blue shadows [kept] chasing each other around the distant mountain peaks." *Courtesy of the New Hampshire Historical Society.*

One July in the mid '80's she left Mama and Fanny in Maine and "steamed away" with her ailing father—now past eighty—to the Maplewood Inn near Bethlehem, New Hampshire. On being ushered into their suite, the old Judge, though exhausted by the long train ride, signaled his approval of the place by announcing: "Well, we've met nothing *crawling* so far."

The hotel was impressive. Not only was it lighted with gas inside, but *electric* lights illuminated the outside as well. Boardwalks stretched off in all directions, one leading to a spectacular view of the Franconia range. It was doubtful that their one little wood stove would produce much heat, but the air was so *"delicious,"* it would probably not be needed.

One of their sitting room windows looked out over the "lawn tennis ground," while the other three commanded a view of the distant mountain peaks around which "the blue shadows keep chasing each other." The first order of business (after "arranging about the seats in the Dining Room") was to "interview the stable man about a carriage," for the hotel was noted for its excellent equipages.

Soon after their arrival she discovered that among the guests were Charles Joseph Bonaparte and his wife. Since he was the younger brother of her erstwhile dinner companion, Col. Jerome Napoleon Bonaparte, she intended to have a chat with him about her "great hero," hoping he would "know & care more about the latter [Napoleon I] than his brother Jerome seemed to."

Within a day Papa showed signs of improvement and could be seen cleaning his nails with an "elegant" knife his grandson Willie had brought him from his recent trip to Jerusalem, along with a "spectacle case made of wood from the Mt. of Olives." After a walk he planned to play "a game of solitaire with glass balls" which Elizabeth had bought for him in Boston.

* * *

Like his younger brother, Harry spent almost as much time abroad as at home—thanks to Aunt Lela's largesse—exploring the rivers of Europe in a jerry-built houseboat. Back in Doylestown, he followed his archeological bent, digging for signs of prehistoric man in the Delaware Valley. In 1885 he wrote his first book, *The Lenape Stone*, in which he attempted to prove the authenticity of an Indian gorget ploughed up by a Bucks County farmer. Aunt Lela "paid Putnam to publish it."[1]

The following year Harry invited his sister, who was touring England with friends, to accompany him on a trip down the Danube. Lela, then twenty-eight, was flattered and quickly joined him. Halted in their journey by a cholera epidemic in Budapest, the two young Mercers spent most of the winter in a picturesque old cloister that had been converted into an inn in Dürnstein, near Vienna.

Remembering her Aunt Lela's lively letters from London and Florence in the '50's and '60's which her family had so carefully saved, Lela felt compelled to emulate them, tuck-

Henry Mercer (left) on his houseboat, moored along a bank of the Danube.

ing into the envelopes headed for Doylestown the occasional photograph or dried flower, just as her aunt had done.

She was sure the family would not be surprised to learn that Harry was conducting an archeological excavation in the mouldering cellars of the old cloister. Even by night, down he went with a lamp and a shovel, while bats swooped through the rusty old gratings overlooking the Danube.

Harry and Lela had an idyllic time, chattering away in execrable German, learning the Austrian dances, listening to the zithers and the guitars in the beer *stübes*, and helping with the winemaking. One day when Lela was strolling along the river with a fellow guest at the cloister, a good-looking army officer approached and was introduced as Ober-Lieutenant Baron Hubert Fidler von Isarborn, temporarily on leave from the Austrian army. Although Lela had once confided to her aunt in Washington that she would never, never marry a foreigner (as so many American girls were doing) because she was too fond of her family ever to leave them, all her resolutions evaporated before this handsome Austrian in his "stunning" uniform, with its flash of turquoise and "tight-fitting trousers."[2] Hubert not only sang beautifully, she discovered, accompanying himself on the zither, but—even more surprising—he was a talented artist, spending hours in his studio just down the corridor from her room.

Lela and her bridegroom, Hubert Fidler von Isarborn, at their wedding reception in the garden at Aldie in the summer of 1888.

Hubert, in turn, was instantly captivated by Lela. When Harry told him she longed for a walking stick carved out of the stem of a rosebush, he climbed the nearby hill, cut down a trunk of proper thickness, and carved it for her. He taught her German; she taught him English.

In the spring, Willie, Jr. joined them, and the two brothers took off with their cumbersome cameras and glass plates to photograph Napoleonic battlefields. When an elderly gentleman who claimed to be a survivor of *la Grande Armèe* turned up to have his picture taken, Harry longed for Aunt Lela to be there.

By the time Judge Chapman, Fanny, and Willie arrived to join them in Vienna, Lela was hopelessly in love. Like her mother in 1853 in Maryland, Lela in 1887 in Austria cared not a whit that the man she loved had no "financial prospects." But now there was a difference: There was always Aunt Lela to fall back on.

The following summer Hubert came to America, and on 24 July 1888, he married Lela at Aldie. The ceremony was performed by a Catholic priest "before forty intimate friends and relatives," the newspaper reported. "The bride wore white silk, the groom his full army regalia, and Hassler's orchestra of Philadelphia provided the music."[3]

Fortunately the sun was shining, so that the wedding reception could be held in the lovely garden, amidst the "cuttings and lily roots" from Washington, the "pinarium" from London, and the terra cotta jars and the antique Corinthian pillar from Florence. If the groom was perspiring under the August sun in his high-necked wool uniform, the wedding picture does not reveal it.

The first part of their honeymoon was spent at Elizabeth's cottage in York Harbor, Maine, before they sailed back to set up housekeeping in Austria the following spring. They returned by way of the Mediterranean, so Hubert could make sketches of the Alhambra.

* * *

In 1891 Judge Chapman died, aged eighty-seven. If he had lived two years longer, he would have been overjoyed, like the rest of the family, at the birth of his first—and only—

Postcard sent by Lela to her parents, showing her home, Walpurgishof, in Hohenaschau, Austria. The building to the left, with its large window, was probably Hubert's studio.

(Above) Willie in Tyrolean dress, with gun and dog, photographed on a visit to Austria to see his daughter Lela and granddaughter Walpurga. (Below) The only Chapman descendant, EL's great-niece, Walpurga von Isarborn, in velvet dress and high-buttoned shoes.

great-grandchild, Lela and Hubert's daughter, Walpurga Mary Elizabeth. Since Fanny was a spinster of forty-seven, Arthur had never married, and Harry and Willie, Jr. showed every sign of retaining their bachelor status, Lela's daughter was cause for great celebration. The baby was born in Munich, and they all sailed over for the event—even Mama! After the "confinement," Elizabeth and Fanny took Mama on to Florence.

When the rest of the family returned home, Elizabeth spent a month in Paris, where she found the "hero of the hour" to be—of all people—Bonaparte! Not only was the little Emperor the subject of three current theatrical productions, but all the bookshops had at least three new "Memoirs paraded in their windows." One which she found *"thrillingly interesting"* she sent on to Agnes Irwin (founder of a well-known girls' school in Philadelphia), and to Dr. Owen Wister (father of the famous novelist), whose "Bonapartist education" she had for a long time "had in charge."

Throughout the 1890's Elizabeth interrupted her travels with a stopover at "Walpurgishof," Lela and Hubert's half-timbered Bavarian chalet, which one suspects she bought for them as a wedding present. Valiantly she was still tackling the language problem. In one room of the chalet, Lela reported, Aunt Lela would be tutored in French, while in another Aunt Fanny labored with German.

When Elizabeth produced the locket that contained Napoleon's hair to show to a guest one day, a few of the fine hairs wafted away. Hubert decided she needed a proper box to house her treasure, so he bought one for her in Munich.

* * *

Harry, too, was perambulating around Europe. In 1892 he was sent as an honorary member of the United States Archeological Commission to the Columbian Exposition in Madrid. From there he visited other archeological sites in Spain, France, and Belgium, studying neolithic tools and comparing them to those he had found in the Delaware Valley.

On his return to the States he was named Curator of American and Prehistoric Archeology at the museum of the University of Pennsylvania in Philadelphia. Though the position was unsalaried, he threw himself with typical fervor into his work, leading the Corwith expedition to the Yucatan in 1895. Aunt Lela followed his career with absorbing interest.

Henry Mercer on a Yucatan "dig" for the museum of the University of Pennsylvania.

When he was working in Philadelphia, he frequently stayed at the Rittenhouse Club, of which he was a member, walking from Rittenhouse Square across the Schuylkill bridge to the museum each day. An attractive bachelor who had turned forty in 1896, he was invited to teas, "at homes," and balls by the descendants of those who had invited his mother and aunt at mid-century.

Sarah Butler Wister of Philadelphia. "Dear Sarah" was the daughter of EL's old friend, actress Fanny Kemble, and the mother of novelist Owen Wister, Jr., Harvard friend of Henry Mercer. *Courtesy of the Historical Society of Pennsylvania.*

During the 1890's Elizabeth often spent the entire season at the Wagner music festival at Bayreuth, where Harry occasionally joined her. One summer she attended the festival not only with Harry, but with a group of her old friends, including the Brimmers from Boston, Lillie de Hegermann, and Lady Paget. At the end of the season she posted a long letter to Philadelphia to Sarah Wister (the wife of Dr. Owen Wister and daughter of her old friend, Fanny Kemble):

> I had the good luck... to see something of the Wagner family, a most charming set of people, & young Siegfried giving great promise as a musician, he having given up architecture last year & taken to the art he was evidently born for.
> I saw him lead an orchestra, given in memory of his grandfather Liszt in the beautiful little rococo theatre of Bayreuth, & when they played two symphonic poems of the latter—one of them we once heard together in Phila.—it was so delightful to see the young master turn & smile twice to his Mother in a neighboring box, as the music played the passages which were evidently the favorites of both.
> I heard also a good deal I thought interesting about Wagner himself from Prof. Todé,... the son-in-law of Frau Cosima [Wagner's wife]. It seems that the great composer was often like all other geniuses... very irritable, & so carried away

with his subject in conversation, & so regardless of his hearer, that many times after visitors had left, his family would say to him: "Those people left offended with what you said to them."

Immediately Wagner would jump up, rush out of the house & down the street, & catching up to his late visitors would say: "My dear friends, indeed I did not mean to hurt your feelings. Do come back & have a cup of tea, & let us talk it all over again together."

One loves to hear such things of the writer of *Parsifal,* who I have come to regard as not only Shakespearean in his genius, but as a great moral reformer.... Perhaps you may smile at this. But I think [this] was Wagner's highest aim, & his family & friends claim this as the aim of his music, & consider Bayreuth as one of the moralizing forces of the Europe of today.... It seems absurd to say the above in the light of the early histories of both Wagner & Liszt, & Frau Cosima [all noted for their liaisons]....

[This moralizing force is] a fact which was new to me... & in the light of such characters as Kundry, Tannhauser, & Parsifal, I am inclined to treat seriously even if I may not agree with all that the creator of them may say.

I did not think the performances, excepting Tannhauser, were quite equal to two years ago—the solos, I mean—the orchestras & the choruses & *mise en scène* as splendid as ever.

Prof. Todé told me that Wagner had made a faithful likeness of himself in the role of Hans Sachs [in *Der Meistersinger*], & even today the family never see it played without being freshly struck by the resemblance.

One day I went on a little Pic Nic of most interesting people to a pine woods about two hours from Bayreuth, & at supper under the flowering lindens I heard many of the points discussed, ... & felt for the first time that I got into the heart of "Wahnfried" (the Wagner house) & heard its tune & inner sentiments.[4]

* * *

That summer Elizabeth accompanied Lady Paget on a tour of Germany. After visiting the homes of Schiller and Goethe, the ladies ended their journey at the residence of Lady P.'s brother, where Elizabeth had her first chance to see a "little of the high life of Germany & in its country homes." She thought it "quite as fine in its way & much more interesting" than that of England. To her delight, Lady Paget's brother turned out to be the grandson of Gen. Blücher's Chief of Staff. After the battle of Waterloo the King of Prussia had given him Napoleon's carriage, along with the field glasses "through which Napoleon must have first caught sight of the Prussian troops coming up!"

When the famous field glasses were produced, Elizabeth dashed up to her room and brought down her lock of Napoleon's hair, which she never traveled without, and laid it beside the field glasses, thinking as she did so, with a *"serrement de coeur,"* that "this was the first time since Waterloo" that these two "interesting relics" had been together.

* * *

Her old friend Henry Adams, a widower since his wife Marian had committed suicide in 1885, turned up at the Wagnerian festival one summer. "I thought my...old sins were long dead and buried," Adams later wrote, "but they rise like Mrs. Bigelow Lawrence, who will die convinced that she was meant as the heroine of that scandalous work [i.e., *Democracy*]. I saw it in her eye at Bayreuth."[5] He was still enjoying his little joke, refusing to admit his authorship, let alone the identity of his heroine, Madeleine Lee.

* * *

In 1896 Elizabeth interrupted her stay in her cottage in Maine to visit old Boston friends who were summering in Bar Harbor and Northeast Harbor. At dinner one night she sat next to young Walter Damrosch, the musician, who had "married a daughter of poor Blaine." The next day Harriet Blaine herself called, wearing a long crepe veil and looking "so sad & so changed" that it brought tears to Elizabeth's eyes. In recent years she had lost her husband and three children, and she was still in deep mourning. The ladies spoke of "old times," and "the poor soul" told Elizabeth she was "linked with the happiest days of her life."[6]

At the dinner tables in Maine conversation invariably turned to "Universal Suffrage." Unless it was soon legalized, it was agreed, "New York City would have to be controlled by a standing army."

The opinion was also expressed that "the most hopeful side of this country today was the flourishing condition of our colleges & universities."

By far the "most inspiring" words came from President Eliot of Harvard, who with "proud scornfulness...swept away any allusion to the idea of there being any lasting defeat or failure for this great strong youthful Republic."

Everyone agreed the Republican McKinley would be elected—hopefully with a "triumphant majority," and expressed the "gravest anxiety" over William Jennings Bryan, the "free-silver" advocate who scorned "the cross of gold." The editor of *The Chicago Tribune*, when asked what he thought of the country's current situation, was heard to say: "Before the Civil War we all feared that we might lose a limb; but the trouble today is *blood poisoning*."

* * *

Throughout the late 1880's and 1890's Elizabeth's interest in art and literature, as well as music, never faltered. When *The Angelus*, Millet's *chef d'oeuvre*, arrived in New York on its tour of America, she went to see it. When an anniversary celebration of the death of Sidney Lanier, the poet–musician, was held in Baltimore, she attended.

In Boston she went to the symphony with Sarah Wyman Whitman, an old friend who had visited Aldie and admired "the constellation...of its gentle and beautiful family," including its "neat-built dog."[7] Sarah was an artist of no mean ability. She worked not only in oils, but in stained glass, a medium rediscovered by the Arts and Crafts Movement about which Elizabeth, the medievalist, was highly enthusiastic.

To Doylestown from Boston came sketches of the stained-glass windows Sarah was working on for the Parish House of Trinity Church, in memory of Phillips Brooks. There had also been a poem, written the day Browning died. To Boston from Doylestown came critiques of Tennyson's most recent verse, and allusions to the latest novel by "H. James," as well as a volume of Dante. With true Victorian sentimentality, Sarah signed her letters to her longtime friend "Constantia." One can only wonder how Elizabeth signed hers!

To another Sarah—Mrs. Owen Wister—she confided that the most recent paintings by John Singer Sargent puzzled her, for they were "so far away from all the Pitti & Uffizi taught me to admire." On a visit to Boston she had seen Sargent's celebrated portrait of Isabella Stewart Gardner:

> [I] found "Mrs. Jack" the *universal* theme—even Mr. Norton [Charles Eliot Norton, the art historian at Harvard] talked of her over his Dantes. I even heard a lady say that certain views of "Mrs. Jack's" face were "exquisitely beautiful."
>
> Sargent has painted her tightly swathed in black satin—like a mummy, with pearls on her dazzling neck & *two* girdles of the same around her waist & two rubies on her slippers, & an arrangement of tapestry in the background which makes a kind of nimbus round her head, so that I heard two or three say the picture reminded them of—a Spanish—Madonna![8]

* * *

In 1896 Elizabeth interrupted her stay in her cottage in Maine to visit old Boston friends who were summering in Bar Harbor and Northeast Harbor. At dinner one night she sat next to young Walter Damrosch, the musician, who had "married a daughter of poor Blaine." The next day Harriet Blaine herself called, wearing a long crepe veil and looking "so sad & so changed" that it brought tears to Elizabeth's eyes. In recent years she had lost her husband and three children, and she was still in deep mourning. The ladies spoke of "old times," and "the poor soul" told Elizabeth she was "linked with the happiest days of her life."[6]

At the dinner tables in Maine conversation invariably turned to "Universal Suffrage." Unless it was soon legalized, it was agreed, "New York City would have to be controlled by a standing army."

The opinion was also expressed that "the most hopeful side of this country today was the flourishing condition of our colleges & universities."

By far the "most inspiring" words came from President Eliot of Harvard, who with "proud scornfulness...swept away any allusion to the idea of there being any lasting defeat or failure for this great strong youthful Republic."

Everyone agreed the Republican McKinley would be elected—hopefully with a "triumphant majority," and expressed the "gravest anxiety" over William Jennings Bryan, the "free-silver" advocate who scorned "the cross of gold." The editor of *The Chicago Tribune*, when asked what he thought of the country's current situation, was heard to say: "Before the Civil War we all feared that we might lose a limb; but the trouble today is *blood poisoning*."

* * *

Throughout the late 1880's and 1890's Elizabeth's interest in art and literature, as well as music, never faltered. When *The Angelus*, Millet's *chef d'oeuvre*, arrived in New York on its tour of America, she went to see it. When an anniversary celebration of the death of Sidney Lanier, the poet–musician, was held in Baltimore, she attended.

In Boston she went to the symphony with Sarah Wyman Whitman, an old friend who had visited Aldie and admired "the constellation...of its gentle and beautiful family," including its "neat-built dog."[7] Sarah was an artist of no mean ability. She worked not only in oils, but in stained glass, a medium rediscovered by the Arts and Crafts Movement about which Elizabeth, the medievalist, was highly enthusiastic.

To Doylestown from Boston came sketches of the stained-glass windows Sarah was working on for the Parish House of Trinity Church, in memory of Phillips Brooks. There had also been a poem, written the day Browning died. To Boston from Doylestown came critiques of Tennyson's most recent verse, and allusions to the latest novel by "H. James," as well as a volume of Dante. With true Victorian sentimentality, Sarah signed her letters to her longtime friend "Constantia." One can only wonder how Elizabeth signed hers!

To another Sarah—Mrs. Owen Wister—she confided that the most recent paintings by John Singer Sargent puzzled her, for they were "so far away from all the Pitti & Uffizi taught me to admire." On a visit to Boston she had seen Sargent's celebrated portrait of Isabella Stewart Gardner:

> [I] found "Mrs. Jack" the *universal* theme—even Mr. Norton [Charles Eliot Norton, the art historian at Harvard] talked of her over his Dantes. I even heard a lady say that certain views of "Mrs. Jack's" face were "exquisitely beautiful."
>
> Sargent has painted her tightly swathed in black satin—like a mummy, with pearls on her dazzling neck & *two* girdles of the same around her waist & two rubies on her slippers, & an arrangement of tapestry in the background which makes a kind of nimbus round her head, so that I heard two or three say the picture reminded them of—a Spanish—Madonna![8]

* * *

Mrs. John L. Gardner, by John Singer Sargent. EL reported that the "nimbus" around the head made her friend "Mrs. Jack" look like "a Spanish Madonna!" *Courtesy of the Isabella Stewart Gardner Museum.*

In the spring of 1899, on one of her European jaunts, she visited Lillie de Hegermann in Paris. Although Elizabeth had turned seventy, she had lost none of her enthusiasms, and was still, as her friend claimed, "interested in everything."[9] Without fail, every day the two ladies went to a museum, or did a little sightseeing.

The presidential *loge* at the Grand Opera was put at their disposal to hear Wagner's *Der Meistersinger* in French. Seated in the luxurious box, where the "huge sofas and the *fauteuils* offered their hospitable arms," they reviewed their impressions of the opera during the *entr'actes*. They were "ultra-enthusiastic." Near them sat Madame Cosima Wagner, who expressed the "greatest pleasure" at the performance, "not concealing her surprise that a representation in French and in France could be so perfect." Lillie could only say that if "that most difficult of ladies" was satisfied, "imagine how satisfied *we* must have been!"

Afterwards Lillie took Elizabeth to Madame Carnot's [the ex-President's widow] evening reception. It was hardly what one could call enlivening. The guests moved in a "procession" through the *salons* until they arrived at the last "melancholy" one, in the middle of which was a piece of marble covered with withered wreaths and faded ribbons, souvenirs of the late President's funeral. Madame Carnot wore a long black veil and received in a "widowed-Empress manner."

At the time of Elizabeth's visit, the talk of Paris was the Dreyfus affair. Public sentiment was running so strongly against Zola that crowds of people stormed through the streets screaming epithets. (Alfred Dreyfus, a French army officer of Jewish blood, was convicted of treason in 1894 and imprisoned on Devil's Island. The novelist Émile Zola forced a retrial, and Dreyfus was exonerated.) One day the two ladies "met a mob"[10] while driving through the Place de la Concorde. Far from being afraid, they were fascinated! It was hardly more threatening than the Indians with their tomahawks, twenty years before.

Later that year, after their return from Europe, the two friends made an excursion to Niagara Falls. Lillie became "perfectly wild" under the excitement created by the foaming water and "bounded ahead everywhere up & down crevices & precipices, the steeper the better, & standing by the Whirlpool rapids, suddenly found her voice again & burst into song."[11]

* * *

Although her vision (and her handwriting) worsened, Elizabeth continued to read the newspaper avidly, never ceasing to champion citizens who clung to their ideals. An outstanding example was Gen. Leonard Wood, the doctor who had been "doing such splendid things in Cuba," and who had helped Theodore Roosevelt organize the Rough Riders. The General had just declined a civil post paying $30,000 a year, in order to return to Santiago to fight the yellow fever and "do his duty" on a mere $6,000. Was that not "truly great"?[12] she asked Sarah Wister.

There was also Georges Picquart, who had been implicated in the Dreyfus case and was later exonerated. In a burst of enthusiasm Elizabeth sent him a cablegram: "God bless Picquart, the prayer of true hearts in America."[13] Carefully couching it in just ten words, she addressed it simply in care of the American Embassy, knowing from past experience that someone there would carry on.

* * *

Before the nineteenth century came to an end Elizabeth helped her nephew in several other ventures. The year 1897 was a turning point in the multifaceted career of Henry C. Mercer, as he was known professionally. One day in April, seeking some fireplace tongs in a jumble of agricultural tools and household utensils at a dealer in "penny lots," he was suddenly struck by the fact that before him lay the material evidence of a pre-industrialized era that was fast becoming obsolete.

Abandoning his interest in prehistoric culture, he gave up his job at the University's museum and concentrated instead on "rummaging the bake-ovens, wagon-houses, cellars, hay-lofts, smoke-houses, garrets, and chimney-corners" for a different kind of artifact, presenting "history from a new point of view." The collecting of Americana was then in its infancy, and largely confined to the decorative arts. Mercer argued that "if we are going to collect old furniture, porcelain, and candlesticks, why not go a step further and gather hoes, axes, tin kitchens, scythes, forks, plows, and bee-hives?" Considered from this point of view, one is "out of mantel decoration" and "knee-deep in science."

With professional expertise he catalogued his growing collection and sorted it into categories he devised, such as articles for survival, for the building of shelter, for the making of clothing, for the cooking of food, for learning, for amusement. He called his collection "Tools of the Nation Maker," because, as he later explained, "in the largest sense the story of Eastern Pennsylvania and of its Bucks County is that of the whole nation." Ultimately he would enlarge the scope to include artifacts from other countries, including China and Africa, for the purpose of comparison or contrast.

His was a new concept of visual history:

> .... You may go down into Independence Hall in Philadelphia, and stand in the room in which the Declaration of Independence was signed and there look up at

the portraits of the Signers. But do you think you are any nearer the essence of the matter there than you are here [in the midst of his collection], when you realize that ten hundred thousand women...spinning upon these wheels...[made] it possible for men to be adequately protected from the cold, so that they could go out and fight any battles at all by sea or land?...Perhaps these things can be adequately described by history, but a sight of the actual object conveys an impression otherwise indescribable.[14]

His collection was exhibited for the first time at a meeting of the Bucks County Historical Society, of which he had been one of the founders in 1880, the year after he graduated from Harvard. The meeting took place in the courthouse in Doylestown, where the Historical Society had a small room. For this special occasion the use of the large courtroom was granted, and there Henry Mercer displayed his collection, with grain cradles overflowing into the prisoner's dock, and mouldboard plows decorating the radiators. Always the artist, he arranged pumpkins, tree boughs, and sheaves of wheat around the exhibit.

Aunt Lela was present that October day in 1897 when her nephew explained to the audience his revolutionary concept of illustrating history. She had undoubtedly seen many of the items in the collection before, because Henry had taken over one of the outbuildings at Aldie and renovated it for a studio, which he called "Indian House."

In the course of his collecting, Henry had become interested in the pottery of the Pennsylvania Germans, a craft fast disappearing. Determined to "resuscitate" it, he apprenticed himself for a brief period to one of the few remaining potters in the upper end of the county, after which he proceeded to construct his own kilns at "Indian House." Experimenting with clays and glazes, he ran into a series of difficulties. The following spring he went to England, where he met the well-known ceramist William de Morgan, with whom, one presumes, he had conversations on technique. Aunt Lela was also in Europe at the time; so they sailed home together.

Henry continued his experiments, switching his concentration from pottery to architectural tiles on the advice of several friends who were Philadelphia architects. He was still struggling with glazes when Aunt Lela, just turned seventy, went back to Europe. Tucked into her luggage were "two little pieces of Bucks County clay" with which she "induced" the Florentine potter, Cantigalli, to experiment.[15] She also obtained "a receipt for a glaze from the kind and helpful Mr. William de Morgan," who was then in Florence. She was in her element: furthering her nephew's enterprise in a city she loved.

By the end of 1899 "The Moravian Pottery and Tile Works" was in operation, taking its name from the first tile motif, a Pennsylvania German tulip, derived from an eighteenth-century Moravian stove plate in Mercer's collection. Designs were later adapted from other sources: from the Aztecs, from ancient English and European abbeys, from American folk art.

The pottery's first sizable commission was Isabella Stewart Gardner's Italian *palazzo* in Boston, for which tile floors were specified in many rooms. How an unknown pottery in Pennsylvania secured the order is not a difficult matter to unravel when one considers Aunt Lela's Boston connections. It is no surprise to find Henry Mercer's name entered five times in "Mrs. Jack's" guest book in 1901.[16]

Elizabeth also focused her attention on another arrow in her nephew's quiver: his ever-growing collection of "tools" and artifacts. By now it literally covered the walls and rafters of "Indian House." A permanent museum was needed, and it must be, above all else, fireproof.

When the Historical Society launched a campaign for a building of its own, in which would be housed many of the items from Mercer's collection, she offered to make a "generous donation"—with the proviso that *she* choose the architect.[17] The trustees had other

(Left) Willie Mercer, Jr., leaning out the window of the family cottage at York Harbor, Maine. (Right) Martha Dana, of Boston, who later married Willie, Jr., painted by Anders Zorn in 1899. *Courtesy of the Museum of Fine Arts, Boston.*

several years at Harvard, he studied sculpture with Charles Grafly, and exhibited his work occasionally in Europe. Like his brother Harry, he, too, had a studio at Aldie, where he fashioned cement garden ornaments, and worked with plaster, glass mosaics, and stained glass. He reinforced the Boston connection by marrying Martha Dana.[2] Twin sons—a Chapman inheritance—died shortly after birth. So the little girl in Austria was still the only descendant.

* * *

Sallie, too, was gone.

In 1885 she married for the fourth and last time. The groom was a wealthy widower, Major George F. Downs, then seventy-one, who had been at her famous fancy-dress ball years before, dressed as a Knight Templar. Supposedly he had been in love with her ever since.

They lived at the Galt House, in Louisville, traveling intermittently. Sallie, though aging, still made good copy for the newspapers, one of which reported that she was the first person to adopt "the fashionable ultra-marine color which soon afterwards made its appearance at the wealthy seaside resorts in the East."[3]

Not long before she died in 1896, she was seen driving around Louisville, her white "enameled"[4] face shining forth from the interior of her colorful landau. It reminded the older folks of the story that had been told and retold over the years. One day, as she walked past a group of laborers, her face whiter and her cheeks rosier than usual, one exclaimed audibly, "By God, painted!" Not losing a step, Sallie said quietly, "Yes, painted by God," and sailed on.[5]

The night before she died in the Galt House, the nurse was forced to ask the hotel clerk to quiet the noise emanating from the barroom, where a chorus girl was showing her knees by kicking at the chandelier. A few hours later Sallie was dead. Many of her mourners arrived two hours ahead of time for the funeral to secure good seats. Her coffin was lavender. Her shroud, stitched up two years before so that she could approve it, was white satin. One of her last requests had been that her body be kept for at least three days, to make sure she had not been buried alive. Interment, of course, took place beside the rococo monument she had erected years before, on the other side of which lay her second and third husbands. The fourth outlived her, and the first she had obliterated from her mind long ago.

* * *

In July 1905, following her lifelong custom of scouring the daily papers, Elizabeth must have read that President Theodore Roosevelt had appointed a new Secretary of the Navy (who would later serve as Attorney General). He was Charles Joseph Bonaparte, the Baltimore lawyer and younger brother of Col. Jerome, whom she had met long ago at the Maplewood Inn in New Hampshire. To have a great-nephew of the Emperor Napoleon occupying high public office in the greatest republic in the world must have struck her as a curiously ironic twist of history. Would this public servant have a Napoleonic silver eagle as the centerpiece of his dinner table, like his older brother?

* * *

Five months later, on 3 December 1905, Elizabeth Chapman Lawrence died. She was seventy-six when she succumbed to a month-long bout with pneumonia. Her obituary in Doylestown's *Daily Republican* of December 4 said in part:

> Among her intimate friends were men and women distinguished in the social and public life of this country and Europe. To the very last Mrs. Lawrence evinced the keenest interest in public affairs and exercised no little influence....
>
> She was quick to give encouragement to every individual or movement tending to make for better government or advancement of the high ideal. Knowing the world from the standpoint of one who enjoyed the advantages of travel and distinguished social connections, she...held to the conviction that personal integrity and an irreproachable character were to be valued above distinction or wealth.
>
> Possessing both wealth and influence, she was able to accomplish great good. While much of her life was spent abroad and the larger cities of this country, she loved her native county....

The Philadelphia *Evening Bulletin* commented:

> [She was] well-known and highly esteemed [and] for nearly half a century has been a conspicuous figure in the social life of this country.... A woman of great beauty, she possessed a mind highly cultivated and wherever she went she gathered around her an agreeable circle of friends....
>
> She spent much of her time in Washington, her summers being passed at Aldie, her beautiful country place, near Doylestown. Her house in Washington was noted for its distinguished guests, and no stranger ever came there without seeking at once an introduction to Mrs. Lawrence. Her house at Doylestown is full of intersting mementos, many of which have been given her by celebrated personages.

* * *

Elizabeth lived just long enough to see her nephew win a Gold Medal for his tiles at the St. Louis World's Fair. Henry Mercer was now well on his way to becoming one of the most famous ceramists in the country. His tiles adorned floors, walls, and fireplaces of such diverse buildings as the State Capitol in Harrisburg, the library and deanery at Bryn Mawr College, the Traymore and Marlborough-Blenheim Hotels in Atlantic City, the Casino at Monte Carlo, and the residence at the Santa Gertrudis ranch in San Antonio.

"Spinning wool," one of four hundred mosaics that cover the floor of the rotunda in the Capitol in Harrisburg. Mercer's tile "carpet" depicts the history of Pennsylvania from Indians to Benjamin Franklin to oil wells.

Mercer's tiles could be found in Grauman's Chinese Theater in Hollywood, in Shepherd's Hotel in Cairo, in the Rockefeller estate at Pocantico Hills. They brightened countless churches, schools, firehouses, bridges, railroad stations, and even gas stations. They embellished the most bizarre movie palaces as well as the smallest vestibule. University clubs had fireplace surrounds of Shakespearean characters; country clubs sported golfing and equestrian motifs.

Some of the tile designs from ancient abbeys were supplied by his good friend Sir Hercules Read of the British Museum. Others were adapted from prints and early manuscripts, or illustrated Dickens's novels and Wagner's operas. Still others sprang from Mercer's own fertile imagination.

* * *

Within a year of his aunt's death, Mercer—now independently wealthy thanks to his share of her inheritance—began to improvise plans for a building that would be a home for himself, a memorial to his aunt, and a museum pertaining to the history of tiles when he died. Since Aunt Lela had so loved the traditions, art, and architecture of the "Old World," and had introduced him to them, what could be more appropriate than a castle?

Keenly aware of the danger of fire, which had destroyed his uncle's armor collection (evidences of which must still have been highly visible when he entered Harvard), he selected a relatively new material, concrete, for his dream building. In addition to being fire-resistant, it had the advantage of plasticity and lent itself admirably to the application of colorful tiling.

With a handful of day laborers (at $1.75 a day), and a horse named Lucy, who powered the hoist, he began construction in 1908 on land he bought not far from Aldie. A plaster model and rough drawings served in lieu of architectural plans. The core of the castle was a 1740 farmhouse that had been on the property when he bought it. He poured cement

(Above) An early photograph of Fonthill, conceived by Henry Mercer in 1907, little more than a year after his aunt's death. He flung up turrets and balconies and dovecotes over and around a small 1740 farmhouse, using a rough plaster model, a handful of day laborers, and a horse named Lucy to "uplift" the cement. (Below) Fonthill today.

around and over the old house, throwing up wings and turrets and balconies in considerable abandon. The citizens of Doylestown thought he was quite mad.

Though the castle was not yet finished, he moved into it in 1910. He called it "Fonthill," after the estate of a distant Mercer relative in Virginia, and devoutly hoped it would not collapse like William Beckford's famous extravaganza of the same name in England. Into it he incorporated elements he remembered from his travels—a house in Salonica, engravings in museums—interweaving them with his own "fancies."[6]

Into the vaulted ceilings, on top of the pillars, around the fireplaces, and even on the stair risers, he set clay tiles from all countries, beginning with examples from Ur, dating to 2400 B.C., which he embedded in a pillar in the "Saloon." Arabian tiles topped a doorway; Delft tiles outlined a window; Spanish tiles sheathed a wall; Chinese roof tiles surmounted a winding staircase; while tiles of his own devising, telling stories like *The Arkansas Traveler* or Dickens's *Pickwick Papers*, surrounded fireplaces.

Fonthill's *pièce de résistance* is the Columbus Room. Its vaulted ceiling blazes with the story of Columbus's discovery of the New World, depicted in Mercer tile. The initials "EL" surmount the capitals of the pillars, and over the doorway is a verse:

Clay and rust in fire burnt bright—
For EL's sake thus flash the light.

Even more had been intended. In one of his many notebooks Mercer wrote:

Ceiling of Columbus
Dedicated to Aunt Lela

A To EL dispenser of my education
B To EL giver of presents
C To EL my guide to Europe
   To EL for many Journeys to Europe
D To EL lover of poetry, helper in art
E To EL inspiring imagination
F To EL the bountiful
G To EL the loving
H To El cultivator of every talent
I In memory of my beloved Aunt EL
J The wise[7]

Soon after Mercer moved into Fonthill, he commenced the building of a new pottery, adjacent to his castle. U-shaped with an open cloister, it is a composite of several Spanish mission churches in California: Santa Barbara, San Juan Capistrano, and San Luis Rey. Built of cement like Fonthill, the Moravian Pottery and Tile Works produced tiles for new buildings, specified by leading architects all over America.[8]

Throughout these years Mercer continued his research, his writing, and his collecting. In 1910 he was elected President of the Bucks County Historical Society, which he had helped to found thirty years before. Four years later he decided to build his own museum and give it to the Society.

For his third structure he again chose a concrete castle. The fact that it towered incongruously above the low-flung Georgian brick Elkins Building bothered him not a bit. He simply connected the two with an arch, then let his imagination soar.

Once again Mercer, a group of day laborers, and Lucy the horse wrought a *tour de force*. Cubicles and alcoves of varying shapes open onto balconies that encircle a central court six stories high. Mercer's museum was built for his collection, and each craft or trade

The letters "EL" set in tile from Mercer's Moravian Pottery adorn the tops of the pillars in the Columbus Room at Fonthill. He dedicated the room to his aunt because it was she who introduced him to the Old World. Columbus's discovery of the New World, depicted in tile, encrusts the vaulted ceiling.

Part of the verse in Mercer tile that tops the doorway in Fonthill's Columbus Room: CLAY AND RUST IN FIRE BURNT BRIGHT / FOR EL'S SAKE THUS FLASH THE LIGHT.

represented in "The Tools of the Nation Maker" was housed in its own area.[9] When space gave out, artifacts were suspended from the ceilings. A whale boat, a Conestoga wagon, and an Indian dugout were slung from hooks imbedded in the cement high overhead, giving the visitor an entirely new view of each artifact. The collection begun at Aldie in 1897 was finally displayed in its own unique way and would eventually number 25,000 items.

Willie Mercer lived just long enough to see his older son's crowning achievement. He died at Aldie the following year (1917), aged ninety.

Lela, in Austria, was the next to go. She died in 1919, after enduring a difficult time in World War 1. She lived just long enough to see her daughter Walpurga married to Baron

The Moravian Pottery and Tile Works, begun in 1910 adjacent to Fonthill. This U–shaped structure, based on the design of three mission churches in southern California, replaced Mercer's first pottery, Indian House, a converted outbuilding at Aldie. From here his decorative architectural tiles were shipped all over the world.

The Mercer Museum, begun in 1914 and finished two years later. A simple archway connects Mercer's monolithic cement castle with the low-flung Georgian brick Elkins Building, built a decade earlier for the Bucks County Historical Society. To display his collection "Tools of the Nation Maker," Mercer created cubicles and galleries and niches that surround a multi-storied court, from the ceiling of which he suspended artifacts as small as a basket and as big as a whale boat.

Edouard von Friesen shortly before the Armistice. The next year Hubert, the artistic zither-playing army officer, died.

Now only Fanny, Henry, and Willie, Jr. (and his wife Martha) were left. Great was the joy in Doylestown in 1922 when word came from Europe that Lela's only child, Walpurga, had a son.

* * *

Two years later Fanny died, alone at Frosterly. She never married—apparently because of her "lasting intimacy" with Carl Schurz, the German–American politician and newspaper editor who had been Secretary of the Interior during the N. R. I. Dining Club days. A widower many years her senior, he corresponded with her for two decades (mostly in German), and until his death in 1906 managed to see her occasionally—a fact which has only recently come to light.

"What a store of happiness is there in the assurance you have given me," Schurz once wrote his "dear *Herzenfanny*," "that my love makes you happy."[10] Why Fanny and Carl Schurz never married is not known. Much of their correspondence has been destroyed, probably by Schurz's daughter, who prohibited any mention of Fanny after her father's death.

That Elizabeth did not know of her sister's liaison is inconceivable. In view of her romantic nature, it is more than likely that she aided and abetted the trysts that took place both in this country and abroad.[11] Not a whisper comes through in her letters, however.

Whether other members of Fanny's family were aware of the affair is problematic. It is curious to note that, among the jumble of photographs in Mercer's library at Fonthill, there is only one of his aunts' Washington friends. It is of Carl Schurz.

* * *

Aldie, too, disappeared. When Willie, Sr. died in 1917, the estate went to his sons. Henry, ensconced at Fonthill, promptly gave his share to Willie, Jr., never imagining that the ensemble would not be preserved intact. In 1927, however, it happened. Willie, Jr. and his wife (who had meanwhile inherited great wealth) built a new house farther back on the property. When the handsome Tudor brick mansion—also called "Aldie"—was finished the following year, Willie, Jr. announced his intention of tearing down "old Aldie."

By then the house Elizabeth had built more than half a century before was a derelict. The wallpaper was "hanging from the walls," plaster was "falling from the ceiling," there were leaks from "garret to basement." In fact, one could see "disintegration on all sides," Willie wrote Henry.[12] In such a condition, no one would buy or rent it, and "when I'm gone who can be expected to keep it up? It might... be turned into a road house or something equally debasing."

Willie, Jr. was surprised that his brother had such an "extraordinary affection for a place you voluntarily left and practically never see," and agreed to "negate" the order to demolish if Henry would restore the building, assume the upkeep, and leave a "fund adequate for its future maintenance." But Henry was by this time past seventy, in failing health, and deeply involved with his own three buildings. The fact that his brother had already given the instruction to raze the house had appalled him. "Mr. Strawbridge does not pull down Graeme Park [built in 1722 for Pennsylvania's Governor, Sir William Keith], Mr. Logan does not pull down Stenton [home of James Logan, William Penn's secretary]," he fulminated. The emotional letter to Willie continued:

Dr. Henry C. Mercer (Sc. D. and LL. D.) in rumpled English tweeds, in front of a tile-bedecked fireplace at Fonthill, not long before his death in 1930.

....Aldie is getting to be a charming relic of the middle 19th century. You can't reproduce it.... If you destroy it something of much historic value and growing interest is gone forever.

Lastly we are all gone except you and me, whatever you may say I have some moral right in this case though at law I have nothing to say—when I think of the memories associated with those walls all those that have been there and all that I have done there and seen there and the thought that you should sweep it all away without consulting me is very dreadful to me.

So the Samuel Sloan landmark came down.
Henry lived less than two years, dying in 1930.

* * *

His will left $100,000 to cover the cost of an expedition to China and the publication of its findings on the tools of one of the last countries not yet industrialized. Called *China at Work*, this undertaking was "in memory of my Uncle Timothy Bigelow Lawrence and of his wish that the Cause of Science advanced by his family as in their foundation of the Lawrence Scientific School at Harvard University, should be promoted by his heirs."[13]

In a sense, Bigelow's will, probated in 1869, had provided for his nephew-by-marriage's education, his travels, his writings, his buildings, his research. Mercer's own will, probated in 1930, demonstrated that he considered himself Bigelow's "heir," carrying on his lifework in the "interest of Science"—an idea nourished by Aunt Lela.

The first of several codicils to his will, written in 1927, excluded his brother Willie from any inheritance, leaving the money instead to the Bucks County Historical Society. Willie contested the will, and one of the witnesses called was Henry's lifelong Harvard friend, the novelist Owen Wister, Jr. (whose mother, Sarah Butler Wister, and grandmother, Fanny Kemble, had played a role in Elizabeth's life). The author of *The Virginian* testified that Mercer had a "beautiful mind, the mind of a genius,"[14] but that his refusal to be reconciled with his brother was a blemish upon it. Before sailing for Europe, Wister testified, he had gone to Fonthill to beg Mercer to "make up" on Christmas morning—to no avail.

The attack on the will was subsequently withdrawn. Willie, Jr. died nine years later, but his wife Martha lived on till 1960. By her will,[15] those Mercer family items that had not already found their way to Fonthill, but had been moved from the old Aldie to the new one, were bequeathed to the only descendant, Lela's daughter, Baroness Walpurga von Friesen, who was then living with her husband and son in Portugal.

* * *

A memorial to Elizabeth can be found in one of Thackeray's letters. On an American tour in 1856 he was reminded of the lady from Doylestown, while being entertained in other company. "Yesterday was a pleasant dinnerkin with a pleasant old gentleman...who has a charming daughter something like Mrs. Bigelow Lawrence, whom it would be very pleasant to fall in love with I daresay."[16]

Thanks to her nephew, a unique memorial graces her hometown. Would she not have loved Henry Mercer's castles?

A photograph of EL, considerably enlarged and hand-colored, hangs on a stairway at Fonthill. At the right may be seen part of Mercer's collection of antique Chinese roof tiles.

The last known photograph of EL.

NOTES

Unidentified quotations are from the original letters of Elizabeth Chapman Lawrence, found in the bread box and now in the Fonthill manuscripts, Spruance Library of the Bucks County Historical Society (BCHS).

CHAPTER 1

1. Edna S. Pullinger, "Edward Hicks, Newtown Coach Painter, Among Friends," *BCHS Journal* 2, no. 6 (Fall 1979): 219–20.
2. For the Chapman genealogy, see "Passengers and Ships prior to 1684," *The Publications of the Welcome Society of Pennsylvania*, no. 1 (Baltimore, 1970), pp.168–75 (the original manuscript is in the BCHS); Todd-Chapman-Mercer Bible (BCHS); *A Collection of Papers Read Before the BCHS* (1932), 6:464–66; *ibid.*, Henry C. Mercer, "John Chapman First Settler of Wrightstown" (1917), 4:441–47; W. W. H. Davis, *History of Bucks County*, 3 vols. (New York, 1905), 3:379–80.
3. A copy of Henry Chapman's diary of his trip to England in 1839 is in the BCHS. The original is in the possession of a descendant in Europe, Baron Bernard von Friesen.
4. W. W. H. Davis, *Doylestown Old and New* (Doylestown, PA, 1904), p. 359.
5. *Ibid.*, p. 192.
6. According to the Philadelphia Directories, the school run by the Misses Gill was located at 427 Spruce St.
7. Davis, *Doylestown*, p. 257.
8. For an account of Mrs. Rush's entertainments see Nicholas B. Wainwright, ed., *A Philadelphia Perspective* (Philadelphia: Historical Society of Pennsylvania [HSP], 1967). Also, Several Anonymous Philadelphians, *Philadelphia Scrapple* (Richmond, VA, 1956), pp. 178–79.
9. Gordon N. Ray, ed., *The Letters and Private Papers of William Makepeace Thackeray*, 3 vols. (Cambridge, MA, 1945–46), 3:118.

CHAPTER 2

1. J. E. Willard, *A Woman of the Century* (Buffalo, 1893), p. 247.
2. Robert Means Lawrence, M.D., *The Descendants of Major Samuel Lawrence* (Cambridge, MA, 1904), pp. 52–57.
3. Nathan Appleton, "Memoir of Abbott Lawrence," *Collections of the Massachusetts Historical Society*, 4th ser. vol. 4, (Boston, 1858): 498.
4. *Ibid.*, p. 501.
5. *New England Historical and Genealogical Register*, vol. 24 (1870), 178; vol. 45 (1891), 177–78; see also the biographical file at Harvard University Library.
6. T. Bigelow Lawrence, *An Exposition of the Difficulties between T.B. Lawrence and his Wife Sallie Ward Lawrence, which led to their Divorce* (Boston, 1850).
7. William Perrine, "A Story of Beautiful Women," *The Ladies Home Journal*, March 1901.
8. *Ibid.*

9. Virginia Tatnall Peacock, *Famous American Belles of the Nineteenth Century* (Philadelphia, 1901), p. 151.

   See also the chapter on Sallie Ward in Mrs. Elizabeth Fries Ellet's *The Queens of American Society* (New York, 1868).
10. Perrine, "Beautiful Women."
11. *Ibid.*
12. *Ibid.*
13. Melville O. Briney, *Fond Recollection* (Louisville, KY, 1955), p. 48, a reprint of articles which had appeared in *The Louisville Times* on 9, 16, and 23 July 1953. The list of wedding guests from Boston appeared in the *Louisville Daily Courier* on 2 December 1848.
14. Briney, *Fond Recollection*, p. 49.
15. *Ibid.*, p. 48.
16. *Ibid.*, p. 49.
17. *Ibid.*
18. *Ibid.*
19. Willard, *Woman of the Century*, p. 248.
20. T. B. Lawrence, *An Exposition of the Difficulties...* p. 11.
21. *Ibid.*, p. 8.
22. *Ibid.*
23. *Ibid.* p. 10.
24. *Ibid.*
25. *Ibid.* p. 13.
26. Briney, *Fond Recollection*, p. 50.
27. Ella Hutchison Ellwanger, "Mrs. Sallie Ward Downs," *Register of the Kentucky Historical Society* 16, no. 46 (1918): 12.
28. T.B. Lawrence, *An Exposition of the Difficulties...*, p. 9.
29. *Ibid.*
30. *Ibid.*, p. 7.
31. *Ibid.*
32. *Ibid.*, p. 13.
33. Briney, *Fond Recollection*, p. 51.
34. Clipping in the Sallie Ward file of the J.B. Speed Art Museum.
35. Briney, *Fond Recollection*, p. 50.
36. *Ibid.*, p. 51.
37. T. B. Lawrence, *An Exposition of the Difficulties...*, p. 7.
38. *Ibid.*
39. *Ibid.*, p. 12.
40. Briney, *Fond Recollection*, p. 51.
41. See London Directories of 1850, '51, and '52 in the Guildhall Library.
42. Ledgers of the Baring Brothers Bank, now in the Guildhall Library, show that £300 rent was paid quarterly to Earl Cadogan. The exorbitant amounts paid to Wimbush &

Co. (carriage hire) and Makepeace & Walford (silversmiths), for example, attest to the Lawrence scale of living.

43. Charles H. Shattuck, ed., *Bulwer and Macready, A Chronicle of the Early Victorian Theater* (Urbana, IL, 1958). See letter from Macready to Bulwer, 20 November 1849, p. 239.
44. Appleton, "Abbott Lawrence," p. 501.
45. Correspondence between Abbott Lawrence, Lord Palmerston, and the State Department may be found on Microfilm #M30, roll 57, National Archives, Washington, D.C.

CHAPTER 3

1. Elizabeth Longford, *Queen Victoria: Born to Succeed* (New York, 1965), p. 205.
2. This book was found in Mercer's library at Fonthill.
3. One of Willie's cousins was Lucy Mercer Rutherford, Mrs. Franklin D. Roosevelt's social secretary. For the Mercer genealogy see James Mercer Garnett, "John Francis Mercer," *Maryland Historical Magazine* 2, no. 3 (September 1907); James Mercer Garnett, "Mercer Genealogy," *Baltimore Sun*, 17 and 24 September 1905; James Mercer Garnett, *Biographical Sketch of Hon. James Mercer Garnett of Elmwood, Essex County, VA, with Mercer–Garnett and Mercer Genealogies*, (Richmond, VA, 1910); J. Reaney Kelly, "Cedar Park, Its People and Its History," *Maryland Historical Magazine* 58, no. 1 (March 1963): 30–53. The Fonthill manuscript contains a notebook compiled by William R. Mercer, Sr. on the Mercer genealogy, a copy of entries in a family Bible printed in Edinburgh in 1726, and a number of photographs of family portraits.
4. R. A. Fletcher, *Steamships and their History* (Philadelphia, 1910), p. 156.
5. Charles Durang, *History of the Philadelphia Stage*, a scrapbook of clippings at the Library Company of Philadelphia, p. 228. Also see George C. D. Odell, *Annals of the N.Y. Stage*, 1850–57 (New York, 1931), 6:242.
6. John Bassett Moore, ed., *The Works of James Buchanan, 1853–55* (Philadelphia and London, 1909), 9:50.
7. *Ibid.*
8. *Ibid.*, p. 62.
9. *Buchanan Papers*, HSP, microfilm roll #20, 24 September 1853.
10. *Ibid.*, roll #21, Boston, 28 January 1854.
11. *The Times* of London, 17 May 1854, reprinted from *New York Daily Times*.
12. For an account of the Ward brothers' trial see Briney, *Fond Recollection*, pp. 87–90; *Full and Authentic Report of the Testimony on the Trial of Matthew F. Ward* (New York, 1854); *Bucks County Intelligencer*, 23 November 1853 and 2, 9, 23 May 1854.
13. *Buchanan Papers*, HSP, microfilm roll #21, 28 January 1854.
14. Moore, *James Buchanan*, p. 76.
15. *Ibid.*, p. 87.
16. *Ibid.*, p. 152.
17. *Ibid.*, pp. 158–59.
18. Letter to James L. Reynolds, U. S. Legation, London, 4 April 1854, Reynolds Collection (uncatalogued), Franklin & Marshall College Library.
19. Undated clipping enclosed with one of EL's letters.

CHAPTER 4

1. Thomas M. Beggs, "Harriet Lane Johnston and the National Collection of Fine Arts," *Annual Report of the Board of Regents of the Smithsonian Institution... for the year ended June 30, 1954* (Washington: Government Printing Office, 1955), p. 445.

2. Longford, *Born to Succeed*, p. 371.

3. The diary of Joshua Bates, the Boston merchant who was a partner of Baring Brothers, contains the following note for 20 May 1855: "Went to Lord Lansdowne's last evening. A full dress party. Saw the Foreign Ministers, Lord Ashburton.... At the drawing room ... there was a great display of American beauty in Mrs. Wadsworth, Mrs. W, Mrs. Lawrence and Mrs. [sic] Lane." The diary is on deposit at the Guildhall Library, London.

CHAPTER 6

1. Henry Wyndham Phillips (1820–68) was the son of the more famous painter, Thomas Phillips (1770–1845). Efforts to find this painting through the Courtauld Institute, the Victoria and Albert Museum, and the National Gallery have proved in vain.

CHAPTER 7

1. Edna Healey, *Lady Unknown: The Life of Angela Burdett-Coutts* (London, 1981), p. 117.

2. See also letter from Harriet Lane to "My dear Ellie," dated 56 Harley St., Wednesday, March 7th/55, Reynolds Collection: "In my *frolics* I took a cold from which I have suffered ever since.... Col. Lawrence has had so severe a cough that he was obliged to go to Torkay [sic] & it has since turned to the whooping cough, I hear.... The last time I was out was to dine with the Queen which I enjoyed very much—her Majesty was most gracious & also Prince Albert.... Of course everything was most magnificent—the Princess Royal came in after dinner & her simplicity & merry tongue was [sic] most agreeable. Uncle sat upon the right of the Queen...."

CHAPTER 9

1. *Buchanan Papers*, HSP, microfilm roll #23, 16 January 1855.

2. *Buchanan Papers*, HSP, microfilm roll #24, 8 Hertford Street, May Fair, 4 September 1855.

3. *Ibid.*, Adelphi Hotel, Liverpool, October 13.

4. *General Register of the United States Navy and Marine Corps (1782–1882)* lists the following dates for William R. Mercer, USNA Class of 1847:

Midshipman	8 December 1841
Passed Midshipman	22 August 1849
Dropped	13 September 1855
Lieutenant Active List	15 September 1855
Resigned	24 January 1859

5. Moore, *James Buchanan*, p. 240.

6. *Buchanan Papers*, HSP, microfilm roll #24, 1 October 1855.

7. Moore, *James Buchanan*, p. 426.

CHAPTER 4

1. Thomas M. Beggs, "Harriet Lane Johnston and the National Collection of Fine Arts," *Annual Report of the Board of Regents of the Smithsonian Institution...for the year ended June 30, 1954* (Washington: Government Printing Office, 1955), p. 445.
2. Longford, *Born to Succeed*, p. 371.
3. The diary of Joshua Bates, the Boston merchant who was a partner of Baring Brothers, contains the following note for 20 May 1855: "Went to Lord Lansdowne's last evening. A full dress party. Saw the Foreign Ministers, Lord Ashburton.... At the drawing room ... there was a great display of American beauty in Mrs. Wadsworth, Mrs. W, Mrs. Lawrence and Mrs. [sic] Lane." The diary is on deposit at the Guildhall Library, London.

CHAPTER 6

1. Henry Wyndham Phillips (1820–68) was the son of the more famous painter, Thomas Phillips (1770–1845). Efforts to find this painting through the Courtauld Institute, the Victoria and Albert Museum, and the National Gallery have proved in vain.

CHAPTER 7

1. Edna Healey, *Lady Unknown: The Life of Angela Burdett-Coutts* (London, 1981), p. 117.
2. See also letter from Harriet Lane to "My dear Ellie," dated 56 Harley St., Wednesday, March 7th/55, Reynolds Collection: "In my *frolics* I took a cold from which I have suffered ever since.... Col. Lawrence has had so severe a cough that he was obliged to go to Torkay [sic] & it has since turned to the whooping cough, I hear.... The last time I was out was to dine with the Queen which I enjoyed very much—her Majesty was most gracious & also Prince Albert.... Of course everything was most magnificent—the Princess Royal came in after dinner & her simplicity & merry tongue was [sic] most agreeable. Uncle sat upon the right of the Queen...."

CHAPTER 9

1. *Buchanan Papers*, HSP, microfilm roll #23, 16 January 1855.
2. *Buchanan Papers*, HSP, microfilm roll #24, 8 Hertford Street, May Fair, 4 September 1855.
3. *Ibid.*, Adelphi Hotel, Liverpool, October 13.
4. *General Register of the United States Navy and Marine Corps (1782–1882)* lists the following dates for William R. Mercer, USNA Class of 1847:

Midshipman	8 December 1841
Passed Midshipman	22 August 1849
Dropped	13 September 1855
Lieutenant Active List	15 September 1855
Resigned	24 January 1859

5. Moore, *James Buchanan*, p. 240.
6. *Buchanan Papers*, HSP, microfilm roll #24, 1 October 1855.
7. Moore, *James Buchanan*, p. 426.

CHAPTER 10

1. *Buchanan Papers*, HSP, microfilm roll #24, Boston, 29 October 1855.
2. *Ibid.*
3. Mary Mercer to Mrs. Henry Chapman, Fonthill mss., 4 April 1856.
4. *Buchanan Papers*, HSP, microfilm roll #24, 97 Beacon St., Boston, 26 April 1856.
5. Willard, *A Woman of the Century*, p. 254.
6. *Antiques Magazine*, November 1947, p. 347.
7. All of these portraits are at the J. B. Speed Art Museum in Louisville. Inscribed on the reverse of Healy's self-portrait: "Portrait of Geo. P. A. Healy. Painted 4th of August, 1860 for his friends Dr. and Mrs. Hunt, Cottage Hill, Ill." Sallie's son, John Wesley Hunt, later became night editor of the *New York World*.
8. *Buchanan Papers*, HSP, microfilm roll #33, Doylestown, July 23.
9. For a description of the visit of "Baron Renfrew" to Boston, see the *Boston Daily Advertiser* and the *Boston Post*, 18–22 October 1860.
10. Homer T. Rosenberger, "Harriet Lane, First Lady: Hostess Extraordinary in Difficult Times," *Records of the Columbia Historical Society of Washington, D.C. 1966-68* (Washington, 1969), pp. 130–41.
11. U.S. Archives, Washington, microfilm T 204, roll #2, Boston, 21 September 1861.
12. Letter in private collection, Boston, 13 June 1861.

CHAPTER 11

1. National Archives, microfilm #T 204, roll 2, 27 October 1862.
2. *Ibid.*, 15 December 1862.
3. *Ibid.*
4. *Ibid.*, roll 3, 1 February 1864.
5. *Ibid.*, roll 2, 2 May 1863.
6. *Ibid.*
7. Fonthill mss., ser. 4, vol. 1. For a further account of Americans in Italy, see Paul R. Baker, *The Fortunate Pilgrims* (Cambridge, MA, 1964); Ernest Earnest, *Ex Patriates and Patriots* (Durham, NC, 1968); and Donald M. Reynolds, *Hiram Powers and His Ideal Sculpture* (New York, 1977).

CHAPTER 12

1. U. S. Archives, microfilm #T 204, roll 2, 27 December 1863.
2. Hiram Powers Papers, Archives of American Art, Smithsonian Institution, roll #1142, frames 923–24.
3. A sheaf of bills paid by Mr. Matteini may be found in the Fonthill mss.

CHAPTER 13

1. National Archives, microfilm #T 204, roll 3, 3 May 1865.
2. *Ibid.*
3. *Ibid.*, 8 May 1865.
4. Samuel Longfellow, ed., *Life of Henry Wadsworth Longfellow* (New York, 1891), 3:204.

5. Mrs. McClellan's note was enclosed in the same envelope with EL's letter.
6. G. H. Fleming, *That Ne'er Shall Meet Again* (London, 1971), p. 211.

CHAPTER 14

1. The quotations on TBL's death are taken from unidentified newspaper clippings on the "Harvard College Library Clipping Sheet."
2. Will #49467, Suffolk Co., MA, 26 April 1864, probated 26 April 1869. Inventory filed 7 May 1869, Rec. Book 34, p. 92.
3. *Col. T. B. Lawrence,* no author (Boston, MA), p. 42.
4. *Ibid.,* p. 19.
5. Mary Mercer to her husband William, Fonthill mss., Florence, 12, June 1870.
6. *Ibid.*
7. *Ibid.*
8. Private collection, Florence, 25 June 1870.
9. *Bucks County Intelligencer,* 14 March 1871. Other buildings designed by Samuel Sloan (1815–'84) are the Philadelphia Savings Fund Society and Episcopal Hospital in Philadelphia; the Fulton Opera House in Lancaster, PA; and "Longwood" in Natchez, MS. It is interesting to note that Addison Hutton (at first an employee, later a partner of Sloan) was designing a new Presbyterian Church in Doylestown at the same time Sloan was designing Aldie. The same builder, Henry D. Livezy, was employed for both.
10. John W. Harshberger, "Some Old Gardens of Pennsylvania," *Pennsylvania Magazine of History and Biography* 47 (1924): 297–98.
11. Fonthill mss., ser. 8, vol. 10. Henry Mercer jotted down these measurements in one of his notebooks when planning Fonthill.
12. Louise and James Bush-Brown, *Portraits of Philadelphia Gardens* (Philadelphia, 1929), pp. 63–68.
13. Fonthill mss., ser. 18, fol. 7. Henry Mercer related this story in a letter to the Society for the Preservation of New England Antiquities, whose president had inquired about a photograph in their possession in 1920.
14. Walter Muir Whitehill, *Museum of Fine Arts, Boston: A Centennial History* (Cambridge, MA, 1970), p. 27. See also Carol Troyen, ed., *The Boston Tradition* (New York, 1980), p. 31. This catalogue, which accompanied an art exhibition by the same name, contains reproductions of Mrs. Abbott Lawrence's portrait (p. 109) and of Meneghelli's painting of "The Lawrence Room" (p. 30).
15. Fonthill mss., ser. 18, fol. 7
16. *New England Historical and Genealogical Register,* vol. 27, 373–75.
17. R.M. Lawrence, *Descendants of Samuel Lawrence,* p. 52.

CHAPTER 15

1. Paul R. Baker, *Richard Morris Hunt* (Cambridge, MA, 1980), p. 15.
2. See *The Connoisseur* 199 (December 1978): 232.

CHAPTER 16

1. Lillie de Hegermann-Lindencrone, *The Sunny Side of Diplomatic Life* (New York,

1914), pp. 71–72. Excerpts containing references to EL appeared in *Harper's Magazine*, October 1914.

2. *Ibid.*, pp. 79–80.
3. Ward Thoron, ed., *The Letters of Mrs. Henry Adams* (Boston, 1936), p. 430.
4. Ernest Samuels, *Henry Adams: The Middle Years* (Cambridge, MA, 1958), p. 30.
5. Thoron, *Mrs. Henry Adams*, p. 176.
6. W. C. Ford, ed., *Letters of Henry Adams, 1858–1891* (Boston, 1930), p. 336n. See also J.C. Levenson, Ernest Samuels, Charles Vandersee and Viola Hopkins Winner, eds., *The Letters of Henry Adams* (Cambridge, MA, 1982–), vol. 2, 502.
7. Thoron, *Mrs. Henry Adams*, p. 339.
8. Harriet S. Blaine Beale, ed., *Letters of Mrs. James G. Blaine* (New York, 1908), 1:62.
9. *Ibid.*, 1:152–53.
10. *Ibid.*, 1:275.

CHAPTER 17

1. Thoron, *Mrs. Henry Adams*, p. 259.
2. Briney, *Fond Recollection*, p. 53.
3. Thoron, *Mrs. Henry Adams*, p. 259.
4. *Ibid.*, p. 338.
5. Beale, *Mrs. James Blaine*, p. 316.
6. *Ibid.*, p. 315.
7. Thoron, *Mrs. Henry Adams*, p. 374.
8. *Ibid.*, p. 425.
9. *Ibid.*, p. 443.
10. *Ibid.*, p. 431.
11. *Ibid.*, p. 427.
12. *Doylestown Democrat*, 6 February 1883.
13. *Ibid.*, 30 January 1883.
14. *Ibid.*, 22 May 1883.
15. Thoron, *Mrs. Henry Adams*, p. 451.
16. *Ibid.*, p. 426.
17. *Ibid.*, p. 383.
18. Mary Mercer to Mrs. Henry Chapman, Fonthill mss., 17 April 1883.
19. A typescript of Milon's letters (now part of the Fonthill manuscripts) was made by EL's great-niece, Walpurga von Friesen. A note attached to the typescript, dated Estoril, Portugal June 1955, says: ".... When she [EL] died, it was in 'Aldie' near Doylestown that she died, the family felt that my father [i.e., Hubert] should have this relic of Napoleon's and my aunt Fanny Chapman, aunt Lela's sister wrapped it in an envelope on which the following is written: 'THE LOCK'—Dear Hubert, Harry, Willy and I (Harry and Willy being my Mother's older and younger brothers) have decided you are to be the posessor *[sic]* of this treasure of dear beloved aunt Lela. F.C. [Fanny Chapman]." The note adds that it was Hubert who had "had a beautiful case made for all the things at Eschenbachs in Munich." The original letters and "the lock" are now in the possession of Walpurga's son, Baron von Friesen.

20. Obituaries for Col. Milon can be found in *The Times—Philadelphia*, 18 March 1887; also *The Philadelphia Press* of the same date. Both refer to the lock of hair given to EL.

CHAPTER 18

1. On page 715 of Battle's *History of Bucks County* may be found an account of *The Lenape Stone*, "published by G. P. Putnam's Sons, 1885." In the margin of the copy in the Spruance Library is scrawled: "Kind! H. C. Mercer Nov. 22—1926—I wrote the book, and my aunt Mrs. T. B. Lawrence paid Putnam to publish it. H.C.M."
2. Copies of letters of Lela Mercer, Spruance Library.
3. *Doylestown Democrat*, 31 July 1888.
4. Wister Papers, HSP, box 13, folder 11, July 7 and September 2.
5. Samuels, *Henry Adams*, pp. 93–94.
6. Wister Papers, HSP, box 13, folder 11, York Harbor, Maine, August 23.
7. For the "Constantia" letters, see Fonthill mss., ser. 19, fol. 6 and 7. For further information on Sarah Wyman Whitman, see Martha J. Hoppin, "Women Artists in Boston: 1870–1900," *The American Art Journal* 13 (Winter 1981): 27–31. A sketch similar to one illustrated in this article for a stained-glass window at Trinity Church, Boston, in memory of Phillips Brooks, was found enclosed in a letter from Sarah Whitman to EL.
8. Wister Papers, HSP, box 13, folder 11, Aldie, July 7.
9. de Hegermann–Lindencrone, *Diplomatic Life*, pp. 252–53.
10. *Ibid.*, p. 264.
11. Wister Papers, HSP, box 13, folder 11, 10 October 1899.
12. *Ibid.*
13. *Ibid.*, Sunday.
14. *Papers Read before...*, Mercer, "Tools of the Nation Maker" (1909), 3:469–81.
15. *Ibid.*, Mercer, "Notes on the Moravian Pottery of Doylestown" (1917), 4:482–87.
16. Two typed letters (dictated) from Mercer to Mrs. Gardner are in her museum's archives. One, dated Fonthill, 24 July 1921, in response to a letter from Mrs. Gardner, describes himself as "very much under the weather," and is signed "Very affectionately yours." Enclosed were five photographs of Fonthill. *Munsey's Magazine* 39, no. 6 (March 1906): 660, says: ".... The story of Fenway Court would tell how a certain factory in Doylestown, Pa., practically came into being because Mrs. Gardner was not content to use an inferior and un-Italian tiling for her floor...." It should be noted that Mercer first signed Mrs. Gardner's guest book 10 September, 1894.
17. Minutes of the board of directors, BCHS, 29 March 1899.

EPILOGUE

1. Beggs, "National Collection of Fine Arts," pp. 443–48. See also Homer T. Rosenberger, "Harriet Lane Johnston and the Formation of a National Gallery of Art, *Records of the Columbia Historical Society of Washington, D.C. 1969–70* (Washington, 1971), pp. 399–442.
2. *Boston Evening Transcript*, 16 December 1904: "At the vestry of St. Cecelia's Church, Dec. 15, William Robert Mercer, Jr. and Martha, daughter of Mr. and Mrs. Charles Stratton Dana."
3. Briney, *Fond Recollection*, p. 53.

4. *Ibid.*, p. 47.
5. Peacock, *Famous American Belles*, p. 156.
6. *Papers Read Before...*, Mercer, "The Building of Fonthill at Doylestown, Pennsylvania" (1932), 6:321–30.
7. Fonthill mss., ser. 8, vol. 10.
8. *Papers Read Before...*, Mercer, "Notes on the Moravian Pottery of Doylestown" (1917), 4:482–87. After a succession of owners following Mercer's death, the moribund tile works was purchased by the County of Bucks in 1967, and was reactivated in 1974 using the original techniques. Mercer's records of the tile works, as well as his personal papers, are preserved at the Spruance Library, and a large portion has recently been microfilmed with a grant from the National Endowment of the Humanities. His correspondence with the Keeper of Medieval Antiquities at the British Museum, who furnished designs from English abbeys, was recently discovered by Cleota Reed, and may be found in her article "Henry C. Mercer's Letters to Sir Hercules Read", *The Bucks County Historical Society Journal*, 2:7, Spring 1980, 272–290.
9. *Ibid.*, Mercer, "Dedication of Mercer Museum," 4: 626–43.
10. Hans L. Trefousse, *Carl Schurz*, (University of Tennessee, 1982), p. 273. For further mention of Fanny, see pp. 249, 253, and 257.
11. Fanny had possession of EL's portrait when she died. In her will she bequeathed "the crayon portrait with green wreath of my sister Lizzie" to her nephew Willie (Bucks County Recorder of Deeds, Will Book 47, p. 154). Henry was left "the portfolio of engravings known as "The Port-folio." When Willie died, he left his house and its contents to his wife Martha (Will Book 65, p. 442). She in turn left "all portraits of members of my husband's family" to "my husband's niece Walpurga von Friesen" (Will Book 115, p. 79).
12. The correspondence between the brothers is in the uncatalogued portion of the Fonthill manuscripts, 6 and 7 May 1928.
13. The will of Henry C. Mercer (Bucks County Will Book 54) was reprinted by BCHS in pamphlet form in 1958. This quotation appears on pp. 11–12. *China at Work*, by Rudolf P. Hommel, was first published in 1937, and re-published in 1969 by the M.I.T. Press (Cambridge, MA). On the flyleaf it says:...Dedicated to the Memory of Timothy Bigelow Lawrence of Boston by his Nephew Henry Chapman Mercer."
14. *Bucks County Intelligencer*, 9 April 1930.
15. Bucks County Will Book 115, p. 79.
16. Ray, *Letters of Thackeray*, 3:536.

INDEX*

A., R. (actor), 106
Adams, Mr. and Mrs. Henry, 1–2, 208–10, 220, 222–23, 238
Agassiz, Louis, 118
Ailesbury, Marchioness of, 57
Albert, Prince, 44, 46, 48, 50, 90
Aldie (Doylestown home), **182**, 178–85, **183**, 234, 246, 252, 254
  house party at, **184**
Alexandra, Princess (Denmark), 133
Alhambra, 234
Alice, Princess, 50
Althorp, (Spencer seat), 132–33, **133**
Americans in Florence, 166, 170
Amory, Mrs. (hostess), 42
Andre, Maj. John, 56
Angelus, The (Millet), 239–40
Annapolis, Assembly at, 10
Antoinette, Marie, 192
Appleton, Thomas Gold, 161, 185, 218
armor, 14, 104, 118, 135, 178–79, 182, 186
Armstrong, Venerando Politza, 220
Ascot (track), 56
Ashburton, Lord & Lady, 78–79, 80–81, 100, 103
Astor, John Jacob, Mr. & Mrs., 2, 214, 215
Atlantic (steamship), **28**, 36, 42
Atlantic City, 247
Augusto (servant), 152

Baden, 154–55
Balaclava, 85
Ballard, Dr. (dentist), 87
Bancroft, George (minister), Mr. & Mrs., 2, 103, 214
Bancroft (historian), 223, 225
Baring, Sir Francis, 85
Baring Brothers, **181**
Barlow, Gen. Francis, 157
Bates, Mrs. Joshua, 43, 73
Bath, Marquis of, 75
Bayard, Senator & Mrs. (Delaware), 2, 204, 214, 215, 228
Bayreuth (Wagner Festival), 237
Bayley's *(sic)*, 23–24
Beacon Street house, **111**, 111–13
Beale, Emily, 209, 210

*Illustrations are referenced in bold face.

Beauclerk, Lord George, 71
Beecher, Henry Ward, 160
Bell, Alexander Graham, 225
Belmont, Augustus, 42–43, 115
Belvoir Castle, 75, 87–88, **88**, 92, 107
Bey, Aristachi (Turkish Minister), 207, 210, 218, 223, 224–25
Bickersleth, Miss, 71
Biddle, Charley, 10
Bierstadt (painter), 174
Bigelow, Hon. Timothy (Bigelow's maternal grandfather), 13
Bismarck, Prince, 191
Black Prince (horse), 124, 130, 138, 178, 244
Blaine, Sen. James G. (Maine), 204, 205, 209, 210–211, **211**, 222, 227–28, 239
  Harriet, 210, 211–12, 214, 219, 222, 225–27
  house, **226**
Blair, Francis, 164
Blessington, Countess of, **51**, 52
Blumenthal (composer), 170
Boboli Gardens, 144–45, **145**
Bonaparte, Charles Joseph, 232, 246
Bonaparte, Col. Jerome, 221, 224
Bonaparte, Joseph, 229
Borghese, Princess, 230
Boston Courier, 20
Boston Herald, 17
Boston Museum of Fine Arts, 2, **185**, 186–87
Boucher, Gen., 192–93
Bowood Park, **83**
Bracciano, 200
Brighton, 71
Brimmer, Mr. & Mrs. Martin (pres., BMFA), 185, 237–38
Brinkman, Lady (hostess), 29
Brontë, Charlotte, 50, 118
Brookfield, Mr. & Mrs., 79–80, 100
Brougham, Lady, 52
Browning, Elizabeth Barrett, 106
Bryan, William Jennings, 239
Bryn Mawr College, 247
Buchanan, James, 32, 33, 35–36, 42–43, 72, 90–91, 99, 107, 108, **108**, 109, 114–115, 116, 120, 121, 126
Buckingham Palace ball, **54**
Bucks County Historical Society, 242, 249, 254

Bulwer-Lytton, Sir Edward, 51, 63–69, 85, 104
Burnside, General, 163–64, 216
Butler, General (S. Carolina), 212–13
Byron, Lord, 82

Cadlands, 75
Caernavon, 71
Cairo, 247
Calhoun, Mrs. John C., 169
calling cards, 43, 86, 121
Cambridge, Duchess of, 48, 50, 92
Cambridge, Princess Mary of, 48, 50, 59, 92–93, **93**
Canterbury, Archbishop of, 57
Cantigalli (potter), 242
Cardigan, Lord, 74, 85
Carnot, Mme. (French Pres. widow), 240
castles, 63–67, 70, 75–78, 87–89, 92, 105, 107, 189, 191
Catharine, Lady, of Wilton, 92
Cavalier (hairdreser), 45
Ceylon, 194
Chambord, Chateau de, 189
Chandler, Sen. Zack (Michigan), 210–11
Chapman, Abraham (grandfather), 5, 115
Chapman, Arthur (half brother), 7, 175, 236
Chapman, Fanny (half sister), 2, 117, **153**, 153–54, 155, 156–57, 159, 168, 169, 175, 176, 188, 197, 199, 203, 205, **206**, 206–207, 209, 212, 215, 221, 234, 256, 251
Chapman, Judge Henry (father), 5, 26, 32, 33–34, 109, 115, 175, 176, 200–203, 231, 234
Chapman, John ("the First"), 5, 202
Chapman, Mary (sister), 6, 8, **25**, 25–26, 108, 109, 112, 113–14, 117, 130, 169, 175, 176, 227, 244
Chapman, Nancy Shunk (stepmother, "Mama"), 6, 26, 116, 120, 121, 236, **244**
Chapman, Rebecca Stewart (mother), 5
Chapman sisters, **177**
Chapman, Tom (brother), 142
Chenonceaux, Countess of, 191
Chestnut Street (Philadelphia), 23
Cheverny (chateau), 191
children, 117, 118, 155, 234–36
China at work, 254
Choate, Rufus (lecturer), 114
church, 5, 171, 202
Church, Frederic (artist), 120, 174
Civil War, 119, 126–31, 134, 138, 142, 152–54, 157, 160, 163–64
Clarendon, Countess of, 44, 45, 46

Clay, Henry, 9
Clementine, Lady, 61
Cleveland, Grover, 227
Clymer, Heister (congressman), 207
Cobden, Richard (economist), 164
Coleman, Miss (hostess), 225
Coliseum, **147**
Collins, Willkie, 106
Commons, House of, 29, 70, 85
Connelly, P. F. (sculptor), **158**, 168, **183**, 186–87
Constable, Lady, 83
Constellation (ship), 140
Contes d'Hoffman, 221
Corie, Mr., 79
Corwith Expedition, 236
cosmetics, 16–17, 33, 245
courtship, 29, 33–34, 156
Coutts, Angela Burdett-, 52, 59, 85–86
Cowper, Earl, 103
Crimean War, 60–61, 74, 85, 107
Croxton Park Races, 92
Crystal Palace Exhibition, 22, **24**, 25, 50, 57, **58**
Cushing, Mrs. (hostess), 118
Cushman, Charlotte (actress), 9, 148–49
Cust, Sir Edward, 45, 74–75

Damrosch, Walter, 239
dancing, 48, 206–207
Dante, 161
Davis, Jefferson, 160–61, 164
deafness, 13–14, 16
death, 5, 107–108, 115, 120, 130, 142, 175, 222, 228, 234, 240, 244–46, 251–252
Delane, John T., 49
Demidoff, Prince, 141
Democracy (novel), 1–2, 209–210
Derby, Lord, 85
Devens, Gen., 216
Devonshire, Duke of, 104
Dexter, Mr. & Mrs. (friends), 152, 155
Dickens, Charles, Mr. & Mrs., 101, **102**, 105–106
Dijon, 194
Disraeli, 49, 61, 85
divorce, 12, 19, **20**, 27, 34, 35, 61
Dönhoff, Count, 207
Downs, Maj. George F., 245–46
Doyle (caricaturist), 49, 70
Doylestown, Pa., 5–6, 7, 110, 169, 176, 182–83, 242
Doylestown Daily Republican, 246
Doylestown Democrat, 224

Doylestown Intelligencer, 36
Drayton, Mr. (suitor), 9
Dreyfuss affair, 240–241
Drontzkoy, Mme. (Russian princess), 149–50, 152
Drummond, Lady Elizabeth, 75
Duff Gordon, Lady, 69
Dumas, Alexander, 167, 191

Ealing Park, 59
Eaton, John (Secretary of War), 169
education, 7, 13, 15, 17, 169–70, 176–77, 203, 239
Edward "the Martyr" (servant), 213–14
Edward II, 244
Egg, Augustus (actor), 106
elections, 115, 116, 155–56, 204–205, 219, 227–29
Elizabeth, Queen, 66
Ellen (maid), 169, 176
Elliot, Mrs. (visitor in Florence), 170
Elliot (Pres. of Harvard), 239
Elvaston Castle, **81, 82,** 81–83
Elwyn, Mr. (*Quarterly Review* Editor), 67
Emma (cook), 53, 60, 98
Emma F. Harriman (ship), 179
entertaining, 60, 104, 118, 143–44, 155, 173, 185, 204, 213, 215, 223, 224–25
Eton Hall, 71
Eugénie, Empress of France, 221
Evans, Dr. Thomas (dentist), 107, 134
Evarts (Secretary of State), Mr. & Mrs., 215, 223
Everett, Edward, 114
Eyre, Mrs. Wilson, 156, 190

Ferdinando (servant), 188, 190, 194, 197, 198, 199, 203
Fillmore, Millard, 105
Fitzpatrick, Emma, 27, 60
Fitzroy, Miss (London belle), 29
Florence, 135–49, **137,** 158, 177–79, 198, 221–22
Florentine society, 145, 149, 156, 159
Fontainebleau, 188
Fonthill, 247–48, **248**
Foster, Mr. (*Examiner* Editor), 67, 105
Fourth of July, 56
Frémont, John C., 115
French Embassy, 57
Freylinghaysen, Mrs. (hostess), 224
Friesen, Edouard von, 251–52
Frosterly, 203, 252

Galt House, 245–46
gardens, 63, 75, 135, 137, 140–41, 144, 154, 195, 207, 234
Gardner, Mrs. Jack, 222, **239,** 242
Garfield, President, 219, 222
Gaskell, Mrs. (biographer), 118–19, 148
Gibbs, Mrs. (Mrs. Astor's mother), 196
Gilbert, Mr., 60
Gill, the Misses, 7
Gilman, Mrs., 155
Gladstone, 85
God Save the Queen, 125
Goodrich Court, 70
gossip, 9, 17, 18, 34, 72, 133, 214
government, 142, 153–54, 157, 188, 204–205, 208, 209–211, 214, 216–17, 222, 228, 239
Grange, The, 78, **79,** 80
Grant, Ulysses S., 160, 164, 188
Granville, Lord, 57
Grauman's Chinese Theater, 247
Greeley, Horace, 142
Greenwich, 56
Groton, 42
Guildhall banquet, 74
Gurney, Samuel, 90
Gwyn, Nell, 71
Gye, Dame Emma (singer), 222

Haddon Hall, 89
Hall, The Rev., 142, 149
Hamilton, Sir William, 104
Hampshire, 78
Hampton Court, 30
Hardy (butler), 114, 116
Harrington, Earl of, 81, 82
Harrisburg Capitol, **247**
Harrison, Mr. (escort), 28–29, 30, 31–32
Hay, John (Undersecretary of State), 21
Hayes, Rutherford B., 204, 205
Haymarket Theatre, 202
Healy, G. P. A. (painter), 118
Heart of the Andes (painting), 120
Hegerman, Johann de (Danish Minister), 206–207
Hegermann, Lillie de, 207, 208, 237, 240–241
Hereford, 71
Hicks, Edward, 5
Hinchinbrook, Lord, 121–22, 144
Hippodrome, 221
Hogarth, 84
holidays, 10, 56, 78–81, 141, 142–43, 146, 152, 157, 196–97, 212
Home, David (medium), 98, 99–100, 101–103
homes, 53, 104, 110–112, 113–114, 127, 135–38, 176, 182–85, 204

Hook, Mrs. (dressmaker), 8
Hôtel des Invalides, 31
Hunt, Holman (artist), **171**, 171–72
Hunt, Mr. & Mrs. Richard Morris (architect), 192–93, 195
Hunt, Dr. Robert, 117
hunting, 89, 92
Hyde Park, 54

illness, 3, 10, 13–14, 16, 43, 87, 90, 92, 103, 110–111, 117, 134, 152, 154, 166, 190, 200
Illustrated London News, 54, 85
"Indian House," 242
Inverness, Duchess of, 44
Isabella, Queen of Spain, 198
Isarborn, Baron Hubert Fidler von, **233**, 233–34, 252
Isarborn, Walpurga von, 234–36, **235**, 251–52, 254

Jackson, Stonewall, 164, 215
James (butler), 60, 104
James, Henry, 223
James-Lorah House (Doylestown), 7
Jerrold, Douglas, 105
Jersey, Lady, 61
Johnson, Andrew, 160
Johnston, Henry Elliott, 244

Kemble, Fanny, 118, 118–19
Kent, Duchess of, 48, 50–51
King, General, 161
Knebworth, 63, **64–66**, 67–69
Koh-i-Noor diamond, 48, 69
Kossuth, Lajos, 23–24

Ladies Home Journal, 15
Lady Moyoress (London), 55
Lambeth Palace, 57
landscaping, 11, 78, 81, 179, 183
Landseer, Sir Edwin, 49, 55, 67, 70, 174
Lane, Harriet (Buchanan's niece), 33, 35, 36, 42, 46, 49, 90–91, 121, 124, **124**, 244
Lane, Richard (lithographer), 78
Langtry, Lily, 227
languages, 6, 7, 140, 167
Lanier, Sidney, 240
Lansdowne House, 49
Lansdowne, Lord, 49, 59, 60, 69, 83, 84, 99
Last Days of Pompeii, The, 67
Last Supper, 146

Lawrence, Abbott (Bigelow's father), 13, 18, 21–22, 34, 38, **40**, 41, 48, 106, 107, 109, 112, 118, 139–40
Lawrence family, **41**
Lawrence family home, 38
Lawrence, Mrs. James (Bigelow's sister-in-law), 41
Lawrence, Katharine Bigelow (Bigelow's mother), 13, 16–17, 34, 38, **39**, 110–112
Lawrence, Kitty (Bigelow's sister), 41
Lawrence, Robert Means, 13
Lawrence, Sallie Ward (*See* Ward, Sallie)
Lawrence, Maj. Samuel (Bigelow's grandfather), 13
Lawrence Scientific School (Harvard), 254
Lawrence, Col. T. Bigelow (EL's husband), 3, 11–12, 13–14, 16–22, **20**, 29, 31, 33–34, 39, 108, 114–115, 119, 124, 126–27, 130, 139, 143, 157–58, 160, 174, 175, 254
Lee, Gen. Robert E., 157, 160–61, 216
Lemon, Mark (actor), 106
Lenape Stone, The (H. Mercer), 232
Leslie, Charles Robert, 44
Lever, Charles James (novelist), 155
Leydon, Count, 224
Light House, The (Dickens), 105
Lincoln, Abraham, 1, 126, 130, 153, 155, 156, 160, 163, 164, 214
Liszt, Franz, 146–48
Literary Fund (London), 43
literature, 50, 67–68, 69, 134
Liverpool, 28, 71
Lloyd, Mr. (sailor), 10
London American, 138
London social life, 61–62, 91
Longshore, Duke of, 107
Lord Mayor of London, 55, 74
Lords, House of, 69
Longfellow, 42, 130, 161
Lords, House of, 69
Lorne, Marquis of (Canada), 224
Louisville Daily Courier, 18–19
Louisville Journal, 19
Louisville Weekly, 27
Lovelace, Lady Ada Byron, 82
Lowell, Augustus, 41
Lowell, Mr. (London minister), 222
Lowndes, James, 209
Lucretia (novel), 51
Lyons, Lord, 121, 192
Lytton, Lord, 200

Macaulay, Thomas B., 69
Macauley, Commodore, 109

MacDonald, Col., 92–93
Maclise, Mr. (painter), 67
Magic Flute, The, 221
Magruder, Col., 127
Mahomet, Prince (Calcutta), 43
Malaret, Mme., 156
manners, 44, 52, 86, 121
Maplewood Inn (New Hampshire), 231
Maquay, Mrs., 170
Marengo (horse), 168, 186–87
Maresfield Park, 71
Marcy, Mrs., 163
Marie, Grand Duchess, 198
Marlboro, Duchess of (Sarah), 132
Marsh, Mrs. (Italian minister's wife), 166, 170, 179
Marsh, Othniel, 223
Maryland, Eastern Shore of, 11
Maryland, Governor of, 10
Matteini, Joseph (clerk), 139, 152, 179
Mayfair home, 104
McClellan, Gen. & Mrs., 142, 149, 155–56, 160, 161–65, **162**, 172–73, 217, 221
McHenry, Mr. (suitor), 10–11
McKinley, President, 239, 244
McLane, Jenny (neighbor), 215
Meissonier (artist), 174
Meistersinger, Der, 240
Mercer, Elizabeth Lawrence (Mary's daughter, "Lela"), 117, 169, 206, 212, 215, 221, 225, 232–233, 234, 251
Mercer, Henry Chapman (Mary's first son), 1, 3, **115**, 139, 169, 176–77, 183, **196**, 203, 212, 224, 225, 232–34, **236**, 236–37, 241–42, 247–48, 251, 252–54, **254**
Mercer, John Francis (Governor of Maryland), 25
Mercer, Martha Dana, **245**, 254
Mercer, Mary (See Chapman, Mary)
Mercer Museum, 249, **251**
Mercer, William Robert (Mary's second son), 131, 169, 225, 227, 234, **244**, 244–245, **245**, 252–54
Mercer, Willie (Mary's husband), **25**, 25–26, 73–74, 108–109, 115–16, 117, 169, 176, 200–203, 212, 227, **234**, 251, 252
Metcalf (landscape gardener), 179, 182
Metternich (memoirs), 216; Princess, 221
Mexican War, 15
military matters, 13–14, 109, 119, 126–28, 134, 140, 216
Millais (painter), 174
Millman, Henry (Dean of St. Paul's), 50
Milnes, Monckton, 85, 107
Milon, Col. Pierre Solidor, 229–230

Monaco, 197
money, 7, 8–9, 18, 19, 21–22, 34, 41, 44, 89, 117, 141, 175–76, 179, 215, 225, 241
Monte Carlo (casino), 247
Montparnasse, 203
Montpensier, Duke and Duchess of, 155
"Moravian Pottery and Tile Works," 242, 249, **251**
Moreau's (costumier), 46
Morgan, Charley (painter), 156
Morgan, William de, 242
Morley, Countess Dowager of, 103
"Mulligan Letters," 228
music, 7, 9, 27, 32, 71, 146, 179

Napoleon Bonaparte, 216, 229, 238
  death mask, **229**
Napoleon, Louis, 51, 83, 101
Nast, Thomas (cartoonist), 228
National Rational International Dining Club, 2, 202, 208, 217–18, 224
Nelson, Lord, 104
Newstead Abbey, 82
New York Mirror, 37
New York Times, 3
Niagara Falls, 241
Nice, 194–98
Nightingale, Florence, 85, **86**
Noailles, Marquise de, 199
Norton, Caroline Sheridan, 75
Norton, Charles Elliot (art historian), 240

Olga, Madame, 154
opera, 44, 51, 159, 166, 172, 221, 238, 240
Opéra Comique, l', 221
Oporto, Duke of, 55
opulence, 15, 48, 49, 50, 58, 88, 149, 220
Orford, Lady, 198–99
Oriental Palace (Brighton), 71–72
Otté, Madame (dressmaker), 8, 36
Outrey (French minister), 213, 216

Paget, Lady, 191, 237, 238
Paget, Sir Augustus, 200
painting, 5, 33, 84, 106, 120, 144, 146, 171–72, 174, 239–40
Palace of St. James, 45
Palmerston, Lord & Lady, 45, 74, 85, 103
Pandolfino, Prince & Princess, 197–98
Panizzi, Mr. (British Museum), 49
Paris, Comte de, 144; and Countess, 155
Paris Exposition, 174

Parliament, 169
Patti, Adelina, 166, 222
Paxton, Sir Joseph, 57
Peabody, Mr., 72
Pendleton, Senator (Ohio), 212, 213–14
Pennsylvania, 91
Perry, Lt., 73
Philadelphia, 8
Philadelphia Evening Bulletin, 246
philanthropy, 90, 179, 185, 187, 198, 229, 241, 242, 254
Phillips, Mr. (artist), 69, 70
Picquart, Georges, 241
Pierce, Franklin, 109
Pierce, General, 127–29
Pisa, 151
Pitti Palace, 158–59
Plunkett, Mrs. (hostess), 205
Pocantico Hills (Rockefeller), 247
poetry, 809, 87, 106, 173, 205
Pompeii, 67
Porter, Col. Fitz-John, 216–17
portraits, 78, 118, 139, 151, 157–58, 168, 187, 187, 255
Portugal, King of, 55
pottery
Powers, Hiram (sculptor), 138–39, **140**, 151, 157–58, 168, 179–80
Powers, Longworth (photographer), 168, 187
presentation (to Victoria), 44–46
Prescott, William (historian), 41, 42, 57–58, 114, 120
Prince Albert's Farm, 105
Pumpelly, Raphael, 223
Punch, 35, 69, 100

Quincy, Josiah, 42

Rachel (actress), 107
Raglan, Lord, 81, 89
Rattazzi, Mme., 167
Read, Sir Hercules (British Museum), 247
Remusat, Mme. de *(Memoires)*, 215–16
"Renfrew, Baron," (Prince of Wales), **126**
Rochefoucauld, Duc de la, 190
Rome, 146
Roosevelt, Theodore, 246
Rose (servant), 188, 190, 194, 221
Rotch, Annie Lawrence, 71, 112
Rotch, Benjamin, 71, 98
Rotten Row, 54
royalty, 44, 48, 55, 69–70, 90–91, 92–93, 121–26, 143, 146, 155, 158–59, 192, 197–98, 199, 202
Rush, Mrs. James (Julia), 9

Russell, Lord John, 85
Rutland, Duke of (& Duchess), 75, 76–78, 87–89, 104, 107

St. Louis World's Fair, 247
St. Moritz, 165–66, 172
Sainte-Beuve, 203
Salvini (tragedian), 172, 225
Sammy (waiter), 213
San Antonio, 247
Sand, George, 107
San Donato (palace), 141, 144, 157
San Jacinto (ship), 73
Sarah (maid), 116, 169
Sargent, John Singer, 240
Schenck, Gen. Robert, 205
Schlözer, Kurt von, 207, 218
Schurz, Carl (Secretary of the Interior), 2, 207–208, 217, **217**, 218, 219, 252
Schwabach, 221
seasickness, 26, 36, 42, 131
Serpentine, The, 85, **87**
servants, 53, 55, 60, 75, 80, 87, 88, 98, 113, 116, 135, 152, 190, 194, 198, 203, 225–26
Seventh Regiment (party), 118
Seward, Secretary of State, 128
Seymour, Lady, 48–49
Shaftesbury, Lord, 103
Shakespeare, 206
Shaw (host), 118
Shelburne, Lord, 84
Shelley, Lady (cousin of poet), 71
Sherman, General, 2, 212, 213, 214–15
Shrewsbury, 70
Shunk, Frank, 120
Shunk, Governor (Penna.), 109
Sickles, Mr. & Mrs. (Legation Secretary), 47, 72
Sidney, Sir Philip, 67, 89
Sistine Chapel, 146
Sloan, Samuel (architect), 176, 178, 179, 182
Smithsonian Institution, 227, 244
Sotheby, Mr. (antiquary), 48
Spencer, Earl and Lady, 132–33
Spencer, Lady Diana, 133
Spencer, William, 10
spiritualism, 98–102
Stanley, Mr. (hunstman), 76
Stanton (Secretary of War), 164
Story, William Wetmore (son of the justice), 148, 160, **173**
Stowe, Mrs., 91
Strafford, Earl of, 67
Strauss, Johann, 179
Strozzi, Marquis de, 156, 167
Surratt, John, 169

Susan (maid), 53, 75
Sutherland, Duchess of, 55, 57, 58
Swinton, James R. (portraitist), **77**
Switzerland, 161–66

Tavistock House, 105
Taylor, Mr. *(Punch* writer), 69
Taylor, Sir Henry, 84
Taylor, Tom, 105
Taylor, Zachary, 102, 254
Thackeray, William Makepeace, 11, 49, 100, 101
Thames, 30
theater, 31, 105–106, 107, 116, 119, 148–49, 172, 191, 225
Théatre Français, 191
Thomas (coachman), 116
Thornton, Sir Edward (English minister) and Lady, 212, 213
Thun, Gen. (Hungary), 167
Tilden, Samuel, 204, 205
tiles, 242, **247**, 249, **250**
Times, The (London), 46, 49, 85
Todé, Prof. (Wagner in-law), 237–38
"Tools of the Nation Maker," 241–42, 251
Torquay, 92
Torrigiani, Villa (Florence), **136**
Tower of London, 73, **201**
Trollope, Mr., 170
Trumbauer, Horace, 242–43
Tuileries, 221
Tussaud's, Mme., 73
Tyler, Bob (son of President Tyler), 9

Usedom, Count & Mme., 172

Vallombrosa, 150
Van Buren, Martin, 104–105
Viardot (singer), 105
Victor Emmanuel II, King, 158–59
Victoria, Queen, 35–36, 44, 46, 48, 50, 51, 55, 69, 70, 85, 90–91, 121, 244
Villard, Henry, 223
Von Schaik, Mrs., 198

Wadsworth, Mrs., 152
Wagner, Cosima, 237, 240
Wagner, Richard, 237–38
"Wahnfried," (Wagner house), 238
Waldegrave, Lady, 205–206
Wales, Prince of (Albert Edward), 50, 121, 125, **125**, 133, 144, 202
Wanamaker, Madame, 230

Ward, Mrs. Robert (Sallie's mother), 17, 19
Ward, Robert, 14, 19
Ward, Sallie, **14,** 14–20, 27–28, 34, 118, 159, 175, 220, 245–46
Warlak, Lady Ann, 68
Washington, 188, 204
Washington, George, 218–19
Washington, Lawrence, 133
weather, 32, 36, 59–60, 70, 86–87, 89, 110, 116, 117, 141, 149, 152, 156, 166, 194, 200
weddings, 6, 13, 14, 16, 38, 234
Wellington, Duchess of, 70
Wellington, Duke of, 75
Westinghouse, Mrs., 221
Westminster Abbey, 56
Westminster, Lord, 106
Westminster, Marchioness of, 61
White House, **234**
Whitman, Sarah Wyman, 240
Wilde, Oscar ("Hosscar"), 220
Wildman, Col. (friend of Byron), 82
Wilton, Countess of, 92
Wilton, Lord, 92
wines, 31, 108, 110, 115, 218
Windsor Castle, 105
Winthrop, Mrs. 222
Wistar, Mary, 27–28
Wister, Dr. Owen, 236
Wister, Owen, 254
Wister, Sarah, **237,** 240
Wood, Gen. Leonard, 241
Wordsworth house, 71
Worth (store), 191, 221
Wye (Maryland plantation), 11

Yorkshire, 202–203